The Metaphysics of Death

THE
METAPHYSICS
OF DEATH

Edited, with an Introduction, by

JOHN MARTIN FISCHER

Stanford University Press, Stanford, California

1993

Stanford University Press
Stanford, California
© 1993 by the Board of Trustees of the
Leland Stanford Junior University
Printed in the United States of America

CIP data appear at the end of the book

I dedicate this book to three physicians who fight against death:

Joseph Fischer,

Edward Fischer, and

Alfred Bochner,

and to my son, who was born as I was finishing this book:

Ariel Marton Fischer

Acknowledgments

I would like to thank Scott Christensen for assistance in preparing the bibliography. Also, I benefited from discussions with my colleagues at the Center for Ideas and Society, University of California, Riverside, during the Winter quarter of 1991: Ben Stolzfus, Carlos Cortes, Mark Gottdiener, Diana Garber, and Dwight Furrow. For the material on science fiction literature I am deeply indebted to George Slusser and also to Ruth Curl.

J.M.F.

Contents

Contributors

Woody Allen is an author, actor, and director.

Anthony L. Brueckner is Associate Professor of Philosophy at the University of California, Santa Barbara.

Joel Feinberg is Professor of Philosophy at the University of Arizona.

Fred Feldman is Professor of Philosophy at the University of Massachusetts, Amherst.

John Martin Fischer is Professor of Philosophy at the University of California, Riverside.

Steven Luper-Foy is Associate Professor of Philosophy at Trinity University, San Antonio, Texas.

Jeff McMahan is Assistant Professor of Philosophy at the University of Illinois, Urbana-Champaign.

Jeffrie G. Murphy is Professor of Philosophy at Arizona State University.

Thomas Nagel is Professor of Philosophy at New York University.

Derek Parfit is Fellow at All Souls College, University of Oxford.

George Pitcher is Professor Emeritus of Philosophy at Princeton University.

Stephen E. Rosenbaum is Associate Professor of Philosophy at Illinois State University.

Harry S. Silverstein is Professor of Philosophy at Washington State University.

J. David Velleman is Associate Professor of Philosophy at the University of Michigan, Ann Arbor.

Bernard Williams is Professor of Philosophy at the University of Oxford.

Palle Yourgrau is Associate Professor of Philosophy at Brandeis University.

The syllogism he had learnt from Kiesewetter's Logic: 'Caius is a man, men are mortal, therefore Caius is mortal,' had always seemed to him correct as applied to Caius, but certainly not as applied to himself. That Caius—man in the abstract—was mortal, was perfectly correct, but he was not Caius, not an abstract man, but a creature quite, quite separate from all others. He had been little Vanya, with a mamma and papa, afterwards with Katenka and with all the joys, griefs, and delights of childhood, boyhood, and youth. What did Caius know of the smell of that striped leather ball Vanya had been so fond of? Had Caius kissed his mother's hand like that, and did the silk of her dress rustle so for Caius? Had he rioted like that at school when the pastry was bad? Had Caius been in love like that? Could Caius preside at a session as he did? "Caius really was mortal and it was right for him to die; but for me, little Vanya, Ivan Ilych, with all my thoughts and emotions, it's altogether a different matter. It cannot be that I ought to die. That would be too terrible." Such was his feeling.   —Leo Tolstoy, *The Death of Ivan Ilych*

A very old Jewish man called his wife to his bed. "I am going to die. Please call a priest—I wish to convert to Catholicism." His wife responded with shock and disbelief, reminding her husband that they had been devout Jews all their lives. "I know, dear," he said, "but isn't it better that one of them should die than one of us?"   —Anonymous

The Metaphysics of Death

CHAPTER ONE

ROS: Do you ever think of yourself as actually *dead*, lying in a box with a lid on it?
GUIL: No.
ROS: Nor do I, really . . . . It's silly to be depressed by it. I mean one thinks of it like being *alive* in a box, one keeps forgetting to take into account the fact that one is *dead* . . . which should make all the difference . . . shouldn't it? I mean, you'd never know you were in a box, would you? It would be just like being *asleep* in a box. Not that I'd like to sleep in a box, mind you, not without any air—you'd wake up dead, for a start, and then where would you be? Apart from inside a box. That's the bit I don't like, frankly. That's why I don't think of it . . . . Because you'd be helpless, wouldn't you? Stuffed in a box like that, I mean you'd be in there for ever. Even taking into account the fact that you're dead, it isn't a pleasant thought. *Especially* if you're dead, really . . . *ask* yourself, if I asked you straight off—I'm going to stuff you in this box now, would you rather be alive or dead? Naturally, you'd prefer to be alive. Life in a box is better than no life at all. I expect. You'd have a chance at least. You could lie there thinking—well, at least I'm not dead! In a minute someone's going to bang on the lid and tell me to come out. (*Banging the floor with his fists.*) "Hey you, whatsyername! Come out of there!"
—Tom Stoppard, *Rosencrantz & Guildenstern Are Dead*

Introduction: Death, Metaphysics, and Morality

John Martin Fischer

The pieces in this collection explore certain puzzles pertaining to death. The puzzles can be described as metaphysical; alternatively, they can be considered normative. But if they are normative issues, they are considerably more abstract than other normative issues. So, for example, the authors of the papers collected here investigate (among other things) the issue of what makes death a bad thing for an individual, if indeed death *is* a bad thing for a person. This issue is more basic and abstract than questions about (for example) the particular conditions under which euthanasia is justified, if it *is* ever justified. Indeed, there are important connections between the more abstract questions addressed in this book and a host of moral problems, such as euthanasia, suicide, and abortion. But the primary focus here will not be on these moral problems. Rather, the focus will be on the more basic and abstract problems concerning the nature of death: Can death be a bad thing for the individual who dies? What is the nature of the evil of death, if it is an evil? If death can harm a person, who is the subject of the harm, and when does the harm occur? If death can be a bad thing for a person, would immortality be good?

Definition of Death

Begin by distinguishing dying, death, and being dead (see, e.g., Rosenbaum, Chapter 7 in this volume). Dying is a process.

Being dead is a condition or state. Death intervenes between dying and being dead; it takes place at the end of dying and the beginning of being dead. For the purposes of the discussion in this book, it is very important to distinguish the process of dying from the latter two things: death and being dead. When one is dying, one is still alive. One can be conscious of dying, and dying can involve significant pain and suffering. It is not particularly puzzling why dying can be a bad thing for a person, insofar as pain and suffering can certainly be bad for an individual. (Perhaps I should also point out that, as Thomas Nagel puts it in his contribution to this volume, dying would not be so bad if it weren't followed by death! But, presumably, this insight is compatible with dying's badness coming from the pain and suffering it involves.) In contrast, it is plausible to suppose that death and being dead do not involve conscious episodes. Of course, some people deny this supposition, but I shall here not explore their positions. (When Isaac Bashevis Singer was asked whether he believes in an afterlife, he said that whatever it is like, it must be better than what we have now.) Rather, I (along with the contributors to this collection) assume that death and being dead are "experiential blanks."[1]

I do not know whether death is a "point," a pointlike event, an extended event, or itself a process. But it does not appear to be important (for our purposes) to resolve this issue. Also, sometimes I (and the authors in this book) will assimilate the notions of death and being dead. For certain purposes this assimilation is innocuous. For example, it is natural to suppose that the considerations pertinent to the question of why death is bad are equally relevant to the issue of why being dead is bad. Indeed, it does not seem inappropriate to say that sometimes death is construed as the *transition* from being alive to being dead, whereas sometimes death is construed as the *state* of being dead.

What exactly is death? It is useful first to distinguish between the *criterion* or *criteria* of death and the *concept* of death. The criterion of death is the test for the existence of death. A criterion is a sign or indication of the presence of something; for example, a fever is a reliable criterion for the presence of some illnesses. In contrast, our concept of death distills our views about the nature of the phenomenon of death. Just as the presence of a fever indicates or points to the presence of something else, an illness, so the presence of the conditions specified in the criterion of death indicates or points to the presence of something else—death itself. Thus, it is important to distinguish various criteria of death from each other and also from our concept (or concepts) of death.

Broadly speaking, there are two criteria of death: the traditional "heart-lung death" criterion and the "brain-death" criterion. Of course, there are different versions of each of these criteria.[2] The basic idea behind the traditional criterion of death is that death occurs when there is the (permanent and irreversible) cessation of heart and lung functioning. Before the inception of mechanical aids to the heart and lungs, this criterion was simpler. Now one should distinguish between a version according to which death occurs when there is the (permanent and irreversible) cessation of heart and lung functioning and a version according to which death occurs when there is such a cessation of *unaided* heart and lung functioning.

In relatively recent times we have developed the technology to keep the respiration and circulation going in individuals whose brains no longer function. Thus, there is a new criterion of death: brain death.[3] But there are various versions of the brain-death criterion. According to one version, death occurs when there is (permanent and irreversible) cessation of the functioning of *all* parts of the brain. According to another version, death occurs when there is such a cessation of the functioning of the part of the brain that sustains *cognitive* functioning (including consciousness). It is possible for an individual to be capable of unaided respiration and circulation without being capable of cognitive functioning of any sort. In such an individual there has been damage to certain (but not all) parts of the brain; this sort of individual is in a "persistent vegetative state." Given this last possibility, it is evident that the traditional criterion and the brain-death criterion can pull in opposite directions.

From the fact that there are different criteria for something, it does *not* follow that there are different concepts of the thing (or different phenomena). Specifically, it does not seem to follow from the fact that there are different criteria of death that we have different concepts of death (associated with the different criteria). Indeed, some argue that the different criteria of death are different ways of "getting to" the same underlying notion of death. (Presumably, insofar as the criteria can sometimes pull in opposite directions, the proponents of the "one-concept" view might hold that certain criteria are *better* ways of detecting the presence of death.) Of course, even if it does not *follow* from the existence of different criteria of death that there are different concepts of death, it may nevertheless be true that there are various different concepts of death. And, indeed, some argue that there *are* different concepts of death, and that the different criteria of death are naturally associated with these different concepts of death.

A very rough stab at an articulation of an abstract concept of death would be as follows. Death is the permanent and irreversible cessation of life.[4] Then the different criteria of death could be construed as "selecting" or "focusing on" certain putatively significant aspects of life. Some would of course suggest that these different aspects actually carve out different concepts of death, whereas others would argue that there is one concept (and one underlying phenomenon) with different associated criteria.

Analytically, it is important to distinguish criteria from concepts. But in discussing the following three different approaches to justifying particular views of human death, I shall speak abstractly of "accounts," where this can refer either to "criteria" or "concepts" or to both. The first approach to justifying particular accounts of human death (its criterion or concept) argues from biological premises. That is, this approach takes the relevant or significant aspects of human life to be those in virtue of which we are *organisms* of a certain kind. The proponents of this approach attempt to derive illumination about death from the notion that it is particularly significant that humans are organisms of a certain sort. Here, the crucial aspects of life are taken to be those pertinent to the capacity for integrated functioning as an organism.[5]

Another approach to justifying particular accounts of human death argues from moral premises. The idea here is to seek illumination of human death by reference to moral intuitions about when it is justifiable to regard and treat a person as dead.[6]

A third approach to elucidating human death proceeds via metaphysical considerations. Specifically, one version of this approach claims that an adequate understanding of the nature and criteria of personal identity will lead to an appropriate account of human death. That is, the proponents of this approach believe that a suitable theory of the nature and conditions of persistence of persons over time will imply the correct account of death.[7]

Note that these approaches are ways of justifying particular accounts of death that "cut across" those accounts. So, for example, some proponents of the biological approach would opt for the traditional account of death, whereas other proponents of this approach would argue for the brain-death account. Similarly, some proponents of the moral approach would opt for the traditional account of death, whereas other proponents of this approach would favor the brain-death account.

I have qualified my description of these three approaches so that they apply merely to human death, and not death per se. This qualification is necessary for various reasons. For example, since such creatures as insects are not persons at all, the third (and probably the second) approaches to justifying accounts of death would not be relevant. Whereas some philosophers have divided their discussions of death so that they have given different accounts of the death of humans and that of (say) cows or insects, others have preferred a unitary account of death that would apply to all living creatures (and not just humans or persons).

It should be noted that the state of public policy about death involves a sort of ambivalence that acknowledges the force of both traditional and brain-death considerations. In many states, a brain-death criterion—originally articulated in the 1968 report of the Ad Hoc Committee of the Harvard Medical School to Examine the Definition of Brain Death—has been "added to" the traditional account of death to form a disjunctive account of death. This is essentially also what was adopted by the 1981 President's Commission for the Study of Ethical Problems in Medicine and Biomedical and Behavioral Research in its report, *Defining Death: Medical, Legal, and Ethical Issues in the Determination of Death*. On page 73, the report says:

An individual who has sustained either (1) irreversible cessation of circulatory and respiratory functions, or (2) irreversible cessation of all function of the entire brain, including the brain stem, is dead.

Clearly, this is to form a disjunctive criterion of death employing the traditional and brain-death criteria discussed above.[8]

It is evident that there are delicate and difficult issues involved in attempting to give a precise account of the nature and criteria of death. Further, there are different approaches to justifying the various putative accounts. For our purposes, here, however, it may be enough to accept the idea that death is the permanent and irreversible cessation of life. More specifically, death is the permanent and irreversible cessation of the relevant aspects of life, where different accounts select different aspects as relevant.

Death and Meaning

There are two connections between death and meaning that I would like briefly to explore. The first is the claim that death gives meaning to life—that death makes life meaningful. (Another claim is that death obliterates meaning—that the fact of our eventual deaths renders all of our strivings pathetic and absurd. I shall not pursue this claim here.)[9] The second is that death can be particularly bad—indeed, tragic—only for creatures who are capable of leading a meaningful life.

Some philosophers have claimed that death is required in order for life to be meaningful. Without death, they have claimed, life would lack the structure and coherence necessary in order for life to be meaningful. On this approach, insofar as leading a meaningful life is desirable, immortality (of any sort) is undesirable. Although there are various versions of this sort of argument, it will be illuminating to focus on the version presented by Bernard Williams (Chapter 5 in this volume).

There are different models of immortality, and different particular considerations will be applicable to the different models. Williams begins with a character in a play by Karel Capek (which was made into an opera by Leoš Janáček). This character had various names with the initials "EM." When she was 42 years old, her father gave her an elixir of life that rendered her capable of living forever (at the biological age of 42). At the time of action of the play, EM is aged 342. As Williams puts it, "Her unending life has come to a state of boredom, indifference, and coldness. Everything is joyless." In the end, she refuses the elixir and dies, and the formula is destroyed by a young woman (despite the protests of some older men!).[10]

Williams's discussion is rich with intriguing insights, but I will attempt to distill (in, regrettably, a somewhat procrustean fashion) a general strategy of argumentation that is alleged to apply in the first instance to EM-type immortality (in which the immortal individual—and not others—is biologically frozen in time in the sense of not biologically aging) as well as to other forms of immortality. Williams's strategy involves positing two criteria that must be met if a given model of immortality is to be genuinely appealing to an individual. First, the future person (posited by the model) must be identical to the individual. Second, the life of the future person must be attractive (in a certain way) to the individual—the life of the future person must be "suitably related" to the goals and projects of the individual, where there is, necessarily, a residuum of vagueness in the specification of the relationship in question.

The problems with EM-type immortality are supposed by Williams to pertain to the second condition. We can construct a dilemma. Either EM's character (her basic goals, projects, dispositions, and interests) remains the same over time, or it changes. If it remains the same, then indefinitely many experiences will lead to detachment or boredom: "a boredom connected with the fact that everything that could happen and make sense to one particular human being of 42 had already happened to her" (Williams, p. 82). But if the character changes, it is unclear whether the second condition is satisfied, because it is unclear how to assess the new projects and goals in light of the old ones.

In general, the strategy can be employed to call into question the appeal of various models of immortality. For instance, on one model an individual (in some sense) leads an indefinite series of lives. Of course, the model has only been very sketchily specified, but it is evident that the strategy suggested by Williams can be deployed here. On some versions of the model, the first condition will not be satisfied; the future persons are not genuinely identical to the current individual (whose attitudes toward the future are at issue). On other versions, the future persons are genuinely identical to the current individual, but then the serial lives become bizarre and unattractive. What would it be like for a single individual—with a single flow and accumulation of memories—to be associated with a series of bodies with the normal biological development (and decay), each of which has an attendant "sub-flow" of experiences?

Although much of science fiction and fantasy literature contains a more hopeful and positive view of immortality (in various forms), there is a particularly striking and unattractive depiction of one version of the "serial-lives" model in Kurt Steiner's *Le disque raye*.[11] In this novel an individual is doomed to repeat the same patterns endlessly; the inevitable cyclical pattern of his life is stultifying. (Note that there are cyclical and noncyclical versions of the serial-lives model.) This cyclical picture of immortality is alluded to by Woody Allen in *Hannah and Her Sisters*:

> Millions of books written on every conceivable subject by all these great minds, and in the end, none of 'em knows anything more about the big questions of life than I do. . . . Nietzsche with his Theory of Eternal Recurrence. He said that the life we live, we're gonna live over and over again the exact same way for eternity. Great. That means I'll have to sit through the Ice Capades again. It's not worth it.

In assessing Williams's argumentative strategy, let us first consider the dilemma pertaining to Williams's second condition in the case of EM. Williams's claim is that immortality is undesirable, whether or not EM's character changes. Suppose, first, that other individuals with whom EM has significant contact *also* are similarly immortal. And suppose that EM's character is (relatively) fixed and unchanging. Under such a condition, Williams claims that EM will either take her experiences of her environment (including human interactions) as objectionably "inevitable" or she will detach herself and ultimately become cold, wooden, and bored.

But I do not see why this dichotomy is exhaustive. Remember that certain (perhaps not all) of one's family and friends also have the relevant sort of immortality. It seems to me that under such circumstances one could live an attractive life characterized by a desirable *mix* of fulfilling activities. Of course, if the mix is not right, the life will be unattractive. For example, if the life consists (almost) solely of contemplative activity, it will not be satisfying. Similarly, if it consists of a single-minded preoccupation with and pursuit of sensual pleasures (even complex and compelling ones), it will not be attractive. In general, single-minded and unbalanced pursuit of any single kind of activity will be unattractive. But of course from the fact that one's life will be *unending* it does not follow that it must *unitary* or *unbalanced*. That one's life is endless clearly does not imply that one must endlessly and single-mindedly pursue some particular sort of activity.

Why can't an immortal life consist in a certain *mix* of activities? Of course, the mix will differ with different individuals, but it might include friendship, love, family, intellectual, artistic, and athletic activity, sensual delights, and so forth. I could imagine that any one of these would be boring and alienating, pursued relentlessly and without some combination of the others. But in the proper mix I do not see that they could not be endlessly interesting—or at least part of a life that is, on balance, desirable and worth living.[12] As Jonathan Glover has put it,

But I am not convinced that someone with a fairly constant character *need* eventually become intolerably bored, so long as they can watch the world continue to unfold and go on asking new questions and thinking, and so long as there are other people to share their feelings and thoughts with. Given the company of the right people, I would be glad of the chance to sample a few million years and see how it went. (*Causing Death and Saving Lives*, p. 57)[13]

Williams says,

Some philosophers have pictured an eternal existence as occupied in something like intense intellectual enquiry. . . . The activity is engrossing, self-justifying, affords, as it may appear, endless new perspectives, and by being engrossing enables one to lose oneself. . . . But if one is totally and perpetually absorbed in such an activity, and loses oneself in it, then as those words suggest, we come back to the problem of satisfying the conditions that it should be me who lives forever, and that the eternal life should be in prospect of some interest. . . . For looking at [a certain person] it seems quite unreasonable to suppose that those activities would have the fulfilling or liberating character that they do have for him, if they were in fact all he could do or conceive of doing. (pp. 88–89)

But why suppose that any one supposedly absorbing activity must be pursued *at the expense of all others*? Why can't such activities be part of a *package* in an immortal life, just as we suppose that they should be in a mortal life? Also, an activity in which it is tempting to say that one "loses oneself" is an activity in which the *content* of one's experiences is focused outward: one is thinking about something besides oneself. (When one is absorbed in such an activity, one is not *self-absorbed*.) But it is quite another thing to claim that these experiences are not one's own. Surely, features of the *content* and *ownership* of experiences must be distinguished.

Now take the second horn of Williams's dilemma and suppose that EM's character changes over time. He claims that it is now unclear that one will find such immortality attractive, given that one's current goals, values, and interests are different from one's future goals, values, and interests. This sort of case raises complex issues.[14] But it seems to me that an individual could value such an existence if he felt that the change in character would result from certain sorts of sequences. That is, if I felt that my future character will be different from my present one as a result of appropriate reflection at future times upon my experiences given my "then-current" character, then I might well value such an existence. One's attitude toward future changes of character depends on *how* the changes take place. Certain sorts of inexplicable or discontinuous changes might issue in future stages or "future selves" to whom one is currently indifferent, but if the changes are the result of certain sorts of sequences, then one may in fact value a life in which changes of character take place. It is not apparent, therefore, that Williams's two conditions entail that EM-type immortality would be unappealing.[15]

I now wish to explore another connection between death and meaning: the claim that death is (or can be) a special sort of harm—a tragedy—for a proper subset of living creatures: those capable of leading *meaningful lives*. These are large issues, and my treatment will necessarily be somewhat panoramic.

We tend to divide living creatures into two categories: "persons" and "nonpersons." We make this sort of division for different purposes, and we draw the boundaries in different ways. One feature of the distinction involves moral responsibility: we hold persons morally responsible for their behavior, whereas we do not hold nonpersons morally responsible. Moral responsibility involves a distinctive set of attitudes (indignation, resentment, hatred, respect, gratitude, love, and so forth) and attendant activities (moral praise and blame, reward and punishment).

Another feature of the distinction involves the right to life: we ascribe the right to life to persons, but not to nonpersons. The right to life gives special protection to the lives of a proper subset of living creatures. And it is not implausible to think that this special protection guards something especially valuable: the capacity to lead a meaningful life. Thus, when this right is violated, something particularly valuable is lost. In general, when a creature who has the capacity to lead a meaningful life dies, something particularly valuable—over and above life per se—is thought to be lost. One of the salient features of personhood is that it can be a particularly bad thing—a tragedy—for a person to die. (Note that I am employing "personhood" in a normative fashion to pick out the property of being such as to have the right to life and be morally responsible. It is here an open question *which* creatures are persons; I do not simply assume as a conceptual matter that all and only *human beings*—members of the species *Homo sapiens*—are persons.)

Now if personhood involves having the right to life and this right is jealous of something particularly valuable—namely, the capacity to lead a meaningful life—then perhaps we can get some idea of the properties necessary for personhood by considering the concept of a meaningful life and the prerequisites of such a life. The problem, of course, is that we are in danger of seeking to explicate the obscure by reference to the equally (or more) obscure.

The notion of a meaningful life is notoriously opaque and contentious.[16] At the risk of being a sort of metaphysical Rambo, I have a few (admittedly very sketchy and speculative) thoughts. Most people think that leading a meaningful life involves freely constructing some sort of "life plan" and freely striving to act in accordance with it. It is in virtue of our life plans (even very sketchy and incomplete ones) that we give meaning to our lives. But in order to freely construct and strive to live in accordance with some sort of life plan, certain minimal capacities are necessary: consciousness, some level of rationality, and free will (of some kind). Only a conscious individual who can think can construct a life plan, and only a free agent can construct and evaluate (and re-evaluate) it freely, and seek to act in accordance with it freely. The absence or attenuation of these capacities implies the absence or attentuation of the capacity to live a meaningful life, and, thus, of personhood. These properties—consciousness, rationality, and free will—can help us to demarcate the boundary between persons and nonpersons. They can point us toward the subclass of living creatures for whom death is a particularly egregious harm or evil.

Of course, the above thoughts are the barest sketch of an argument, leaving many issues untouched and questions unanswered. Some such questions are as follows. Why exactly suppose that a meaningful life is associated with freely constructing and seeking to live in accordance with a life plan? And why should the particular badness of death be associated with the capacity to lead a meaningful life?

Certainly, various philosophers have suggested alternative accounts of personhood, some of which select or emphasize cognitive capacities of certain kinds, others of which select or emphasize affective or executive capacities of various sorts. All of these philosophers attempt to identify certain properties putatively possessed by all and only persons. Although I cannot fully defend this suggestion here, perhaps it is an advantage of the account adumbrated above that it explains in a natural and direct manner why death can be a particularly bad thing for those individuals who are persons.[17]

It can presumably be bad to some extent for any living creature to die; that is, it can be bad to some (possibly minuscule) amount *for the creature itself* that it dies. But I have suggested above that it can be *particularly bad* for certain living creatures (persons) to die. If this is in fact so, it becomes more interesting and pressing to inquire into the nature of the badness of death.

Why—and How—Death Is Bad

An individual's death can be bad for the person's family, friends, and acquaintances. This is uncontroversial. But it seems also that death can (although it need not) be bad for the individual who dies. The controversy concerns whether (and how) this can be so.

It is plausible that death is not a bad thing for someone suffering from a terminal and horribly painful and debilitating disease. Both the person's family and he himself may welcome death as a relief from the pain and suffering. But for a normal child or an adult human being, death is typically a bad thing (in some sense). That is, we reasonably hope that death takes place later rather than earlier (within a certain range), and we look to its prospective occurrence with a certain trepidation and regret. It is generally thought to be rational to take our own prospective death as a bad thing. And even though it certainly should not become a preoccupying, driving anxiety, it may be rational to fear death (see, e.g., Murphy, Chapter 3 in this volume).

We apply a number of different notions to death. We think of it as a bad thing, a misfortune, an evil, or a harm to an individual. Also, we judge it an appropriate object of regret and (some degree of) fear. I shall here not distinguish these different concepts, although for some purposes they might usefully be distinguished. For instance, some philosophers might deny that death can *harm* someone, but they concede that it can be a misfortune or bad thing for the individual. This distinction might be useful in certain contexts.

When someone dies, this can cause terrible grief, pain, and suffering among others. It is evident that such things are bad for persons. But how exactly can death itself (as opposed to dying) be bad *for the individual who dies*? Of course, *if* death and being dead involve a "conscious" afterlife in which there is "pain" or unpleasant experiences, then it could easily be seen how death could be bad: it would be bad in the same way that (for example) painful dying would be bad. But our assumption here is that death is an *experiential blank*. Given this, how can death be bad for the individual who dies?

In thinking about this larger question, it might be useful to distinguish three questions. First, what is the nature of the harm or bad involved in death? (If it is not pain, what is it, and how can it be bad?) Second, who is the subject of the harm or evil? (If the person is no longer alive, how can he be the subject of the bad? And if he is not the subject, who is? Can one have a harm with no subject?) Third, when does the harm take place? (Can a harm take place after its subject ceases to exist? If death harms a person, can the harm take place before the death occurs?) This family of questions helps to frame the puzzle of why—and how—death is bad. Many of the chapters in this book address these questions, and I shall sketch here some of the salient strategies. It will be seen that often an answer to one question in the family of questions entails answers to the others.

As a point of departure, let us take note of the view which *denies* that death is bad for the person who dies and that it is rational to fear death or regard its prospective occurrence as a bad thing. The most prominent proponents of this position in the history of philosophy are Lucretius (ca. 96–ca. 55 B.C.) and Epicurus (341–270 B.C.). Stephen Rosenbaum (author of Chapters 7 and 15 in this volume) is a contemporary Epicurean (as regards death). Even if they ultimately reject the conclusion of Lucretius and Epicurus that death is not bad for the person who dies, many philosophers have considerable respect for the position developed by these two men, and they undertake to show *why* it is untenable. I shall call the position that death is not a harm or evil for the person who dies and is thus not appropriately feared the "Epicurean view" or "skepticism about death's badness."

There are various considerations that have attracted philosophers to the Epicurean view. One is the idea that, in order for something to be bad for a person, it must be *experienced* as bad or in some way unpleasant by the person. On this view, since all bads must be experienced and death is an experiential blank, death is not a bad for the person who dies. Another (perhaps intimately related) consideration is the idea that, if some event or process is bad for a person, then the person must exist when the event or process takes place. On this view, death cannot be a bad for a person, since the person does not exist when death (as opposed to dying) occurs. How can a harm take place at a time when its alleged subject has ceased to exist?

Most philosophers have wished to resist the Epicurean conclusion. I shall begin by considering the response to the Epicurean view developed by Bernard Williams in Chapter 5. Williams distinguishes between "conditional" and "categorical" desires. Among conditional desires, some are conditional upon one's being alive. For example, one might want to be treated well, if one remains alive, but wish, all things considered, that one were dead. Williams claims, however, that not all desires are conditional upon being alive. Some desires are *categorical*: they (implicitly) answer the question of whether one wishes to remain alive. (See also Luper-Foy, Chapter 14, and Rosenbaum,

Chapter 15, in this volume.) The desires to raise a family, write a great book, help to eradicate poverty and starvation, and so forth are categorical desires in that they presuppose that one does indeed desire to continue to live. When one has a categorical desire to (say) raise a family, it is not that one merely desires to raise a family, *if* one should continue to live; rather, one wishes to continue to live (in part) because one desires to raise a family.

Williams claims that death's badness consists in its frustration of an individual's categorical desires. This provides a nice way of explaining the particular badness of death for certain living creatures: only certain creatures (persons) can form categorical (and not merely conditional) desires about the future. Further, the frustration of a desire (in the sense that is relevant to Williams's explanation) need not be *experienced*; on this approach, a desire is frustrated insofar as the object of the desire is not secured, but this need not issue in any awareness of this situation or any unpleasant experiential state.

Many of us have what might be called "impersonal" categorical desires: desires that some condition obtain in the future irrespective of its causal genesis. So, for example, we want it to be the case that poverty, starvation, and disease are eradicated, that political oppression is ended, that our environment is preserved, that our families, friends, and nations prosper, and so forth. But there are other categorical desires that might be called "egocentric categorical desires." Despite the name, these desires are not centered or focused on states of oneself. Rather, these desires are specific as regards the ways in which certain desired states of affairs are brought about. So, for example, I may wish not just that a book is written, but that a book is written *by me*, and I may wish not just that a family is raised, but that a family is raised *by me*, and so forth.[18] In certain contexts death can be bad to the extent that it frustrates one's impersonal categorical desires. But in other contexts those desires will be satisfied quite independently of one's continued life (for example, the desire that a book will be written); in these contexts it may nevertheless be true that death is bad insofar as it frustrates one's egocentric categorical desires.[19]

There are some problems with this "desire-frustration" account of death's badness. For example, when exactly does the evil or harm of death take place? The problem is that when the desire is frustrated, the person putatively possessing the desire does not exist. If the bad takes place when the object of the desire is not secured, then one must say that someone is harmed at a time when he does not exist and *a fortiori* does not have the desire in question. Alternatively, one could say that the evil or harm takes place at some time *before* death takes place—perhaps when the individual in question first forms the desire (or when it becomes an *interest* of the individual). On this approach, the harm of death takes place *before* death, even if the individual (and no one else) knows that the individual has in fact been harmed. (For illuminating discussions of these issues, see Pitcher, Chapter 9, and Feinberg, Chapter 10, in this volume.)

Although the desire-frustration model seems to capture part of death's badness, it is not evident that it distills the essence of it. This is because it seems that death could be bad for someone who (inappropriately) lacks any categorical desires. If a person lacks any such desires and we deem him rational in lacking these desires, perhaps death is not bad for him. But if a person is (inappropriately) depressed or for some other reason simply lacks any categorical desire, we may still think that death is bad for him. Indeed, we may think that he *should* have such desires, and thus he is *doubly* unfortunate. Thus, the mere lack of such desires does not show that death is not bad. And this indicates that the essence of death's badness is not the frustration of existing desires.[20]

Another approach to answering the question about the nature of death's badness might be called the "deprivation" theory of death's badness. On this view, death is bad insofar as it deprives the person of the goods of life, where these goods might be specified in various ways. A mere deprivation need not be experienced as unpleasant or bad, and thus it is compatible with death's being an experiential blank.

The first task of the proponent of the deprivation theory is to convince us that something can be bad for a person, can harm him, even though it is not experienced as bad or unpleasant by the person. One of the nicest defenses of the deprivation theory is by Thomas Nagel in Chapter 4 of this volume. Nagel argues that there can be bads and harms that are not experienced as bad by the individual who is (allegedly) the subject of the bad in question. Regarding the view that all bads must be experienced by their subjects, Nagel says:

It means that even if a man is betrayed by his friends, ridiculed behind his back, and despised by people who treat him politely to his face, none of it can be counted as a misfortune for him so long as he does not suffer as a result. It means that a man is not injured if his wishes are ignored by the executor of his will, or if, after his death, the belief becomes current that all the literary works on which his fame rests were really written by his brother, who died in Mexico at the age of twenty-eight. . . .

Someone who holds that all goods and evils must be temporally assignable states of the person may of course try to bring difficult cases into line by pointing to the pleasure or pain that more complicated goods and evils cause. Loss, betrayal, deception, and ridicule are on this view bad because people suffer when they learn of them. But it should be asked how our ideas of human value would have to be constituted to accommodate these cases directly instead. One advantage of such an account might be that it would enable us to explain *why* the discovery of these misfortunes causes suffering—in a way that makes it reasonable. For the natural view is that the discovery of betrayal makes us unhappy because it is bad to be betrayed—not that betrayal is bad because its discovery makes us unhappy. (pp. 64–65)

Similarly, Joel Feinberg says (Chapter 10 in this volume):

How can a person be harmed, it might be asked, by what he can't know? Dead men are permanently unconscious; hence they cannot be aware of events as they occur; hence (it will be said) they can have no stake one way or the other in such events. That this argument employs a false premise can be shown by a consideration of various interests of *living* persons that can be violated without their ever becoming aware of it. Many of these are "possessory interests" whose rationality can be doubted, for example, a landowner's interest in the *exclusive* possession and enjoyment of his land—an interest that can be invaded by an otherwise harmless trespasser who takes one unobserved step inside the entrance gates; or the legally recognized "interest in domestic relations" which is invaded when one's spouse engages in secret adulterous activity with a lover. The latter is an interest in being the exclusive object of one's spouse's love, and has been criticized by some as implying property in another's affections. But there is no criticizing on such grounds the interest every person has in his own reputation, which is perhaps the best example for our present purposes from the purely self-regarding category. If someone spreads a libelous description of me among a group whose good opinion I covet and cherish, altogether without my knowledge, I have been injured in virtue of the harm done my interest in a good reputation, even though I *never* learn what has happened. That is because I have an interest, so I believe, in having a good reputation *as such*, in addition to my interest in avoiding hurt feelings, embarrassment, and economic injury. And *that* interest can be seriously harmed without my ever learning of it. (p. 180)

Also, Robert Nozick says:

Suppose we read the biography of a man who *felt* happy, took pride in his work, family life, etc. But we also read that his children, secretly, despised him; his wife, secretly, scorned him having innumerable affairs; his work was a subject of ridicule among all others, who kept their opinion from him; *every* source of satisfaction in this man's life was built upon a falsehood, a deception. Do you, in reading about this man's life, think: "What a *wonderful* life. I wish I, or my children, could lead it"? And don't say that you wouldn't want to lead the life because all the deceptions and falsehoods might come out making the man unhappy. They didn't. Of course, it is difficult to imagine the others behaving appropriately, and the person himself not being nagged by doubts. But is *this* the ground of one's reaction? Was it a good life? . . .

This man lived a lie, though not one that he told. We can imagine other cases. You have what you believe is a private relationship with someone. However, unbeknownst to you, I am filming it with my super-duper camera and sound equipment, and distributing the film to people whom you will never encounter. Nothing in your life is changed by the fact that people are packing the pornographic movie theaters in Outer Mongolia to keep up with the latest serial installment in your life. So, should anyone care? And is the only ground on which my action can be criticized, the nature of all viewers' experience? ("On the Randian Argument," p. 221)

All of these examples purport to render plausible the idea that something that is never actually experienced as unpleasant by an individual can nevertheless be a bad thing for that individual. This would make it plausible that death can be bad for a person, even though it is a mere experiential blank. But some opponents of the deprivation theory agree that certain things never actually experienced as unpleasant by a person can be bad for that person, but *disagree* with the claim that this renders it plausible that death can be bad for a person. These theorists argue that it is a necessary condition of something's being bad for a person that that person *can* (in some sense) experience it as unpleasant or bad (see, e.g., Silverstein, Chapter 6, and Rosenbaum, Chapter 7, in this volume). And they point out that none of the examples adduced by proponents of the deprivation theory are cases in which it is *impossible* for the relevant individuals to experience the things as unpleasant or bad; in all of these cases (except of course the controversial case of death), it is *possible* for the agents to experience the bad things as bad, even though they do not *in fact* have such experiences. There is then an apparently crucial asymmetry between death and the relatively (although not entirely) uncontroversial examples of non-experienced bad adduced by the proponents of the deprivation theory.

Another way of putting the deprivation-theory opponent's point is as follows. He argues that the only way something can be bad for an agent is if it is possible for the agent to experience it as bad. This seems to follow from the "existence requirement": the occurrence of something at a time can be a bad for a person only if the person exists at the time (see, e.g., McMahan, Chapter 13, and Feldman, Chapter 16, in this volume). But death—being an experiential blank that occurs after the agent is alive or exists—cannot be experienced by the one who dies as bad. Thus, death cannot be a bad for the individual who dies. Now the proponent of the deprivation theory adduces examples in which it is allegedly true that persons suffer misfortunes of which they are unaware. But since none of these examples is an example in which the individual has ceased to exist and thus it is *impossible* for the relevant person to experience the thing as a bad, none of the examples refutes the pertinent premise of the argument.

It must be conceded that none of the proponent's examples decisively defeats the premise of the argument, so construed. But it seems to me that nevertheless the examples call it into question. In all of the examples, it appears that what explains the misfortune which the relevant person suffers is something "objective" and independent of either actual *or possible* experience. What makes the things in question bads or evils for the relevant individuals has (intuitively speaking) nothing to do with whether the things are actually or even possibly experienced. Insofar as the examples have this property, they render it reasonable to reject the premise, although they do not *entail* the falsity of the premise.

The dialectical situation seems to me to be as follows. A claim is made by the opponent of the deprivation theory: that it is a necessary condition of something's being bad for a person that it be possible for the person to experience it as bad. The proponent then produces a number of examples in which it seems that something is bad for a person and yet he never actually experiences the thing as bad. Further, in these examples it is intuitively plausible to suppose that the badness of the things is quite independent even of the *possibility* of experiencing them as bad: in the cases there is no reason to suppose that the things are bad at least in part because the agents might experience them as bad (or somehow suffer as a result of them). Now the opponent responds by saying that strictly speaking the examples do not *require* the rejection of the claim at issue, since none of the examples is one in which it is uncontroversially true that something is bad for an agent but it is *impossible* for the agent to experience it as bad. Indeed, the opponent claims that it is the obligation of the proponent to produce (nonquestion-begging) examples in which something is bad for a person but impossible for the person to experience as bad.

But it seems to me that the demand is unreasonably strong. It would be ideal for the proponent of the deprivation theory to have such examples available, but they are not necessary to call the premise (and thus the corresponding conclusion) into question. How many interesting philosophical claims are such that one can produce *decisive* counterexamples (or supporting examples)—examples that *require* either the rejection or adoption of the claim in question? If the proponents of the deprivation theory have provided examples in which it is reasonable to think that certain things are bad for agents and the agents never experience them as bad, and if they are examples in which it is plausible that whether or not the agents *can* experience the things is not relevant to their badness, then the proponents would have rendered their position appealing (if not ineluctable). Thus, it is at least reasonable to think that death (although an evil) is interestingly different from "standard" evils or harms in that it is impossible to experience it as bad (and the existence requirement is not met).

Another way in which death is different from "standard" evils or harms is in its apparent "noncomparative" nature. Some philosophers have argued that all evils or harms are by their very nature "comparative." Thus, to say that something harms someone is (on this view) in part at least to say that the person is worse off given that this thing has occurred than he would be in certain relevant alternatives. The essence of the view is that something's being a bad or harm requires a comparison between (at least) two scenarios in both of which the person exists. On this view, however, death cannot be bad for an individual, since he does not exist in the death scenario: there is nothing to which to compare his continued existence.

Some philosophers have concluded from the essentially comparative notion of bads and harms, the existence requirement, and the view that the person who dies ceases to exist that death cannot be a bad for a person. Harry Silverstein (Chapter 6 in this volume) argues for the comparative view and the existence requirement, but he denies that dead people no longer exist. On his view, temporal distance is on a par with spatial distance with regard to existence. Thus, death is a bad thing for an existing person—the person who dies. Although this view gives a clear answer to the question about the subject of the evil of death, it does so at the price of consequences that some will find implausible. There are interesting critical discussions of Silverstein's "spatialization" approach to temporal distance by Palle Yourgrau and Stephen Rosenbaum (Chapters 8 and 7 in this volume, respectively). According to Yourgrau, dead persons do not exist, and yet they are not nothing (as are, for example, mere fictional characters). For Yourgrau, there is a realm of being that is not existence. Other philosophers wish to deny that death is comparative but maintain that it can nevertheless be a harm to the person who dies (see, e.g., Chapters 13 and 16). On this view, harms are divided into two subclasses: comparative and noncomparative.

An interesting methodological issue emerges from the above discussion. On the one hand, some philosophers claim that it is true of various different harms or evils that there is the possibility of experiencing them as bad, the existence requirement holds, and they are comparative in nature. They further note that death has none of these properties, and they conclude that it cannot be a harm. Others grant the first two claims, but deny the conclusion. They say that harms or evils are to be divided into two proper subclasses. First, there are the "standard" harms of which the following is true: there is the possibility of experiencing them as bad, the existence requirement holds, and they are comparative in nature. Second, there are "nonstandard harms," of which death is putatively an example. It is interesting to ask why one should adopt one of these approaches rather than the other. Of course, a philosopher who opts for the second approach will claim that the sorts of examples discussed above at least render his approach attractive, even if they fall short of rendering it irresistible. Further, he might claim that the intuitive view that death can be a harm or misfortune for the individual who dies is on much firmer ground than such delicate matters as the existence requirement, the condition of the possibility of experiencing any bad, and the putative comparative nature of all bads.

If death is indeed a bad for the individual who dies, it is in the subclass of bads that cannot be "read off" the temporally intrinsic states and properties of an individual at a time. Thus, it is not a "current-time-slice" notion. Other bads are similarly not matters simply of the current time-slice. For example, Nagel argues that a persistent state of vegetative contentment may be a misfortune for someone who used to be (say) a great scientist but was *reduced* to such a state (pp. 65–66 in this volume). Thus, whether a state or condition is a bad or misfortune may not depend solely on temporally non-relational or current-time-slice features of an individual. Rather, there is an interesting and important dependence on facts about *history* and *possibilities*. Death would thus be similar to other bads (and certain other phenomena) in not having its normative properties issue solely from current-time-slice features.[21]

Fred Feldman has recently proposed an interesting version of the deprivation theory. In general, his view is that something is bad for someone insofar as his welfare level is lower in the nearest possible world in which it occurs than in the nearest world in which it does not occur. (For the details, see his "Some Puzzles About the Evil of Death," Chapter 16 in this volume; there is also a discussion of such a view in Jeff McMahan's "Death and the Value of Life," Chapter 13.) On this view, a state of affairs can be bad for a person whether it occurs before he exists, while he exists, or after he exists.

Consider a final problem for the deprivation account. Death is supposed to be an experiential blank that is bad insofar as it deprives the person who dies of the goods of life. Presumably, if one dies later rather than earlier, one can have more of the goods of life. But prenatal nonexistence seems in these ways precisely symmetric to death (conceived as posthumous nonexistence). That is, prenatal nonexistence is an indefinitely long experiential blank that is a deprivation of the goods of life: if one is born earlier rather than later, one can have more of the goods of life. (Of course, this presupposes that we hold fixed one's death date, but this assumption is simply the mirror image of the assumption above that one holds fixed the birth date in assessing the first conditional.) But we do not regard prenatal nonexistence as a bad, misfortune, or harm; we do not tend to think it rational to regret it. Given this and the apparent symmetry between prenatal nonexistence and death (on the deprivation theory), it seems that we cannot consistently hold that death can be a bad thing for the person who dies, on the deprivation theory.

Nagel has attempted to respond to this worry by suggesting that, although it is conceptually and metaphysically possible for an individual to die later than he actually dies, it is conceptually and metaphysically *impossible* for a given individual to be born earlier than he actually is born. That is, the time of birth is taken to be essential to personal identity. Given this, the asymmetry in our attitudes toward prenatal and posthumous nonexistence can be explained.

But it is certainly unclear that the claim about the essentiality of the time of an individual's birth is true. Why should one suppose that this is true? Even if it is a necessary condition of personal identity that one issue from the particular sperm and egg cells from which one actually issues, this in itself would not imply that the particular time at which one is born is essential to personal identity. (Why couldn't those sperm and egg cells have existed earlier?)[22]

The following is another strategy for explaining the apparent asymmetry in our attitudes toward prenatal and posthumous nonexistence (which would render the deprivation theory consistent with such asymmetric attitudes). In general, we tend to have temporally asymmetric attitudes toward our own pains and pleasures (see Parfit, Chapter 11 in this volume). We prefer our pains to have been in the past rather than in the present or future. Also, we prefer our pleasures to be in the present or future, rather than in the past. Further, this asymmetry (which manifests itself from a "temporally located perspective"—the perspective of an individual located at a particular point in time) is evidently a deep feature of ourselves whose rationality is not in doubt.

Given the rationality of our temporally asymmetric attitudes, the rationality of our asymmetric attitudes toward prenatal and posthumous nonexistence can be understood. Of course, death itself is here being construed as an experiential blank, and thus our temporally asymmetric attitudes toward pains are not relevant. But since death is a deprivation of (among other things) pleasures and pleasant experiences, then it is not irrational to have asymmetric attitudes toward prenatal nonexistence and posthumous nonexistence, insofar as it is not irrational to have asymmetric attitudes toward past and future pleasures. If we are relatively indifferent to past pleasures but have a more vivid appreciation of the prospect of future pleasures, then it is not mysterious why we would regard prenatal and posthumous nonexistence differently. (For a development and defense of this approach, see Brueckner and Fischer, Chapter 12 in this volume.)[23] Of course, this explanation takes for granted the underlying rationality of our temporally asymmetric attitudes toward pleasurable experiences; relative to this assumption, the asymmetry in our attitudes toward death and prenatal nonexistence can be rendered compatible with the deprivation theory.

Despite its manifest attractions, the deprivation theory is not without problems. Who exactly is the subject of the misfortune? Perhaps it is the "person-before-he-dies" or the "ante-mortem person" (see Chapters 9 and 10). But if so, then this individual is harmed *after* he ceases to exist, which is a somewhat jarring idea. Alternatively, the harm occurs while the individual dies. But then the harm occurs before death does, and this is also somewhat difficult to swallow, especially on the deprivation theory (as opposed perhaps to the desire-frustration theory).[24] Some proponents of the deprivation theory have been attracted to the idea that some bads or harms are not "dated" at all. On this view, we should not attempt always to attach a precise and specific time to the occurrence of all sorts of bads or harms, and, in particular, to the evil or harm of death (see Nagel, Chapter 4 in this volume). While it may be clear when death occurs and that death harms a person, it may not be determinate when the *harm* occurs.

Death and Morality

There are many connections between the metaphysical issues we have been charting above and the moral issues pertaining to death.[25] If the Epicurean position is correct, then it might lead to very implausible results concerning the moral status of killing. Presumably, killing another person might be considered wrong to the extent that *others* suffer as a result of the death, but it could not be considered morally objectionable to the person who is killed (insofar as the death is quick and painless). Further, it would seem that on the skeptical view about the badness of death no suicide could be considered unfortunate or irrational (except insofar as it has an impact on *others*). Indeed, it is controversial whether a sincere Epicurean can consider his own life meaningful and worthwhile (see Chapters 14 and 15). (Of course, even if death is considered possibly a bad thing for a person, there is much controversy about the conditions under which killing is morally unjustified. For example, it is contentious whether and under what circumstances euthanasia is morally permissible.)[26]

Here I wish briefly to sketch a connection between the metaphysical issues discussed above and one of the most contentious moral issues: abortion.[27] Let us suppose we accept some version of the deprivation theory of death's badness. Now it might be argued that all abortions are morally wrong in virtue of the fact that killing the fetus deprives a living thing of a "future like ours."[28] Somewhat more carefully, the argument is as follows. In general (and apart from countervailing moral reasons), killing another human being is wrong insofar as death is a deprivation of the good things of life. But just as the death of a child or an adult human being deprives it of future goods (including future pleasurable experiences), so the death of a fetus deprives it of such goods. That is, the deprivation theory of the badness of death seems to apply symmetrically to born and unborn living things—it would appear to apply to the fetus as much as to children and adults. Thus, if intentionally killing a child or adult is (other things being equal) morally wrong, then abortion is as well.

If one accepts the argument and the deprivation theory, this might lead one to conclude that abortion is morally unacceptable. Alternatively, if one is convinced that abortion is not in general morally unacceptable, this might lead one to question the deprivation theory or the argument. Here, I shall briefly lay out some reasons to question the argument. If the argument is problematic, it might ultimately emerge that one can simultaneously embrace the deprivation theory and the denial of the general impermissibility of abortion.

One way of arguing that abortion need not always be morally impermissible is to focus on the claims, rights, and interests of the mother as well as that of the fetus. On this approach, one might concede that the death of the fetus is bad for the fetus insofar as it deprives it of the goods of life. Thus, abortion is prima facie morally wrong. On the other hand, the mother has certain rights; perhaps the relevant rights are those of autonomy or privacy or simply the right to determine what happens in and to her body. In any case, it is not evident that the deprivation to the fetus must be considered a morally weightier consideration than the rights and interests of the mother. Thus, abortion may be *all-things-considered* permissible in certain contexts, even though the deprivation theory is true and abortion is prima facie morally objectionable.[29]

Consider, as an analogy, killing in self-defense. It seems that there are some cases of killing in self-defense in which the killing is morally permissible. This is entirely compatible with the claim that the person who dies suffers a misfortune that consists in the deprivation of future goods. In this case, by hypothesis, the deprivation is all-things-considered justified; other moral considerations are weightier than the misfortune of the person who dies. (I am not here claiming that all or any cases of abortion are in *all* relevant respects analogous to killing in self-defense; my point is the more restricted claim that the deprivation of future goods is not the only or necessarily the decisive moral consideration in other contexts, and thus it may not be the only or the decisive moral consideration in the context of abortion.)

Alternatively, one could argue that the fetus is not yet a person and thus the deprivation of future goods is not relevant to it. (McMahan employs this strategy in Chapter 13.) When an adult human being dies, the deprivation of future goods is a deprivation suffered by the person associated with the human body in question; the future goods would have been experienced by the person whose body died. But the same cannot be said of the fetus, since no person is associated with the fetus; it is *not* the case that the future goods would have been experienced by the person whose body died (since there is no such person). Of course, this strategy depends on the (controversial) claim that the fetus is not a person.

Finally, the severity of the deprivation of future goods might reasonably be thought to depend on the relationship between the individual who dies and those future goods. But since the fetus has no mental life at all, it could be argued that the sorts of psychological relationships between past and future mental states that make death particularly bad for children and adults do not obtain in the case of a fetus (see Chapter 13).

Death, Humor, and Ambivalence

Notoriously, death elicits ambivalence. One such ambivalence manifests itself in our humor about death. Arguably, part of the function of such humor is to make death less terrifying. One way in which this is done is to treat death as continuous with and similar to ordinary life; insofar as death is like ordinary life, it can seem less mysterious and frightening.

This tendency to treat death as a mere extension of life is seen in the humor of Woody Allen. In the movie *Love and Death*, he says, "We all die eventually. I just hope I'm alive when it happens." Also in *Love and Death*, Allen asks, "What happens to us after we die? Is there a hell? Is there a God? Do we live again? Where do we go? Do I need a toothbrush? . . . Are there girls?" In his book *Without Feathers*, Allen says:

While taking my noon walk today, I had more morbid thoughts. What *is* it about death that bothers me so much? Probably the hours. Melnick says the soul is immortal and lives on after the body drops away, but if the soul exists without my body I am convinced all my clothes will be too loose-fitting. Oh well. (p. 6)

Also in *Without Feathers* Allen asks, "After death is it still possible to take showers? . . . I keep wondering if there is an afterlife, and if there is will they be able to break a twenty?" (p. 4). And in *Getting Even*, he says, "It is impossible to experience one's own death objectively and still carry a tune" (p. 32).

Similarly, consider this passage from *White Noise* by Don Delillo:

"They've grown comfortable with their money," I said. "They genuinely believe they're entitled to it. This conviction gives them a kind of rude health. They glow a little."

"I have trouble imagining death at that income level," she said.

"Maybe there is no death as we know it. Just documents changing hands." (p. 6)

These remarks treat death as if it were like ordinary life, filled with mundane matters. (Also, one sees this sort of tendency in certain funerary practices, especially those that involve preservation of the dead body.) To this extent one can feel some comfort and protection against the mystery and fear of death. On the other hand, the humor of these remarks depends essentially on the *inappropriateness* of this sort of assimilation of death to life. Thus, we are also reminded of death's radical difference from life. In some of the humor about death, then, there is the impetus both to treat death as fundamentally similar to ordinary life and to remind us of death's fundamental difference from ordinary life.

In this humor, however, it is the impetus to find death similar to life (and, ultimately, to laugh at death) that mitigates our fear of it. Ironically, it is the project of the Epicurean to argue that death is fundamentally *dissimilar* to ordinary life. Indeed, the Epicurean argues that it is precisely in virtue of this dissimilarity between death and ordinary life that we should not fear it.

CHAPTER TWO

I feel that life is divided up into the horrible and the miserable. Those are the two categories. . . . The horrible would be . . . terminal cases . . . and blind people, crippled. . . . I don't know how they get through life. It's amazing to me. . . . And the miserable is everyone else. That's all. So when you go through life you should be thankful that you're miserable, because . . . you're very lucky to be miserable. —Woody Allen, *Annie Hall*

Death Knocks

Woody Allen

(*The play takes place in the bedroom of the Nat Ackermans' two-story house, somewhere in Kew Gardens. The carpeting is wall-to-wall. There is a big double bed and a large vanity. The room is elaborately furnished and curtained, and on the walls there are several paintings and a not really attractive barometer. Soft theme music as the curtain rises. Nat Ackerman, a bald, paunchy fifty-seven-year-old dress manufacturer, is lying on the bed finishing off tomorrow's* Daily News. *He wears a bathrobe and slippers, and reads by a bed light clipped to the white headboard of the bed. The time is near midnight. Suddenly we hear a noise, and Nat sits up and looks at the window.*)

Nat: What the hell is that?
(*Climbing awkwardly through the window is a sombre, caped figure. The intruder wears a black hood and skintight black clothes. The hood covers his head but not his face, which is middle-aged and stark white. He is something like Nat in appearance. He huffs audibly and then trips over the windowsill and falls into the room.*)
Death (*for it is no one else*): Jesus Christ. I nearly broke my neck.
Nat (*watching with bewilderment*): Who are you?
Death: Death.
Nat: Who?
Death: Death. Listen—can I sit down? I nearly broke my neck. I'm shaking like a leaf.

Reprinted by permission from *Getting Even* (New York: Random House, 1966): 41–53.

Nat: Who *are* you?

Death: *Death.* You got a glass of water?

Nat: Death? What do you mean, Death?

Death: What is wrong with you? You see the black costume and the whitened face?

Nat: Yeah.

Death: Is it Halloween?

Nat: No.

Death: Then I'm Death. Now can I get a glass of water—or a Fresca?

Nat: If this is some joke—

Death: What kind of joke? You're fifty-seven? Nat Ackerman? One eighteen Pacific Street? Unless I blew it—where's that call sheet? (*He fumbles through pocket, finally producing a card with an address on it. It seems to check.*)

Nat: What do you want with me?

Death: What do I want? What do you think I want?

Nat: You must be kidding. I'm in perfect health.

Death (*unimpressed*): Uh-huh. (*Looking around*) This is a nice place. You do it yourself?

Nat: We had a decorator, but we worked with her.

Death (*looking at picture on the wall*): I love those kids with the big eyes.

Nat: I don't want to go yet.

Death: *You* don't want to go? Please don't start in. As it is, I'm nauseous from the climb.

Nat: What climb?

Death: I climbed up the drainpipe. I was trying to make a dramatic entrance. I see the big windows and you're awake reading. I figure it's worth a shot. I'll climb up and enter with a little—you know . . . (*Snaps fingers*) Meanwhile, I get my heel caught on some vines, the drainpipe breaks, and I'm hanging by a thread. Then my cape begins to tear. Look, let's just go. It's been a rough night.

Nat: You broke my drainpipe?

Death: Broke. It didn't break. It's a little bent. Didn't you hear anything? I slammed into the ground.

Nat: I was reading.

Death: You must have really been engrossed. (*Lifting newspaper Nat was reading*) "NAB COEDS IN POT ORGY." Can I borrow this?

Nat: I'm not finished.

Death: Er—I don't know how to put this to you, pal . . .

Nat: Why didn't you just ring downstairs?

Death: I'm telling you, I could have, but how does it look? This way I get a little drama going. Something. Did you read *Faust*?

Nat: What?

Death: And what if you had company? You're sitting there with important people. I'm Death—I should ring the bell and traipse right in the front? Where's your thinking?

Nat: Listen, Mister, it's very late.

Death: Yeah. Well, you want to go?

Nat: Go where?

Death: Death. It. The Thing. The Happy Hunting Grounds. (*Looking at his own knee*) Y'know, that's a pretty bad cut. My first job, I'm liable to get gangrene yet.

Nat: Now, wait a minute. I need time. I'm not ready to go.

Death: I'm sorry. I can't help you. I'd like to, but it's the moment.

Nat: How can it be the moment? I just merged with Modiste Originals.

Death: What's the difference, a couple of bucks more or less.

Nat: Sure, what do you care? You guys probably have all your expenses paid.

Death: You want to come along now?

Nat (*studying him*): I'm sorry, but I cannot believe you're Death.

Death: Why? What'd you expect—Rock Hudson?

Nat: No, it's not that.

Death: I'm sorry if I disappointed you.

Nat: Don't get upset. I don't know, I always thought you'd be . . . uh . . . taller.

Death: I'm five seven. It's average for my weight.

Nat: You look a little like me.

Death: Who should I look like? I'm your death.

Nat: Give me some time. Another day.

Death: I can't. What do you want me to say?

Nat: One more day. Twenty-four hours.

Death: What do you need it for? The radio said rain tomorrow.

Nat: Can't we work out something?

Death: Like what?

Nat: You play chess?

Death: No, I don't.

Nat: I once saw a picture of you playing chess.

Death: Couldn't be me, because I don't play chess. Gin rummy, maybe.

Nat: You play gin rummy?

Death: Do I play gin rummy? Is Paris a city?

Nat: You're good, huh?

Death: Very good.

Nat: I'll tell you what I'll do—

Death: Don't make any deals with me.

Nat: I'll play you gin rummy. If you win, I'll go immediately. If I win, give me some more time. A little bit—one more day.

Death: Who's got time to play gin rummy?

Nat: Come on. If you're so good.

Death: Although I feel like a game . . .

Nat: Come on. Be a sport. We'll shoot for a half hour.

Death: I really shouldn't.

Nat: I got the cards right here. Don't make a production.

Death: All right, come on. We'll play a little. It'll relax me.

Nat (*getting cards, pad, and pencil*): You won't regret this.

Death: Don't give me a sales talk. Get the cards and give me a Fresca and put out something. For God's sake, a stranger drops in, you don't have potato chips or pretzels.

Nat: There's M&M's downstairs in a dish.

Death: M&M's. What if the President came? He'd get M&M's, too?

Nat: You're not the President.

Death: Deal.

(*Nat deals, turns up a five.*)

Nat: You want to play a tenth of a cent a point to make it interesting?

Death: It's not interesting enough for you?

Nat: I play better when money's at stake.

Death: Whatever you say, Newt.

Nat: Nat. Nat Ackerman. You don't know my name?

Death: Newt, Nat—I got such a headache.

Nat: You want that five?

Death: No.

Nat: So pick.

Death (*surveying his hand as he picks*): Jesus, I got nothing here.

Nat: What's it like?

Death: What's what like?

(*Throughout the following, they pick and discard.*)

Nat: Death.

Death: What should it be like? You lay there.

Nat: Is there anything after?

Death: Aha, you're saving twos.

Nat: I'm asking. Is there anything after?

Death (*absently*): You'll see.

Nat: Oh, then I will actually see something?

Death: Well, maybe I shouldn't have put it that way. Throw.

Nat: To get an answer from you is a big deal.

Death: I'm playing cards.

Nat: All right, play, play.

Death: Meanwhile, I'm giving you one card after another.

Nat: Don't look through the discards.

Death: I'm not looking. I'm straightening them up. What was the knock card?

Nat: Four. You ready to knock already?

Death: Who said I'm ready to knock? All I asked was what was the knock card.

Nat: And all I asked was is there anything for me to look forward to.

Death: Play.

Nat: Can't you tell me anything? Where do we go?

Death: We? To tell you the truth, *you* fall in a crumpled heap on the floor.

Nat: Oh, I can't wait for that! Is it going to hurt?

Death: Be over in a second.

Nat: Terrific. (*Sighs*) I needed this. A man merges with Modiste Originals . . .

Death: How's four points?

Nat: You're knocking?

Death: Four points is good?

Nat: No, I got two.

Death: You're kidding.

Nat: No, you lose.

Death: Holy Christ, and I thought you were saving sixes.

Nat: No. Your deal. Twenty points and two boxes. Shoot. (*Death deals.*) I must fall on the floor, eh? I can't be standing over the sofa when it happens?

Death: No. Play.

Nat: Why not?

Death: Because you fall on the floor! Leave me alone. I'm trying to concentrate.

Nat: Why must it be on the floor? That's all I'm saying! Why can't the whole thing happen and I'll stand next to the sofa?

Death: I'll try my best. Now can we play?

Nat: That's all I'm saying. You remind me of Moe Lefkowitz. He's also stubborn.

Death: I remind him of Moe Lefkowitz. I'm one of the most terrifying figures you could possibly imagine, and him I remind of Moe Lefkowitz. What is he, a furrier?

Nat: You should be such a furrier. He's good for eighty thousand a year. Passementeries. He's got his own factory. Two points.

Death: What?

Nat: Two points. I'm knocking. What have you got?

Death: My hand is like a basketball score.

Nat: And it's spades.

Death: If you didn't talk so much.

(*They redeal and play on.*)

Nat: What'd you mean before when you said this was your first job?

Death: What does it sound like?

Nat: What are you telling me—that nobody ever went before?

Death: Sure they went. But I didn't take them.

Nat: So who did?

Death: Others.

Nat: There's others?

Death: Sure. Each one has his own personal way of going.

Nat: I never knew that.

Death: Why should you know? Who are you?

Nat: What do you mean who am I? Why—I'm nothing?

Death: Not nothing. You're a dress manufacturer. Where do you come to knowledge of the eternal mysteries?

Nat: What are you talking about? I make a beautiful dollar. I sent two kids through college. One is in advertising, the other's married. I got my own home. I drive a Chrysler. My wife has whatever she wants. Maids, mink coat, vacations. Right now she's at the Eden Roc. Fifty dollars a day because she wants to be near her sister. I'm supposed to join her next week, so what do you think I am—some guy off the street?

Death: All right. Don't be so touchy.

Nat: Who's touchy?

Death: How would you like it if I got insulted quickly?

Nat: Did I insult you?

Death: You didn't say you were disappointed in me?

Nat: What do you expect? You want me to throw you a block party?

Death: I'm not talking about that. I mean me personally. I'm too short, I'm this, I'm that.

Nat: I said you looked like me. It's like a reflection.

Death: All right, deal, deal.

(*They continue to play as music steals in and the lights dim until all is in total darkness. The lights slowly come up again, and now it is later and their game is over. Nat tallies.*)

Nat: Sixty-eight . . . one-fifty . . . Well, you lose.

Death (*dejectedly looking through the deck*): I knew I shouldn't have thrown that nine. Damn it.

Nat: So I'll see you tomorrow.

Death: What do you mean you'll see me tomorrow?

Nat: I won the extra day. Leave me alone.

Death: You were serious?

Nat: We made a deal.

Death: Yeah, but—

Nat: Don't "but" me. I won twenty-four hours. Come back tomorrow.

Death: I didn't know we were actually playing for time.

Nat: That's too bad about you. You should pay attention.

Death: Where am I going to go for twenty-four hours?

Nat: What's the difference? The main thing is I won an extra day.

Death: What do you want me to do—walk the streets?

Nat: Check into a hotel and go to a movie. Take a *schvitz*. Don't make a federal case.

Death: Add the score again.

Nat: Plus you owe me twenty-eight dollars.

Death: *What?*

Nat: That's right, Buster. Here it is—read it.

Death (*going through pockets*): I have a few singles—not twenty-eight dollars.

Nat: I'll take a check.

Death: From what account?

Nat: Look who I'm dealing with.

Death: Sue me. Where do I keep my checking account?

Nat: All right, gimme what you got and we'll call it square.

Death: Listen, I need that money.

Nat: Why should you need money?

Death: What are you talking about? You're going to the Beyond.

Nat: So?

Death: So—you know how far that is?

Nat: So?

Death: So where's gas? Where's tolls?

Nat: We're going by car!

Death: You'll find out. (*Agitatedly*) Look—I'll be back tomorrow, and you'll give me a chance to win the money back. Otherwise I'm in definite trouble.

Nat: Anything you want. Double or nothing we'll play. I'm liable to win an extra week or a month. The way you play, maybe years.

Death: Meantime I'm stranded.

Nat: See you tomorrow.

Death (*being edged to the doorway*): Where's a good hotel? What am I talking about hotel, I got no money. I'll go sit in Bickford's. (*He picks up the* News.)

Nat: Out. Out. That's my paper. (*He takes it back.*)

Death (*exiting*): I couldn't just take him and go. I had to get involved in rummy.

Nat (*calling after him*): And be careful going downstairs. On one of the steps the rug is loose.

(*And, on cue, we hear a terrific crash. Nat sighs, then crosses to the bedside table and makes a phone call.*)

Nat: Hello, Moe? Me. Listen, I don't know if somebody's playing a joke, or what, but Death was just here. We played a little gin . . . No, *Death.* In person. Or somebody who claims to be Death. But, Moe, he's such a *schlep!*

CURTAIN

CHAPTER THREE

Who will die first?

This question comes up from time to time, like where are the car keys. It ends a sentence, prolongs a glance between us. I wonder if the thought itself is part of the nature of physical love, a reverse Darwinism that awards sadness and fear to the survivor. Or is it some inert element in the air we breathe, a rare thing like neon, with a melting point, an atomic weight?

· · ·

Sometimes I think our love is inexperienced. The question of dying becomes a wise reminder. It cures us of our innocence of the future. Simple things are doomed, or is that a superstition?

· · ·

Who will die first? She says she wants to die first because she would feel unbearably lonely and sad without me, especially if the children were grown and living elsewhere. She is adamant about this. She sincerely wants to precede me. She discusses the subject with such argumentative force that it's obvious she thinks we have a choice in the matter. She also thinks nothing can happen to us as long as there are dependent children in the house. The kids are a guarantee of our relative longevity. We're safe as long as they're around. But once they get big and scatter, she wants to be the first to go. She sounds almost eager. She is afraid I will die unexpectedly, sneakily, slipping away in the night. It isn't that she doesn't cherish life; it's being left alone that frightens her. The emptiness, the sense of cosmic darkness.

· · ·

"I do want to die first," she said, "but that doesn't mean I'm not afraid. I'm terribly afraid. I'm afraid all the time."

"I've been afraid for more than half my life."

"What do you want me to say? Your fear is older and wiser than mine?"

"I wake up sweating. I break out in killer sweats."

"I chew gum because my throat constricts."

"I have no body. I'm only a mind or a self, alone in a vast space."

"I seize up," she said.

"I'm too weak to move. I lack all sense of resolve, determination."

"I thought about my mother dying. Then she died."

"I think about everyone dying. Not just myself. I lapse into terrible reveries."

"I felt so guilty. I thought her death was connected with my thinking about it. I feel the same way about my own death. The more I think about it, the sooner it will happen."

"How strange it is. We have these deep terrible lingering fears about ourselves and the people we love. Yet we walk around, talk to people, eat and drink. We manage to function. The feelings are deep and real. Shouldn't they paralyze us? How is it we can survive them, at least for a while? We drive a car, we teach a class. How is it no one sees how deeply afraid we were, last night, this morning? Is it something we all hide from each other, by mutual consent? Or do we share the same secret without knowing it? Wear the same disguise."

"What if death is nothing but sound?"

"Electrical noise."

"You hear it forever. Sound all around. How awful."

"Uniform, white."

"Sometimes it sweeps over me," she said. "Sometimes it insinuates itself into my mind, little by little. I try to talk to it. 'Not now, Death.' "

—Don Delillo, *White Noise*

Rationality and the Fear of Death

Jeffrie G. Murphy

> Cowards die many times before their deaths;
> The valiant never taste of death but once.
> Of all the wonders that I yet have heard,
> It seems to me most strange that men should fear;
> Seeing that death, a necessary end,
> Will come when it will come.
> —Shakespeare, *Julius Caesar*

"To philosophize," writes Montaigne, "is to learn to die."[1] This remark forms part of a long-standing tradition in philosophy which teaches that a truly wise or rational man will not fear death, and this tradition has found its way into our ordinary language—e.g., it is common to describe a person who accepts a terminal illness with patience as "philosophical" about his death. And most people would, I think, so describe the attitude expressed in the quoted remark given to Caesar—a remark particularly interesting because, in addition to telling us a great deal about the kind of person Shakespeare conceived Caesar to be, it appears to contain what has often been offered as an *argument*

Reprinted by permission from *The Monist* 59 (1976): 187–203. I wish to thank Lewis W. Beck, Peter Laska, Barbara Levenbook, Ronald D. Milo, George Panichas, and Anthony D. Woozley for the kindness in commenting on an earlier draft of this paper. I am particularly grateful to Lars Hertzberg for commenting on several previous drafts and for prolonged and instructive conversations on the issues involved.

that one is irrational in fearing death. The argument is that death is necessary or inevitable in the natural order of things and that, once one sees this, one will also see that fearing death is irrational.[2] Such an idea is found in the Stoics and the Epicureans among others and is, in many respects, interestingly different from the way of thinking about death that Christianity introduced into our civilization. The most illustrious and systematic defender of the pagan conception, of course, is Spinoza:

A free man, that is to say, a man who lives according to the dictates of reason alone, is not led by fear of death, but directly desires the good, that is to say, desires to act, to live, and to preserve his being in accordance with the principle of seeking his own profit. He thinks, therefore, of nothing less than death, and his wisdom is a meditation upon life. (*Ethics*, Four, LXVII)[3]

From Spinoza we get the idea, not merely that it is irrational to fear death, but that the absence of such irrational fearing is the mark of a kind of freedom or human liberation—the only kind of freedom or liberation possible in the realm of necessity. This idea of freedom as rational understanding, though a part of earlier philosophical traditions, is at the heart of Spinoza's philosophy.

My primary purpose in this paper is sympathetically to develop this pagan way of thinking about death—a way of thinking that many writers (e.g. Carl Jung)[4] regard as excessively rationalistic. This charge of excessive rationalism in part no doubt grows out of a desire to be as obscurantist as possible on important matters—a desire to convince ourselves, as J. L. Austin once remarked, of how clever we are by showing how obscure everything is. But part of the charge I suspect (particularly when it comes from psychiatrists and psychoanalysts) is based on the belief that rational thinking about death can ultimately provide no genuine solace or comfort to those troubled about the matter. (Why, for example, should the fact that death is a "necessary end" ease our minds? It might, if anything, seem to make matters worse, since inevitability precludes hope.) As the continued prevalence of sexual guilt and neurosis in a supposedly "sexually enlightened" age seems to indicate, intellectual understanding does not guarantee emotional peace.

I should certainly agree that there are no guarantees here. But surely there is evidence that rational thinking sometimes provides solace for some people—e.g., witness the lives and deaths of Spinoza, Hume, and Freud. It is not to be expected that all men will derive comfort from the same source, but this is no reason unjustly to discriminate against those who might find comfort in being reasonable. The primary goal of philosophy, of course, is not comfort but understanding; and understanding does not necessarily comfort. However, I am convinced that it is a fact that judging a fear to be irrational can sometimes be instrumental either in directly extinguishing that fear or in prodding a person to gain help (e.g. through therapy) in extinguishing that fear. For this reason, it will perhaps be of some practical use if it can be shown that it is irrational to fear death. I should not, of course, want to overestimate the probability here—something that "rationalists" are indeed perhaps inclined to do.

Judging the rational status of the fear of death has its most obvious practical utility, however, not in providing immediate comfort to people experiencing the fear, but rather in coming to terms with such issues as recommending therapy for others or in planning programs of education for children. Should we try to desensitize children to a certain degree by, for example, exposing them to the deaths of others rather than, as is our present practice, shielding them from such unpleasantness?⁵ I take it that we cannot properly answer this sort of question unless we first make a judgment concerning the rationality (i.e. the appropriateness and utility) of this fear and the role it may play in human life. The fear of death makes people "feel bad," but not all feelings that are unpleasant to those who experience them are to be extinguished. Neurotic feelings of guilt or shame (i.e., feeling guilty or ashamed when one has really done nothing wrong), for example, should surely be extinguished. They are inappropriate and harmful. However, genuine moral feelings (e.g., outrage over unjust treatment of self or others, guilt over *real* injury or wrongdoing to others) are appropriate and moreover probably produce good consequences—e.g., action against injustice, restitution for injury. And yet these feelings, though perfectly rational, are just as unpleasant to feel as those that are irrational. Thus the question of what feelings to extinguish is not to be answered solely by a consideration of whether they make the person feeling them suffer. Some suffering is appropriate and beneficial. This is not to say that suffering is irrelevant to rationality; for it is irrational to approve of suffering, either for oneself or others, for no good reason. My only point is that, since in some cases there may be good reasons, the appropriateness or desirability or rationality of a feeling is not solely a function of that feeling's hedonic tone.

Before beginning my development of the argument that (in a certain sense) it is irrational to fear death, it is necessary that I indicate what I mean to include, for purposes of this chapter, under the expression "the fear of death." The phrase is used in ordinary language to cover a very heterogeneous group of phenomena, and it is obviously not true that all feelings that could be characterized by the phrase "fear of death" are irrational. When Spinoza, for example, claimed that it is irrational to fear death, he surely did not mean to suggest that it is irrational to do such things as look both ways before crossing a street—i.e., he surely wanted to distinguish a reasonably prudent concern for one's safety from that fear of death which he regarded as contrary to reason. It is presumably not irrational to fear a *premature* death and thus take certain steps—e.g., give up smoking cigarettes, reduce cholesterol intake, exercise—in order to prolong life as long as possible. Thus these concerns, even if they are properly characterized as involving a fear of death, are not directly my concern in this paper. I am rather concerned simply with the fear that one will die *simpliciter*, the fear based on the certain fact of human mortality—not the fear that one might die early (perhaps avoidable) but the fear that one will die sometime (certainly unavoidable). Thus my concern lies in assessing the rationality of fearing death in the sense in which death is *unavoidable*. Unavoidability is dramatically illustrated for the man who knows that he has a terminal illness, but the certainty of death is no greater for such a person than for the rest of us. He simply has a better guess as to the time. My subject, then, is man's necessary mortality as an object of fear and of the kind of self-deception that fear induces.

The syllogism he had learnt from Kiesewetter's Logic: "Caius is a man, men are mortal, therefore Caius is mortal," had always seemed to him correct as applied to Caius, but certainly not as applied to himself. That Caius—man in the abstract—was mortal, was perfectly correct, but he was not Caius, not an abstract man, but a creature quite, quite separate from all others. He had been little Vanya, with a mamma and papa, afterwards with Katenka and with all the joys, griefs, and delights of childhood, boyhood, and youth. What did Caius know of the smell of that striped leather ball Vanya had been so fond of? Had Caius kissed his mother's hand like that, and did the silk of her dress rustle so for Caius? Had he rioted like that at school when the pastry was bad? Had Caius been in love like that? Could Caius preside at a session as he did? "Caius really was mortal and it was right for him to die; but for me, little Vanya, Ivan Ilych, with all my thoughts and emotions, it's altogether a different matter. It cannot be that I ought to die. That would be too terrible." Such was his feeling. (Leo Tolstoy, *The Death of Ivan Ilych*)

I shall now proceed by arguing in the following stages. First, I shall develop a general account of the concepts "rational fearing" and "irrational fearing." Second, I shall attempt to analyze the concept of *death*—what is it and why do people tend to regard it as a terrible and thus fearful thing? Finally, I shall apply the general account of rational fearing to the topic of death.

I

I should like to develop a general account of the distinction between rational fearing and irrational fearing in the hope that this account may ultimately be used to illuminate the fear of death. The account that I shall offer purports to capture and distinguish between some intuitively acceptable cases of fearings that are clearly rational and fearings that are clearly irrational. If the account looks correct for the clear cases, then we may have some confidence that it will help us come to terms with the rational status of the fear of death—a case where pretheoretical convictions no doubt are in conflict.

Now at the outset, it is important to realize that the expression "Jones is irrational in fearing" is crucially ambiguous. On the one hand, we can mean that the *fear itself* is irrational—i.e. inappropriate or not fitting to its object. On the other hand, we can mean that the *person* is irrational in the *role* that he allows his fears (however rational in the first sense) to have in his life. Spinoza, remember, does not say that the fear of death is itself irrational. What he says is that a rational man will not let himself be *led* by the fear of death. There is a sense in which fear of death is obviously rational—i.e. obviously fitting or appropriate. Indeed, as I shall later suggest, one's own death and suffering in part define the concept of the fearful. However, just because fear is rational in this sense, it does not follow that a person is rational in being led by this fear. This sense of "rational," characterizing persons, involves more than fittingness or appropriateness and requires a consideration of *utility*. (Again we have a parallel with the moral feeling of guilt. Are Dostoevskiian characters—e.g. Stavrogin—who live a life dominated by guilt for their wrongdoings to be judged rational or irrational? In one sense, I should argue, they are rational; for guilt is the appropriate or fitting feeling for moral wrongdoing toward others. They are not like persons who feel guilt when they have really done nothing wrong, and thus they are not irrational in *that* sense. However, though their guilt feelings may not themselves be irrational, the *characters* seem irrational because they allow themselves to be dominated and destroyed by those feelings.) In this chapter, I am interested primarily in the question "When is a *person* rational in fearing?" and am interested in the rationality of feelings themselves only insofar as this issue is relevant to the rationality of persons.[6]

My controlling assumption throughout is that Spinoza is fundamentally correct, at least in this context, in his attempt to analyze the concept of rationality (for persons) in such a way as to give a central place to concepts of self-interest or self-realization—what he calls "profit."[7] The basic idea in some ways anticipates Darwin and Freud in claiming that man is basically an animal whose reason functions, as instincts function in other animals, primarily for self-preservation and self-enrichment. A similar concept of rationality is found in Hobbes, who argues that no rational man could knowingly frustrate his own long-range self-interest. And Philippa Foot has recently reiterated this view: "Irrational actions are those in which a man in some way defeats his own purposes, doing what is calculated to be disadvantageous or to frustrate his ends."[8] This "egoistic" analysis of rationality might be challenged by philosophers of Kantian sympathies who believe (as I am inclined to) that *moral* rationality involves something different. However, since I do not see the problem of the rationality of fearing death as a moral problem, I do not think that Kantian scruples need detain us on this particular issue. Fear, after all, is not a likely candidate for a moral feeling. Its primary significance, unlike that of such genuine moral feelings as guilt and shame, lies simply in the avoidance of danger.

Having laid my controlling assumption on the table, I shall now offer the following as an account of the distinction between rational and irrational fearing.

It is rational for a person P to fear some state of affairs S if and only if:

(1) P holds the reasonable belief that S obtains or is likely to obtain,

(2) P holds the reasonable belief that S (a) is not easily avoided and (b) is very undesirable, bad, or evil for P,

(3) the fear of S could be instrumental in bringing about some behavior or action that would allow P to avoid S, and

(4) the fear of S is compatible, at least in the long run, with the satisfaction of the other important desires of P.[9]

If conditions (1) and (2) obtain, the fear is rational in the sense of being fitting or appropriate to its object. Conditions (3) and (4) have to obtain, however, in order for the *person* to be rational in his fearing.

Since this general account is probably not intuitively obvious, I shall comment upon each of the four conditions separately.

(1) P *holds the reasonable belief that* S *obtains or is likely to obtain.* This, I take it, is the least controversial of the conditions I have put forth. Perhaps paradigm examples of people who suffer fears we regard as irrational are those who suffer from psychotic delusions. Paranoids, or alcoholics experiencing delirium tremens, for example, may fear the demons in the water faucets, the Martians in the closet, or the pink spiders on the wall. The best reason we have for thinking that these fears are irrational is the absence of any grounds or evidence that there might be demons in the water faucets, Martians in the closet, or pink spiders on the wall.

(2) P *holds the reasonable belief that* S *(a) is not easily avoided and (b) is very undesirable, bad, or evil for* P. Except for one problem to be noted shortly, this condition also seems fairly noncontroversial. Phobias, I take it, are acceptable examples of irrational fears. We should tend to characterize as irrational persons who are "scared to death" of (nonpoisonous) snakes or of high places. This is not because, as was the case in (1) above, there are no snakes or high places, but is rather because snakes and high places are normally harmless. Typically we pass these fears

off as "silly" and would not regard a person experiencing them as seriously irrational unless they had other harmful effects—a point to be explored when I discuss (4) below.

Now what may appear to some as a problem with the condition is the claim that S must be bad *for P*. This may strike some as too egoistic, and they might argue that it is perfectly rational to fear that something bad will happen to another. On this point I am inclined to argue as follows: One can certainly care deeply (perhaps on moral grounds) that others not die, but this caring typically is not, in my judgment, to be explicated as a kind of *fearing*. Wanting others in general not to die is, I suppose, simply part of what it means to be a morally sensitive person placing a high value on human life. One's own fear of dying, however, is hardly to be understood in this way. Fear is a very personal (self-regarding) feeling, and thus it seems to be tautological that one can literally fear only that which deeply involves oneself. The following conversation, for example, would be extremely odd: "I am terribly afraid." "Why?" "Because people are continuing to die in Bangladesh." One's own suffering and death, it could be said, *define* the concept of the fearful.

Thus I am inclined to think that one can literally *fear* evil happening to another only if that other is so close to one (a wife or child perhaps) that what happens to that other in a sense happens to oneself. As Freud says about the death of a child: "*Our* hopes, *our* pride, *our* happiness, lie in the grave with him, we will not be consoled, we will not fill the loved one's place." [10] For reasons that will become apparent when I later analyze the nature of death, I think there is a sense in which it is true (at least for some parents) that a part of them would die in the death of their child.

It is perhaps morally regrettable that most of us do not identify a very wide range of persons (perhaps the whole human race) with ourselves to such an extent that we could fear their deaths. It is surely not psychologically regrettable, of course, since if we did make such an identification we could probably not stand the emotional damage that would result. However, regrettable or not, it is false that very many people would sincerely agree with John Donne's observation that each man's death diminishes me. We may not be islands, but neither are we continents or worlds.

(3) *The fear of S could be instrumental in bringing about some behavior or action that would allow P to avoid S.* This condition is at the heart of Spinoza's concept of rationality as involving self-preservation, as securing a "profit" in one's life. One way to characterize an activity as rational is to see that it has a point or purpose—that it at least appears to accomplish something. And surely it is avoidance behavior that gives fearing its significance. Suppose we imagined ourselves to be in a position of a Creator giving man the instinct of fear. What could this be except giving man the general capacity to make self-protective responses to danger? Fear's primary biological function is found in self-defensive behavior—what physiologists call the "fight or flight" reflex. And surely such fear, in addition to being biologically functional, is a part of what we understand by a rational approach to danger. If one discovers a hungry and aggressive tiger in the room, a state of affairs that surely satisfies conditions (1) and (2), who would doubt that the resulting fear is appropriate and that a person is rational in being "led" by the fear to the extent that he attempts to get out of the room as quickly as possible?

Since this condition will (not surprisingly) play a role in my later argument that it is irrational to fear death, I shall defer further discussion of it until later.

(4) *The fear of S is compatible, at least in the long run, with the satisfaction of the other important desires of P.* If the first three conditions are unsatisfied, we can perhaps, some may argue, conclude nothing more than that in such fearing the person is *non*-rational. The present condition, however, surely gives us a test for genuine *ir*rationality with respect to fearing; and indeed its nonsatisfaction is a mark of fearings that we should call *neurotic*. A phobia, for example, becomes clearly a neurotic symptom, and not just something silly or eccentric, when it so pervades the life of the person who experiences it that he is rendered incapable of leading a successful and satisfying life. A person who merely shudders when he sees a spider, for example, is perhaps just a little silly. A person who is so afraid that he might see a spider that he never leaves his home and has that home visited by a pest exterminator several times a week is something more than silly. He is pathetic and is in need of help.

Even fearings that would normally be quite rational become

irrational when this condition is unsatisfied. A certain fear of germs, for example, is certainly rational. There are germs, many germs are very harmful, and a fear of them can prompt a person to take reasonable precautions against disease. However, a person who is so afraid of germs that he washes twenty times a day, sprays all items in his house with germicide, refuses to leave his sanitized bedroom, etc., has crossed the boundary between reasonable prudence and irrational fearing.

As with condition (3), this condition will play an important role in my later discussion of the fear of death.

II

The conditions I have outlined above provide a very rough way of distinguishing two very different ways of attempting to come to terms with death—what I shall call the "other-worldly" and the "naturalistic." Other-worldly Christians, for example, who counsel that at least certain persons (the saved) should not fear death, tend to argue that the fear of death fails to satisfy conditions (1) or (2)—i.e., they argue either that there is no such thing as death or that death is a good thing. In practice, of course, these two claims—insofar as they are intelligible at all—tend to be collapsed together. Naturalistic writers, such as Spinoza, tend to argue that a rational person will not be led by the fear of death because such fearing fails to satisfy conditions (3) or (4)—i.e., they argue that the fear of death is pointless (since it cannot help us to avoid death) or harmful (because it interferes with the satisfactions that life offers).

Although my primary purpose is to develop the pagan naturalistic tradition represented by Spinoza, it might be worth pausing a few moments over the obvious weaknesses in the other-worldly tradition. First, and most obvious, the set of beliefs that underlie that tradition (distinction between soul and body, immortality of the soul, etc.) are not very likely candidates for reasonable beliefs. Indeed, if they are held in a literal or "fundamentalist" sense, they might better be offered as candidates for obscurantist superstition. Second, and more important for our present purposes, is the following: Even if these beliefs are accepted, there is an important sense in which they really do not provide answers to the question "How are we to come to terms with death?" For they are, after all, *denials* that there is such a thing as genuine death. Socrates (at least according to Plato) seemed to have this kind of other-worldly outlook—e.g., he says in *Apology* that, after his body passes away, it is not unlikely that his soul (his true person) will pass to a kind of heaven where he will converse with such departed luminaries as Hesiod and Homer. This seems to me to be a way of *not* facing death and certainly does not deserve to be characterized, as many people have characterized it, as facing death with *courage*. For what is courageous about accepting the fact that one will move to a place where one will be better off than ever before? And what is intellectually commendable about believing such things in the absence of any shred of evidence? [11]

There is one other argument that condition (2) is not satisfied which, though also found in naturalistic writers (e.g. Lucretius [12] and Hobbes), shares a common feebleness with the arguments noted above. It is, very generally, the argument that the death of *P* is not bad for *P* because it cannot *hurt P*. Hobbes puts the argument in the following way:

There be few lingeringe diseases or sudden paynes that be not more sensible and paynefull then death, and therefore I see little reason why a man that lives well should feare death more then sicknesse.
("Of Death")

Even more comforting thoughts are expressed by the Christian poet John Donne:

From rest and sleep, which but thy picture be,
Much pleasure; then from thee much more must flow.
("Death, Be Not Proud")

These arguments are so far beside the point that they at most demonstrate only one thing—that the fear of death must be very terrible indeed for some people if they are willing to grab at such small straws and take comfort in such inanity. Though it is natural that some people might confuse a fear of death with a fear of pain (or, in our own day, with a fear of winding up one's days being treated as a nonperson in one of our contemporary hospitals), it is quite obvious on reflection that the fear of death and the fear of pain are quite distinct. It should also be clear on reflection that all things bad for us (e.g. loss of reputation) do not necessarily have to "hurt" in any literal sense. If the fear of death just was the fear of pain, then there would indeed be little reason why anyone should fear death. For death is not always a painful affair, and, in most of those cases where it might be, we have drugs or (if it comes to it) suicide. Thus Hobbes and Donne have perhaps provided us with reasons why we should not fear a *painful* death, but these are not reasons why we should not fear death *simpliciter*. They have not given us reasons why death itself, independent of suffering, is not a very undesirable, bad, or evil thing for a person.

III

What, then, is death such that it is a very undesirable, bad, or evil thing for a person? *That* it is bad is, I take it, obvious; for death, along with suffering, in part define the very concept of what is a bad thing for a person and (as I suggested earlier) the very concept of the fearful. Thus, I should argue, explaining what is bad or fearful about death is part of explaining what death itself is.

The death of a *person*, unlike the death of a beast, represents not merely the extinction of an organism. It also represents the end of a conscious history that transcends itself in thought. All I mean by this high-sounding phrase is that, to use the language of Sartre, persons define themselves in large measure in terms of their future-oriented *projects*. What I am is in large measure what I want to accomplish. This is perhaps a very "bourgeois" conception of personality, for it is a definition in terms of individual agency. In more collectivist societies, the conception of a person might well (for better or worse) be different and the fear of death correspondingly different.[13] However, the analysis I am offering does seem to me true of at least a great many persons in society as we now find it. Our self-identifying projects may be bound up with persons very close to us, and this explains why we sometimes, as I noted earlier, see the deaths of our children or wives as a partial death of our own persons. But it is rare (and perhaps regrettable) that the range of such persons included in self-identification is anything but quite narrow.

If I am correct that a person is self-defined largely in terms of certain projects—e.g., the desire to accomplish something in one's profession, to provide for one's family, to achieve certain satisfactions, to redress moral injuries done—then we can see wherein much of the badness of death lies: death represents *lost opportunity*. My death might prevent me from finishing a book, from getting my children through school, from rendering aid to those who have a claim on my benevolence, from making amends for moral wrongs against others. It is this idea that death means *no more chances* that tormented Ivan Ilych—a man who had already thrown away the chances he had to live the right sort of life:

His mental sufferings were due to the fact that that night, as he looked at Gerasim's sleepy, good-natured face with its prominent cheekbones, the question suddenly occurred to him: "What if my whole life has been wrong?" It occurred to him that what had appeared perfectly impossible before, namely that he had not spent his life as he should have done, might after all be true. It occurred to him that his scarcely perceptible attempts to struggle against what was considered good by the most highly placed people, those scarcely noticeable impulses which he had immediately suppressed, might have been the real thing, and all the rest false. . . . "But if that is so," he said to himself, "and I am leaving this life with the consciousness that I have lost all that was given me and it is impossible to rectify it—what then?" (Tolstoy, *The Death of Ivan Ilych*)

Mary Mothersill has put the point in the following way:

Death is the deadline for all my assignments. . . . To know what it is like to hope that one will not be interrupted is to know something about (one sort) of fear of death. We may think of death (rather grandiosely) as the person from Porlock but for whose untimely visit, *Kubla Khan*, or so Coleridge claimed, would have been much, much longer than it is.[14]

At this point, I should like to raise the following query: Would one fear death more than (or in a way different from) the fear of permanent coma resulting from massive brain damage? If, as I suspect, most people would answer *no*, then this is support for the account I have been offering.

Now one thing we can learn from this account is in keeping with the Christian message that we should (within reason of course) live each day as though it may be our last. Knowing that death will come, we can make an effort to accomplish what we feel we need to accomplish—realizing that there will not always be chances to "do it later." There are, of course, those unfortunate and generally neurotic individuals who have no sense of self-worth, who feel that they never can accomplish anything that matters, who feel that their very existence is an injury to others. These persons, unless they are helped by therapy, really lack self-defining projects and thus really lack a strong sense of themselves as persons. Not surprisingly, such individuals tend to fear death with the greatest intensity of all. For they fear, not simply that they will not finish, but that they will never even get started.[15]

Even if we are fortunate and are not plagued by neurotic self-doubts, and even if we make a prudent effort to accomplish what we think important with some sense of urgency in order to "beat death," we shall never be completely successful. Not only will we always fail to get something done that we think we ought to have done, but we shall also (as long as we remain persons) continue to generate new self-defining projects as we grow older. Thus, though with diligence we can perhaps prevent death from being as bad as it might be, for most of us it will, when it comes, be bad enough.

IV

What does all of this tell us about the rationality of fearing death? Applying conditions (3) and (4) of the previously developed analysis, conditions that I regard as perhaps doing little more than formalizing Spinoza's general account of the fear of death, I should conclude that a prudent fear of death is perfectly rational. By a prudent fear of death I mean simply (a) one that provokes people into maintaining a reasonable (though not neurotic compulsive) diligence with respect to living the kind of life they regard as proper or meaningful (e.g., maintaining their health, not making the mistake of Ivan Ilych) and (b) one that is kept in its proper place (i.e., does not sour all the good things in one's life). If the fear of death, even if initially inspired by the desire to accomplish important things in time, becomes a neurotic compulsion, then the saying "In the midst of life we are in death" is exemplified.

Fear of death is irrational and properly extinguished, then, when it can serve no legitimate purpose in our lives—when it cannot aid us in avoiding bad things (e.g. failed assignments) in a way that is consistent with the successful and satisfying integration and functioning of our person. As Spinoza would put it, the fear of death is irrational when it redounds, not to our profit, but to our loss. For, other things (especially moral things) being equal, the pursuit of loss rather than profit could not be the goal of any rational man.[16]

To call the fear of death irrational is not, of course, moralistically to *condemn* those who feel it. A man is fairly to be blamed only for that which is in his control, and typically feelings are not in our control—at least not in our direct control. The irrational fear of death, if it pervades the life of a person, becomes a kind of neurosis, and normally the proper response to a fearful neurotic is not blame but, rather, a suggestion that he seek therapeutic help in extinguishing his fears.[17]

If a person can extinguish or have extinguished such irrational fears of death he will move toward being, in Spinoza's sense, liberated or free. To fear irrationally is to be a kind of prisoner to one's pointless passions, in bondage to feelings that preclude the enjoyment of what is now valued and the pursuit of what is wanted for the future. The meaningfulness of the present and the future are destroyed, and one is put in the pitiful position, described by Socrates, of caring so much about simply living that one loses whatever it is that makes life *worth* living. To quote Montaigne again:

The thing I fear most is fear. . . . He who has learned how to die has unlearned how to be a slave. . . . For as it is impossible for the soul to be at rest when she fears death, so, if she can gain assurance against it, she can boast of a thing as it were beyond man's estate: that it is impossible for worry, torment, fear, or even the slightest displeasure to dwell in her. . . . She is made mistress of her passions and lusts, mistress over indigence, shame, poverty, and all other wounds of fortune. Let us gain this advantage, those of us who can; this is the true and sovereign liberty, which enables us to thumb our noses at force and injustice and to laugh at prisons and chains.[18]

V

I am not sure how much comfort or solace, if any, can be derived from the way of thinking about death that I have outlined. One small comfort, at least to me, is that this way of thinking about death under some circumstances renders *suicide* a reasonable option, not merely for coming to terms with such misfortunes as pain, but also as a way of fulfilling (or at least not compromising) one's conception of oneself as a person. For if what one really values is the preservation of oneself as a certain *kind* of person (e.g., one who does not become a vegetable as a result of a debilitating illness, one who does not dishonor oneself and betray one's friends under torture) one can see, in voluntary death, at least this comfort—that one will end as the person one is and perhaps admires, not as another person that one perhaps would despise. What this shows is that the general reasons we have for not wanting to die may, in a particular case, constitute reasons for wanting to die. An American journalist, Charles Wertenbaker, wrote the following before his own suicide:

Problem with death is to recognize the point at which you can die with all your faculties, take a healthy look at the world and people as you go out of it. Let them get you in bed, drug you or cut you, and you become sick and afraid and disgusting, and everybody will be glad to get rid of you. It shouldn't be such a problem if you can remember how it was when you were young. You wouldn't give up something for instance to add ten years to your life. All right, don't ask for them now. You wouldn't give up drinking and love-making and eating—and why should you have given them up? Nothing is ever lost that has been experienced and it can all be there at the moment of death—if you don't wait too long.[19]

In a case like this, it is possible to see suicide not merely as reasonable but even as noble. This way of thinking, found in Greek, Roman, and some Oriental civilizations, and eloquently defended by David Hume (*Of Suicide*), provides the man who accepts it with an ultimate "out." And having an out is having a certain kind of limited freedom. For at least one's bondage is not total.

In closing, I must admit that even the above provides precious little in the way of comfort. The universe is impersonal, and is thus not kind. And it is just false that there is to be found, even by the exercise of our reason, a comfort for every sorrow. Even a man who clearly recognizes the irrationality of fearing death will sometimes, I am sure, be tormented by that fear anyway, and I make no pretense that I am any different. However, I am confident of one thing: that any occasional comfort, however little, that may be derived from rational understanding, unlike that which may flow from various forms of superstitious obscurantism, is at least consistent with human dignity and intellectual integrity.[20] And that, I think, is something.

CHAPTER FOUR

There's an old joke. Uh, two elderly women are at a Catskills mountain resort, and one of 'em says: "Boy, the food at this place is really terrible." The other one says, "Yeah, I know, and such . . . small portions." Well, that's essentially how I feel about life. Full of loneliness and misery and suffering and unhappiness, and it's all over much too quickly.

—Woody Allen, *Annie Hall*

Death

Thomas Nagel

If death is the unequivocal and permanent end of our existence, the question arises whether it is a bad thing to die.

There is conspicuous disagreement about the matter: some people think death is dreadful; others have no objection to death per se, though they hope their own will be neither premature nor painful. Those in the former category tend to think those in the latter are blind to the obvious, while the latter suppose the former to be prey to some sort of confusion. On the one hand it can be said that life is all we have and the loss of it is the greatest loss we can sustain. On the other hand it may be objected that death deprives this supposed loss of its subject, and that if we realize that death is not an unimaginable condition of the persisting person, but a mere blank, we will see that it can have no value whatever, positive or negative.

Since I want to leave aside the question whether we are, or might be, immortal in some form, I shall simply use the word *death* and its cognates in this discussion to mean *permanent* death, unsupplemented by any form of conscious survival. I want to ask whether death is in itself an evil, and how great an evil, and of what kind, it might be. The question should be of interest even to those who believe in some form of immortality, for one's attitude toward immortality must depend in part on one's attitude toward death.

Reprinted by permission from *Mortal Questions* (Cambridge, Engl.: Cambridge University Press, 1979): 1–10.

If death is an evil at all, it cannot be because of its positive features, but only because of what it deprives us of. I shall try to deal with the difficulties surrounding the natural view that death is an evil because it brings to an end all the goods that life contains. We need not give an account of these goods here, except to observe that some of them, like perception, desire, activity, and thought, are so general as to be constitutive of human life. They are widely regarded as formidable benefits in themselves, despite the fact that they are conditions of misery as well as of happiness, and that a sufficient quantity of more particular evils can perhaps outweigh them. That is what is meant, I think, by the allegation that it is good simply to be alive, even if one is undergoing terrible experiences. The situation is roughly this: There are elements that, if added to one's experience, make life better; there are other elements that, if added to one's experience, make life worse. But what remains when these are set aside is not merely *neutral*: it is emphatically positive. Therefore life is worth living even when the bad elements of experience are plentiful and the good ones too meager to outweigh the bad ones on their own. The additional positive weight is supplied by experience itself, rather than by any of its contents.

I shall not discuss the value that one person's life or death may have for others, or its objective value, but only the value it has for the person who is its subject. That seems to me the primary case, and the case that presents the greatest difficulties. Let me add only two observations. First, the value of life and its contents does not attach to mere organic survival: almost everyone would be indifferent (other things equal) between immediate death and immediate coma followed by death twenty years later without reawakening. And second, like most goods, this can be multiplied by time: more is better than less. The added quantities need not be temporally continuous (though continuity has its social advantages). People are attracted to the possibility of long-term suspended animation or freezing, followed by the resumption of conscious life, because they can regard it from within simply as a *continuation* of their present life. If these techniques are ever perfected, what from outside appeared as a dormant interval of three hundred years could be experienced by the subject as nothing more than a sharp discontinuity in the character of his experiences. I do not deny, of course, that this has its own disadvantages. Family and friends may have died in the meantime; the language may have changed; the comforts of social, geographical, and cultural familiarity would be lacking. Nevertheless, these inconveniences would not obliterate the basic advantage of continued, though discontinuous, existence.

If we turn from what is good about life to what is bad about death, the case is completely different. Essentially, though there may be problems about their specification, what we find desirable in life are certain states, conditions, or types of activity. It is *being* alive, *doing* certain things, having certain experiences, that we consider good. But if death is an evil, it is the *loss of life*, rather than the state of being dead, or nonexistent, or unconscious, that is objectionable.[1] This asymmetry is important. If it is good to be alive, that advantage can be attributed to a person at each point of his life. It is a good of which Bach had more than Schubert, simply because he lived longer. Death, however, is not an evil of which Shakespeare has so far received a larger portion than Proust. If death is a disadvantage, it is not easy to say when a man suffers it.

There are two other indications that we do not object to death merely because it involves long periods of nonexistence. First, as has been mentioned, most of us would not regard the *temporary* suspension of life, even for substantial intervals, as in itself a misfortune. If it ever happens that people can be frozen without reduction of the conscious lifespan, it will be inappropriate to pity those who are temporarily out of circulation. Second, none of us existed before we were born (or conceived), but few regard that as a misfortune. I shall have more to say about this later.

The point that death is not regarded as an unfortunate *state* enables us to refute a curious but very common suggestion about the origin of the fear of death. It is often said that those who object to death have made the mistake of trying to imagine what it is like to *be* dead. It is alleged that the failure to realize that this task is logically impossible (for the banal reason that there is nothing to imagine) leads to the conviction that death is a mysterious and therefore terrifying prospective state. But this diagnosis is evidently false, for it is just as impossible to imagine being totally unconscious as to imagine being dead (though it is easy enough to imagine oneself, from the outside, in either of those conditions). Yet people who are averse to death are not usually averse to unconsciousness (so long as it does not entail a substantial cut in the total duration of waking life).

If we are to make sense of the view that to die is bad, it must be on the grounds that life is a good and death is the corresponding deprivation or loss, bad not because of any positive features but because of the desirability of what it removes. We must now turn to the serious difficulties that this hypothesis raises, difficulties about loss and privation in general, and about death in particular.

Essentially, there are three types of problems. First, doubt may be raised whether *anything* can be bad for a man without being positively unpleasant to him: specifically, it may be doubted that there are any evils that consist merely in the deprivation or absence of possible goods, and that do not depend on someone's *minding* that deprivation. Second, there are special difficulties, in the case of death, about how the supposed misfortune is to be assigned to a subject at all. There is doubt both as to *who* its subject is and as to *when* he undergoes it. So long as a person exists, he has not yet died, and once he has died, he no longer exists; so there seems to be no time when death, if it is a misfortune, can be ascribed to its unfortunate subject. The third type of difficulty concerns the asymmetry, mentioned above, between our attitudes to posthumous and prenatal nonexistence. How can the former be bad if the latter is not?

It should be recognized that, if these are valid objections to counting death as an evil, they will apply to many other supposed evils as well. The first type of objection is expressed in general form by the common remark that what you don't know can't hurt you. It means that even if a man is betrayed by his friends, ridiculed behind his back, and despised by people who treat him politely to his face, none of it can be counted as a misfortune for him so long as he does not suffer as a result. It means that a man is not injured if his wishes are ignored by the executor of his will, or if, after his death, the belief becomes current that all the literary works on which his fame rests were really written by his brother, who died in Mexico at the age of 28. It seems to me worth asking what assumptions about good and evil lead to these drastic restrictions.

All the questions have something to do with time. There certainly are goods and evils of a simple kind (including some pleasures and pains) that a person possesses at a given time simply in virtue of his condition at that time. But this is not true of all the things we regard as good or bad for a man. Often we need to know his history to tell whether something is a misfortune or not; this applies to ills like deterioration, deprivation, and damage. Sometimes his experiential *state* is relatively unimportant— as in the case of a man who wastes his life in the cheerful pursuit of a method of communicating with asparagus plants. Someone who holds that all goods and evils must be temporally assignable states of the person may of course try to bring difficult cases into line by pointing to the pleasure or pain that more complicated goods and evils cause. Loss, betrayal, deception, and ridicule are on this view bad because people suffer when they learn of them. But it should be asked how our ideas of human value would have to be constituted to accommodate these cases directly instead. One advantage of such an account might be that it would enable us to explain *why* the discovery of these misfortunes causes suffering—in a way that makes it reasonable. For the natural view is that the discovery of betrayal makes us unhappy because it is bad to be betrayed—not that betrayal is bad because its discovery makes us unhappy.

It therefore seems to me worth exploring the position that most good and ill fortune has as its subject a person identified by his history and his possibilities, rather than merely by his categorical state of the moment—and that while this subject can be exactly located in a sequence of places and times, the same is not necessarily true of the goods and ills that befall him.[2]

These ideas can be illustrated by an example of deprivation whose severity approaches that of death. Suppose an intelligent person receives a brain injury that reduces him to the mental condition of a contented infant, and that such desires as remain to him can be satisfied by a custodian, so that he is free from care. Such a development would be widely regarded as a severe misfortune, not only for his friends and relations, or for society, but also, and primarily, for the person himself. This does not mean that a contented infant is unfortunate. The intelligent adult who has been *reduced* to this condition is the subject of the misfortune. He is the one we pity, though of course he does not mind his condition—there is some doubt, in fact, whether he can be said to exist any longer.

The view that such a man has suffered a misfortune is open

to the same objections that have been raised in regard to death. He does not mind his condition. It is in fact the same condition he was in at the age of three months, except that he is bigger. If we did not pity him then, why pity him now; in any case, who is there to pity? The intelligent adult has disappeared, and for a creature like the one before us, happiness consists in a full stomach and a dry diaper.

If these objections are invalid, it must be because they rest on a mistaken assumption about the temporal relation between the subject of a misfortune and the circumstances that constitute it. If, instead of concentrating exclusively on the oversized baby before us, we consider the person he was, and the person he *could* be now, then his reduction to this state and the cancellation of his natural adult development constitute a perfectly intelligible catastrophe.

This case should convince us that it is arbitrary to restrict the goods and evils that can befall a man to nonrelational properties ascribable to him at particular times. As it stands, that restriction excludes not only such cases of gross degeneration but also a good deal of what is important about success and failure, and other features of a life that have the character of processes. I believe we can go further, however. There are goods and evils that are irreducibly relational; they are features of the relations between a person, with spatial and temporal boundaries of the usual sort, and circumstances that may not coincide with him either in space or in time. A man's life includes much that does not take place within the boundaries of his body and his mind, and what happens to him can include much that does not take place within the boundaries of his life. These boundaries are commonly crossed by the misfortunes of being deceived, or despised, or betrayed. (If this is correct, there is a simple account of what is wrong with breaking a deathbed promise. It is an injury to the dead man. For certain purposes it is possible to regard time as just another type of distance.) The case of mental degeneration shows us an evil that depends on a contrast between the reality and the possible alternatives. A man is the subject of good and evil as much because he has hopes that may or may not be fulfilled, or possibilities that may or may not be realized, as because of his capacity to suffer and enjoy. If death is an evil, it must be accounted for in these terms, and the impossibility of locating it within life should not trouble us.

When a man dies we are left with his corpse, and while a corpse can suffer the kind of mishap that may occur to an article of furniture, it is not a suitable object for pity. The man, however, is. He has lost his life, and if he had not died, he would have continued to live it, and to possess whatever good there is in living. If we apply to death the account suggested for the case of dementia, we shall say that although the spatial and temporal locations of the individual who suffered the loss are clear enough, the misfortune itself cannot be so easily located. One must be content just to state that his life is over and there will never be any more of it. That *fact*, rather than his past or present condition, constitutes his misfortune, if it is one. Nevertheless if there is a loss, someone must suffer it, and *he* must have existence and specific spatial and temporal location even if the loss itself does not. The fact that Beethoven had no children may have been a cause of regret to him, or a sad thing for the world, but it cannot be described as a misfortune for the children that he never had. All of us, I believe, are fortunate to have been born. But unless good and ill can be assigned to an embryo, or even to an unconnected pair of gametes, it cannot be said that not to be born is a misfortune. (That is a factor to be considered in deciding whether abortion and contraception are akin to murder.)

This approach also provides a solution to the problem of temporal asymmetry, pointed out by Lucretius. He observed that no one finds it disturbing to contemplate the eternity preceding his own birth, and he took this to show that it must be irrational to fear death, since death is simply the mirror image of the prior abyss. That is not true, however, and the difference between the two explains why it is reasonable to regard them differently. It is true that both the time before a man's birth and the time after his death are times when he does not exist. But the time after his death is time of which his death deprives him. It is time in which, had he not died then, he would be alive. Therefore any death entails the loss of *some* life that its victim would have led had he not died at that or any earlier point. We know perfectly well what it would be for him to have had it instead of losing it, and there is no difficulty in identifying the loser.

But we cannot say that the time prior to a man's birth is time in which he would have lived had he been born not then but earlier. For aside from the brief margin permitted by premature labor, he *could* not have been born earlier: anyone born substantially earlier than he was would have been someone else. Therefore the time prior to his birth is not time in which his subsequent birth prevents him from living. His birth, when it occurs, does not entail the loss to him of any life whatever.

The direction of time is crucial in assigning possibilities to people or other individuals. Distinct possible lives of a single person can diverge from a common beginning, but they cannot converge to a common conclusion from diverse beginnings. (The latter would represent not a set of different possible lives of one individual, but a set of distinct possible individuals, whose lives have identical conclusions.) Given an identifiable individual, countless possibilities for his continued existence are imaginable, and we can clearly conceive of what it would be for him to go on existing indefinitely. However inevitable it is that this will not come about, its possibility is still that of the continuation of a good for him, if life is the good we take it to be.[3]

We are left, therefore, with the questions whether the nonrealization of this possibility is in every case a misfortune, or whether it depends on what can naturally be hoped for. This seems to me the most serious difficulty with the view that death is always an evil. Even if we can dispose of the objections against admitting misfortune that is not experienced, or cannot be assigned to a definite time in the person's life, we still have to set some limits on *how* possible a possibility must be for its nonrealization to be a misfortune (or good fortune, should the possibility be a bad one). The death of Keats at 24 is generally regarded as tragic; that of Tolstoy at 82 is not. Although they will both be dead forever, Keats's death deprived him of many years of life that were allowed to Tolstoy; so in a clear sense Keats's loss was greater (though not in the sense standardly employed in mathematical comparison between infinite quantities). However, this does not prove that Tolstoy's loss was insignificant. Perhaps we record an objection only to evils that are gratuitously added to the inevitable; the fact that it is worse to die at 24 than at 82 does not imply that it is not a terrible thing to die at 82, or even at 806. The question is whether we can regard as a misfortune any limitation, like mortality, that is normal to the species. Blindness or near-blindness is not a misfortune for a mole, nor would it be for a man, if that were the natural condition of the human race.

The trouble is that life familiarizes us with the goods of which
death deprives us. We are already able to appreciate them, as a
mole is not able to appreciate vision. If we put aside doubts
about their status as goods and grant that their quantity is in
part a function of their duration, the question remains whether
death, no matter when it occurs, can be said to deprive its victim
of what is in the relevant sense a possible continuation of life.

The situation is an ambiguous one. Observed from without,
human beings obviously have a natural lifespan and cannot live
much longer than a hundred years. A man's sense of his own
experience, on the other hand, does not embody this idea of a
natural limit. His existence defines for him an essentially open-
ended possible future, containing the usual mixture of goods
and evils that he has found so tolerable in the past. Having been
gratuitously introduced to the world by a collection of natural,
historical, and social accidents, he finds himself the subject of a
life, with an indeterminate and not essentially limited future.
Viewed in this way, death, no matter how inevitable, is an
abrupt cancellation of indefinitely extensive possible goods.
Normality seems to have nothing to do with it, for the fact that
we will all inevitably die in a few score years cannot by itself
imply that it would not be good to live longer. Suppose that we
were all inevitably going to die in *agony*—physical agony lasting
six months. Would inevitability make *that* prospect any less unpleasant? And why should it be different for a deprivation? If
the normal lifespan were a thousand years, death at 80 would
be a tragedy. As things are, it may just be a more widespread
tragedy. If there is no limit to the amount of life that it would be
good to have, then it may be that a bad end is in store for us all.

CHAPTER FIVE

"Do you think your death is premature?" he said.

"Every death is premature. There's no sufficient reason why we can't live a hundred and fifty years. Some people actually do it, according to a headline I saw at the supermarket."

"Do you think it's a sense of incompleteness that causes you the deepest regret? There are things you still hope to accomplish. Work to be done, intellectual challenges to be faced."

"The deepest regret is death. The only thing to face is death. This is all I think about. There's only one issue here. I want to live."

. . .

"So you're saying, Jack, that death would be just as threatening even if you'd accomplished all you'd ever hoped to accomplish in your life and work?"

"Are you crazy? Of course. That's an elitist idea. Would you ask a man who bags groceries if he fears death not because it is death but because there are still some interesting groceries he would like to bag?"

"Well said."

"This is death. I don't want it to tarry awhile so I can write a monograph. I want it to go away for seventy or eighty years."

"Your status as a doomed man lends your words a certain prestige and authority. I like that. As the time nears, I think you'll find that people will be eager to hear what you have to say. They will seek you out."

"Are you saying this is a wonderful opportunity for me to win friends?"

"I'm saying you can't let down the living by slipping into self-pity and despair. People will depend on you to be brave. What people look for in a dying friend is a stubborn kind of gravel-voiced nobility, a refusal to give in, with moments of indomitable humor. You're growing in prestige even as we speak.

You're creating a hazy light about your own body. I have to like it."

We walked down the middle of a steep and winding street. There was no one around. The houses were old and looming, set above narrow stone stairways in partial disrepair.

"Do you believe love is stronger than death?"

"Not in a million years."

"Good," he said. "Nothing is stronger than death. Do you believe the only people who fear death are those who are afraid of life?"

"That's crazy. Completely stupid."

"Right. We all fear death to some extent. Those who claim otherwise are lying themselves. Shallow people."

"People with their nicknames on their license plates."

"Excellent, Jack. Do you believe life without death is somehow incomplete?"

"How could it be incomplete? Death is what makes it incomplete."

"Doesn't our knowledge of death make life more precious?"

"What good is a preciousness based on fear and anxiety? It's an anxious quivering thing."

"True. The most deeply precious things are those we feel secure about. A wife, a child. Does the specter of death make a child more precious?"

"No."

"No. There is no reason to believe life is more precious because it is fleeting. Here is a statement. A person has to be told he is going to die before he can begin to live life to the fullest. True or false?"

"False. Once your death is established, it becomes impossible to live a satisfying life."

"Would you prefer to know the exact date and time of your death?"

"Absolutely not. It's bad enough to fear the unknown. Faced with the unknown, we can pretend it isn't there. Exact dates would drive many to suicide, if only to beat the system."

—Don Delillo, *White Noise*

The Makropulos Case: Reflections on the Tedium of Immortality

Bernard Williams

This essay started life as a lecture in a series "on the immortality of the soul or kindred spiritual subject."[1] My kindred spiritual subject is, one might say, the mortality of the soul. Those among previous lecturers who were philosophers tended, I think, to discuss the question whether we are immortal; that is not my subject, but rather what a good thing it is that we are not. Immortality, or a state without death, would be meaningless, I shall suggest; so, in a sense, death gives the meaning to life. That does not mean that we should not fear death (whatever force that injunction might be taken to have, anyway). Indeed, there are several very different ways in which it could be true at once that death gave the meaning to life and that death was, other things being equal, something to be feared. Some existentialists, for instance, seem to have said that death was what gave meaning to life, if anything did, just because it was the fear of death that gave meaning to life; I shall not follow them. I shall rather pursue the idea that from facts about human desire and happiness and what a human life is, it follows both that immortality would be, where conceivable at all, intolerable, and that (other things being equal) death is reasonably regarded as an evil. Considering whether death can reasonably be regarded as

Reprinted by permission from *Problems of the Self* (Cambridge, Engl.: Cambridge University Press, 1973): 82–100. I am grateful to the Committee for inviting me to give the 1972 lecture in this series.

an evil is in fact as near as I shall get to considering whether it should be feared: they are not quite the same question.

My title is that, as it is usually translated into English, of a play by Karel Capek which was made into an opera by Janáček and which tells of a woman called Elina Makropulos, alias Emilia Marty, alias Ellian Macgregor, alias a number of other things with the initials "EM," on whom her father, the Court physician to a sixteenth-century emperor, tried out an elixir of life. At the time of the action she is aged 342. Her unending life has come to a state of boredom, indifference, and coldness. Everything is joyless: "In the end it is the same," she says, "singing and silence." She refuses to take the elixir again; she dies; and the formula is deliberately destroyed by a young woman among the protests of some older men.

EM's state suggests at least this, that death is not necessarily an evil, and not just in the sense in which almost everybody would agree to that, where death provides an end to great suffering, but in the more intimate sense that it can be a good thing not to live too long. It suggests more than that, for it suggests that it was not a peculiarity of EM's that an endless life was meaningless. That is something I shall follow out later. First, though, we should put together the suggestion of EM's case, that death is not necessarily an evil, with the claim of some philosophies and religions that death is necessarily not an evil. Notoriously, there have been found two contrary bases on which that claim can be mounted: death is said by some not to be an evil because it is not the end, and by others, because it is. There is perhaps some profound temperamental difference between those who find consolation for the fact of death in the hope that it is only the start of another life, and those who equally find comfort in the conviction that it is the end of the only life there is. That both such temperaments exist means that those who find a diagnosis of the belief in immortality, and indeed a reproach to it, in the idea that it constitutes a consolation, have at best only a statistical fact to support them. While that may be just about enough for the diagnosis, it is not enough for the reproach.

Most famous, perhaps, among those who have found comfort in the second option, the prospect of annihilation, was Lucretius, who, in the steps of Epicurus, and probably from a personal fear of death that in some of his pages seems almost tangible, addresses himself to proving that death is never an evil. Lucretius has two basic arguments for this conclusion, and it is an important feature of them both that the conclusion they offer has the very strong consequence—and seems clearly intended to have the consequence—that, for oneself at least, it is all the same whenever one dies, that a long life is no better than a short one. That is to say, death is never an evil in the sense not merely that there is no one for whom dying is an evil, but that there is no time at which dying is an evil—sooner or later, it is all the same.

The first argument[2] seeks to interpret the fear of death as a confusion, based on the idea that we shall be there after death to repine our loss of the *praemia vitae*, the rewards and delights of life, and to be upset at the spectacle of our bodies burned, and so forth. The fear of death, it is suggested, must necessarily be the fear of some experiences had when one is dead. But if death is annihilation, then there are no such experiences: in the Epicurean phrase, when death is there, we are not, and when we are there, death is not. So, death being annihilation, there is nothing to fear. The second argument[3] addresses itself directly to the question of whether one dies earlier or later, and says that one will be the same time dead however early or late one dies, and therefore one might as well die earlier as later. And from both arguments we can conclude *nil igitur mors est ad nos, neque pertinet hilum*—death is nothing to us, and does not matter at all.[4]

The second of these arguments seems even on the face of things to contradict the first. For it must imply that if there *were* a finite period of death, such that if you died later you would be dead for less time, then there *would* be some point in wanting to die later rather than earlier. But that implication makes sense, surely, only on the supposition that what is wrong with dying consists in something undesirable about the condition of being dead. And that is what is denied by the first argument.

More important than this, the oddness of the second argument can help to focus a difficulty already implicit in the first. The first argument, in locating the objection to dying in a confused objection to being dead, and exposing that in terms of a confusion with being alive, takes it as genuinely true of life that the satisfaction of desire, and possession of the *praemia vitae*, are good things. It is not irrational to be upset by the loss of home, children, possessions—what is irrational is to think of death as, in the relevant sense, *losing* anything. But now if we consider two lives, one very short and cut off before the *praemia* have been acquired, the other fully provided with the *praemia* and containing their enjoyment to a ripe age, it is very difficult to see why the second life, by these standards alone, is not to be thought better than the first. But if it is, then there must be something wrong with the argument which tries to show that there is nothing worse about a short life than a long one. The argument locates the mistake about dying in a mistake about consciousness, it being assumed that what commonsense thinks about the worth of the *praemia vitae* and the sadness of their (conscious) loss is sound enough. But if the *praemia vitae* are valuable, even if we include as necessary to that value consciousness that one possesses them, then surely getting to the point of possessing them is better than not getting to that point, longer enjoyment of them is better than shorter, and more of them, other things being equal, is better than less of them. But if so, then it just will not be true that to die earlier is all the same as to die later, nor that death is never an evil—and the thought that to die later is better than to die earlier will not be dependent on some muddle about thinking that the dead person will be alive to lament his loss. It will depend only on the idea, apparently sound, that if the *praemia vitae* and consciousness of them are good things, then longer consciousness of more *praemia* is better than shorter consciousness of fewer *praemia*.

Is the idea sound? A decent argument, surely, can be marshaled to support it. If I desire something, then, other things being equal, I prefer a state of affairs in which I get it from one in which I do not get it, and (again, other things being equal) plan for a future in which I get it rather than not. But one future, for sure, in which I would not get it would be one in which I was dead. To want something, we may also say, is to that extent to have reason for resisting what excludes having that thing: and death certainly does that, for a very large range of things that one wants.[5] If that is right, then for any of those things, wanting something itself gives one a reason for avoiding death. Even though if I do not succeed, I will not know that, nor what I am missing, from the perspective of the wanting agent it is rational to aim for states of affairs in which his want is satisfied, and hence to regard death as something to be avoided; that is, to regard it as an evil.

It is admittedly true that many of the things I want, I want only on the assumption that I am going to be alive; and some people, for instance some of the old, desperately want certain things when nevertheless they would much rather that they and their wants were dead. It might be suggested that not just these special cases, but really all wants, are conditional on being alive; a situation in which one has ceased to exist is not to be compared with others with respect to desire-satisfaction— rather, if one dies, all bets are off. But surely the claim that all desires are in this sense conditional must be wrong. For consider the idea of a rational forward-looking calculation of suicide; there can be such a thing, even if many suicides are not rational, and even though with some that are, it may be unclear to what extent they are forward-looking (the obscurity of this with regard to suicides of honor is an obscurity in the notion of shame). In such a calculation, a man might consider what lay before him, and decide whether he did or did not want to undergo it. If he does decide to undergo it, then some desire propels him on into the future, and *that* desire at least is not one that operates conditionally on his being alive, since it itself resolves the question of whether he is going to be alive. He has an unconditional, or (as I shall say) a *categorical* desire.

The man who seriously calculates about suicide and rejects it, only just has such a desire, perhaps. But if one is in a state in which the question of suicide does not occur, or occurs only as total fantasy—if, to take just one example, one is happy—one has many such desires, which do not hang from the assumption of one's existence. If they did hang from that assumption, then they would be quite powerless to rule out that assumption's being questioned, or to answer the question if it is raised; but clearly they are not powerless in those directions—on the contrary they are some of the few things, perhaps the only things, that have power in that direction. Some ascetics have supposed that happiness required reducing one's desires to those necessary for one's existence, that is, to those that one has to have granted that one exists at all; rather, it requires that some of one's desires should be fully categorical, and one's existence it-self wanted as something necessary to them.

To suppose that one can in this way categorically want things implies a number of things about the nature of desire. It implies, for one thing, that the reason I have for bringing it about that I get what I want is not merely that of avoiding the unpleasant-ness of not getting what I want. But that must in any case be right—otherwise we should have to represent every desire as the desire to avoid its own frustration, which is absurd.

About what those categorical desires must be, there is not much of great generality to be said, if one is looking at the happy state of things: except, once more against the ascetic, that there should be not just enough, but more than enough. But the ques-tion might be raised, at the impoverished end of things, as to what the minimum categorical desire might be. Could it be *just* the desire to remain alive? The answer is perhaps "no." In say-ing that, I do not want to deny the existence, the value, or the basic necessity of a sheer reactive drive to self-preservation: hu-manity would certainly wither if the drive to keep alive were not stronger than any perceived reasons for keeping alive. But if the question is asked, and it is going to be answered calculatively, then the bare categorical desire to stay alive will not sustain the calculation—that desire itself, when things have got that far, has to be sustained or filled out by some desire for something else, even if it is only, at the margin, the desire that future desires of mine will be born and satisfied. But the best insight into the effect of categorical desire is not gained at the impoverished end of things, and hence in situations where the question has actu-ally come up. The question of life being desirable is certainly transcendental in the most modest sense, in that it gets by far its best answer in never being asked at all.

None of this—including the thoughts of the calculative sui-cide—requires my reflection on a world in which I never occur at all. In the terms of "possible worlds" (which can admittedly be misleading), a man could, on the present account, have a reason from his own point of view to prefer a possible world in which he went on longer to one in which he went on for less long, or—like the suicide—the opposite; but he would have no reason of this kind to prefer a world in which he did not occur at all. Thoughts about his total absence from the world would have to be of a different kind, impersonal reflections on the value *for the world* of his presence or absence: of the same kind, essentially, as he could conduct (or, more probably, not manage to conduct) with regard to anyone else. While he can think egoistically of what it would be for him to live longer or less long, he cannot think egoistically of what it would be for him never to have existed at all. Hence the somber words of Sophocles, "Never to have been born counts highest of all,"[6] are well met by the old Jewish reply, "How many are so lucky? Not one in ten thousand."

Lucretius's first argument has been interestingly criticized by Thomas Nagel,[7] on lines different from those that I have been following. Nagel claims that what is wrong with Lucretius's argument is that it rests on the assumption that nothing can be a misfortune for a man unless he knows about it, and that misfortunes must consist in something nasty *for* him. Against this assumption, Nagel cites a number of plausible counter-instances, of circumstances that would normally be thought to constitute a misfortune, though those to whom they happen are and remain ignorant of them (as, for instance, certain situations of betrayal). The difference between Nagel's approach and mine does not, of course, lie in the mere point of whether one admits misfortunes that do not consist of or involve nasty experiences: anyone who rejects Lucretius's argument must admit them. The difference is that the reasons a man would have for avoiding death are, on the present account, grounded in desires—categorical desires— that he has; he, on the basis of these, has reason to regard possible death as a misfortune to be avoided, and we, looking at things from his point of view, would have reason to regard his actual death as his misfortune. Nagel, however, if I understand him, does not see the misfortune that befalls a man who dies as necessarily grounded in the issue of what desires or sorts of desires he had; just as in the betrayal case, it could be a misfortune for a man to be betrayed, even though he did not have any desire not to be betrayed. If this is a correct account, Nagel's reasoning is one step farther away from Utilitarianism on this matter than mine,[8] and it rests on an independent kind of value that a sufficiently Utilitarian person might just reject, whereas my argument cannot merely be rejected by a Utilitarian person, it seems to me, since he must if he is to be consistent, and other things being equal, attach disutility to any situation that he has good reason to prevent, and he certainly has good reason to prevent a situation that involves the nonsatisfaction of his desires. Thus, granted categorical desires, death has a disutility for an agent, although that disutility does not, of course, consist in unsatisfactory experiences involved in its occurrence.

The question would remain, of course, with regard to any given agent, whether he had categorical desires. For the present argument, it will do to leave it as a contingent fact that most people do: for they will have a reason, and a perfectly coherent reason, to regard death as a misfortune, while it was Lucretius's claim that no one could have a coherent reason for so regarding it. There may well be other reasons as well; thus Nagel's reasoning, though different from the more Utilitarian type of reason I have used against Lucretius, seems compatible with it and there are strong reasons to adopt his kind of consideration as well. In fact, further and deeper thought about this question seems likely to fill up the apparent gap between the two sorts of argument; it is hard to believe, for one thing, that the supposed contingent fact that people have categorical desires can really be as contingent as all that. One last point about the two arguments is that they coincide in not offering—as I mentioned earlier—any considerations about worlds in which one does not occur at all; but there is perhaps an additional reason why this should be so in the Utilitarian-type argument, over and above the one it shares with Nagel's. The reason it shares with Nagel's is that the type of misfortune we are concerned with in thinking about X's death is X's misfortune (as opposed to the misfortunes of the state or whatever); and whatever sort of misfortune it may be in a given possible world that X does not occur in it, it is not X's misfortune. They share the feature, then, that for anything to be X's misfortune in a given world, then X must occur in that world. But the Utilitarian-type argument further grounds the misfortune, if there is one, in certain features of X, namely his desires, and if there is no X in a given world, then *a fortiori* there are no such grounds.

But now: if death, other things being equal, is a misfortune, and a longer life is better than a shorter life, and we reject the Lucretian argument that it does not matter when one dies, then it looks as though—other things always being equal—death is at any time an evil, and it is always better to live than die. Nagel indeed, from his point of view, does seem to permit that conclusion, even though he admits some remarks about the natural term of life and the greater misfortune of dying in one's prime. But wider consequences follow. For if all that is true, then it looks as though it would be not only always better to live, but better to live always, that is, never to die. If Lucretius is wrong, we seem committed to wanting to be immortal.

That would be, as has been repeatedly said, with other things equal. No one need deny that since, for instance, we grow old and our powers decline, much may happen to increase the reasons for thinking death a good thing. But these are contingencies. We might not age; perhaps, one day, it will be possible for some of us not to age. If that were so, would it not follow then that, more life being per se better than less life, we should have reason so far as that went (but not necessarily in terms of other inhabitants) to live forever? EM indeed bears strong, if fictional, witness against the desirability of that; but perhaps she still labored under some contingent limitations, social or psychological, that might once more be eliminated to bring it about that really other things were equal. Against this, I am going to suggest that the supposed contingencies are not really contingencies, that an endless life would be a meaningless one, and that we could have no reason for living eternally a human life. There is no desirable or significant property that life would have more of, or have more unqualifiedly, if we lasted forever. In some part, we can apply to life Aristotle's marvelous remark about Plato's Form of the Good: "Nor will it be any the more good for being eternal: that which lasts long is no whiter than that which perishes in a day."[9] But only in part; for, rejecting Lucretius, we have already admitted that more days may give us more than one day can.

If one pictures living forever as living as an embodied person in the world rather as it is, it will be a question, and not so trivial as may seem, of what age one eternally is. EM was 342; because for 300 years she had been 42. This choice (if it was a choice) I am personally, and at present, well disposed to salute—if one had to spend eternity at any age, that seems an admirable age to spend it at. Nor would it necessarily be a less good age for a woman: that at least was not EM's problem, that she was too old at the age she continued to be at. Her problem lay in having been at it for too long. Her trouble was, it seems, boredom: a boredom connected with the fact that everything that could happen and make sense to one particular human being of 42 had already happened to her. Or, rather, all the sorts of things that could make sense to one woman of a certain character; for EM has a certain character, and indeed, except for her accumulating memories of earlier times, and no doubt some changes of style to suit the passing centuries, seems always to have been much the same sort of person.

There are difficult questions, if one presses the issue, about this constancy of character. How is this accumulation of memories related to this character that she eternally has, and to the character of her existence? Are they much the same kind of events repeated? Then it is itself strange that she allows them to be repeated, accepting the same repetitions, the same limitations—indeed, *accepting* is what it later becomes, when earlier it would not, or even could not, have been that. The repeated patterns of personal relations, for instance, must take on a character of being inescapable. Or is the pattern of her experiences not repetitious in this way, but varied? Then the problem shifts, to the relation between these varied experiences, and the fixed character: how can it remain fixed, through an endless series of very various experiences? The experiences must surely happen to her without really affecting her; she must be, as EM is, detached and withdrawn.

EM, of course, is in a world of people who do not share her condition, and that determines certain features of the life she has to lead, as that any personal relationship requires peculiar kinds of concealment. That, at least, is a form of isolation which would disappear if her condition were generalized. But to suppose more generally that boredom and inner death would be eliminated if everyone were similarly becalmed, is an empty hope: it would be a world of Bourbons, learning nothing and forgetting nothing, and it is unclear how much could even happen.

The more one reflects to any realistic degree on the conditions of EM's unending life, the less it seems a mere contingency that it froze up as it did. That it is not a contingency is suggested also by the fact that the reflections can sustain themselves inde-

pendently of any question of the particular character that EM
had; it is enough, almost, that she has a human character at all.
Perhaps not quite. One sort of character for which the difficulties of unending life would have less significance than they
proved to have for EM might be one who at the beginning was
more like what she is at the end: cold, withdrawn, already frozen. For him, the prospect of unending cold is presumably less
bleak in that he is used to it. But with him, the question can shift
to a different place, as to why he wants the unending life at all;
for, the more he is at the beginning like EM is at the end, the
less place there is for categorical desire to keep him going, and
to resist the desire for death. In EM's case, her boredom and
distance from life both kill desire and consist in the death of it;
one who is already enough like that to sustain life in those conditions may well be one who had nothing to make him want to
do so. But even if he has, and we conceive of a person who is
stonily resolved to sustain forever an already stony existence,
his possibility will be of no comfort to those, one hopes a larger
party, who want to live longer because they want to live more.

To meet the basic anti-Lucretian hope for continuing life that
is grounded in categorical desire, EM's unending life in this
world is inadequate, and necessarily so relative to just those desires and conceptions of character which go into the hope. That
is very important, since it is the most direct response, that which
should have been adequate if the hope is both coherent and
what it initially seemed to be. It also satisfied one of two important conditions that must be satisfied by anything that is to be
adequate as a fulfillment of my anti-Lucretian hope, namely that
it should clearly be *me* who lives forever. The second important
condition is that the state in which I survive should be one that,
to me looking forward, will be adequately related, in the life it
presents, to those aims I now have in wanting to survive at all.
That is a vague formula, and necessarily so, for what exactly that
relation will be must depend to some extent on what kind of
aims and (as one might say) prospects for myself I now have.
What we can say is that since I am propelled forward into longer
life by categorical desires, what is promised must hold out some
hopes for those desires. The limiting case of this might be that
the promised life held out some hope just to that desire mentioned before, that future desires of mine will be born and sat-

isfied; but if that were the only categorical desire that carried me forward into it, at least this seems demanded, that any image I have of those future desires should make it comprehensible to me how in terms of my character they could be my desires.

This second condition the EM kind of survival failed, on reflection, to satisfy; but at least it is clear why, before reflection, it looked as though it might satisfy the condition—it consists, after all, in just going on in ways in which we are quite used to going on. If we turn away now from EM to more remote kinds of survival, the problems of those two conditions press more heavily right from the beginning. Since the major problems of the EM situation lay in the indefinite extension of one life, a tempting alternative is survival by means of an indefinite series of lives. Most, perhaps all, versions of this belief that have actually existed have immediately failed the first condition: they get nowhere near providing any consideration to mark the difference between rebirth and new birth. But let us suppose the problem, in some way or another, removed; some conditions of bodily continuity, minimally sufficient for personal identity, may be supposed satisfied. (Anyone who thinks that no such conditions could be sufficient, and requires, for instance, conditions of memory, may well find it correspondingly difficult to find an alternative for survival in this direction that both satisfies the first requirement, of identity, and also adequately avoids the difficulties of the EM alternative.) The problem remains of whether this series of psychologically disjoint lives could be an object of hope to one who did not want to die. That is, in my view, a different question from the question of whether it will be him—which is why I distinguished originally two different requirements to be satisfied. But it is a question; and even if the first requirement be supposed satisfied, it is exceedingly unclear that the second can be. This will be so, even if one were to accept the idea, itself problematical, that one could have reason to fear the future pain of someone who was merely bodily continuous with one as one now is.[10]

There are in the first place certain difficulties about how much a man could consistently be allowed to know about the series of his lives, if we are to preserve the psychological disjointness that is the feature of this model. It might be that each would in fact have to seem to him as though it were his only life, and that he could not have grounds for being sure what, or even that, later lives were to come. If so, then no comfort or hope will be forthcoming in this model to those who want to go on living. More interesting questions, however, concern the man's relation to a future life of which he did get some advance idea. If we could allow the idea that he could fear pain which was going to occur in that life, then we have at least provided him with one kind of reason that might move him to opt out of that life and destroy himself (being recurrent, under conditions of bodily continuity, would not make one indestructible). But physical pain and its nastiness are to the maximum degree independent of what one's desires and character are, and the degree of identification needed with the later life to reject that aspect of it is absolutely minimal. Beyond that point, however, it is unclear how he is to bring this later character and its desires into a relation to his present ones, so as to be satisfied or the reverse with this marginal promise of continued existence. If he can regard this future life as an object of hope, then equally it must be possible for him to regard it with alarm, or depression, and—as in the simple pain case—opt out of it. If we cannot make sense of his entertaining that choice, then we have not made sense of this future life being adequately related to his present life, so that it could, alternatively, be something he might want in wanting not to die. But can we clearly make sense of that choice? For if we—or he—merely wipe out his present character and desires, there is nothing left by which he can judge it at all, at least as something *for him*; whereas if we leave them in, we—and he—apply something irrelevant to that future life, since (to adapt the Epicurean phrase), when they are there, it is not, and when it is there, they are not. We might imagine him considering the future prospects and agreeing to go on if he found them congenial. But that is a muddled picture. For whether they are congenial to him as he is now must be beside the point, and the idea that it is not beside the point depends on carrying over into the case features that do not belong to it, as (perhaps) that he will remember later what he wanted in the earlier life. And when we admit that it is beside the point whether the prospects are congenial, then the force of the idea that the future life could be something that he *now* wanted to go on to, fades.

There are important and still obscure issues here,[11] but per-

haps enough has been said to cast doubt on this option as coherently satisfying the desire to stay alive. While few will be
disposed to think that much can be made of it, I must confess
that out of the alternatives it is the only one that for me would, if
it made sense, have any attraction—no doubt because it is the
only one which has the feature that what one is living at any
given point is actually *a life*. It is singular that those systems of
belief that get closest to actually accepting recurrence of this sort
seem, almost without exception, to look forward to the point
when one will be released from it. Such systems seem less interested in continuing one's life than in earning one the right to a
superior sort of death.

The serial and disjoint lives are at least more attractive than
the attempt some have made to combine the best of continuous
and of serial existence in a fantasy of very varied lives that are
nevertheless cumulatively effective in memory. This might be
called the *Teiresias* model. As that case singularly demonstrates,
it has the quality of a fantasy, of emotional pressure trying to
combine the uncombinable. One thing that the fantasy has to
ignore is the connection, both as cause and as consequence, between having one range of experiences rather than another,
wishing to engage in one sort of thing rather than another, and
having a character. Teiresias cannot have a character, either con-
tinuously through these proceedings or cumulatively at the end
(if there were to be an end) of them: he is not, eventually, a
person but a phenomenon.

In discussing the last models, we have moved a little away
from the very direct response that EM's case seemed to provide
to the hope that one would never die. But perhaps we have
moved not nearly far enough. Nothing of this, and nothing
much like this, was in the minds of many who have hoped for
immortality; for it was not in this world that they hoped to live
forever. As one might say, their hope was not so much that they
would never die as that they would live after their death, and
while that in its turn can be represented as the hope that one
would not really die, or, again, that it was not really oneself that
would die, the change of formulation could point to an afterlife
sufficiently unlike this life, perhaps, to ease the current of
doubt that flows from EM's frozen boredom.

But in fact this hope has been and could only be modeled on
some image of a more familiar untiring or unresting or unflag-

ging activity or satisfaction, and what is essentially EM's problem, one way or another, remains. In general we can ask what it is about the imagined activities of an eternal life that would stave off the principal hazard to which EM succumbed, boredom. The Don Juan in Hell joke, that heaven's prospects are tedious and the devil has the best tunes, though a tired fancy in itself, at least serves to show up a real and (I suspect) a profound difficulty, of providing any model of an unending, supposedly satisfying, state or activity that would not rightly prove boring to anyone who remained conscious of himself and who had acquired a character, interests, tastes, and impatiences in the course of living, already, a finite life. The point is not that for such a man boredom would be a tiresome consequence of the supposed states or activities, and that they would be objectionable just on the utilitarian or hedonistic ground that they had this disagreeable feature. If that were all there was to it, we could imagine the feature away, along no doubt with other disagreeable features of human life in its present imperfection. The point is rather that boredom, as sometimes in more ordinary circumstances, would be not just a tiresome effect, but a reaction almost perceptual in character to the poverty of one's relation to the environment. Nothing less will do for eternity than something that makes boredom *unthinkable*. What could that be? Something that could be guaranteed to be at every moment utterly absorbing? But if a man has and retains a character, there is no reason to suppose that there is anything that could be that. If, lacking a conception of the guaranteedly absorbing activity, one tries merely to think away the reaction of boredom, one is no longer supposing an improvement in the circumstances, but merely an impoverishment in his consciousness of them. Just as being bored can be a sign of not noticing, understanding, or appreciating enough, so equally not being bored can be a sign of not noticing, or not reflecting, enough. One might make the immortal man content at every moment, by just stripping off from him consciousness that would have brought discontent by reminding him of other times, other interests, other possibilities. Perhaps, indeed, that is what we have already done, in a more tempting way, by picturing him just now as at every moment totally absorbed—but that is something we shall come back to.

Of course there is in actual life such a thing as justified but necessary boredom. Thus—to take a not entirely typical example—someone who was, or who thought himself, devoted to the radical cause might eventually admit to himself that he found a lot of its rhetoric excruciatingly boring. He might think that he ought not to feel that, that the reaction was wrong and merely represented an unworthiness of his, an unregenerate remnant of intellectual superiority. However, he might rather feel that it would not necessarily be a better world in which no one was bored by such rhetoric and that boredom was, indeed, a perfectly worthy reaction to this rhetoric after all this time; but for all that, the rhetoric might be necessary. A man at arms can get cramp from standing too long at his post, but sentry duty can after all be necessary. But the threat of monotony in eternal activities could not be dealt with in that way, by regarding immortal boredom as an unavoidable ache derived from standing ceaselessly at one's post. (This is one reason why I said that boredom in eternity would have to be *unthinkable*.) For the question would be unavoidable, in what campaign one was supposed to be serving, what one's ceaseless sentry watch was for.

Some philosophers have pictured an eternal existence as occupied in something like intense intellectual enquiry. Why that might seem to solve the problem, at least for them, is obvious. The activity is engrossing, self-justifying, affords, as it may appear, endless new perspectives, and by being engrossing enables one to lose oneself. It is that last feature that supposedly makes boredom unthinkable, by providing something that is, in that earlier phrase, at every moment totally absorbing. But if one is totally and perpetually absorbed in such an activity, and loses oneself in it, then as those words suggest, we come back to the problem of satisfying the conditions that it should be me who lives forever, and that the eternal life should be in prospect of some interest. Let us leave aside the question of people whose characteristic and most personal interests are remote from such pursuits, and for whom, correspondingly, an immortality promised in terms of intellectual activity is going to make heavy demands on some theory of a "real self" that will have to emerge at death. More interesting is the content and value of the promise for a person who *is*, in this life, disposed to those activities. For looking at such a person as he now is, it seems quite unreasonable to suppose that those activities would have the fulfilling or liberating character that they do have for him, if they were in fact all he could do or conceive of doing. If they are genuinely fulfilling, and do not operate (as they can) merely as a compulsive diversion, then the ground and shape of the satisfactions that the intellectual enquiry offers him, will relate to *him*, and not just to the enquiry. The *Platonic introjection*, seeing the satisfactions of studying what is timeless and impersonal as being themselves timeless and impersonal, may be a deep illusion, but it is certainly an illusion.

We can see better into that illusion by considering Spinoza's thought, that intellectual activity was the most active and free state that a man could be in, and that a man who had risen to such activity was in some sense most fully individual, most fully himself. This conclusion has been sympathetically expounded by Stuart Hampshire, who finds on this point a similar doctrine in Spinoza and in Freud.[12] In particular, he writes, "[One's] only means of achieving this distinctness as an individual, this freedom in relation to the common order of nature, is the power of the mind freely to follow in its thought an intellectual order." The contrast to this free intellectual activity is "the common condition of men that their conduct and their judgments of value, their desires and aversions, are in each individual determined by unconscious memories"—a process that the same writer has elsewhere associated with our having any character at all as individuals.[13]

Hampshire claims that in pure intellectual activity the mind is most free because it is then least determined by causes outside its immediate states. I take him to mean that rational activity is that in which the occurrence of an earlier thought maximally explains the occurrence of a later thought, because it is the rational relation between their contents that, granted the occurrence of the first, explains the occurrence of the second. But even the maximal explanatory power, in these terms, of the earlier thought does not extend to total explanation: for it will still require explanation why this thinker on this occasion continued on this rational path of thought at all. Thus I am not sure that the Spinozist consideration that Hampshire advances even gives a very satisfactory sense to the *activity* of the mind. It leaves out, as the last point shows, the driving power that is needed to sustain one even in the most narrowly rational thought. It is still further remote from any notion of creativity, since that, even within a theoretical context, and certainly in an artistic one, precisely implies the origination of ideas that are not fully predictable in terms of the content of existing ideas. But even if it could yield one sense for "activity," it would still offer very little, despite Spinoza's heroic defense of the notion, for *freedom*. Or—to put it another way—even if it offered something for freedom of the intellect, it offers nothing for freedom of the individual. For when freedom is initially understood as the absence of "outside" determination, and in particular understood in those terms as an unquestionable *value*, my freedom is reasonably not taken to include freedom from my past, my character, and my desires. To suppose that those are, in the relevant sense, "outside" determinations is merely to beg the vital question about the boundaries of the self, and not to prove from premises acceptable to any clear-headed man who desires freedom that the boundaries of the self should be drawn round the intellect. On the contrary, the desire for freedom can, and should, be seen as the desire to be free in the exercise and development of character, not as the desire to be free of it. And if Hampshire and others are right in claiming that an individual character springs from and gets its energies from unconscious memories and unclear desires, then the individual must see them too as within the boundaries of the self, and themselves involved in the drive to persist in life and activity.

With this loss, under the Spinozist conception, of the individual's character, there is, contrary to Hampshire's claim, a loss of individuality itself, and certainly of anything that could make an eternity of intellectual activity, so construed, a reasonable object of interest to one concerned with individual immortality. As those who totally wish to lose themselves in the movement can consistently only hope that the movement will go on, so the consistent Spinozist—at least on this account of Spinozism—can only hope that the intellectual activity goes on, something that could be as well realized in the existence of Aristotle's prime mover, perhaps, as in anything to do with Spinoza or any other particular man.

Stepping back now from the extremes of Spinozist abstraction, I shall end by returning to a point from which we set out, the sheer desire to go on living, and shall mention a writer on this subject, Unamuno, whose work *The Tragic Sense of Life*[14] gives perhaps more extreme expression than anyone else has done to that most basic form of the desire to be immortal, the desire not to die.

I do not want to die—no, I neither want to die nor do I want to want to die; I want to live for ever and ever and ever. I want this "I" to live—this poor "I" that I am and that I feel myself to be here and now, and therefore the problem of the duration of my soul, of my own soul, tortures me.   (p. 60)

Although Unamuno frequently refers to Spinoza, the spirit of this is certainly far removed from that of the "sorrowful Jew of Amsterdam." Furthermore, in his clear insistence that what he desperately wants is this life, the life of this self, not to end, Unamuno reveals himself at equal removes from Manicheanism and from Utilitarianism; and that is correct, for the one is only the one-legged descendant of the other. That tradition—Manichean, Orphic, Platonic, Augustinian—which contrasts the spirit and the body in such a sense that the spiritual aims at eternity, truth, and salvation, while the body is adjusted to pleasure, the temporary, and eventual dissolution, is still represented, as to 50 percent, by secular Utilitarianism: it is just one of the original pair of boots left by itself and better regarded now that the other has fallen into disrepair. Bodies are all that we have or are: hence for Utilitarianism it *follows* that the only focus of our arrangements can be the efficient organization of happiness. Immortality, certainly, is out, and so life here should last as long as we determine—or eventually, one may suspect, others will determine—that it is pleasant for us to be around.

Unamuno's outlook is at the opposite pole to this and, whatever else may be wrong with it, it salutes the true idea that the meaning of life does not consist either in the management of satisfactions in a body or in an abstract immortality without one. On the one hand he had no time for Manicheanism and admired the rather brutal Catholic faith that could express its hopes for a future life in the words he knew on a tombstone in Bilbao:

Aunque estamos in polvo convertidos
en Ti, Señor, nuestra esperanza fía,
que tornaremos a vivir vestidos
con la carne y la piel que nos cubria.
(p. 79)

On the other hand, his desire to remain alive extends an almost incomprehensible distance beyond any desire to continue agreeable experiences:

> For myself I can say that as a youth and even as a child I remained unmoved when shown the most moving pictures of hell, for even then nothing appeared quite so horrible to me as nothingness itself.   (p. 28)

The most that I have claimed earlier against Lucretius is not enough to make that preference intelligible to me. The fear of sheer nothingness is certainly part of what Lucretius rightly, if too lightly, hoped to exorcise; and the *mere* desire to stay alive, which is here stretched to its limit, is not enough (I suggested before) to answer the question, once the question has come up and requires an answer in rational terms. Yet Unamuno's affirmation of existence even through limitless suffering[15] brings out something that is implicit in the claim against Lucretius. It is not necessarily the prospect of pleasant times that creates the motive against dying, but the existence of categorical desire, and categorical desire can drive through both the existence and the prospect of unpleasant times.

Suppose, then, that categorical desire does sustain the desire to live. So long as it remains so, I shall want not to die. Yet I also know, if what has gone before is right, that an eternal life would be unliveable. In part, as EM's case originally suggested, that is because categorical desire will go away from it: in those versions, such as hers, in which I am recognizably myself, I would eventually have had altogether too much of myself. There are good reasons, surely, for dying before that happens. But equally, at times earlier than that moment, there is reason for not dying. Necessarily, it tends to be either too early or too late. EM reminds us that it can be too late, and many, as against Lucretius, need no reminding that it can be too early. If that is any sort of dilemma, it can, as things still are and if one is exceptionally lucky, be resolved, not by doing anything, but just by dying shortly before the horrors of not doing so become evident. Technical progress may, in more than one direction, make that piece of luck rarer. But as things are, it is possible to be, in contrast to EM, *felix opportunitate mortis*—as it can be appropriately mistranslated, lucky in having the chance to die.

CHAPTER SIX

Of all the famous men who ever lived, the one I would most like to have been was Socrates. Not just because he was a great thinker, because I have been known to have some reasonably profound insights myself, although mine invariably revolve around a Swedish airline stewardess and some handcuffs. No, the great appeal for me of this wisest of all Greeks was his courage in the face of death. His decision was not to abandon his principles, but rather to give his life to prove a point. I personally am not quite as fearless about dying and will, after any untoward noise such as a car backfiring, leap directly into the arms of the person I am conversing with. In the end, Socrates' brave death gave his life authentic meaning; something my existence lacks totally, although it does possess a minimal relevance to the Internal Revenue Department.   —Woody Allen, *Side Effects*

The Evil of Death

Harry S. Silverstein

> So death, the most terrifying of ills, is nothing to us,
> since so long as we exist, death is not with us; but
> when death comes, then we do not exist. It does not
> concern either the living or the dead, since for the
> former it is not, and the latter are no more.
>
> —Epicurus, *Letter to Menoeceus*

The common-sense view is that a person's death is one of the
greatest evils that can befall him. Most of us, to be sure, would
concede that in extreme circumstances—e.g., when one is suffering from a terminal, excruciatingly painful, illness—death
can rationally be welcomed; and one can always find a few persons who are willing to claim that life is inherently more of a
burden than a blessing. But the fact remains that, in Joel Feinberg's words, "there is nothing a normal person (in reasonable
health and tolerable circumstances) dreads more than his own
death."[1] Yet there is a notorious difficulty with the view that
death is an evil for the person who dies, a difficulty recognized
long ago by Epicurus and brought out in the famous passage
quoted above. While one is still alive one has not, of course,
suffered the evil of death; yet when one is dead one does not

Reprinted by permission from *Journal of Philosophy* 77, no. 7 (July 1980): 401–24.
I am grateful to several participants at a meeting of the Washington State Uni-
versity/University of Idaho Philosophy Colloquium, and particularly to Marv
Henberg and Michael Ferejohn, for helpful criticisms of an earlier draft.

exist to be the recipient of goods or evils. But if the supposed subject of the evil thus fails to exist, then the claim that death is an evil for the person who dies would seem to be not (merely) false, but incoherent.

The view that death cannot intelligibly be claimed to be an evil for the person who dies I shall label the *Epicurean view*, and the conflict between this view and our common-sense view I shall label the *Epicurean dilemma*. Despite these labels, however, it should be emphasized that my concern is substantive, not exegetical; I neither affirm nor deny that any of the claims and arguments I shall be discussing can correctly be attributed to Epicurus.[2]

The Epicurean view presupposes—and I shall therefore assume in what follows—that death is the total and permanent annihilation of consciousness and, thus, of the person. For if there were "life after death," one would not cease to exist, and thus one would not cease to be a possible value recipient, at death; depending on the nature of one's "afterlife," one's death could be accounted evil, good, or indifferent in the standard way. However, the fact that one can avoid the Epicurean view by postulating life after death does not, of course, constitute an acceptable resolution of the Epicurean dilemma. For the common-sense fear of death *is* the fear of permanent annihilation, a fear that religious views concerning an afterlife did not create, but are rather intended to overcome. The common-sense view is that death is an evil not because (or if) there is an afterlife, but because (or if) there is not.

The Problem

To resolve the Epicurean dilemma we must show (a) that our common-sense view of death is false, or at any rate that it can be abandoned, and the Epicurean view accepted, without undue moral or philosophical discomfort; (b) that the Epicurean view is false, the plausibility of the argument supporting it notwithstanding; or (c) that, despite first appearances, common sense and the Epicurean view are not really incompatible. Alternative (c) seems clearly hopeless, and since the discomfort involved in accepting the Epicurean view is considerable, as I shall emphasize below, alternative (a) is at best an unpleasant last resort. Thus, alternative (b) represents the only hope for a "happy" or fully satisfactory resolution of the Epicurean dilemma. I shall attempt such a resolution in the next section. The present section, whose underlying purpose is to demonstrate the seriousness of the Epicurean dilemma, is devoted to further clarification and to criticism of unsatisfactory "resolutions."

The following judgment (or schema) can be taken to represent the claim whose intelligibility is at issue:

S_1: A's death is an evil for A.

This judgment has two crucial features. First, and obviously, it is an "A-relative" value judgment, a judgment that asserts something to be good, bad, or indifferent *for A*. The claim common sense supports, but whose intelligibility is denied by the Epicurean view, is not that A's death is an evil *for B*, a claim whose intelligibility, if B survives A, is unproblematic; nor is it that A's death is an evil *simpliciter*, a claim that, though perhaps not unproblematic (for how can something be evil if it is not evil *for* anyone or anything?), at any rate avoids the "no subject" difficulty with which the Epicurean view is concerned. Rather, the claim in question is that A's death is an evil *for A*. Second, and perhaps less obviously, S_1 must be interpreted, for our purposes, as *life-death comparative*; i.e., it must be interpreted as asserting in part:

S_2: A's death is worse for A than A's (continued) life is (bad) for A.

(I say "in part" because S_2 alone, unlike S_1, is consistent with the claim that neither A's death nor his life is an evil for him.) This is not the only interpretation of S_1 common in everyday life; it is sometimes interpreted as a "death-death comparative" claim, a claim asserting that a certain sort of death (more accurately: a certain sort of dying) is worse than another. But any "death-death comparative" use is, of course, irrelevant to the Epicurean dilemma; a supporter of the Epicurean view can cheerfully concede S_1's intelligibility if it is used, for instance, to claim that A's slow painful dying at the hands of an extreme sadist is worse than normal sorts of dying. The concern of the Epicurean dilemma, as we might put it, is not with the evaluation of one sort of death as compared with another, but with the evaluation of death as such.

Our justification for insisting on the life-death comparative interpretation, however, is not merely the negative one that the death-death comparative interpretation, the only plausible alternative, is irrelevant; ample positive justification is provided by the facts that (a) S_2 is as central to our common-sense view of death as is S_1; and yet (b) the Epicurean view must be taken to reject the intelligibility of S_2 as well as that of S_1, since the same "no subject" difficulty applies in both cases—since A does not exist when he is dead, it would seem that we cannot coherently claim that his death is worse *for him* than (or is better *for him* than, or has the same value *for him* as) anything whatever. In short, if we cannot defend the intelligibility of S_2 against the Epicurean view, we will not have resolved the Epicurean dilemma.

It is the combination of "A-relativity" and "life-death comparativity" that makes the Epicurean dilemma so serious, for it is this combination that undermines what I shall call the *standard argument* against the Epicurean view. According to the standard argument, death is simply an evil of deprivation, an evil consisting in the loss, or lack, of a positive good, namely, life. By claiming that death is not a "positive" evil, but merely the lack of a positive good, the standard argument seems to avoid the mistake of confusing the permanent annihilation of consciousness—i.e., death—with the permanent consciousness of nothingness (permanent solitary confinement in total darkness, as it were); that is, it seems to recognize that death is not a peculiarly terrifying state that one somehow exists to suffer from, but is rather simply nonexistence. It is by focusing on the value of life, moreover, that the standard argument claims to avoid the "no subject" difficulty and, thus, to get around the Epicurean view. There is nothing problematic, so the argument goes, about the intelligibility of the following claim:

S_3: A's life is (or is a) good for A.

For while A is alive, he exists, and is thus a possible value recipient. But if A's life can intelligibly be regarded as a good, its loss can intelligibly be regarded as an evil; hence the Epicurean dilemma is resolved.[3] The fatal difficulty with this argument, however, is that if S_3 is to be relevant to the Epicurean dilemma, it must be interpreted as life-death comparative, and the combination of this with A-relativity makes S_3 vulnerable to exactly the same Epicurean attack as S_1 and S_2. Interpreted as life-death comparative, S_3 asserts in part:

S_4: *A*'s life is better for *A* than *A*'s death is (good) for *A*.

And the second term of this comparative suffers from the same "no subject" difficulty as the first term of S_2; indeed, S_2 and S_4 make equivalent claims. If the fact that *A* does not exist when he is dead entails that *A*'s death cannot intelligibly be evaluated relative to *A* (i.e., that it cannot intelligibly be said to be good, bad, or indifferent for *A*), then it also entails that *A*'s death is not something to which the value of *A*'s life can intelligibly be compared, relative to *A*.

There is, of course, an alternative interpretation of S_3 in common use, a "life-life comparative" interpretation paralleling the death-death comparative interpretation of S_1. In some contexts a life-life comparative use of S_3 asserts merely that *A*'s life is (equal to or) better than some vaguely understood "average"; in other contexts it asserts, or at least implies, something more concrete (e.g., if *A* has just made a happy second marriage after a disastrous first one, one might use S_3 to express the view that *A*'s life is better for him now than it used to be, and better than it would be now if he were still married to his first spouse). But although the life-life comparative interpretation of S_3, as exemplified by any such instance, is straightforwardly intelligible, it is irrelevant to the life-death interpretation of S_1 and, thus, is irrelevant to the Epicurean dilemma. The fact that one sort of life can intelligibly be said to be better for *A* than another does nothing to show that life as such can intelligibly be said to be better for *A* than death, or, therefore, that *A*'s death can intelligibly be said to be an evil for him.

Perhaps the best way to explain the motivation for the standard argument is to say that its supporters are guilty of conflating the life-death comparative and life-life comparative interpretations of S_3. It is this conflation, at any rate, which gives the argument its persuasiveness, for it is only on the basis of this conflation that one could plausibly suppose S_3 to be both unproblematically intelligible and relevant to the Epicurean dilemma at the same time. And if these interpretations are kept properly distinct, the failure of the standard argument is, of course, clear: on the one hand, if S_3 is given its life-life comparative interpretation, then, though it is straightforwardly intelligible, it is irrelevant to the Epicurean dilemma; on the other hand, if it is given its life-death comparative interpretation, then, though it has the desired relevance, it suffers from the same "no subject" problem as S_1 and S_2 and, hence, cannot be assumed to be intelligible without simply begging the question. Moreover, since to conflate these two interpretations is, in effect, to conflate death with an alternative sort of life, it is doubtful whether the standard argument really does avoid the mistake of thinking of death as a mode of existence, as a state from which one suffers. And this mistake, indeed, is implicit in its original description of the evil of death as the "loss," or "lack," of life. For whereas there is nothing wrong with the statement "A has lost (or lacks) his life" if it is construed merely as an idiomatic way of saying that A no longer exists, it cannot be taken in the literal sense required by the view that death is an ordinary evil of deprivation, the sense used when one says that a person has lost a friend, a job, or a leg. An existing person, a person who is, for example, actually enduring permanent solitary confinement, can literally be said to have lost, or to lack, (the goods of) his (previous mode of) life; but a dead person no longer exists and hence cannot literally be said to have lost, or to lack, anything whatever.[4]

Bernard Williams's preliminary argument in "The Makropulos Case: Reflections on the Tedium of Immortality" [Chapter 5 in this volume] provides a nice illustration of the standard argument and the conflation that motivates it. Contending that the argument underlying the Epicurean view "seeks to interpret the fear of death as a confusion, based on the idea that we shall be there after death to repine our loss of the *praemia vitae*, the rewards and delights of life," Williams continues:

[This] argument, in locating the objection to dying in a confused objection to being dead, . . . takes it as genuinely true of life that the satisfaction of desire, and possession of the *praemia vitae*, are good things. . . . But now if we consider two lives, one very short and cut off before the *praemia* have been acquired, the other fully provided with the *praemia* and containing their enjoyment to a ripe age, it is very difficult to see why the second life, by these standards alone, is not to be thought better than the first. . . . If the *praemia vitae* are valuable . . . then surely getting to the point of possessing them is better than not getting to that point, longer enjoyment of them is better than shorter, and more of them, other things being equal, is better than less of them. But if so, then it just will not be true . . . that death is never an evil. (pp. 75–76)[5]

The conflation occurs here with respect to the claim that possession of the *praemia vitae* is a good for the possessor, a claim that, Williams contends, is conceded even by supporters of the Epicurean view. In our schematic form, this "*praemia*" judgment becomes:

S_5: *A*'s possession of the *praemia vitae* is a good for *A*.

But S_5 has two possible interpretations, viz., (i) a life-life comparative interpretation according to which it asserts in part:

S_6: A life containing the *praemia vitae* is better for *A* than a life that lacks that *praemia vitae* is (good) for *A* [i.e., *A*'s living in possession of the *praemia* is better for *A* than *A*'s living without the *praemia* is good for *A*]

and (ii) a life-death comparative interpretation according to which it asserts in part:

S_7: A life containing the *praemia vitae* is better for *A* than death is (good) for *A*.

And the plausibility of Williams's argument depends entirely on the conflation of these two interpretations; if they are properly distinguished, his argument is vitiated. On its life-life comparative interpretation S_5 should indeed be acceptable to everyone, Epicureans included, for on this interpretation its intelligibility is unproblematic; but on this interpretation S_5 is, of course, entirely compatible with the Epicurean view and does nothing to show that death is an intelligible evil for the person who dies. On its life-death comparative interpretation, on the other hand, S_5 is indeed incompatible with the Epicurean view; but there is no plausibility whatever in the supposition that, on this interpretation, S_5 is accepted by supporters of, or is implicit in the argument underlying, this view. Thus, to hold that its supporters presuppose a claim that undermines the Epicurean view itself is simply to conflate these two interpretations.

Williams's contention that life is desirable for its possessor because the *praemia vitae* are desirable can be thought of as an instance of the common claim that life is good for its possessor because it is a precondition for all (other) goods. And the obvious Epicurean retort is that, in just the sense that life is a precondition for all (other) goods, so it is a precondition for all (other?) evils (and also for all things of indifferent value). The point, a supporter of the Epicurean view would say, is that A's life is a presupposition of all A-relative evaluation and, precisely for that reason, cannot itself be given any A-relative value. And this point is nicely illustrated by the contrast between S_6 and S_7. S_6, which gives only a comparative A-relative evaluation of the *praemia vitae* and their lack on the assumption of A's continued life, is, according to the Epicurean view, perfectly intelligible; but S_7, which attempts a comparative A-relative evaluation of A's life itself, is not.

To desire something for one's own sake—i.e., to have what I shall call a *prudential desire* for something—is to regard that thing as in one's own interest, and to regard it as in one's own interest is to regard it as a good for oneself. Hence, what goes for value, in the context of the Epicurean dilemma, goes also for rational desire. Just as the Epicurean view does not deny that one's death may be an evil for others, so it does not deny that one can have a rational altruistic desire to continue living; but just as it does deny that one's death can be an intelligible evil for oneself, so it denies that one can have a rational prudential desire to continue living.[6] Moreover, and more generally, the Epicurean view implies that A's prudential desires (indeed, anyone's desires "for A's sake"), like A-relative evaluations, presuppose A's (continued) existence. Williams criticizes these claims in his concluding attack on the Epicurean view:

It is admittedly true of many of the things I want, I want only on the assumption that I am going to be alive. . . . It might be suggested that not just these special cases, but really all [prudential] wants, are conditional on being alive; a situation in which one has ceased to exist is not to be compared with others with respect to desire-satisfaction— rather, if one dies, all bets are off. But surely the claim that all [prudential] desires are in this sense conditional must be wrong. For consider the idea of a rational forward-looking calculation of suicide; there can be such a thing, even if many suicides are not rational. . . . In such a calculation, a man might consider what lay before him, and decide whether he did or did not want to undergo it. If he does decide to undergo it, then some desire propels him on into the future, and *that* desire at least is not one that operates conditionally on his being alive, since it itself resolves the question of whether he is going to be alive. He has an unconditional, or (as I shall say) a *categorical* desire. (p. 77)

But the Epicurean view does not deny that one can—indeed, most of us do—desire to continue living; nor does it deny that one might—indeed, again, most of us do—construe this desire, at least in part, as a prudential desire. What the Epicurean view denies is that one can *coherently* construe such a desire as prudential; what it denies, that is, is that a desire to continue living can be given a coherent prudential rationale or justification. And Williams's appeal to the notion of "rational forward-looking calculation" does nothing to undermine this denial. For although one can always construct prudential calculations that are "rational" in the sense that they contain no factual or arithmetic mistakes, Williams provides no argument against the Epicurean contention that such calculations are not coherently applicable to life-death choices. Suppose, for instance, that, using a scale from $+10$ to -10, A calculates correctly that his average A-relative value level (e.g., his average happiness level), if he continues living, will be $+2$. What the Epicurean view claims— and what Williams does nothing to disprove—is that A cannot coherently use such a calculation as the basis for a prudential choice between life and death, since, as no value on the scale (including 0, the "midpoint" value of neutrality or indifference) can intelligibly be assigned to A's death, there is nothing against which the value $+2$, however "rationally" derived, can intelligibly be weighed.

Our discussion here is relevant to another attempt to undercut, or at least evade, the Epicurean view, an attempt consisting essentially in the claim that the prudential desire to continue living is a basic given, an essential feature of human nature, perhaps even implicit in the concept of a human being as a "self-maintaining" being, and is therefore a desire that needs no (further) defense or justification.[7] In the first place it must be emphasized, again, that the Epicurean view denies no factual claims concerning what people desire or how they construe, explain, and defend their desires; hence, it is consistent even with the extreme claim that every human being, in virtue of being human, necessarily has a prudential desire (or a desire that he takes to be prudential) to continue living. All that the Epicurean

view contends is that, *if* a prudential desire (or a desire construed as prudential) to continue living is an essential ingredient
in human nature, then human nature is essentially irrational.
Thus, the point in contention is not the claim that such a desire
is essential to human nature, but the further claim that, *since* (or
if) such a desire is essential to human nature, it requires no (further) justification or defense. Yet, construed as a response to the
Epicurean view, this claim simply begs the question. For any
claim concerning how much, or what sort of, justification the
prudential desire to continue living does or does not require presupposes that this desire is at least coherent; and it is precisely
this presupposition that the Epicurean view denies. Hence, although this claim might constitute an adequate response to,
e.g., the "noncognitivist" contention that the goal of preserving
one's own life cannot be shown to be "objectively" obligatory or
required by reason, a contention that is consistent with the same
presupposition, it patently does not constitute an adequate response to the Epicurean view. Nor can one object: "But the
coherence of the prudential desire to continue living is demon-
strated simply by its existence; for whatever is actual is possible,
and whatever is possible is noncontradictory, and thus coherent." For to describe a desire as prudential is not to claim, e.g.,
that it has a certain phenomenological character, but rather that
it has a certain sort of justification; hence, the existence of a (coherent) prudential desire to continue living cannot, as this objection assumes, be regarded as a "datum," as something "given
in experience." What is "given" is at most (i) that nearly everyone desires to continue living, and (ii) that nearly everyone who
has such a desire *believes* that it has a coherent prudential justification. But the question with which the Epicurean view is concerned is the question whether this belief is correct, and this
question cannot, of course, be settled by "experience," but only
by philosophical argument.

The incoherence claimed by the Epicurean view is perhaps its
most disturbing feature and is, therefore, perhaps the greatest obstacle to "resolving" the Epicurean dilemma simply by
accepting this view. Since common sense is notoriously fal-
lible, the mere fact that the Epicurean view conflicts with the
common-sense claim that A's death is an evil for A might leave
some readers unmoved. But it is one thing simply to deny that

A's death is an evil for *A*; it is quite another to imply, as does the Epicurean view (for the "no subject" difficulty holds across the board), that *A*'s death cannot intelligibly be ascribed any *A*-relative value, positive, negative, or neutral. The counter-intuitiveness of this implication is most strikingly illustrated, I think, by its application to prudential decisionmaking. For it entails not (merely) that the common-sense prudential assessment of life-death choices is mistaken, but that no coherent prudential assessment of such choices—including the claim that they are prudentially indifferent—is possible in principle; it entails, in short, that such choices are simply outside the realm within which prudential reasoning can intelligibly be employed. Thus, if a supporter of the Epicurean view is asked by a depressed friend, "From a prudential point of view, do you think I should kill myself?" then, just as he cannot consistently respond "From a prudential point of view you ought not to kill yourself," so he cannot consistently respond either "From a prudential point of view you ought to kill yourself" or (and this is where many people go wrong) "From a prudential point of view it makes no difference whether you kill yourself or not; it's prudentially permissible to do either." His only consistent response is "Your very question is incoherent, since it makes the confused assumption that prudential reasoning can intelligibly be applied to your choice." To put the difficulty another way, the Epicurean view rejects any "principle of sufficient prudential reason," and does so in a far stronger and more alarming sense than that in which, say, noncognitivist ethical theories reject a "principle of sufficient moral reason." For whereas noncognitivists make the comparatively benign claim that there is no rational ground for choice among rival systems of moral reasons or principles where each such system is both internally consistent and complete ("complete" in the sense that, for every alternative, it yields a judgment as to whether the alternative is morally required, morally prohibited, or morally indifferent), the Epicurean view makes the far more virulent claim that, since prudential reasoning is not coherently applicable to life-death alternatives, there *cannot be* a system of prudential reasons or principles that is both internally consistent and complete.

Thus, we seem to have reached an impasse. Acceptance of the Epicurean view now seems clearly to be an unhappy last resort, if not flatly intolerable;[8] but since we cannot refute it by thinking of death as an ordinary evil of deprivation, we seem to have no acceptable argument against it. Hence, the Epicurean dilemma constitutes a serious problem.

The Resolution

If A is dead, he *no longer* exists; but he did exist at an earlier time. Hence, the Epicurean view is clearly based on a "temporality assumption" at least as strong as the following:

An A-relative value must have a temporal location or extent at least part of which is prior to A's death.[9]

In this section I shall attempt to resolve the Epicurean dilemma by showing that, and how, we can justifiably reject this *temporality assumption*.

It is sometimes suggested that the problem with which this paper is concerned is simply a special case of the general problem of posthumous reference.[10] On this view S_1 is comparable to

S_8: A is being eulogized at his funeral,

the common problem being that, since A does not exist at the time in question, "A" apparently fails to refer. But posthumous evaluation (ascribing a value to something that entirely postdates its recipient) seems clearly to be problematic in a way that posthumous reference and, thus, posthumous predication in general, is not; whereas everyone agrees at once that "ordinary" posthumous predication, as exemplified by S_8, is in fact intelligible—the problem here merely concerns the *explanation* of this fact—the intelligibility of posthumous evaluation is open to genuine—and serious—doubt. And the obvious explanation of this discrepancy is that values must, it would seem, make a difference to, or affect, their recipients in a way that most other predicates (or the properties and relations these predicates express) need not, and in a way that seems clearly to require the temporality assumption. More precisely: there appears to be a conceptual connection of some sort between x's having a certain value for A (e.g., x's being an evil for A) and A's having an appropriate experience or feeling (e.g., A's suffering) as a result of x; but A's having an appropriate feeling from, or as a result of,

x seems to require that A coexist either with x or with x's causal effects; and this seems to be precisely what the temporality assumption demands.

Thus, if we are to justify the rejection of the temporality assumption we must focus, not on the problem of posthumous reference (though I shall discuss this problem briefly later on), but on the view that there is a value-feeling connection of the sort just described (the "Values Connect with Feelings" view, or VCF). Specifically, we must show either that VCF is false or that there is an acceptable interpretation of it that is consistent with the denial of the temporality assumption. The first approach is attempted by Thomas Nagel in his well-known paper "Death" [Chapter 4 in this volume]. Nagel's central argument against VCF is an argument by counterexample. If we accept the claim that an A-relative evil must result in A's suffering, then we are forced, Nagel says, to accept all the implications of the "common remark that what you don't know can't hurt you," implications that Nagel plainly finds intolerable:

> Even if a man is betrayed by his friends, ridiculed behind his back, and despised by people who treat him politely to his face, none of it can be counted as a misfortune for him so long as he does not suffer as a result. (p. 64)

But even if we agree that these implications are unacceptable, Nagel's argument has force only against the strongest and least plausible version of VCF, the version that requires that the value-recipient *actually have* the appropriate feeling. It has no force against more plausible versions, e.g., a version according to which x can intelligibly be said to have a certain A-relative value provided merely that it be possible, or possible under certain conditions, for A to have the appropriate feeling as a result of x.[11] For A's suffering from, e.g., undetected betrayal is possible in the sense that he may later discover the betrayal and suffer as a result—indeed, he may then suffer, not merely from the fact that he was betrayed but from the fact that the betrayal was undetected until that time. Thus, Nagel's examples are quite consistent with, and therefore constitute no argument against, this weaker version of VCF; yet this version, like the stronger, appears to require the temporality assumption.

Hence, Nagel's argument by counterexample is insufficient,

and although the rest of his discussion is suggestive—indeed, much of what he says fits in perfectly with what I think is the correct view—it does not contain a persuasive argument against VCF. One of the points he emphasizes, for instance, is that

> It is arbitrary to restrict the goods and evils that can befall a man to nonrelational properties. . . . As it stands, that restriction excludes not only . . . cases of gross degeneration but also a good deal of what is important about success and failure, and other features of a life that have the character of processes. . . . There are goods and evils that are irreducibly relational. (p. 66)

But there are, of course, many relations—being the wife of a domineering antifeminist, a billionaire's sole beneficiary, an intermediary between two quarreling Mafia leaders, etc.—that conform to VCF. Hence, the claim that values may be relational, though quite correct, constitutes no argument against VCF (and, therefore, constitutes no argument against either the temporality assumption or the Epicurean view).

Perhaps Nagel's most striking thesis is that values need not have a determinate spatial *or temporal* location; although a value recipient himself, Nagel says,

> can be exactly located in a sequence of places and times, the same is not necessarily true of the goods and ills that befall him. . . .
> A man's life includes much that does not take place within the boundaries of his body and his mind, and what happens to him can include much that does not take place within the boundaries of his life. These boundaries are commonly crossed by the misfortunes of being deceived, or despised, or betrayed. (If this is correct, there is a simple account of what is wrong with breaking a deathbed promise. It is an injury to the dead man. For certain purposes it is possible to regard time as just another type of distance.) . . . A man is the subject of good and evil as much because he has hopes that may or may not be fulfilled, or possibilities that may or may not be realized, as because of his capacity to suffer and enjoy. If death is an evil, it must be accounted for in these terms, and the impossibility of locating it within life should not trouble us. . . .
> [A]lthough the spatial and temporal locations of the individual who suffered the loss [of life] are clear enough, the misfortune itself cannot be so easily located. One must be content just to state that his life is over and there will never be any more of it. That *fact*, rather than his past or present condition, constitutes his misfortune, if it is one. Nevertheless, if there is a loss, someone must suffer it, and *he* must have existence and specific spatial and temporal location even if the loss itself does not. (pp. 65–67)

It is the claim that values may be atemporal, of course, that is relevant to the problem of death; and as I shall point out below, the framework that makes possible a successful resolution of the Epicurean dilemma implies that, on one significant interpretation, this claim is quite correct. But the above passage, though providing various assertions of this claim, hardly provides an adequate defense of it, particularly given the failure both of the standard argument, as discussed in the last section, and of Nagel's earlier argument against VCF. Indeed, it is doubtful whether Nagel succeeds even in showing this claim to be coherent, at least as it applies to the death case. For A's death does have a temporal location—i.e., we can in principle identify the temporal period during which A lives, the temporal point (or perhaps short stretch?) during which he passes from life to death, and the open-ended temporal period during which he is dead. And though one may indeed be puzzled about assigning a temporal location to the *loss* involved in death, this is simply a reflection of the fact that, as we noted in the first section, death does not involve a literal loss at all (and where there is a literal loss—such as the loss of a friend, a job, or a leg—assigning it a temporal location poses no difficulty).

Hence, something more—or something different—is needed if we are to mount a successful attack against the temporality assumption. And, in my view, any attempt, such as Nagel's, to undermine this assumption by attacking VCF is doomed at the outset simply because VCF, at least in some suitably weak version, must be accepted as true. Our only hope, then, is to find some way of showing that, and how, the denial of the temporality assumption can be made consistent with the acceptance of VCF; that is what I shall attempt here. Specifically, I shall argue that *temporally* distant—and hence posthumous—events (states, objects, etc.) can coherently be accorded the same status, with respect to VCF—and hence, with respect to A-relative evaluation—as spatially distant events (states, objects, etc.). Thus, since spatially distant events (etc.) satisfy VCF and, hence, can intelligibly be ascribed A-relative value, so, I shall claim, can posthumous events.[12]

One obvious difference between posthumous and spatially distant events is that, unless the concept of "cause" is radically revised, only the latter can be said to *cause* A's present feelings and experiences. But where A's "appropriate feeling" results from his apprehension or consciousness of the event (etc.) in question, what seems important in any case is not the event's being the *cause*, but its being the *object*, of this feeling. Thus, if we can show, for example, that A's death can be the *object* of his grief in the same way that the death of a spatially distant friend can be such an object, we will have shown that S_1 conforms to a reasonable version of VCF and thus is perfectly intelligible. But the claim that a posthumous event can be the object of an appropriate feeling faces an obvious, and now familiar, difficulty: so long as A is alive, and thus is capable of having appropriate feelings, events posthumous to A *do not (yet) exist*; and if a posthumous event does not exist, it can hardly be an object of feeling or experience (there is no "it" there to be such an object). Hence, Epicureans will contend, there remains a radical difference between, e.g., the death of A's spatially distant friend Jones and A's own death, so far as A-relative evaluation is concerned. In the former case we are confronted not merely with A's feelings of grief but with Jones's death; Jones's death actually obtains—it is an "objective fact"—and thus is both a possible object of A's feelings and an intelligible A-relative evil. But in the latter case the relevant "objective facts" do not include A's death, which has not occurred, but only A's feelings about his death; hence, although these *feelings* can intelligibly be regarded as A-relative evils (though if A's death cannot be regarded as evil, such feelings would seem to be irrational),[13] A's death itself, it will be claimed, cannot.

The view that spatially distant events exist, whereas posthumous (and, in general, temporally distant) events do not, brings us to the heart of the matter. For by refusing to treat space and time equally—that is, by refusing to say: "Just as spatially distant events exist though they do not exist *here*, so temporally distant, including posthumous, events exist though they do not exist *now*"—this view presupposes a conceptual/ontological framework that is significantly biased in favor of space, a framework according to which we inhabit an essentially three-dimensional, spatial universe and which condemns time to a purely ancillary treatment befitting its status as space's poor relation. Yet of course it is not merely possible, but on various counts desirable, to adopt a framework that takes a four-dimensional, spatiotemporal view of the universe. A powerful defense of such a framework is provided by W. V. Quine:

There are overwhelming reasons for treating time on a par with space; reasons of clarity and convenience, having nothing to do with Einstein's relativity theory. We say Elsa Lanchester is the widow of Charles Laughton; but there is no Charles Laughton for her to be the widow of, and there never was any, either, as long as she was his widow. We say that Charles Laughton married Elsa Lanchester, moreover, and yet we refuse to conclude that he married his own widow. We say there have been fifty-five kings of England, though there never once were more than three people who had been kings of England or ever would be. The simplest way of putting all this mess in order is by viewing people and other physical objects as deployed in four-dimensional space-time and all as coexisting in an eternal or timeless sense of the word. Temporal segments or stages of physical objects are physical objects in turn, temporally shorter ones. Elsa Lanchester's widowhood is a part of her, the later part. . . . In these terms my little anomalies are easily straightened out. . . .
    Another point in favor of the four-dimensional view is the relativity of rest and motion. This is . . . the doctrine that there is no absolute rest or motion. . . . Now granted this, we must concede that strictly speaking there are no places; for if there were, we could define absolute motion as change of place. On the other hand there is here no impediment to saying that there are place-times. One could thus claim for four-dimensional space-time a reality that cannot be claimed for three-dimensional space.
    Einstein's relativity comes in only at the end, as the clincher. The four-dimensional view was already overwhelmingly advantageous, as we see, but Einstein's special theory of relativity makes it imperative. For, in Einstein's theory, one's very distinction between space and time depends on how one is moving.[14]

The adoption of this four-dimensional framework, then, is the key to the resolution of the Epicurean dilemma. For, apart from phenomenalist objections that apply as much to spatial as to temporal distance[15] and are therefore irrelevant here, the problem of existence constitutes the sole obstacle to the claim that posthumous events, like spatially distant events, can be objects of appropriate feelings and experiences in the sense required by a reasonable version of VCF. And the four-dimensional framework allows, indeed requires, us to view posthumous objects and events, like spatially distant objects and events, as existing—in Quine's words, it views objects, events, etc. from all places and times (or better, from all place-times) "as coexisting in an eternal or timeless sense of the word." Thus, we seem to have solved our problem. By adopting the four-dimensional framework we can say (a) that posthumous events exist; (b) that posthumous events can therefore be objects of appropriate feeling in the sense required by VCF; (c) that VCF thus does not require the temporality assumption; (d) that the temporality assumption can therefore justifiably be rejected; and, hence, (e) that the Epicurean view can justifiably be rejected. In brief, A's death coexists with A ("in an eternal or timeless sense of the word"), and is therefore a possible object of A's suffering, and is therefore an intelligible A-relative evil.

All that remains, then, is to consider whether there is any serious objection to the adoption of the four-dimensional framework. Now the only doubts about this framework that are both relevant and plausible, I think, are doubts as to whether it might not be as incompatible with common sense as is the Epicurean view. Yet even these doubts should quickly be stilled. For it is common sense, after all, not some esoteric theory, which holds that Elsa Lanchester is the widow of Charles Laughton though there is no Charles Laughton for her to be the widow of, that there have been fifty-five, yet never more than three, kings of England—and that A's death is an intelligible A-relative evil despite the fact that it entirely postdates A. To say that this "mess" is best organized in terms of the four-dimensional framework is therefore tantamount to saying that this framework is a central presupposition of common sense itself. Thus, philosophers who set out and defend this framework are not engaging in radical revisionary metaphysics or exhibiting obsequious subservience to science, but are simply articulating and clarifying what is implicit in much of our everyday conceptual practice.

I lack the space for a full discussion of the relation between common sense and the four-dimensional framework; but to illuminate the framework, and to emphasize its importance, I should like to conclude by considering two matters pertinent to this relation that have special relevance to the concerns of this paper. The first involves the general problem of posthumous reference, the problem of explaining how "A" in S_8—or "Charles Laughton" in "Elsa Lanchester is the widow of Charles Laughton"—can be referentially satisfactory. Now if this problem is approached from the perspective of the three-dimensional framework, it seems thoroughly intractable. For since the three-

dimensional framework does not view time as an essential characteristic of objects—on its view, objects are simply spatial entities—it must provide an alternative way of dealing with time;
and it does this by viewing time as a characteristic of predicate
ascriptions. Thus, on the three-dimensional framework statements of the form "*A* has property *P*" (e.g., "*A* is asleep") are
construed as "*A has-at-t P*" (e.g., "*A* is now asleep"), where *t*
is the appropriate time. But when we combine this temporal
view of predication with the view, also implicit in the three-
dimensional framework, that existence is restricted to the present, then posthumous reference becomes impossible. S_8 is construed as "*A* has *now* the property 'being eulogized at one's
funeral'"; yet on this framework *A* does not exist now (i.e., at
the time of the eulogy); and thus the term "*A*" simply fails to
refer. The adoption of the four-dimensional framework, however, eliminates these difficulties. Since time, on this framework, *is* a characteristic of objects, predicate ascriptions can
be viewed as "timeless" or atemporal; e.g., "A is asleep" is
no longer construed as "A has now the property of 'being
asleep,'" but rather as "The now-segment of *A* has *atemporally*
the property 'being asleep.'" And when this atemporal view of
predication is combined with the four-dimensional framework's
atemporal view of existence, posthumous reference poses no
difficulty; since *A* has atemporal or "timeless" existence, though
he may now be dead, the term "*A*" in "*A* has atemporally the
property 'being eulogized at one's funeral'" is referentially unproblematic. And a more complete "four-dimensional" analysis,
an analysis that includes the temporal claims implicit in normal
uses of S_8 but not contained in "*A* has atemporally the property
'being eulogized at one's funeral'"—e.g., that the eulogy is occurring now (i.e., at the time of the utterance) and that both the
eulogy and the utterance postdate *A*—can be provided as follows (where the subscript "a" signifies that the predication is
atemporal):

S_9: *A* is$_a$ eulogized at his funeral; and if *A*'s temporal dimension ex-
tends$_a$ from t_1 to t_2, the eulogy's temporal dimension extends$_a$ from t_3
to t_4, and the temporal location of this utterance is$_a$ t_5, then t_2 is$_a$
earlier than t_3 and t_5 is$_a$ between t_3 and t_4.

Now the special interest for us in all this lies not in the fact that
the four-dimensional framework resolves the problem of post-

humous reference (for as we noted above, to explain how posthumous reference is intelligible is not in itself sufficient to show that and how posthumous evaluation is intelligible) but in the fact that it does so via the medium of *atemporal* predication. For this provides a basis on which we can give a clear sense to the notion of atemporal values, the notion emphasized, yet never adequately explained, by Nagel. If we say (i) that values are, to follow the standard jargon, "supervenient" upon the "natural" properties or relations on which they are based; (ii) that a property or relation is expressed by its "correlated predicate"; and (iii) that a predicate is "atemporal" if, perhaps because of reference problems, its ascription is intelligible *only* where it is construed atemporally and thus *only* in the context of the four-dimensional framework; then we can define "an atemporal value" very simply as "a value supervenient upon a property or relation whose correlated predicate is atemporal." Thus, the value ascribed by, e.g., "A's being eulogized at his funeral is an evil for A," unlike that ascribed by, e.g., "A's being asleep is a good for A," is an atemporal value; for the predicate "being eulogized at one's funeral" is, whereas the predicate "being asleep" is not, an atemporal predicate in this sense.[16] And since "being dead" is, of course, an atemporal predicate—a four-dimensional unpacking of "A is dead" on the model of S_9 would be "(A exists$_a$; and) if A's temporal dimension extends$_a$ from t_1 to t_2 and the time of this utterance is$_a$ t_3, then t_3 is$_a$ later than t_2"—the value ascribed by S_1 is, as Nagel would wish, an atemporal value. Now what it is most important to recognize here is that, although the four-dimensional framework countenances (indeed requires) atemporal-predicate ascriptions—and therefore presumably countenances atemporal truths and facts— it does not countenance atemporal events (including losses!), states, and objects; on the contrary, it emphasizes the temporality of events, etc., in the clearest possible way. And it is, I think, Nagel's failure to draw an adequate distinction between predicate ascriptions, facts, and truths on the one hand and events, states, and objects on the other which constitutes the major mistake in his discussion (contrast, e.g., his claim that "this *fact* [that the subject's life is over] constitutes his misfortune," together with its implicit suggestion that this fact is atemporal—which is all quite reasonable—with his claim that death is, or involves, an atemporal *loss*—which is not). Nor is this failure particularly surprising, given our use of value terms. For one of the intriguing aspects of this use, which I cannot elaborate here, is that values are idiomatically characterizable either as events (etc.) or as facts; if *A* has a bad cold, one can say either "*A*'s cold is (an) evil for *A*" or "The fact that *A* has a cold is (an) evil for *A*" with perfect linguistic propriety.

The second, and final, matter concerns what I shall call *duration predicates*, predicates that focus on temporal duration itself. Consider, for instance, the statement "*A* is serving a 20-year prison sentence." Since there is no temporal point at which *A* serves his entire sentence, no temporal, three-dimensional, construal of the form "*A* serves-at-*t* a 20-year sentence" will work; thus, duration predicates are atemporal predicates in the above sense, predicates intelligible only on the four-dimensional framework. Now to say that duration predicates require the four-dimensional framework seems just to say that this framework is essential to viewing objects and events as temporal wholes, as entities that retain their identities over time. Thus, if we reject this framework we seem forced to the view that *A* has no existence except in the present, that his past and future are not, strictly speaking, *his* at all, but belong to distinct selves; if it is *A* who is now going to sleep, it will not be *A* who awakes in the morning. And this implies, in turn, that a consistent adherence to the three-dimensional framework forces one not merely to reject posthumous evaluation, and thus to accept the Epicurean view, but to reject *A*-relative evaluation involving future times within the span of *A*'s life. For since, e.g., the target of the tongue-lashing *A* fears from his boss next Monday will be a self distinct from *A*, the recipient of the evil "supervenient" thereupon will likewise be a self distinct from *A*; in short, values involving future times, such as the negative value of next Monday's tongue-lashing, cannot be *A*-relative values.

Now since all of this is, of course, supremely counterintuitive, this discussion should remove any lingering doubts about the importance of the four-dimensional framework for common sense. But the fact that duration predicates are atemporal has a further implication of special significance for us, viz., that the values supervenient upon durational properties and relations are likewise atemporal; since "serves a 20-year sentence" is atemporal, so is the A-relative evil constituted by A's serving a sentence of this duration. Thus, the four-dimensional framework required by any A-relative evaluation of A's death (required, indeed, not merely by all posthumous, but, as we have now seen, by all "future" A-relative evaluation), is also required by any A-relative evaluation of duration. And if we consider the connection between death and duration, this fact will hardly be surprising. For the reason one fears death, of course, is that it shortens the duration of one's life; if A contracts terminal cancer at the age of 30—or at the age of 75, for that matter—his approaching death would typically be the object of negative feelings precisely because of his awareness of the brevity of his life as a whole, and the consequent sparsity of its content, in comparison with alternative imaginable lives. In short, it is the "four-dimensional" ability to understand life in durational terms, to view one's life as a temporal whole and to make evaluative comparisons between it and alternative possible life-wholes, which ultimately accounts for the fact that statements of the form "A's death is an evil for A" are commonly regarded as not merely intelligible, but true.

CHAPTER SEVEN

AGATHON: But all that talk about death being the same as sleep.

ALLEN: Yes, but the difference is that when you're dead and somebody yells, "Everybody up, it's morning," it's very difficult to find your slippers.

—Woody Allen, *Side Effects*

How to Be Dead and Not Care: A Defense of Epicurus

Stephen E. Rosenbaum

Non fui; fui; non sum; non curo.   —Roman epitaph

The prospect of death is at best a disquieting annoyance; it is at worst a terrifying mystery. However we react to the prospects of our deaths, we try to suppress our thoughts about death, and live as if our time were endless. Long ago, Epicurus offered a remedy for our attitudes toward our deaths. He apparently argued that since death is neither good nor bad for the person dead and since the fear of that which is not bad for one is groundless, it is unreasonable to fear death; consequently, no one should fear death. If Epicurus were correct in this, we should perhaps try to revise our attitudes toward our deaths. Without regard to what we can do or what we should do about our attitudes, I wish to discuss Epicurus's view that one's death is not bad for one. Since Thomas Nagel's article, "Death," published in 1970,[1] Epicurus's view has come under strong attack from various sources, but has not yet received a sound defense.[2] I undertake to supply that defense.

Before reconstructing Epicurus's argument, it would be well to make explicit certain basic assumptions and certain basic

Reprinted by permission from *American Philosophical Quarterly* 23, no. 2 (April 1986): 217–25.

concepts involved in the issue to be discussed. First, I suppose that being alive is generally good. Some argue against Epicurus partly on the ground that life is good, and I wish to make clear at the outset that I shall not challenge that supposition. Second, I accept the proposition that when one dies, one ceases to exist, in some important sense. Although this proposition is not completely unproblematic, it is one of the bases for the discussion of Epicurus's doctrine. Those who find death frightful and evil find it so precisely because they consider it, or think it might be, the end of their existence as persons. Epicurus finds death harmless partly because it brings about (or is) nonexistence. The issue between Epicurus and his antagonists is how to view one's death, if it leads to nonexistence. Of course, if one could justifiably believe in life after death, the issue would be different, though if one knew merely that one would continue to exist after one's death, one would not thereby know whether one's death is good, bad, or neither.

It is useful additionally to distinguish three concepts from one another, those of dying, death, and being dead. Attempting a careful explication of the issue raised by Epicurus using only the word "death" would be futile, for the term is ambiguous, being used to mean sometimes dying, sometimes death, and sometimes being dead, as I shall explain those terms. Dying, we may say, is the process whereby one comes to be dead or the process wherein certain causes operate to bring about one's being dead. As such, dying takes place during, and at or near the end of, one's lifetime, however extensive it may be. The time dying takes may be short or long. The process of dying may be comfortable or uncomfortable. When we say about a person that it took a long time for the person to die, we are commenting about the person's dying. An important truth about dying is that it takes place during a person's lifetime and may thus be experienced. We should distinguish dying from death. Doing so is not perfectly in accord with common usage, but this is insignificant, since common usage is not perfectly unambiguous. When we say, for example, "Her death took a long time," we could substitute the word "dying" for that of "death" with no loss of meaning. Nevertheless, I want to focus on that sense of "death" in which the word might be used to say, "Though he had had a long, fatal illness, his death came unexpectedly." In this context, death is roughly the time at which a person becomes dead, and is different from dying, the process leading to death. Metaphorically, death is the portal between the land of the living and the land of the dead; the bridge over the Styx. Several facts should be noted about death, in this sense. It is not clearly a part of a person's lifetime, although it may be a (very) small part. Also, it is not clear that it takes time or, if so, how much time it takes. It may be a mere moment in time separating being alive from being dead. Distinct from dying or death is being dead. Being dead is the state in which one finds oneself (so to speak) after one dies. Being dead is clearly not part of a person's life, in the normal sense, though we might say that it is part of a person's history. The differences among these concepts may be summarized easily: death comes at the end of a person's dying and at the beginning of a person's being dead. There are two points in making these distinctions. One is that doing so will enable us to understand Epicurus's view about death in the clearest way. The other is that it will enable us to notice ambiguous uses of the term "death" which embody rhetorically, but not logically, persuasive ways of insinuating the falsity of Epicurus's view.

Now we are in a position to formulate Epicurus's argument after reminding ourselves of what he said in his "Letter to Menoeceus":

Accustom thyself to believe that death is nothing to us, for good and evil imply sentience, and death is the privation of all sentience, . . . Death, therefore, the most awful of evils, is nothing to us, seeing that, when we are, death is not come, and when death is come, we are not. It is nothing, then, either to the living or to the dead, for with the living it is not and the dead exist no longer.[3]

I offer the following reconstruction of Epicurus's argument. In formulating the arguments as I do, I attempt to do justice to Epicurus's philosophical insight, caring less for historical accuracy than for verisimilitude. The reconstruction runs as follows:

(A) A state of affairs is bad for person P only if P can experience it at some time.

Therefore, (B) P's being dead is bad for P only if it is a state of affairs that P can experience at some time.

(C) P can experience a state of affairs at some time only if it begins before P's death.

(D) *P*'s being dead is not a state of affairs that begins before *P*'s death.

Therefore, (E) *P*'s being dead is not a state of affairs that *P* can experience at some time.

THEREFORE, *P*'s being dead is not bad for *P*.

Before discussing objections to this argument, several comments are in order. First, the conclusion does not entail that *P*'s being dead is not bad for others or that *P*'s being dead is not bad in any way in which something might be bad but not *for* anyone, if there is such a way. So, the argument, if sound, should not inhibit our thinking that a person's being dead is bad in these other ways. Second, the conclusion is not about death or dying, but rather it is about being dead. So it does not rule out a person's dying being bad for the person, as painful experience makes obvious it should not. Neither does it rule out a person's death being bad for the person. There are several reasons why I express the conclusion in this way. It makes Epicurus's argument clearly sensible in a way in which it would not otherwise be. When Epicurus said that "death . . . is nothing to us, seeing that, when we are, death is not come, and when death is come, we are not,"⁴ he is most plausibly interpreted as talking about being dead. Taking death to be a sort of tertiary period in one's history, one could construe Epicurus as being concerned about death (in my sense), but I believe that it would be an exceedingly uncharitable way of making him look silly. The term "death" as ordinarily used, is ambiguous, being used sometimes to mean dying, sometimes death, and sometimes being dead, as I have explicated the terms. There is no reason to expect Epicurus thoughtfully to have distinguished these and to have selected the Greek equivalent of "being dead" to express his view.⁵ Second, the issue would be much less interesting if it concerned death instead of being dead. What people seem to think bad is not the moment of death itself, but rather the abysmal nonexistence of being dead. That, at any rate, is what they fear, and that fear is what Epicurus wished to extinguish. In addition, I am not sure that a person's death (in my sense) could be bad for a person, since the death of a person may have no temporal duration, being a mere moment in time separating being alive from being dead. Even if death endured a fraction of a second, most rational beings would not be very concerned about it no matter how much agony were believed to be involved. Finally, there are sympathetic proponents of Epicurus's view who take him to be concerned about being dead, not death. Lucretius, for example, understood Epicurus's view about death as a view about being dead.[6] So we have good reason to express the conclusion in the way we do.[7]

It is important, furthermore, to spend some time explaining and commenting on the concept of experience, which plays a crucial role in the argument. Comments about experience should be made in full realization of the woes that can befall one who attempts to look too deeply into Pandora's box. The word "experience" is ambiguous, and it is not possible to review the analysis of the concept briefly, nor is it useful to do so.[8] Nevertheless, some helpful remarks can be made in the context of an argument for (A), that a state of affairs is bad for a person only if the person can experience it at some time.

Suppose that a person P cannot hear and never will hear. Then the egregious performance of a Mozart symphony cannot causally affect P at any time, supposing that what makes the performance bad is merely awful sound, detectable only through normal hearing, and supposing further that the performance does not initiate uncommon causal sequences that can affect the person. It is clear that the person cannot experience the bad performance, auditorily or otherwise. Furthermore, it seems clear that the performance cannot be bad for the person in any way. It cannot affect the person in any way. The reason why it is not bad for him is that he is not able to experience it. The person's being deaf insulates him from auditory experiences that might otherwise be bad for him. Similarly, a person born without a sense of smell cannot be causally affected by, and thus cannot experience, the stench of a smoldering cheroot. The stench cannot be an olfactory negativity for her. We could imagine indefinitely many more such cases.

Since I see nothing eccentric about these cases, I believe that we are entitled to generalize and claim that our judgments about these cases are explained by the principle that if a person cannot experience a state of affairs at some time, then the state of affairs is not bad for the person. Dead persons cannot experience any states of affairs; they are blind, deaf, and generally insentient. So no state of affairs is bad for a dead person. The principle that explains these cases is, moreover, logically equivalent to (A), a state of affairs is bad for a person only if the person can experience it at some time. We may take it that we thus have a positive reason for believing (A).

Now, clearly there are certain suppositions about experience used in this argument. Foremost is the assumption that one experiences a state of affairs only if it can affect one in some way. There is supposed to be a causal element in experience. In this sense of "experience," then, one does not experience a situation merely by believing that the situation has occurred or will occur, or by imagining a certain situation. A person can believe that a state of affairs has occurred or will occur even if the state of affairs has had no causal effects on the person. The event may not have occurred and may never occur. Thus, in the sense of "experience" presupposed here, one does not experience just by believing. Similarly, one does not experience a situation just by imagining it. One might imagine oneself basking lazily on a sunny beach, but that situation is not thereby a situation that one experiences. The apparently required causal connection between the situation and the person is missing.

Notice that I have assumed here only a necessary condition for experiencing a situation, not a sufficient condition. Hence, one might be causally affected by a situation and not experience it. Perhaps awareness of the causal effects is also required. I believe there may be one sense of the term "experience" in which awareness is required, another in which it is not. It is difficult to think that one could perceptually experience something, for example, without being aware of it. However, there is that way of experiencing in which we are said to undergo an experience, of which we need not be aware. If one undergoes (as we say) the experience of being irradiated by low level radioactivity, one might well not be aware of it. It seems to me that one clear requirement of experience, at least in one clear sense, is that one be causally affected in some way by situations one experiences.

Finally, if a requirement of experiencing a state of affairs is that the state of affairs be able to have causal effects on one, then we can express a positive reason for believing not only premise (A) but also premise (C), that P can experience a state of affairs at some time only if it begins before P's death. Surely a state of affairs can causally affect a person only if the person exists after the state of affairs begins to occur, for effects occur only after their causes. To be sure, a person's dead body can be affected after the person ceases to be, but a person is not identical to its lifeless body. A person exists after a state of affairs begins to occur only if the state of affairs begins before the person's death. Therefore a state of affairs can causally affect a person only if the state of affairs begins before the person's death. So a person can experience a situation only if the situation begins to occur before the person's death. Obviously, this is (C). According to one reasonably clear concept of experience, then, we have reasons to believe basic premises in the argument.

Before considering objections to the Epicurean argument, I want to characterize what I take to be the purpose of Epicurus's argument. I do this because some discussions of the issue seem to have misunderstood entirely what Epicurus was trying to do. Simply, he was trying to show us the truth about being dead so that we might not be excessively troubled about it. His general philosophical aim seems to have been much the same as that of Lucretius, his disciple, to know the truth and thereby achieve *ataraxia*. There is no reason to believe he would have been willing to peddle *ataraxia* by means of rhetorical trickery, not that he may not have done so inadvertently. Indicative of his purpose is a comment in his "Letter to Herodotus," in which he discussed metaphysics. He said that "mental tranquillity means being released from all . . . troubles and cherishing a continual remembrance of the highest and most important truths."[9] Thus, I believe that Mary Mothersill seriously misunderstood Epicurus when announcing her view that his argument "will hardly bear looking into, but may have been intended as little more than an eristic flourish," and that "Epicurus was not much interested in logic."[10] Epicurus did have a serious purpose, to establish the truth and thereby gain mental tranquillity and show the way to mental tranquillity. In fairness to Mothersill, we should admit that there would be more to her comment if Epicurus's argument were to be understood only as he expressed it. There is not much there. Nevertheless, I think that it is uncharitable caviling to dismiss his argument without an attempt to state the argument clearly.

Others have not fully appreciated the revisionistic character of Epicurus's philosophy. Harry Silverstein, for example, sees the matter raised by Epicurus as a sort of contest between the Epicurean view and the common sense view "that a person's death is one of the greatest evils that can befall him." [11] Seeming to believe that the philosopher's task is to bolster the deliverances of common sense against all antagonists, Silverstein is driven to extreme lengths in the effort to undermine Epicurus's view. Epicurus believed, however, that unreflective common sense frequently was a source of bemusement and misery, and he wished to make common sense conform to the results of philosophical reflection. He believed that one of the results was a realization that death is not bad for the person who dies. I do not want to argue for Epicurus's apparent view of philosophy, and I certainly do not wish to dismiss arguments against Epicurus on the ground that they presuppose a distinct view of philosophy. I merely note that the argument is offered in a revisionistic spirit and that those who conjure ways to defend common sense against Epicurus are arguing in a very different context from that of Epicurus. Whether one takes philosophy to be revisionistic or not, perhaps one should approach philosophical arguments from the point of view of possible discovery, not from that of the infrangibility of one's own prereflective inclinations. However this may be, the philosophical issue is whether the argument is sound. To objections against the argument I now turn.

Given the Epicurean argument as I have stated it, there are only three premises one could question. Those are the basic ones, (A), (C), and (D). The others, (B) and (E), are merely logical consequences of (A), (C), and (D). Since (D) is true by definition, we shall consider only (A) and (C), which have, in fact, been attacked by Epicurus's adversaries.

Thomas Nagel argues that what a person does not know may well be bad for the person. [12] Nagel seems thereby to object to premise (A). He gives plausible cases in which something can be bad for a person even if the person is unaware of it. Unknown betrayal by friends and destruction of one's reputation by vile, false rumors of which one is unaware are examples of evils which a person might not consciously experience. Strictly, however, such cases are logically compatible with (A) and hence do not refute (A), since all (A) requires for something to be bad for a person is that the person *can* experience it (perhaps not consciously) at some time, not that he actually experience it consciously.[13] We can grant that what one *does not* consciously experience can hurt one without granting that what one *cannot* experience can hurt one. All (A) requires for an event or state of affairs to be bad for a person, implicitly, is that the person be able to experience it at some time, not that the person be aware or conscious of the causal effects at some time.

Nagel tries to deny the conclusion directly by characterizing death as a loss to the person who suffers it, and, taking losses to be bad, concludes that a person's death is bad for the person. He seems relatively unconcerned about the proposition that once a person dies, that person no longer exists, and thus does not and *cannot* experience the loss, a proposition which he accepts.[14] L. S. Sumner is more explicit about the issue and claims that though the person who dies no longer exists, "the only condition essential to any loss is *that there should have been a subject who suffered it*."[15] It is all right, I suppose, to *call* a person's death a loss for the person, but it is clearly not like paradigmatic cases of losses that are bad for persons. Consider the case in which one loses one's business to creditors. One has the business, the creditors get it, and then one does not have it. We may suppose that the loss is bad for the person. Such cases are common. We should note that in such cases the loss is something the person is able to experience after it occurs. Typical losses that are bad for persons seem to instantiate the following principle: A person *P* loses good *g* only if there is a time at which *P* has *g* and there is a later time at which *P* does not have *g*. If *P* ceases to exist when *P* dies, then being dead cannot be considered a loss of this typical sort in which losses are bad for persons, for in typical cases *P* exists after the loss and is able to experience it. If being dead is a loss, it is so insufficiently similar to paradigm cases of loss which are bad for persons that we need special reasons or arguments why treating death as a loss enables us to reject (A). Neither Nagel nor others offer such reasons. Therefore, the argument that death is a loss and is thus bad is not convincing.

Nagel believes further that by treating death as a loss for a person, he has a way of resolving *the symmetry problem*, noted by Lucretius.[16] Considering this problem will help us understand more clearly the problems in holding that death is bad for one.

Taking being dead to be nonexistence, Lucretius compared the nonexistence after death to that before conception, and apparently thought that since prenatal nonexistence is not bad for a person (and no one finds it distressing), then posthumous nonexistence is not bad either (though people *do* find it distressing). He seemed to have thought that we should rectify our unjustifiably asymmetrical attitudes toward the two symmetrical states. The argument would be that if being dead (when one is nonexistent) is bad for one, then not having had life before one's conception (when one is also nonexistent) should be bad for one. Since the latter is not bad for one, then the former is not.

Nagel's response to this argument is that "the time after his [a person's] death is a time of which his death deprives him. It is a time in which, had he not died then, he would be alive. Therefore any death entails the loss of *some* life that its victim would have led had he not died at that or any earlier point."[17] By this, Nagel intends to suggest implicitly that we cannot say something similar about birth, hence, there is an asymmetry, contrary to Lucretius. However, we can say something quite analogous about birth: The time before a person's birth is a time of which his not having been born earlier deprives him. It is a time in which, had he not been born as late as he was, he would be alive. Therefore any delay in being born entails the loss of some life that its beneficiary would have led had he been born earlier. To be clear about the analogy, if life is a good, then, given a living person, if losing life so soon is bad for the person, then not having acquired life earlier should be bad for the person. In either case, one misses out on life. Shall we say that the issue is whether it is worse to have lived and lost than never to have lived at all? No, because it is not true of a living person that that person *never* lived at all. A living person can live longer not only by dying later but also by being born earlier. The issue really is whether it is worse to have lived and lost than not *yet* to have lived. I do not see that it is worse. What makes the symmetry is, in part, the fact that a living person who *was* prenatally nonexistent *was going to live*, just as the living person who *will be* posthumously nonexistent *has lived*. The symmetry is plausible because the analogy between the two relevant states seems quite sound.

Nagel objects to the proposed symmetry by insisting that "we cannot say that the time prior to a man's birth is a time in which he would have lived had he been born not then but earlier. . . . He *could* not have been born earlier: anyone born substantially earlier than he would have been someone else. Therefore, the time prior to his birth is not time in which his subsequent birth prevents him from living." [18] The reply to this is obvious. If the time at which we are born is *essential* to who we are, to our identity, then the time at which we die should be also. If *we* could not have been born earlier (because if "we" had been, "we" would have been someone else), then *we* could not have died later (and still have been us). Nagel's answer relies on the view that there is an asymmetry between time of birth and time of death, implicitly because time of birth is not essential to us while time of death is. But *this* putative asymmetry is invisible. Thus it cannot be used to argue for the asymmetry between prenatal and posthumous nonexistence. If Lucretius's symmetry thesis is correct, as it seems to be, then there is no reason to think that being dead is any worse than not having been born yet.

A recent objection to the Epicurean argument is that of Harry Silverstein, who, defending common sense, apparently believes that a person can in some way, experience posthumous states of affairs, thus seeming to reject (C). He apparently argues against (C) by proposing an analogy between spatially distant events and temporally distant (future) events. He believes that the view that spatially distant events exist (but not *here*) and that temporally distant events do not exist "presupposes a conceptual ontological framework that is significantly biased in favor of space, a framework according to which we inhabit an essentially three-dimensional, spatial, universe and which condemns time to a purely ancillary treatment befitting its status as space's poor relation." [19] Wishing for a less biased ontology, Silverstein proposes to treat time on a par with space and to say that just as spatially distant events exist so too do future events. Thus, he has a possible way of negating (C): A person can experience states of affairs or events that begin after that person's death, because such things *exist* atemporally ("during") a person's life.

There is much to say about Silverstein's argument, which is, at points, quite complex. However, I shall be content to make a few points, one of which seems to me quite telling against his argument. Silverstein wishes to show, as he puts it, "that A's death can be the *object* of his grief in the same way that the death of a spatially distant friend can be such an object."[20] He wants to make this point because he thinks that "where A's 'appropriate feeling' results from his apprehension or consciousness of the event (etc.) in question, what seems important in any case is not the event's being the *cause*, but its being the *object*, of this feeling."[21] To make the point, he feels he must hold a metaphysical view according to which it is possible that future events or states of affairs exist now, atemporally. There are several appropriate comments to be made about Silverstein's view. First, one of his basic assumptions goes without support, that assumption, namely, that an event's being an object of feeling, not a cause, is what is important in saying whether posthumous events are bad for a person. It seems to me that unless this hypothesis receives some support, we are free to reject it, especially since I have already argued that a causal relationship between the event and the person is necessary. Second, he assumes that a person's having, at some time, an actual feeling about an event is necessary for the event to be bad for the person. This assumption, too, is without support. To be sure, it is his interpretation of Epicurus's view that bad is associated with sentience, but it is not the only or the most obvious interpretation. If we say, for example, that one must experience an event consciously for it to be bad for one, it does not follow from what we say that one must have certain feelings about the event, about one's awareness of the event, or about anything. It should be argued that feelings of some sort are involved.

Finally, it is clear that events which have never occurred and will never occur *can*, in some sense, be *objects* of our psychological attitudes. For example, Britons in the early 1940's feared an invasion of Britain by the Nazis. Yet that event never occurred. They dreaded being governed by Hitler, yet that state of affairs did not obtain and never will. Silverstein insists that "the problem of existence constitutes the sole obstacle to the claim that posthumous events, like spatially distant events, can be objects of appropriate feelings and experiences."[22] But should we say that the events and state of affairs in the previous examples had to exist (and existed) for them to have been objects of fear and dread? We can say so, if we like, but whether we say thus that the Nazi invasion of Britain existed (or exists), atemporally, it is nevertheless an event that Britons never experienced (it is natural to say), because it never occurred. This suggests that something is seriously wrong with Silverstein's objection to premise (C). Very simply, he fails to distinguish the existence of an event or state of affairs from the occurrence of an event or state of affairs. Certainly, there might be no need to make such a distinction for one who takes it that the class of occurring events is identical to the class of existing events. Without such a distinction, one would hold that an event exists if, and only if, it occurs. If Silverstein identifies the classes of events, then he would seem forced to the view that if events exist atemporally (as he believes) then events occur atemporally. But if events occurred and existed atemporally, what would be the difference between past and future events? There would be none, which is absurd. Therefore, Silverstein should distinguish existing from occurring events or find some other way of distinguishing past from future events. It would be most plausible to say that for events or states of affairs, to exist is one thing, to occur is another. One might hold that all events *exist* atemporally but that among the existing events, some have already occurred (past events) and some have not yet occurred (future events). With this distinction, moreover, it is easy to defend (C) against Silverstein's attack. (C) could be interpreted in terms of an event occurring instead of an event existing. As stated, (C) should be understood to be slightly elliptical for this: *P* can experience a state of affairs at some time only if it begins *to occur* before *P*'s death. In fact, this is how I have taken it. So understood, it is no good to object to (C) that posthumous events or states of affairs exist timelessly (during a person's life). This would be logically compatible with (C). One would have to show that a person can experience a state of affairs or an event that does not begin *to occur* before the person's death. I do not see how *this* can be done. Therefore, I conclude that Silverstein's metaphysical proposal is ineffective against premise (C), whatever its merits independently.

In spite of the apparent soundness of Epicurus's argument, one might object against Epicurus's argument on the ground that it misses the point. One might claim that the badness of our deaths lies in our anticipation of losing the capacity to experience, to have various opportunities and to obtain various satisfactions. It does seem quite obvious that such anticipation is bad, for it is a source of displeasure, as much as is the experience of anticipating the tortures of the dental chair. However, the anticipation of either bad experiences or of the inability to experience *simpliciter* is something that can occur only while we are alive. It cannot occur when we are dead if being dead entails nonexistence. Therefore, we do not experience the anticipation of being dead when we are dead. So, the badness of the anticipation of death does not show the badness of death itself. This point may be understood more clearly when one compares the anticipation of dental pain to the anticipation of being dead. For the former, there are two bad experiences, the anticipation and the pain of the root canal; for the latter, there is only one bad experience, the anticipation of being dead. Indeed, Epicurus may be thought to have believed that the anticipation of death is a pointless bad, since it is a bad with no genuine basis, the object of it not being bad. Epicurus hoped that understanding this could free us from one bad, one baseless source of anxiety. One could say, I suppose, that one's death is bad, meaning that anticipation of one's death is bad. However, not only would it be unduly misleading to say this, but also, it would not be a way of undermining Epicurus's view that one's death itself is not bad for one.

Now that objections to the Epicurean argument have been shown to fail, we might think of trying to account for what seems a widespread and well-entrenched fear of death or being dead. It is perhaps useful to remind ourselves that people may fear what is not really bad for them; they might fear what they only believe to be bad for them. We might thus speculate that people fear death out of ignorance. This seems somewhat too facile and insensitive, however true. Perhaps a few conjectures may help explain the fear of being dead in a way both sympathetic to human anguish and consistent with the Epicurean view.

Lucretius offered a very interesting psychological explanation of the terror of death. He hypothesized that we have a very difficult time thinking of ourselves distinct from our bodies.

Accordingly, when you see a man resenting his fate, that after death he must either rot with his body laid in the tomb, or perish by fire or the jaws of wild beasts, you may know that he rings false, . . . although he himself deny the belief in any sensation after death. He does not, I think, admit what he professes to admit . . . : he does not wholly uproot and eject himself from life, but unknown to himself he makes something of himself to survive. For when he in life anticipates that birds and beasts will mangle his body after death, he pities himself; for he does not distinguish himself from that thing, he does not separate himself sufficiently from the body there cast out, he imagines himself to be that and, standing beside it, infects it with his own feeling. Hence he . . . does not see that in real death there will be no other self that could live to bewail his perished self, or stand by to feel pain that he lay there lacerated or burning.[23]

Lucretius may have believed that we so habitually identify ourselves with our bodies that we have a psychologically difficult time separating ourselves from them. So we think that since bad things can happen to our bodies in death, bad things can happen to us. This way of thinking is perhaps exemplified in the custom, in some societies, of placing a dead person's body inside a sturdy, well-sealed box, fitted with comfortable bedding. Why would there be this practice if there were not at least some psychological basis for associating a living person with that person's lifeless body? If Lucretius were correct in his hypothesis, then it would help to alleviate our fear of our deaths if we could sufficiently separate ourselves from our dead bodies.

Another possible explanation for the fear of death in at least our society, broadly speaking, is that people have been exposed for so long to the thesis that there is a life after death that even if they do not explicitly accept the view, they are somehow strongly affected by it. Since they have no information about what really happens to a person after the person dies, they feel that what happens then could well be awful. Wanting desperately not to experience the awful, and not knowing that they will not, they fear. If this is so, then, ironically, fear of death has its psychological roots in the belief in a life after death.

One might try to account for our fear of death based on the fact that the conclusion of the Epicurean argument leaves plenty of room for maneuver. It would allow, for example, dying or death (possibly), but not being dead, to be bad for a person. One might hypothesize that those who view being dead as a bad for them and thus fear it do so out of confusion. They take dying or death with being dead, and then think that being dead is bad. On that basis they may fear it. Their fear could be based on a truth, that dying or death is (or could be) bad for them, and at the same time a confusion, that there is no difference between dying or death and being dead. Such a confusion might well receive aid from the fact that "death," as commonly used, is ambiguous, as I noted at the outset. Nagel's argument benefits from such a confusion. Whatever the explanation or explanations, it is obviously possible to account for our fear of death while at the same time accepting the conclusion of the Epicurean argument.

I have resurrected and reconstructed an Epicurean argument that death is not bad for one. I have given reasons for believing basic premises in the argument, and I have laid to rest all the objections of which I am aware. (*Requiescant in pace*). Finally, I have offered conjectures that may enable us to account for our fear of being dead compatibly with the conclusion of the argument. This effort should bury the myth that death is bad for us. If we do not believe, as did many of the ancients, that a Stygian passage will take us to a nether realm of being, then, though we may not relish the idea of not being able to experience, we should find in the contemplation of our journey no cause for thanatophobia, as we might if we could reasonably believe that a disorientingly different and possibly quite displeasing set of experiences awaited us.

CHAPTER EIGHT

Why do some men go through life immune to a thousand mortal enemies of the race, while others get a
migraine that lasts for weeks? Why are our days num-
bered and not, say, lettered?

—Woody Allen, *Getting Even*

The Dead

Palle Yourgrau

> His soul had approached that region where dwell
> the vast hosts of the dead. He was conscious of, but
> could not apprehend, their wayward and flickering
> existence.   —James Joyce, *Dubliners*: "The Dead"

Death opens the door to metaphysics. We must be bold and step
through it. Plato has already traced for us, in the *Phaedo*, some
of the intricate strands that tie together death and philosophy,
the master insisting even that philosophy is itself a kind of cul-
tivation of dying. There are, indeed, at least three topics that an
analysis of death can be expected to shed light on: (1) through
the meaning of death, the meaning of life; (2) the nature of nonexistence; and (3) the relation of living to temporality. By (1) I
have in mind the Ecclesiastes problem: How can one's life have
meaning if after all is said and done one is simply dead? "Seeing
that which now is in the days to come shall all be forgotten, and
how dieth the wise man? As the fool." The second problem concerns the fact that the dead no longer exist, and mere thought
about the nonexistent (never mind what the appropriate attitude
to adopt toward them may be) has been a thorn in the side of

Reprinted (with some modifications) by permission from *Journal of Philosophy* 86,
no. 2 (February 1987): 84–101. The paper was read at Philosophy Colloquia at
Columbia University, Rice University, and Amherst College. I am grateful to
these audiences for the healthy skepticism of their responses.

philosophers at least since the time of Parmenides, the Prince
of Being. Finally, one can hardly expect to unravel the mystery
of death without coming to grips with the even greater mystery of time—since it is, after all, the past that receives the dead
and the future that holds the clue to our own mortality. More
specifically, there is the problem, associated with Lucretius, of
why we fear death but not the seemingly symmetric phenomenon of our prenatal nonexistence.

In what follows I will attempt to shed some light on the second and third problems. Thomas Nagel, in "The Absurd,"[1] has
offered some interesting suggestions concerning the first, but
this will not be our focus here. I will, however, be concerned to
defend the following three theses: (1) Death is an evil, a misfortune, and one that befalls the nonexistent themselves. (2) The
dead, appearances to the contrary, are not nothing. (3) Most
people will never exist. The significance of these sobering facts
is something that I hope will emerge as a consequence of the
ensuing discussion.

To begin, then, with the problem of nonexistence, note that
we are naturally inclined to feel sorrow for the very person who
has died, to continue to talk about him (or her), and to continue
to adopt attitudes such as love and honor toward him. Our
hearts here see more clearly than our heads, for these natural attitudes are disturbed by a beleaguering metaphysical con-
science. How can one even assert, for example, that Socrates is
dead? If this is a truth, whom is it supposed to be a truth about?
Socrates? But there is, there exists, no such person. For, precisely because he is dead, he is no longer, and therefore there is
no one of whom we may truly predicate death, or nonexistence.
Further, how could death be an evil for Socrates? Nonexistent
objects cannot feel anything, so how can they be expected to
suffer from any evil, including the evil of death? Finally, how
can one continue to love Socrates? There is no one there to love.
There is, of course, in W. V. Quine's sense, a "notional" kind
of love, which we can feel even for Pegasus.[2] One should not
underestimate the importance of such notional attitudes. As
Sidney Morgenbesser and Mary Mothersill have pointed out,[3]
one feels a definite sorrow at the death of (the fictional) Anna
Karenina. Clearly, one can appreciate in Anna Karenina traits
that real people have, or can have, and we can, while reading

the novel, momentarily suspend our realization that the characters are merely fictional. This accounts for the fact that, as Mothersill reminds us, we recover from our grief with remarkable ease. Such attitudes should not tempt us, therefore, toward a theory that attributes to fictional characters the property of being real people, like us; we would, indeed, if this were done, lose the precise difference (as well as similarity) that exists between our irretrievable sorrow at the death of Jesus or Socrates, and our attitude to Anna Karenina. (Note, further, that as Charles Parsons has remarked,[4] the dead of the remote past play a role in our lives not unlike that of fictional characters. The mists of time lay an epistemological mantle over the distant dead, and we scarcely know whether we are grieving over fiction or reality.) But there is also, clearly, a "relational sense" of "love" according to which it is the object itself that we love, and how could one be expected to maintain this relationship when one of the terms is missing?

There are two prominent responses to these problems, both of which, I shall suggest, are misguided: (a) skepticism and paraphrase; and (b) what I will call *spatialization*. Before discussing these approaches, however, it is well to make certain that we have a clear concept of death itself. By "death" I will mean precisely: "permanent postnatal nonexistence." By this definition, however, I do not mean to settle either the linguistic issue of what the English word "really means" or the factual question of whether, in this sense, anyone ever really dies. If Plato's suspicion (in the *Phaedo*) that the soul is immortal is correct, and if he is correct in suggesting that I am to be identified with my soul, then our discussion of death here will at least indicate exactly what misfortune it is that Plato has shown us we have been spared.

With these preliminaries out of the way, what is the first approach to our problem? The paraphrastic refuses to take our attitudes to the dead at face value. To say that Socrates is dead is to indicate that the name "Socrates" no longer has a bearer.[5] Those who pity Socrates are wasting their sorrow on one who suffers no evil; better to extend our pity to those who can suffer—the bereaved survivors. And to say that we still cling to Socrates himself, goes this way of thinking, is to speak loosely: we cling to all we have left, namely, our memories of Socrates, our impressions of him, and the impressions he has left on others.

I confess to finding this line of thinking shallow and unconvincing. To start with, the intuitions it challenges are clear, unequivocal, and quite literal: talk of the dead is of an entirely different order from, say, talk of the tooth fairy, which cries out for paraphrase. There is, moreover, a form of argument associated with Plato's *Euthyphro* that suggests the error in the paraphrastic approach. Surely Plato was saddened *because of* Socrates' misfortune, not: Socrates' death was a misfortune *because* of the ensuing sadness of Plato. The grievers grieve over the misfortune of death; death is not a misfortune because it gives rise to so many unhappy grievers.

Indeed, we find here a clue to one of our puzzles: death, as Thomas Nagel points out,[6] like many other evils, is intrinsically relational. The lover betrayed by a lover has suffered a harm, even when ignorant of the harm done. To apply the *Euthyphro* again: the lover is grieved *because* he discovers the injury done to him; not: the lover is injured *because* he becomes grieved over his discovery. The grief is due to the wrong, not the wrong to the grief. With purely relational evils, then, we are harmed because of what happens in relation to us, not because of a felt condition of our present state. Death, clearly, will be an evil of this sort. But what is it the dead relate to, which explains their misfortune? Surely it is precisely the life they have been denied—the possibility of enjoying all that life is a precondition for. But surely this is too much! Is one really expected to swallow an account of death as a purely relational phenomenon between an object that *no longer* exists and a life that *never will* exist? In fact, yes, but the elucidation of these metaphysical mysteries will have to wait for later.

Nagel, as we have seen, recognizes the relational character of the evil of death, but his insufficient attention to metaphysics weakens his final account. Who is it, after all, that suffers from this (relational) evil? "If there is a loss, someone must suffer it, and he must have existence."[7] But the dead, alas, do not have existence, and so this account is as yet incomplete. Further, Nagel is led by his theory to deny to the unborn the right to suffer the evil of nonexistence. Whether or not he is right about this point is something we will come to shortly, but to complete his intuitions about the misfortunes of the dead it may become overwhelmingly tempting to try to find a way out by which the dead really can be seen to exist. If we could do this, Nagel's approach could be saved, and without any excessive metaphysical cost. This is indeed precisely what Harry Silverstein tries to do in "The Evil of Death,"[8] where he succumbs to temptation and maintains that Socrates, though dead, exists.

Silverstein accomplishes this feat by what I call the spatialization of time: treating time as if it were a kind of mere fourth dimension of space, he takes location in time to be as ontologically neutral as location in space. In this scheme of things, your existence in the past tells us *where* (in time) you exist, not *whether* you exist (now—i.e., at all), just as to exist in New Jersey tells us where you are (in space) and not whether you are.[9] To exist at all, then, is to exist somewhere and somewhen. Silverstein gathers this conception from the weighty authority of Quine (with the "tenseless" existence of the quantifier) and Einstein (with the static geometry of the four-dimensional spacetime continuum).

I must say that I find this approach to Socrates' death just as unpalatable as its predecessor. My objections to it are as follows: (1) I find it exceedingly difficult to give up my intuition that dead people simply do not exist. ("For living things it is living that is existing" [Aristotle, *De Anima*, 415b12].) And I do not mean merely that the dead do not *now* exist; for objects in time, what does not exist now does not exist at all. Since I find that my intuition that Socrates, as dead, no longer exists, is unshakable, I am more inclined to reject any philosophy that rejects this intuition than to give up the intuition itself. (2) The dead are not the only nonexistent objects that we seem compelled to admit. There are also, I will urge, (a) the unborn, (b) the (merely) possible worlds, and (c) the past and future themselves. How should we analyze these apparent nonexistents? The temptation may again be to spatialize—and this is, in effect, exactly what David Lewis has achieved with his possible-world theory.[10] However, although the reasons for spatialization here closely resemble those in regard to time, philosophers have been (justifiably) wary of following Lewis in his extremely unintuitive spatialization of modality, according to which to exist in a possible world is really to exist. (This is not to say that anyone has successfully refuted Lewis—a point I have argued elsewhere.)[11] But then we must find some *ad hoc* device to account for these apparent nonexistents. Better to find a theory that will maximize our analysis of the nonexistent. (3) Finally, we should recall that Special Relativity is an empirical theory. It might have been false. If the four-dimensional Einstein-Minkowski view had been false of the actual world, would not death still have posed its problems? Is death not a problem already for Newton? Further, is there not something exceedingly paradoxical in the claim that certain experimental results, dealing with principles of symmetry in physics and results about the speed of light, should bear on the question of whether Socrates, as dead, really exists? Moreover, there are alternative philosophical accounts of the interpretation of Special Relativity (see, for example, the work of Milic Čapek, Lawrence Sklar, and Karl Popper),[12] especially as regards the verificationism that seems to imbue standard reconstructions of the theory. Thus (for reasons 1–3) Silverstein's spatialization approach is not satisfactory. The clue to explaining the correct subject of the evil of death lies elsewhere.

The approach I favor is what the facts themselves seem to be urging us to accept: that death concerns the nonexistent as well as the existent; that, therefore, some things do not exist—i.e., that there are nonexistent objects. We should distinguish, therefore, between being something, being an *object* (which we express by "there is," or "$(\exists x)$"), and being an *existing* object. Existence is that property, delicate as an eyelid, which separates the living from the dead. I express it with the predicate "E!" When I say "Some objects do not exist," I write it as follows: $(\exists x){\sim}(E!x)$. I thus preserve existential generalization: from "Fa" I can always conclude "$(\exists x)(Fx)$," and thus from "Socrates is dead" I conclude: "There is an object that is dead and this object is Socrates." That one can adopt this practice has been shown recently by the neo-Meinongian logicians. Here I follow Terence Parsons's notation in *Nonexistent Objects*.[13] I can agree, therefore, with Ludwig Wittgenstein that Socrates' death is not an event in his *life*; but it is, for all that, a genuine event, and it does befall *Socrates*.[14]

I believe, indeed, that talk of the dead, not talk of fiction, is the proper introduction to nonexistents. In discussing Socrates, for example, we clearly have a particular object in mind to refer to. He is a perfectly specific object. Having admitted this, we remind ourselves that he is, after all, dead, and hence no longer exists. "Ah," comes the reply, "but he used to exist." Precisely, and, therefore, since he no longer exists, he does not exist at all! (How easily one is tempted here to deny where this argument leads us, and to suddenly "spatialize" time, pretending that "past existence" is a kind of existence, "located" in the past.) Thus we are led to the conclusion that we have been referring all along to a specific nonexistent object and that to be is to be an object, whereas to exist is to be an existent object. Do not say "But if we're referring to Socrates he *must* exist," nor "Since he doesn't exist, we *cannot* be referring to him." The facts are in front of us: We *are* referring to him, and he really *does not* exist. There simply is such a person as Socrates, and nothing, not even his death, can ever erase this fact. (If the bad news is that you are going to die, the good news is that you will not "disappear"—i.e., become nothing.) Of course, had he never come to exist perhaps we would never have known him, nor been able to single him out and refer to him (but see below). But these semantic/epistemic facts do not touch the question of ontology. For surely we do not want to say that if Socrates had never existed there would never have been such a person as Socrates to come to exist (which is not to be confused with "If Socrates had never existed there would have *existed* no such person as Socrates").

Now the plausibility of this approach turns on our ability to make sense of the quantifier, "($\exists x$)," which no longer expresses existence, but rather "being" (which is *not* to be considered a kind of *existence*). Parsons does little to explicate this notion, and he could hardly be expected to define it, any more than classical logicians could define existence. Clearly, we are dealing here with logically primitive notions. Nevertheless, one can go some way toward explicating this new quantifier of "being." Charles Parsons sheds some light on this distinction.[15] He, too, invites us to consider the quantifier as expressing not existence but rather "being" and relegates existence to a special predicate. I find useful his comparison of the being/existence distinction with the Kantian-Fregean contrast of existence with actuality (*Wirklichkeit*). Moreover, I agree with him that we must distinguish the concept of objects-in-general from the concept of existent objects, and that "if we use the devices of singular terms, predication, identity and quantifiers to make serious statements, then we are speaking about genuine objects." [16] Further, just as we refuse naively to admit objecthood to the referent of just any singular term (see text below), Parsons notes that, if our pure existential quantifier of "being" is to be applicable to abstract mathematical objects, it must be more restricted than Meinong's (since, for example, "$\sqrt{4}$" denotes a mathematical object but "the largest integer" does not). But where Parsons seems to express sympathy with what he sees as Kant's view, that mathematical objects are "beyond possibility and actuality," I find my instincts to be more Platonic. I am more inclined to believe that, for such objects (as, perhaps, for God and the soul), their possibility implies their actuality. (See *Phaedo*, 105A–107B, as well as my text, below, on the ontological argument.) It is an interesting question, indeed, whether anything that lacks "matter" can ever be merely potential. Aristotle, for example, in *Metaphysics* λ, concludes that the "unmoved mover," lacking matter, must be pure actuality. But how can what lacks matter be actual, active, (causally) effective? For Aristotle, the answer is: The unmoved mover is a "final cause," inspiring lesser beings to imitate its divinity. Similarly, Frege explains the peculiar "actuality" of the Platonic realm of pure thought: "Thoughts are not wholly unactual . . . their action is brought about by a performance of the thinker [who 'grasps' them] . . . and yet the thinker does not create them but must take them as they are" ("The Thought," in *Logical Investigations* [Oxford, 1977], pp. 29–30, with modifications in translation by Parsons). [17] Indeed, "unmoved mover" is an excellent way to describe a "Platonic" object—a genuine yet "nonactual" object capable of being contemplated by us.

The dead, then, we can now see, are not nothing. But what are they being contrasted with? What is nothing? (If I may be allowed to put it thus.) A partial answer is: Pegasus. My ontology is thus more Parmenidean than Meinongian. Names in fiction (and myth), I believe, are not genuine names for specific nonexistents but "mock-names" with which we pretend to refer to existent objects. (There is no easy road to metaphysics; certainly, semantic naiveté is no substitute for ontological insight.) I thus agree with Keith Donnellan and Saul Kripke that to speak of Pegasus is to speak of nothing. [18] That is why, as Kripke urged long ago, in a Parmenidean moment, Pegasus, being nothing, not only does not exist but could not come to exist. (What was not there in the first place cannot come to be there.) To say this, however, is not yet to assert that one could not coin some new names and attempt to refer to the "incomplete" objects that Terence Parsons has theorized about, objects defined by arbitrary sets of "nuclear" (i.e., safe, non-paradox-generating) properties, not necessarily closed under implication. This is an open question of metaphysics worthy of investigation. Indeed, this is just part of a fundamental question in metaphysics, to wit: Which essences define possible objects?

Progress on this problem would help us gain some insight into an important special case, in which the essence in question is God's and the subject is the ontological argument. It is worthwhile to linger on this issue. Assuming, as is reasonable, that God's essence, as the greatest possible being, includes necessary existence, the question arises whether such an essence defines a possible being. Instead of investigating this pressing concern, however, too many philosophers have focused their attention on addressing "fallacies" in the argument—such as that some of its proponents have assumed too quickly that one can know that God is possible simply because we know he has an essence. And Kant, and others, have denied that existence is a property, or predicate, that can be included in an essence. But we have already seen that the mere advent of the existential quantifier by no means established Kant's thesis, since on our account we preserve both the quantifier and the predicate for existence. It is not a fallacy then, but an unresolved question of pure metaphysics whether or not a necessary being (such as God) is possible. And that it follows from the possibility of such a being that it does exist necessarily and, therefore, actually is, remains, I take it, a valid conclusion, given a plausible modal logic, like C. I. Lewis's S5 (with Kripke's semantics),[19] where we have:

$$\Diamond \Box \, P \supset \Box P \text{ and also } \Box P \supset P$$

(i.e., if possibly necessarily P, then necessarily P; and if necessarily P, then P).

There are those who question the importance of the ontological argument even if it is sound. They argue that (1) they cannot recognize their God in the God of the argument, and (2) in particular they do not believe (their) God *necessarily* exists. I find this attitude puzzling in the extreme. Call their God "Jehovah," and that of our argument, "God." Now, first, I find it incredible that the prophets would have considered themselves lucky that they found themselves in a world where Jehovah just happens to exist. At any rate, given that God and Jehovah both exist and are not identical, how can the pious not bow to God? For God, by definition, is perfect, and so it follows that Jehovah is not. Thus whatever divine attributes adorn Jehovah that make him worthy of worship, they are surpassed by God. Piety, I would think, compels us to worship not Jehovah, but God.

Before quitting this subject we should note an important lesson to be gathered from the ontological argument (as from the study of death): that what is possible is a genuine feature of the actual world, a feature that contributes to what is of value in it. What could be (or could have been) is as much a feature of our lives as what is. This constitutes, I believe, the "romantic" conception of life, and it leads, inevitably, to a certain melancholy. For in this sublunar world of ours, nothing is ever all it could be. (This, I take it, is at the heart of Plato's philosophy.)

There are, then, some important open problems about which objects there are (are possible). But, I have been suggesting, not all beings, even the nonexistent, are as mysterious as God. The dead, for example, are a set of nonexistents easier to grasp than the unborn. We can name specific dead people and we know many detailed facts about them, whereas it is difficult to find a single unborn whom we can isolate and refer to with a name. This is no doubt part of why Thomas Nagel and others are skeptical of the assertion that there are specific unborn, and, hence, that there is anyone there to suffer the deprivation of nonexistence. Indeed, some have been moved to assert that concerning the merely possible, there are only purely general facts. For myself, however, I find that this attitude comes dangerously close to the sin of conflating ontology with epistemology. The most that the above considerations show is that we cannot know, or refer to, specific unborn. (Though there may be certain exceptions. Given a suitable theory of counterfactuals, and the appropriate view of determinism, perhaps after an abortion we could name the very would-be person, say, "Newman," and thus refer to him.) But why assume that there are any unborn in the first place?

The point is that, once we admit the category of the nonexistent, we see that, as Plato notes in the *Phaedo*, the existent "come from" the nonexistent. Now, I find it exceedingly implausible to deny either that more people always could come to be born than already exist, or that we could never "run out" of persons to be born. The "supply" of souls is unchanging; clearly, it must also be inexhaustible (what would it be to "run out" of [possible] people to be born?). In fact, their number is awesome, and that explains the assertion with which this paper began, that most people will never exist. Indeed, from the point of view of pure ontology, the realm of existence is the merest dot of an "i" in the vast sea of being. All the more reason not to chauvinistically narrow our metaphysical preoccupations to what exists.

Those readers who are skeptical of my Platonism (which is not to be confused with Lewis's spatialization) will find great comfort in Hidé Ishiguro's contrary approach, elegantly presented in "Possibility."[20] "I do not hold," Ishiguro says, "that the actual world is one among the possible worlds. Possible worlds are ideal entities." Again, "Possible worlds, then, . . . are, I suggest, abstract entities, partially described, whose existence is invoked in my modal theories as models of my imaginative thoughts." And, finally, "Since possible worlds and possible objects are constructs of thought, they are not the kind of things to which actual things and the actual world can stand in any relation."[21] My reaction to this, in a nutshell, is that it conflates abstract existents with concrete nonexistents. Possible people, like the dead and the unborn, are not a peculiar kind of abstract existent, but rather a perfectly ordinary kind of concrete object like you and me, who merely have the bad luck not to enjoy existence. When I contemplate having a child I do not turn my thoughts away from real, concrete children to the realm of (existent) *abstracta*; the (possible) children I am thinking of are of the ordinary garden variety, and really do not exist. What separates actual, living people from merely possible people is precisely their existence. As Kant's famous remark has it, "The real contains no more than the merely possible. A hundred real dollars do not contain the least coin more than a hundred possible dollars."[22] Curiously, Ishiguro cites this very dictum of Kant's, in disapproval: "As Brentano says, possible dollars are not sums of dollars at all. They are not a kind of dollar—as a 1979 Hong Kong dollar or an 1800 U.S. dollar would be. Similarly, a possible world is not a kind of world like a chaotic world or a far-away world."[23] As I read him, Kant seems to be making just the opposite point here. It is not Kant but rather Ishiguro who maintains that possible people are a "special kind of object." For it is she, not Kant, who claims that possible persons are *abstract, ideal constructs of our thoughts*. Kant, contrariwise, says that merely possible people are *just like you and me*—except for their non-existence—and he is at pains to insist that the existent and the nonexistent do not constitute "special kinds" of object. Ishiguro may, of course, be correct that we sometimes think about possible people *by* mentally manipulating more accessible ideal constructs that stand in their place. But this only serves to highlight the fact that our intentional objects—that is, the targets of our thoughts—are not the symbolic middlemen but rather the possible persons themselves.

It may be thought, however, that there are in fact too many nonexistents—that Terence Parsons's theory is beset with Cantorian cardinality problems. George Bealer's incisive review takes advantage of Parsons's generous formalistic schema for objecthood: "For any set of [nuclear] properties there is an object having exactly those properties," to raise threats from diagonalization.[24] I am inclined to believe, however, that these problems concern not the nonexistents themselves but rather the abstract schematizations of Parsons.[25] When similar crises befell set theory, Kurt Gödel urged that we not be hoodwinked by shadows into ignoring what remains in the light: "Despite their remoteness from sense experience, we do have something like a perception of the objects of set theory. . . . The set theoretical paradoxes are hardly any more troublesome for mathematics than deceptions of the senses are for physics."[26] Moreover, my concern in this essay is not with recondite metaphysical curiosities like Pegasus and the man in the moon (which are highlighted in Parsons's theory). Though my intuition may indeed falter in regard to these wayward and flickering objects, this hardly inclines me to doubt the reality of my deceased parents. Our intuition of the dead arises not from reflection on language or logical form, but rather from more direct epistemic contact: we know them in the same way we know many of the living, having at some time made their acquaintance.

We are now in a position to address the question that Nagel was forced to dismiss: whether the unborn suffer from the evil of nonexistence. Assuming that life, as such, is a good (which is not to say that more life is always better than less), my answer, then, is yes. This leaves open the question of whether the deprivation of nonexistence endured by the unborn is as great as that suffered by the dead, and here the issue becomes more complex. That nonexistence is a misfortune at all for the unborn should by now no longer seem paradoxical. If one objects that the unborn *are* nothing, we respond that this is to confuse that which lacks existence with what really is nothing—as egregious an error as to conflate Socrates with Pegasus. If the reply comes that, nevertheless, the unborn *feel* nothing, then we remind ourselves that nonexistence, like death and betrayal, is a purely relational evil that requires no inner sensation to be endured. This still leaves us, however, with the issue of the comparative weight of the evil of nonexistence. Here, we may develop a suggestive conception of Nagel's. Certain misfortunes are not merely relational but require a certain pattern in one's life. Thus, someone who, as an adult, has a terrible accident and is reduced to a state of total dependency has suffered a misfortune, even though there is nothing intrinsically unfortunate about his final state (babies, for example, suffer no misfortune in enduring this state).

As I would put it, some evils are a function of the "curve," or "acceleration," of one's world-line, not of its static properties at an instant. Thus, to "picture" certain misfortunes, one must display the curvature of one's world-line:

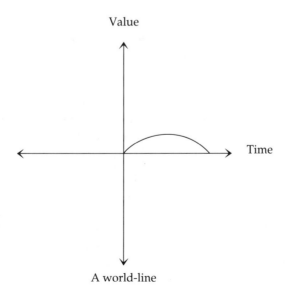

A world-line

Certain curves, it turns out (like the one described above), we take to be instances of misfortunes. Further, the curve will have to have a modal as well as a temporal dimension—possibilities that have been cut off from one's life. Thus, for example, if a woman with a great potential as a violinist acquires a spouse who cuts off this career prematurely, she has (all else being equal) suffered a great harm, even though (1) her "inner state," for all her married life, may never be unpleasant, and (2) the life denied her is a purely possible life that never came to exist. (Recall Marlon Brando, in *On the Waterfront*: "I could have been a contender.") Death, itself, of course, would have to be analyzed by just such a "modal curve," except that in that case we would have a nonexistent person's relationship to a possible but non-actual continuation of his or her life.[27] We can now approach our question. The obvious problem is how to compare a being (the unborn) that has a modal but no temporal curve with a being that has both (the dead): Is having no curve worse than having the worst curve? The poet seems to think so when he says in a similar context that "'Tis better to have loved [lived] and lost than never to have loved [lived] at all." But, as the philosopher says, "It is proverbial that bards tell many a lie." The fact is that we want to use different categories of evaluation for those with (temporal) curves that indicate misfortune and those with no such curves at all: an untimely death, for example, can be *tragic*, but never to have been born is better described as unfortunate. (We speak of a tragic loss of life, but not of a tragic failure to join the living.) But we must be careful not to be prejudiced here, since we are all creatures of existence and can therefore much more easily sympathize with the deprivations of the living than with the beinglessness (to coin a slightly misleading expression) of those unfortunate enough never to have been born. A bridge case here is the aborted; for, although they too lack a temporal curve, their modality, as it were, has itself a temporal dimension, since (for a time) the strength of the possibility of their coming to exist surpassed that of the average unborn. They have thus suffered a genuine *loss*, and that is at least part of the reason that we are less hesitant to speak of an abortion as tragic (even if the fetus was never a person). To proceed any further into these issues, however, would take us too far from the project at hand, which is merely to illustrate the fuller evaluational problematic that emerges from the metaphysical picture I have been suggesting. The silence of the dead is as nothing to the eternal quiet of the unborn, and I have thus tried to engage the reader on their behalf.

A few words are perhaps in order, at this point, concerning the unfashionable metaphysical generosity of this conception. Much of my thinking here was provoked by Kripke's pioneering work, formal and informal, on the semantics and metaphysics of modality. In his writings one finds echoes of the traditional doctrine of essence and accident, of substances, not reducible to their properties, which retain their identity as they take on shifting and even unrecognizable attributes through temporal and modal wanderings. And, of course, there is the frequent formal and informal quantification over those creatures of ontological darkness, the possible worlds. But in spite of these suggestive conceptions Kripke himself has proved surprisingly shy of committing himself to an explicit ontology, even to the point of a suspect forbearance in acknowledging the legitimacy of his own brain child: the worlds. In fact there seems to be in his thinking a peculiar (and fruitful) tension between a formalistic scheme of things that suggests a classical metaphysic and a neo-Wittgensteinian urge to flee from ontology into the vernacular. Indeed in a related context concerning the philosophy of language he goes so far as to acknowledge this ambivalence: "I find myself torn between two conflicting feelings—a 'Chomskyan' feeling . . . and a contrary (late) 'Wittgensteinian' feeling."[28] But the (ontological) silence this has induced leads not to a more sober metaphysics but rather to unexamined commitments; for, as Stanley Rosen observes in his commentary on Kripke, "We in turn must say that common sense is here a catchphrase concealing a philosophical ideology."[29] It is my aim in this essay to go in the other direction, to bring to the light and so develop some of the metaphysical turns I have found unconcealed in the classical line in Kripke's philosophy.

The problem of the nonexistence of the dead thus beckons us along the path of metaphysics. But another mystery awaits us, since we have still to explore Lucretius's problem and the strange facts about time that it discloses. Why then do we fear our deaths, but not the seemingly indistinguishable period of nonexistence that preceded our births? We cannot, I suggest, grasp this problem if we insist on a spatialized conception of time, like that alluded to earlier, in connection with Silverstein. For if we treat time as a mere fourth spatial dimension, death and prenatal nonexistence are indeed mirror images of each other, and it would be irrational to fear the one and not the other. But if we do not adopt this conception of time, we open the door to the rationality of assuming an asymmetrical attitude here.

Let us follow John McTaggart and distinguish two fundamental features of time, the B-series and the A-series.[30] The B-series characterizes times in terms of the (fixed and immutable) relation of "before and after" and is the subject of the mathematical physics of space-time (indeed Minkowski speaks of the *geometry* of the four-dimensional space-time continuum). To recognize the B-series alone *is* to spatialize time. (Those who point out that the time variable in the definition of the interval in Special Relativity—viz. $ds^2 = dx^2 + dy^2 + dz^2 - c^2dt^2$—has a different numerical sign than have the spatial dimensions, have hardly refuted my characterization. For this shows only that there are special *geometrical* constraints [with respect to time] on the space-time paths allowed by Special Relativity, not that we are not being offered a four-dimensional geometrical space.) The A-series, on the other hand, characterizes times in terms of their shifting realizations as "now," or "past"/"present"/"future." The A-series gives us the time we experience and live in, and it carries with it some distinctive concomitants: (1) time passes, or "flows"—what was present is now past—and it flows toward the future; (2) the future, unlike the past and the present, is still open; and (3) location in the A-series is not ontologically neutral (to be in the past is not only not to exist now; for temporal objects, it is not to exist at all).

Now, the Fundamental Problem of Time, I would suggest, is the relationship of the A-series to the B-series. Are both real, both objective, or is only one real, the other subjective? What is disturbing is that the logic and metaphysics of the B-series have received increasing elucidation, especially since Einstein, but not only has the A-series not enjoyed such a renaissance, it has also suffered from increasingly severe attacks from the friends of the B-series. These attacks come from logic, semantics, and physics. The attack from logic was launched by Aristotle. Intuitively, the past is now "necessary," in the sense of (now) unalterable (not because we cannot *get* there, but because it is already a fact, and you cannot change the facts). Now for any seemingly future contingent proposition, P, by excluded middle: $P \lor \sim P$. But, however things turn out, either P or $\sim P$ will have been true in the past. Yet, since past truths are necessary, so is this past truth about the future. So the future, too, turns out to be necessary, contradicting condition (2) of the A-series.

If, with Aristotle, we reject such "logical determinism," the picture that results is one of a "moving," open future in which, so to speak, Reality itself "grows by accretion of facts."[31] Indeed, even Truth would have to expand, or Aristotle's ghost would return to haunt us. But how is this possible? Attempts to formalize this intuitive idea, even those as sophisticated as Richmond Thomason's model of "branching time," of which Jeffrey's seems to be a version, do not quite work.[32] Worse, reflection suggests that no standard logico-mathematical approach to the dynamic of time will succeed in capturing this feature: one cannot trap water with a net. Only a fool, it would seem, or a philosopher, would continue to pursue so elusive a quarry. But have I not overstated the recalcitrance of the problem? If the Big Bang Theory is correct, as well as General Relativity, then the Universe itself, i.e., space-time, has been "expanding" for eons. (Do not ask: Where to? That would only betray mathematical innocence.) But an expanding universe is one thing, an "accumulation of Reality" (and thus of Truth) another. Mathematics can describe the former; the latter seems always to slip through its fingers.

The attack from semantics comes from the recent revolt against Frege, which led to the Kaplan-Perry theory of indexicals, like "now" and "present."[33] According to this theory, to call an event "now" is not to *say* anything about it—it is not to attribute any "property" or Fregean "sense" to it. Rather, the simple truth is given by the rule: at any time t, "now" refers (simply, or "directly") to t. Since this rule obviously characterizes all times equally, no one time is ever "really" the one time that is now, or in the present: each time is now with respect to itself. For a critique of this theory, see my "Frege, Perry, and Demonstratives" and "The Path Back to Frege."[34] In the first essay I drew attention to the fact that the ubiquitous Kaplan-Perry semantics for indexicals would lead inevitably to a spatialization of time (via "now") and modality (via "actual"—assuming the indexicality of actuality). David Lewis was already peddling the latter, and in due course D. H. Mellor tried to sell us the former.[35] Now, although this is not the place to rehearse the detailed argument, we can illustrate at least briefly why Perry's theory does not get off the ground (and thus provide some semantic breathing room for the beleaguered A-series). The Kaplan-Perry rule for "now," if put precisely, would be "For all times t and speakers s, if s employs 'now' correctly at t, he refers to t." A rule is no good unless you can use it, but, if you try to employ this rule, it becomes obvious that, in grasping it, you get a handle not on any particular time but only on a universal conditional on times (and speakers). The problem is that to use the rule to get to a specific time you must *instantiate* the universal quantifier, but, to accomplish this instantiation, you must already have a particular time t in mind. But how do you get to have it in mind? By describing it (e.g., as Saturday, 10 A.M.)? (This is vigorously denied by Kaplan and Perry.) By taking t to be the present moment—i.e., now? (This is circular; it is the rule itself that was supposed to show how we use "now" to get to a particular time.) It seems, rather, that Kaplan and Perry have mistaken a necessary constraint on a mode of designation for a particular use of "now" (that if "now" is used at t, the mode of designation should determine t) for the mode of designation itself.

Curiously, Kaplan, in "Demonstratives,"[36] prides himself on his sharp separation of semantics from epistemology and insists that his theory of "direct reference" needs no epistemological buttressing, like Russell's notion of acquaintance. Even Kripke, it will be remembered, had little use for the notion of a speaker's knowing who his referent is.[37] Thus it is that in post-Fregean semantics the competent speaker is relieved of the burden of knowing what he is talking about. Small wonder, then, that Hilary Putnam, always on the cutting edge, having contributed to the dissolution of the speaker-world relationship, has recently given up the world itself.[38]

This leaves us with the argument from physics. Given the relativity of simultaneity in Special Relativity, there is no unique set of events simultaneous with the present. "The now," the present, is no longer an absolute feature of reality. There remains, only, for each inertial frame, "the now" relative to that frame. These are serious challenges to the ontological credentials of the A-series. Can it survive them? This is not the place to settle the question.[39] Given that the resolution of Lucretius's puzzle requires a solution to this dilemma, we can see why the problem of death is so profound. Without offering an analysis of this problem about time I will simply content myself with the extreme plausibility of the A-series, and for the sake of the present discussion assume its legitimacy.

It will be recalled, then, that an important aspect of the time of the A-series is that it is future-directed. We live in the "direction" of the future, and we attach different values to events, positive and negative, according to their position in our pasts or futures. Each of us knows, for example, the different attitude we would take if told we had had a terrifying toothache as a child, as opposed to being told that such a pain awaits us in ten minutes. In general, it is a fundamental feature of the human condition to focus our fear on future evils. If this is true for evils in general, how much more must it be so for the ultimate evil of death? It is thus precisely the futurity of death that renders it a more fearful evil than prenatal nonexistence. Moreover, we can see that no matter how long we may extend our lives, we will not lessen the fear of death, since at the final moment one's death will still be "now." (Of course, unlike toothaches, we will never experience our own death—but by now this problem should not require any further attention.)

Note, further, that it is the mere futurity of death, coupled with the fact that we live in the direction of the future, which is relevant here, and not the openness of the future. For, to begin with, this is one aspect of our futures that is not open at all; as mortal creatures we are not free not to (eventually) die. Next, the fact that we may have some freedom in choosing when to die does not go to the heart of the matter, for the fear of death I am investigating here is not that of premature, or untimely, dying, but of the fact of (ultimate) death itself—i.e., of our mortality. One can cheat the angel of death with the small movement of a sharp blade, but one has not thereby tricked God out of our mortality. Nor will it avail to reverse this line of reasoning and argue from the very inevitability of death to the enormousness of its significance, since, of course, our prenatal nonexistence is every bit as inevitable.

The futurity of death, therefore, is its distinguishing feature, as opposed to prenatal nonexistence, and this is a feature invisible to the spatialized time of the B-series. Further, without the direction of time provided by the A-series, we will not be able to produce a full account of the "curves" of our lifelines discussed earlier. For it is essential to the evaluation of these "life-diagrams" that we note which direction is the future. A life, for example, that opens in misery and works its way to serenity is surely to be preferred to one that proceeds in the opposite direction. The evaluative study of such lifelines, then, cannot be reduced to a kind of pure geometry.

With these geometrical reflections, however, our study of the meaning of death draws to a close. Many questions, of course (especially of a valuational nature), remain open; my primary concern has been to provide a metaphysical framework with which to approach the dead. In attempting to unravel these mysteries we have pursued being into the nonexistent and come to grips with the most ephemeral and elusive of things: the flow of time. Being ourselves the future dead, it behooves us to engage (while we can) in serious philosophizing about death. And if we are thereby beckoned down the path of metaphysics we should not fear to tread it. It is indeed a narrow and treacherous way, but it is the only one there is.

CHAPTER NINE

Exactly what do we mean when we say, man is mortal? Obviously it's not a compliment.
—Woody Allen, *Side Effects*

The Misfortunes of the Dead

George Pitcher

I assume, as most people nowadays do, that one's death means the permanent end not only of one's physical life, but also of one's conscious life. Death, so conceived, has its obvious drawbacks, but also its benefits; for the dead are at least free from pain, grief, despair, and other unpleasant sensations, moods, emotions, and so on. But we have conflicting intuitions on the question of whether the dead can be harmed, on the question of whether an event that occurs after a person's death can count as a misfortune for him. (I shall, throughout, use the terms "harm" and "misfortune" so as to render these two questions equivalent.) On the one hand, we think that if the business Mrs. White established and was proud of in her lifetime should collapse in ruins soon after her death, that really cannot be a disaster *for her*. She is beyond disasters of any kind. On the other hand, we cannot rest quite content there: we think that in some way we do not wholly understand, it would have been better for Mrs. White if her business had not failed so soon after her death. We feel positively sorry for her when the employees are laid off, the petition for bankruptcy filed, the windows are boarded up.

In this paper, I want to defend the thesis that the dead can be harmed, and to explain how this can be, and is, so. (I think the

Reprinted by permission from *American Philosophical Quarterly* 21, no. 2 (April 1984): 183–88. Joel Feinberg, Dale Jamieson, Gilbert Harman, Thomas Nagel, and Thomas Scanlon made helpful comments on earlier versions of this paper. I am extremely grateful to Ernest Partridge for his painstaking criticisms and also to Edward T. Cone for several useful suggestions.

dead can also be benefited, but I shall concentrate on the gloomy side of things.) First, however, I shall discuss a second thesis about the dead—namely, that they can be wronged. ("To wrong someone" will be used as a generic term to cover such actions as being unjust to someone, maligning or slandering someone, betraying someone's trust, and so on.)

If we allow our unfettered intuition to operate on certain examples, it becomes abundantly clear that we think the dead can indeed be wronged. Bill Brown promises his dying father that he will bury him in the family plot when he dies. Bill instead sells his father's corpse to a medical school for dissection by students. Our intuition tells us that Mr. Brown has been badly betrayed by his son. A second example: in the Olympic Games five years ago, End won the mile run and received the gold medal. He has since died. Now, an international panel of corrupt judges, all of whom hated End, falsely charge that he committed a foul on the third lap, and officially declare Red, who finished second, the winner. End, though dead, is the victim of a gross injustice, we naturally think. The dead, then, can be wronged: they can be the victims of injustice, slander, betrayal, and so on. (They can also be honored, justice can be rendered to them, and so on, but again I shall accentuate the negative.)

Notice, by the way, that the dead can be the targets of actions that may not count as wrongs committed against them, but that are anyway hostile to them. For example, suppose that after Mrs. Tisdale's death, her husband reveals all her secret vices, because he has always hated her (perhaps with good reason) and wants the good reputation she enjoyed in her church to be demolished. This deliberate wrecking of Mrs. Tisdale's reputation constitutes an act of vengeance against her. So we may say that the dead can be attacked, as well as wronged. To simplify matters, however, I shall not be concerned in what follows with the fact that the dead can be attacked.

Although we take for granted, in our unreflective moments, that the dead can be wronged, perhaps we should not. The dead, if they exist at all, are so much dust. How is it possible for so much dust to be wronged? I shall maintain that it is not possible for so much dust to be wronged, but that it is possible for the dead to be wronged, even though the dead are now just so much dust. Let me explain.

Consider the linguistic act of describing a dead person. There are two different things a person might do if he sets out to describe a friend of his who is now dead:

(a) He can describe the dead friend as he was at some stage of his life—i.e., as a living person.

(b) He can describe the dead friend as he is now, in death—mouldering, perhaps, in a grave.

In (a), we may say that there is a description of an *ante*-mortem person after his death, while in (b) there is a description of a *post*-mortem person after his death.

I maintain that although both ante-mortem and post-mortem persons can be described after their death, only ante-mortem persons can be wronged after their death. Suppose, for example, that Mrs. Blue, now dead, was not in the least anti-semitic, but that her spiteful neighbor now maliciously asserts that she was. This charge is a lie and since it is a lie about a person who is now dead, it may be said to constitute a wrong perpetrated against a dead person. Her neighbor wrongs the dead Mrs. Blue when he falsely states that she was anti-semitic. But he wrongs the ante-mortem Mrs. Blue, not the post-mortem Mrs. Blue: he falsely charges that Mrs. Blue when alive was anti-semitic, and so it is the living Mrs. Blue who is wronged. Her neighbor says nothing either true or false about Mrs. Blue as she is now, in death. Indeed, it would be nonsense to suggest that Mrs. Blue, after her death—the post-mortem Mrs. Blue—could be anti-semitic.

All wrongs committed against the dead are committed against their ante-mortem selves. Thus when young Brown sells his father's corpse to the medical school, he breaks a promise he made to his father before the old man died: so it is the living Mr. Brown who is betrayed by his son's action. Again, it is the End who actually won the race—i.e., the living End—who is wronged when the judges unjustly strip him of his victory. It is impossible to wrong a post-mortem person. Post-mortem persons, we said, are, if anything, just so much dust; and dust cannot be wronged.

Let us turn, now, to the first thesis about the dead—namely, that they can be harmed. We can see that just as there is a distinction to be made between a post-mortem person's being wronged after his death and an ante-mortem person's being wronged after his death, so there is a distinction between a post-mortem person's being harmed after his death and an ante-mortem person's being harmed after his death. I take it that no one would want to argue seriously that a post-mortem person can be harmed after his death, any more than one would maintain that a post-mortem person can be *wronged* after his death. Dust can neither be wronged nor harmed.

A serious question can arise only over the issue of whether or not an *ante*-mortem person can be harmed after his death. The question is this: Is it possible for something to happen after a person's death that harms the living person he was before he died? I want to urge that it is possible.

I shall construe harm, or misfortune, in the following more or less orthodox way: an event or state of affairs is a misfortune for someone (or harms someone) when it is contrary to one or more of his more important desires or interests. This very rough characterization could be endlessly refined, but I hope the intuitive idea is clear enough for our purposes. I think it does capture most of the cases that we would, upon reflection, consider to be cases of a person's being harmed (or suffering a misfortune). For example: if someone swears out a warrant against me, falsely accusing me of murder, I am thereby harmed, provided I have the usual desires to be well thought of, to be able to pursue my normal life, to be calm and free from anxiety and anger, and so on; for the accusation works against those desires.

There are, to be sure, certain ways in which a living person, after his death, cannot be harmed: it is easy to see, for example, why one cannot, after one's death, be killed or wounded, or be caused to feel pain. But we all have desires and interests that can be thwarted (or satisfied) after we have died. Consider Mrs. White, for instance. Mrs. White, remember, was very proud of the business that she had established. We may assume that she had a strong desire that it should survive for a long time after her death, as a kind of monument to her industry and skill. This desire is defeated when the business collapses soon after her death. I maintain that the wrecking of her business thus harms Mrs. White—the living (ante-mortem) Mrs. White—even though it occurs when she is dead.

The view that an ante-mortem person can be harmed after his

death is one that we all find, or can anyway be made to find, entirely plausible, if we do not stop to examine it too closely. Consider, for example, two possible worlds. In World I, a philosopher spends his entire life working on a metaphysical system that he believes to be, and desperately wants to be, the Truth about reality. And it is! After his death, his system is universally accepted, endlessly discussed, and he is acclaimed as the greatest philosopher who ever lived. World II is exactly the same as World I up to the time of the philosopher's death; but in this world, a disgruntled neighbor burns the philosopher's house down the day after his death, and his writings are destroyed. We may imagine that he never revealed his metaphysical views to anyone; so his system is irretrievably lost, and the philosopher is remembered only by a few friends and the hostile neighbor. We would all, I think, judge that the philosopher's life in World I is better than his life in World II, and that the neighbor's vicious action in World II really harms the philosopher. What would be more natural than to feel sorry for the dead thinker? The labor of a lifetime, that for which he sacrificed everything, all reduced to a heap of ashes! Poor man!

The idea that the dead can be harmed goes back, in the philosophical literature, at least to Aristotle:

Since, then, a man's own misfortunes sometimes have a powerful influence upon his life, and sometimes seem comparatively trivial; and the same applies also to the misfortunes of all his friends alike; although it makes a difference whether a particular misfortune befalls people while they are alive or after they are dead—a far greater difference than it makes in a tragedy whether the crimes and atrocities are committed beforehand or carried out during the action; then we must take into our reckoning this difference too; or rather, perhaps, the fact that it is questionable whether the departed have any participation in good or its opposite. For the probable inference from what we have been saying is that if any effect of good or evil reaches them at all, it must be faint and slight, either in itself or to them—or if not that, at any rate not of such force and quality as to make the unhappy happy or to rob the happy of their felicity. So it appears that the dead are affected to some extent by the good fortunes of those whom they love, and similarly by their misfortunes; but that the effects are not of such a kind or so great as to make the happy unhappy, or to produce any other such result.[1]

Aristotle obviously, and not surprisingly, has serious qualms about attributing misfortune (or good fortune) to the dead. He thinks it "questionable" whether anything good or bad can happen to them; but, in the end, he concedes that "it appears that the dead are affected to some (small) extent" by things that happen to those that they loved. I can understand Aristotle, here, only by construing him as claiming (to put it in my terminology) that an ante-mortem person can be harmed (or benefited) after his death. No doubt this is what he does mean.

But we still need something that Aristotle does not try to provide—an account that explains how, exactly, a living person can be affected in any way by things that happen after he dies. It might well seem that there could not, in principle, be any such account: once a person dies, his life is completed, and nothing can be added to it or subtracted from it. But that is an oversimplified picture of a person's life. For example, we have already seen that an ante-mortem person can be wronged after his death—and why should that not count as something new that happens to him? It can easily seem as though being wronged and being harmed are relevantly different, however. Being wronged, it might be thought, does not necessarily involve any change in one's intrinsic condition: if someone tells lies about me, he wrongs me—but that, in itself, leaves me just as I was. And so it is not difficult to see that an ante-mortem person can be wronged after his death. But being harmed, so this line of reasoning continues, is different. Just as damaging a vase changes its condition for the worse, so harming a person changes his condition for the worse. Therefore, if an ante-mortem person could be harmed after his death, this would mean that an event at a later time could actually change a person's condition at an earlier time—in other words, there would be backward causation, an altering of the past. But since the past cannot be changed, an ante-mortem person cannot be harmed after his death.

Certainly the main obstacle to accepting the thesis that an ante-mortem person can be harmed after his death is the disturbing notion that it would involve backward causation. I do not know whether or not there is such a thing as backward causation, or backward quasi-causation, but fortunately there is no need for us to debate that issue—for harming a living person after his death does not involve any such process. The idea that it must involve such a process rests on the wholly misleading picture of being harmed as a kind of alteration in one's metaphysical state. To see how misleading this picture is, consider the following. Suppose that Mr. Black's son Jack is killed in an airplane crash many miles away. Given that his son's welfare is one of Black's strongest interests, the son's death harms Black (is a great misfortune for him). There should be no temptation to think that this harming of Black requires instantaneous causation at a distance—the plane crash sending out infinitely rapid waves of horror, as it were, diminishing Black's metaphysical condition. If that idea is absurd, so is the idea that if the son's death should occur after Mr. Black's, and should thus harm the ante-mortem Black after his death, it must do so by a process of backward causation.

Perhaps the picture of harm as a kind of diminishing of one's condition is abetted by the notion that if something harms a person, he must both know about it ("What I don't know can't hurt me!") and mind it. But it is just false that in order to be harmed, the victim must be aware of the harm. To be sure, in most cases of misfortune, the victim is aware of the (for him) unfortunate state of affairs. But a misfortune can befall a person who is totally ignorant of it. If, for example, one has the usual desire to go on living, then it is a misfortune to be stricken with an incurable fatal disease, even though one is unaware that one has it. Consider, too, the man described by Thomas Nagel—let us call him Purple—who is "betrayed by his friends, ridiculed behind his back, and despised by people who treat him politely to his face."[2] Nagel suggests, quite rightly, that this would be reckoned a misfortune for (or harm done to) Purple, even if he never discovers the horrible truth.

Once the misleading picture associated with the idea that an ante-mortem person can be harmed after his death—a picture that makes such harming seem utterly mysterious—is cleared away, the idea itself emerges with great plausibility and power. To see how plausible it is, consider the sad example of Bishop Berkeley's son William, who was his treasure, and who died at the tragically early age of fourteen. Let us imagine, what I think was actually false, that Berkeley knew for the last few years of the boy's life that the lad was going to die when he was still very young. Let us imagine further that the contemplated death was not to be from a lingering illness: he had, let us say, a rare allergy to a certain virus and Berkeley knew that the child was bound to come into contact with the virus and to die quickly when he did. During those years, the fact that William was going to die young was surely a misfortune for Berkeley. He might have said at any time in that period, "The fact that William is going to die before he grows up is the greatest tragedy of my life"—and mightn't he well have been right? We must avoid the mistake of supposing that it was his *knowing* that William was going to die young that was Berkeley's only misfortune during the years before William's death. To be sure, his knowing that the boy was going to die young *was* a misfortune for Berkeley: it must have made him miserable. But it was not the only misfortune. Indeed, this knowledge was a torment to Berkeley precisely because he regarded it as a great misfortune that his son was going to die young. It would also be a mistake to think that the only misfortune for Berkeley, here, apart from the misery caused by his knowledge of William's fate, was the actual death of his son. If that were so, then if he had not known ahead of time that his son was going to die young, there would have been no misfortune in Berkeley's life until the boy actually died. But surely if his friends knew, though Berkeley did not, that his son was fated to die young, they would have felt very sorry for Berkeley—and not just because there would eventually be the tragedy of his son's early death, but also because *then* (i.e., *before* his son's death) there was a grave misfortune in Berkeley's life. What was it? It was the fact that his adored and adoring child, so full of promise, was going to die young. This fact was one that Berkeley passionately did not want to exist, it was totally against his interests (whether or not he knew of its existence). Therefore, it was a very real misfortune for him.

William Berkeley's early death may be viewed as casting a shadow of misfortune backward over the life of Bishop Berkeley (and over the lives of the others who had an important interest in William's living or dying). Within the shadow, the misfortune was that William was going to die young, not that William died young.

Before going on, we might ask how far back in the life of Bishop Berkeley this shadow of misfortune falls: how much of his life is darkened by the early death of his son William? It certainly seems wrong to say that when Bishop Berkeley was himself a child, he was harmed by the fact that the son, William, he would one day have was going to die young. Why? Because when he was a child, the long life of his own future children was presumably not one of his major interests. I am not sure when this did become one of Berkeley's important interests. It surely was one from the time of William's birth, and no doubt for some time before that. But I doubt that there is any non-arbitrary way, or for our purposes any need, to fix the precise time at which a long life for William first became one of Berkeley's important interests and hence to fix the precise time at which the early death of William first harmed Bishop Berkeley.

To continue: if my account of our example is accepted, then there should be no further resistance to the idea that an ante-mortem person can be harmed after his death. To see this, let us change the example. Suppose now that although William Berkeley dies young, as before, Bishop Berkeley dies before him. The early death of the boy means, as it meant in the original example, that during the time before his death there was a misfortune in the lives of all who cared strongly about William—the misfortune, namely, that William was going to die young. For the part of this time that Bishop Berkeley was still alive, he was obviously one of those who had that misfortune (whether or not he knew that William was to die young). So the shadow of harm that an event casts can reach back across the chasm even of a person's death and darken his ante-mortem life.

It is important to see that the death of young William, on the view I am defending, does not mean that the ante-mortem Berkeley suffers the misfortune that his beloved son dies young. Only someone alive at the time of the boy's death can suffer that misfortune. No, the misfortune that darkens the life of the ante-mortem Berkeley in virtue of his son's early death is the backward shadow misfortune that his son is going to die young. This is important to see because it is all too easy to suppose that any view committed to the proposition that the dead can be harmed must hold that when William dies, *his death* is the misfortune that the ante-mortem Berkeley suffers. Perhaps one reason why these views are so often dismissed is that they are thought to commit their defenders to such a judgment. But as we have seen, they are not so committed. The ante-mortem Berkeley is harmed by William's early death not because he therefore suffers the misfortune of that death, but because he therefore suffers the misfortune that his beloved son is going to die young.

Incidentally, this example reveals a defect in Aristotle's account. He said, remember, that the effect of an unfortunate occurrence on the dead is "faint and slight" and "not of such a kind or so great as to make the happy unhappy." He was undoubtedly thinking of the normal case, where the unfortunate post-mortem occurrence was not foreseen by the ante-mortem person. But if Berkeley had known, before his own death, that William was going to die young, the effect on him of the boy's death would not have been "faint and slight"; it might well have converted him from a happy man into an unhappy one.

I confess that the thesis "An ante-mortem person can be harmed by events that happen after his death" seems to suggest that when an unfortunate post-mortem even happens, then *for the first time* the ante-mortem person is harmed. The alleged suggestion, in other words, is that the person goes to his death unharmed and only when the unfortunate post-term event takes place is he (i.e., the ante-mortem person) harmed, retroactively. I admit that this is a natural way to construe the words of the thesis, but of course, the thesis as I have been defending it does not carry the alleged suggestion. On my view, the sense in which an ante-mortem person is harmed by an unfortunate event after his death is this: the occurrence of the event makes it true that during the time before the person's death, he was harmed—harmed in that the unfortunate event was going to happen. If the event should not occur, the ante-mortem person would not have been so harmed. So the occurrence of the post-mortem event is responsible for the ante-mortem harm. The sense of "make true" and "responsible," here, is non-mysterious. If the world should be blasted to smithereens during the next presidency after Ronald Reagan's, this would make it true (be responsible for the fact) that even now, during Reagan's term, he is the penultimate president of the United States. Only if one bears this straightforward sense of "make true" and "responsible" in mind can one properly understand the thesis that "An ante-mortem person can be harmed by events that happen after his death."

CHAPTER TEN

IKE: Well, all right, why is life worth living? That's a very good question. . . . Well, there are certain things I—I guess that make it worthwhile . . . like what? Okay . . . for me . . . oh, I would say . . . what, Groucho Marx, to name one thing . . . and Willie Mays, and . . . the second movement of the Jupiter Symphony, and . . . Louie Armstrong's recording of "Potatohead Blues" . . . Swedish movies, naturally . . . *Sentimental Education* by Flaubert . . . Marlon Brando, Frank Sinatra . . . those incredible apples and pears by Cézanne . . . the crabs at Sam Wo's . . . Tracy's face. . . .   —Woody Allen, *Manhattan*

Harm to Others

Joel Feinberg

Death and Posthumous Harms

Can a person be harmed by his own death? On the one hand, we are inclined to answer unhesitatingly, "of course." To murder a person, we think, is to inflict on him what is in general the most serious harm a person can suffer. On the other hand, a moment's reflection makes us hesitate. In order to be harmed, common sense reminds us, a person must be in existence at the time, but death (real total death of the person, not the mere "apparent death" of theological teachings) is the cessation of one's existence, the first moment of a state of nonbeing, which is beyond harm or gain. Thus there is another tendency, opposite to the first, to suppose that death is *not* a harm. Ordinary usage gives support to both these tendencies, and philosophers line up on both sides with reinforcing arguments. If their disagreements are over their descriptions of pretheoretical ordinary thinking (or "common sense"), then it may never be resolved, for the issue may be inherently indeterminate.[1] In that case our task will be to propose a further refinement of ordinary thinking in the interest of our emerging general theory of harm, and to support that proposal with the best reasons we can find.

First, consider the case against classifying death as a harm. Even ordinary language gives it some backing. If a murderer is asked whether he has harmed his victim, he might well reply:

Reprinted by permission from *Harm to Others* (Oxford: Oxford University Press, 1984): 79–95.

"Harmed him? Hell no; I killed him outright!" The victim's mourners too might feel that it is something of an understatement to describe the death of their loved one as a harm (to him). The death of the victim, it would seem, is not a mere "harmed condition" he is put in, and certainly not a "harmful" one; it is no "condition" of him at all, but rather his total extinction. Ordinary language, to be sure, is not univocal, but the main case against calling death a harm is not based on ordinary language, but rather on a very simple and powerful argument: there cannot be harm without a subject to be harmed, and when death occurs it obliterates the subject, and thus excludes the possibility of harm. Even this way of speaking is misleading, the argument goes, for it suggests that death *does something* to the subject and that therefore there is a period of time during which they are both coexistent. Actually, death is defined simply as the first moment of the subject's nonexistence,[2] so it is not something that ever coexists with the dying person for the time required for it to have a directly harmful effect on him.

Consider the purest possible hypothetical case of the infliction of death, where all extraneous and distracting harms have been excluded from the example. A woman in the prime of her life, with many ongoing projects and enterprises, but with no dependents or friends close enough to mourn her, is shot in the head by an unseen assailant, while she is asleep. Without ever being aware that she was even in danger, much less that she has been fatally wounded, she dies instantly. Right up to the very instant she was shot she was unharmed, then at that very moment, perhaps one second after the killer squeezed the trigger, she was dead. At the very most, she was in a "harmed condition" for the one-half second or so before she died. As for death itself, one might agree with the ancient Epicureans: "Where she was, death was not, and where death was, she was not."

This powerful argument against classifying death as a harm is indeed a problem for the position on the other side, a difficulty commonly called "the problem of the subject." Like a rock withstanding the lashings of a storm it stands resistant to all counterarguments, maintaining and reiterating that there cannot be a harm without a subject to be harmed.[3] Indeed, if the argument has any weakness at first sight, it consists in its tendency to prove too much. The ancient Epicureans, after all, were not quibbling over the word "harm." They used the problem of the subject to argue more sweepingly that death is not *any kind of evil* to the one who dies, and therefore nothing to be feared or regretted, a conclusion generally thought to be paradoxical.[4]

The case in favor of classifying death as a harm can be put almost equally quickly. To begin with, ordinary language lends some support to this side of the controversy too. It is so natural, almost unavoidable, to speak in idioms that seem to imply this view, that there must be some point in it (at least points of analogy). For example, we sometimes say of a person who has been killed that "he was deprived of his life," or of years of happiness he might otherwise have enjoyed. Incurably ill persons, on the other hand, are said to "seek release" and when they find it, to be "better off dead," since their "lives were of no further use to them." People killed in accidents are often characterized in the language of loss: "Hundreds lost their lives in the storm." We can, of course, avoid these idioms and talk only of the destruction of the person, not harm or benefit to the person, as the evil or good in question, because there is no survivor to be the proper subject of harm or benefit. But this linguistic strictness would deprive us of metaphors of striking aptness and utility.

The main support for the view of death as harm, however, comes not from ordinary language, but from whatever support has already been mustered for the analysis of harm as set-back interest, which, given the universal interest in not dying, implies that death is a harm. The continuance of our lives for most of us, at most moments in our lives, is something manifestly in our interests, and that being so, the sudden extinction of life would, as a thwarting of that interest, be a harm. (The skeptical question, harm to whom? must for the moment be put aside.) Consider again the sleeping victim of a murder who dies instantaneously. One second before the trigger was pulled, it was true of the victim (as it is now true of both the author and reader of these words) that continued life was something in her *interest*. Indeed, there is nothing a normal person (in reasonable health and tolerable circumstances) dreads more than his own death, and that dread, in the vast majority of cases, is as rational as it is unavoidable, for unless we continue alive, we have no chance whatever of achieving those goals that are the ground of our ultimate interest. Some of these goals, perhaps, might be achieved for us by others after our deaths, publicly oriented and other-regarding goals in particular. But most of our interests require not simply that some result be brought about, but rather that it be brought about *by* us, or if not by us, then *for* us. My interest in producing an excellent book, or a beautiful art object, is not fully satisfied by another person's creation of such objects. My interest was not simply that such objects exist, but that *I* bring them into existence. Similarly my aim to build a dream house, or to achieve leisure in security, is not satisfied when such a house or such leisure comes into existence, but only when I am present to enjoy and use it. Our interest in avoiding death is a supreme welfare interest, an indispensable condition for the advancement of most, if not all, of the ulterior interests that constitute our good. There is something bare minimal about it on the one hand, yet something supremely important on the other. Apart from the interests it serves, it has no value in itself; yet unless it is protected, hardly any of a person's ulterior interests will be advanced. To extinguish a person's life is, at one stroke, to defeat almost all of his self-regarding interests: to ensure that his ongoing projects and enterprises, his long-range goals, and his most earnest hopes for his own achievement and personal enjoyment, must all be dashed.

If the prior interests set back by death justify our characterization of death as a harm (even without a subject), then equally some of them warrant our speaking of certain later events as posthumous harms. On the other hand, if the absence of a subject (even given prior interests whose targets postdate death) prevents us from speaking of death as a harm, then it equally precludes talk of posthumous harms. Death and developments after death are alike in coming into existence during a period when there is no longer a subject. If the absence of a subject precludes our speaking of posthumous harms, then equally it precludes our speaking of death as a harm (a rather harder pill to swallow) since both death and posthumous events are post-personal. Either death and posthumous harms both alike can be harms or neither can.[5] (I discuss posthumous harms in more detail below.)

There is a case, then, for saying both that death is not (ever) a harm and that it is (often) a thwarting of the antecedent interest in staying alive. That makes death a very hard case indeed for the analysis of harm as set-back or thwarted interest. The writer who has strong theoretical incentives for saving the set-back interest theory of harm has only two alternative moves at this point. He might simply stipulate an admittedly extended sense of "harm" broad enough to include death as a harm, or he might search for a way to solve "the problem of the subject" by explaining how a person can be harmed by events that occur subsequent to his own existence. Failing both of these moves, he must revise or supplement the harm principle so as to make it more adequate as a liberal principle of liberty-limitation. He could do that by a simple amendment to his formulation of that principle so that it certifies as a relevant reason for the restriction of liberty that it is necessary to prevent *harm or death* to others (implying that they are not the same thing). The cost of this amendment, clearly, would be the abandonment of the analysis of a harm (which has been so useful thus far) as any setback to interest, for there *is* an interest in avoiding death, yet the amendment implies that death is not a harm.

Stipulating a new sense of "harm" broad enough to include death would be but a minor and quite excusable departure from the conventions of ordinary language for the sake of theoretical economy, similar perhaps to the restriction of the sense of "fish" to exclude whales and seals, which were once commonly and properly called "fish." Still it would make things tidier all around if we could show that first appearance to the contrary, there *is* a plausible subject for harmful deaths and posthumous events. Although a whiff of paradox may still attach to it, there is a way of conceiving death, even without the assumption of survival or immortality, that lends plausibility to the description of death as sometimes harmful to the one who dies. That is all that can be claimed for the theory suggested in sections below.

To be sure, death is not always and necessarily a harm to the one who dies. To the person in hopeless, painful illness, who has already "withdrawn his investments" in all ulterior interests, there may be nothing to lose, and cessation of agony or boredom to be "gained," in which case death is a blessing. For the retired nonagenarian, death may not exactly be ardently desired, but still it will be a nontragedy. Those who mourn his death will not think of themselves as mourning *for him*, but rather for his dependents and loved ones, if any, or simply in virtue of the capacity of any *memento mori* to evoke sadness. In contrast, when a young vigorous person dies, we think of *him* as chief among those who suffered loss. The strength of that conviction provides much of the motivation for the search for a solution to the problem of the subject.

Surviving Interests

I would like to suggest that we can think of some of a person's interests as surviving his death, just as some of the debts and claims of his estate do, and that in virtue of the defeat of these interests, either by death itself or by subsequent events, we can think of the person who was, as harmed. I no longer wish to say that these interests themselves are the "true subjects of harm,"[6] because that suggests a bizarre ontological reification, as if each interest were a little person in its own right. Ernest Partridge is understandably impatient with this view and quite right when he says, "But surely by 'interests themselves' he [Feinberg] cannot mean interests of no one."[7] All interests are the interest of some persons or other, and a person's surviving interests are simply the ones that we identify by naming *him*, the person whose interests they were. He is of course at this moment dead, but that does not prevent us from referring now, in the present tense, to his interests, if they are still capable of being blocked or fulfilled, just as we refer to his outstanding debts or claims, if they are still capable of being paid. The final tally book on a person's life is not closed until some time after his death.

Even Partridge finds himself obliged, when speaking of a hypothetical violation of the will of Alfred Nobel, to use the idiom "contrary to the wishes of the late Alfred Nobel,"[8] implying that what is done *now* can affect ("be contrary to") what was wished *then*. There *are* such wishes, in a kind of timeless propositional sense, rendered, by grammatical convention merely, in the present tense, even though there is no longer an Alfred Nobel. The conditions of the will "exist" and are binding now, and they give present expression to the wishes that Nobel had *then*. That does not imply a peculiar metaphysical status for the wishes as being still consciously experienced in some universal mind, or in the head of a decaying corpse, or whatever.

Similar comments can be made about surviving interests. In this section I shall try to explain more fully what it is for interests to survive before tackling head-on, in the next section, the problem of the subject.

What then does it mean to say that a "surviving interest" has been set back or defeated? Our answer to this question will depend on which of two conceptions of interest enhancement and impairment we adopt. As we have seen, interests are "stakes" that are derived from and linked to wants, in the case of ulterior interests to more ulterior goals or focal aims. Now we can apply to these wants W. D. Ross's distinction between want-fulfillment and want-satisfaction.[9] The *fulfillment* of a want is simply the coming into existence of that which is desired. The *satisfaction* of a want is the pleasant experience of contentment or gratification that normally occurs in the mind of the desirer when he believes that his desire has been fulfilled. When the object of a want does not come into existence, we can say that the want has been *unfulfilled* or *thwarted*; the experience in the mind of the desirer when he believes that his desire has been thwarted is called *frustration* or *disappointment*. Notoriously, fulfillment of desire can fail to give satisfaction. There is no more melancholy state than the disillusionment that comes from getting what we wanted and finding it disappointing. Such disillusionment can usually be explained as the consequence of a rash or ill-considered desire and unrealistic expectations. On other occasions, the original desire will bear up under retrospective scrutiny, and yet its fulfillment gives no pleasure. Indeed, the occurrence of subjective satisfaction is a highly contingent and unreliable phenomenon. Sometimes when our goals are achieved, we do not experience much joy, but only fatigue and sadness, or an affective blankness. Some persons, perhaps, are disposed by temperament normally to receive their achievements in this unthrilled fashion. Still, even in these cases, reexamination of the goal whose fulfillment failed to satisfy may disclose no hidden defects, no reasons for regret, in a word, no disillusionment. Not only can one have fulfillment without satisfaction; one can also have satisfaction of a want in the absence of its actual fulfillment, provided only that one is led to believe, falsely, that one's want has been fulfilled. Similarly, pleasant states of mind resembling "satisfaction" can be induced by drugs, hypnosis, and

178   FEINBERG

other forms of manipulation that have no relation whatever to prior wants.

Similarly, one's wants can be thwarted without causing frustration, or disappointment, and one can be quite discontented even when one's wants have in fact been fulfilled. These negative cases are perfectly parallel with the positive ones. Nonfulfillment of a want yields no disappointment when the want was ill-advised in the first place. In such a case, the want can happily be renounced after rational reassessment. Disillusionment, however, is often not involved. A perfectly genuine and well-considered goal may be thwarted without causing mental pain when the desirer has a placid temperament or a stoic philosophy. And discontent does not presuppose thwarting of desire any more than satisfaction presupposes fulfillment. One can have feelings of frustration and disappointment caused by false beliefs that one's wants have been thwarted, or by drugs and other manipulative techniques.

For these reasons, harm to an interest is better defined in terms of the objective blocking of goals and thwarting of desires than in subjective terms; and the enhancement or advancing of an interest is likewise best defined in terms of the objective fulfillment of well-considered wants rather than in terms of subjective states of pleasure. Most persons will agree, I think, that the important thing is to get what they want, even if that causes no joy.[10] The pleasure that normally attends want-fulfillment is a welcome dividend, but the object of our efforts is to fulfill our wants in the external world, not to bring about states of our own minds. Indeed, if this were not the case, there would be no way to account for the pleasure of satisfaction when it does come; we are satisfied only because we think that our desires are fulfilled. If the object of our desires were valuable to us only as a means to our pleasant inner states, those glows could never come.

The object of a focal aim that is the basis of an interest, then, like the object of any want, is not simply satisfaction or contentment, and the defeat of an interest is not to be identified with disappointment or frustration. Hence, death can be a thwarting of the interests of the person who dies, and must be the total defeat of most of his self-regarding interests, even though, as a dead man, he can feel no pain.

This account helps explain, I think, why we grieve for a

young, vigorous "victim of death" himself, and not *only* for those who loved him and depended on him. We grieve for him in virtue of his unfulfilled interests. We think of him as one who has invested all his energies and hopes in the world, and then has lost everything. We think of his life as a whole as not as good a thing as it might have been had he lived on. In some special circumstances, death not only does its harm in this wholly "negative" way, preventing the flowering of the interests in which a person's lifetime good consists, it also does direct and "positive" harm to a person by undoing or setting back important interests that were already prospering. Death, in these cases, leads to the harming of surviving interests that might otherwise have been prevented.[11]

Because the objects of a person's interests are usually wanted or aimed-at events that occur outside his immediate experience and at some future time, the area of a person's good or harm is necessarily wider than his subjective experience and longer than his biological life. The moment of death is the terminating boundary of one's biological life, but it is itself an important event within the life of one's future-oriented interests. When death thwarts an interest, the harm can be ascribed to the person who is no more, charged as it were to his "moral estate."

The interests that die with a person are those that can no longer be helped or harmed by posthumous events. These include most of his self-regarding interests, those based, for example, on desires for personal achievement and personal enjoyment, and those based on "self-confined" wants that a person could have "if he were the only person that had ever existed,"[12] for example, the desire to be a self of a certain kind, or the desire for self-respect. Other self-regarding wants, in contrast, seem more like other-regarding and publicly oriented wants, in that they can be fulfilled or thwarted after the death of the person whose wants they are. I refer to some of a person's desires to stand in certain relations to other people where "the concern is primarily with the self . . . and with others only as objects or as other terms in a relation to me."[13] These desires can be called "self-centered" and include as a class such wants as the desire to assert or display oneself before others, to be the object of affection or esteem of others, and so on. In particular, the desire to maintain a good reputation, like the desire that some social or political cause triumph, or the desire that one's loved ones flourish, can be the basis of interests that survive their owner's death, in a manner of speaking, and can be promoted or harmed by events subsequent to that death. Fulfillment and thwarting of interest, after all, may still be possible, even when it is too late for satisfaction or disappointment.

The above account might still contain elements of paradox, but it can be defended against one objection that is sure to be made. How can a person be harmed, it might be asked, by what he can't know? Dead men are permanently unconscious; hence they cannot be aware of events as they occur; hence (it will be said) they can have no stake one way or the other in such events. That this argument employs a false premise can be shown by a consideration of various interests of *living* persons that can be violated without their ever becoming aware of it. Many of these are "possessory interests" whose rationality can be doubted, for example, a landowner's interest in the *exclusive* possession and enjoyment of his land—an interest that can be invaded by an otherwise harmless trespasser who takes one unobserved step inside the entrance gates; or the legally recognized "interest in domestic relations" which is invaded when one's spouse engages in secret adulterous activity with a lover. The latter is an interest in being the exclusive object of one's spouse's love, and has been criticized by some as implying property in another's affections. But there is no criticizing on such grounds the interest every person has in his own reputation, which is perhaps the best example for our present purposes from the purely self-regarding category. If someone spreads a libelous description of me among a group whose good opinion I covet and cherish, altogether without my knowledge, I have been injured in virtue of the harm done my interest in a good reputation, even though I *never* learn what has happened. That is because I have an interest, so I believe, in having a good reputation *as such*, in addition to my interest in avoiding hurt feelings, embarrassment, and economic injury. And *that* interest can be seriously harmed without my ever learning of it.

How is the situation changed in any relevant way by the death of the person defamed? If knowledge is not a necessary condition of harm before one's death why should it be necessary afterward? Suppose that after my death, an enemy cleverly forges documents to "prove" very convincingly that I was a philanderer, an adulterer, and a plagiarist, and communicates this "information" to the general public that includes my widow, children, and former colleagues and friends. Can there be any doubt that I have been harmed by such libels? The "self-centered" interest I had at my death in the continued high regard of my fellows, in this example, was not thwarted by my death itself, but by events that occurred afterward. Similarly, my other-regarding interest in the well-being of my children could be defeated or harmed after my death by other parties overturning my will, or by thieves and swindlers who cheat my heirs of their inheritance. None of these events will embarrass or distress me, since dead men can have no feelings; but all of them can harm my interests by forcing nonfulfillment of goals in which I had placed a great stake.

This liability, to which we are all subject, to drastic changes in our fortune both before and after death was well understood by the Greeks. Aristotle devotes a chapter of his *Nicomachean Ethics* to a saying already ancient in his time, and attributed by some to Solon, that we can "call no man fortunate before his death."[14] On one interpretation, this dark saying means that "only when he is dead is it safe to call a man . . . beyond the arrows of outrageous fortune." On the day before he dies, his interests can be totally smashed and his life thus ruined. But as Aristotle shrewdly observes (attributing the point to the general popular wisdom), some of a person's interests are not made safe even by his death, and we cannot call him fortunate with perfect confidence until several more decades have passed; "For a dead man is popularly believed to be capable of having both good and ill fortune—honor and dishonor and prosperity and the loss of it among his children and descendants generally—in exactly the same way as if he were alive but unaware or unobservant of what was happening."[15]

Three hypothetical cases can illustrate the "popular belief" mentioned by Aristotle, and the case for posthumous harm can rest with them.

Case A: A woman devotes thirty years of her life to the furtherance of certain ideals and ambitions in the form of one vast undertaking. She founds an institution dedicated to these ends and works single-mindedly for its advancement, both for the sake of the social good she believes it to promote, and for the sake of her own glory. One month before she dies, the "empire of her hopes" collapses utterly as the establishment into which she has poured her life's energies crumbles into ruin, and she is personally disgraced. She never learns the unhappy truth, however, as her friends, eager to save her from disappointment, conceal or misrepresent the facts. She dies contented.

Case B: The facts are the same as in Case A, except that the institution in which the woman had so great an interest remains healthy, growing and flourishing, until her death. But it begins to founder a month later, and within a year, it collapses utterly, while at the same time, the woman and her life's work are totally discredited.

Case C: The facts are the same as in Case B, except for an additional surmise about the cause of the decline and collapse of the woman's fortune after her death. In the present case, a group of malevolent conspirators, having made solemn promises to the woman before her death, deliberately violate them after she has died. From motives of vengeance, malice, and envy, they spread damaging lies about her and her institution, reveal secret plans, and otherwise betray her trust in order to bring about the ruin of her interests.

It would not be very controversial to say that the woman in Case A had suffered grievous harm to her interests although she never learned the bad news. Those very same interests are harmed in Case B to exactly the same extent, and again the woman does not learn the bad news, in this case because she is dead, and dead people hear no news at all. There seems no relevant difference between Case A and Case B except that in Case B there might seem to be no subject of the harm, the woman being dead at the specific moment when the harm occurred. (But see the next section below.) We have seen, however, that there is a sense in which some of her interests survive her, and that these, like all interests, are harmed by thwarting or nonfulfillment rather than by subjective disappointment. But if that point is not convincing, the argument must depend on its reinforcement by Case C. In that example, the woman is not *merely* harmed (if she is harmed at all); rather she is exploited, betrayed, and wronged. When a promise is broken, someone is wronged, and who if not the promisee? When a confidence is revealed, someone is betrayed, and who, if not the person whose confidence it was?

When a reputation is falsely blackened, someone is defamed, and who, if not the person lied about? If there is no "problem of the subject" when we speak of wronging the dead, why should there be when we speak of harming them, especially when the harm is an essential ingredient of the wrong?

The Proper Subject of Surviving Interests

The motivation for thinking of death and some posthumous events as harms should now be clear, but the central puzzle still remains. The surviving interests, like the interests instantly squelched by death itself, must be the interests of someone or other. If they are the interests of the person who is now dead, then we are faced with the impossible problem of explaining how a mere physical thing—a decaying body six feet underground—can have any want-based interests. If the interests are those of the living person who is no more, then the problem is to explain how his lot can be made better or worse, as it were *retroactively*. If, on the contrary, the detached interests themselves are the only proper subjects of the harm, then either they are nobody's interests at all (the view Partridge derides) or they are the interests of some Absolute Mind, a metaphysical assumption that is uneconomical, to put it mildly.

The view I would like to defend is that the interests harmed by events that occur at or after the moment a person's nonexistence commences are interests of the living person who no longer is with us, not the interests of the decaying body he left behind. (The latter attribution of course is utterly absurd.) As George Pitcher points out (in an important article from which I shall now proceed to borrow heavily),[16] a dead person can be described in two different ways: (1) "as he was at some stage of his life—i.e. as a living person" or (2) "as he is now, in death—mouldering, perhaps, in a grave." Pitcher calls the first "a description of an *ante*-mortem person after his death" and the second "a description of a *post*-mortem person after his death."[17] All antemortem persons are subject not only to being described, but also to being wronged after their deaths, by betrayals, broken promises, defamatory lies, and the like, but no "postmortem person" can be wronged at all. (How could one break a promise to a corpse, or wrong the corpse by misdescribing it?) Postmortem persons cannot be *harmed* either, for no "mere thing" can be harmed directly in its own right, but only in a "derivative sense." The only troublesome category is that of acts after death that harm the antemortem person. As Pitcher puts it, the question is whether it is possible "for something to happen after a person's death that harms the living person he was before he died."[18] The main obstacle to an affirmative answer is its apparent implication that "posthumous harms" are *retroactive*, "that when an unfortunate post-mortem event happens, then *for the first time* the ante-mortem person is harmed,"[19] though he was unharmed when he died. Pitcher wisely rejects this apparent implication.

Retroactivity is as puzzling and paradoxical a concept, or worse, than the concepts it is meant to clarify, and we are well advised to follow Pitcher in disowning it. We especially should avoid that version of the retroactivity thesis which interprets posthumously harmful events as standing in the relation of *backward causation* to the earlier harms they are said to inflict on the antemortem person. It is probably not possible to conceive of posthumous harms in this way and fortunately not necessary to do so. When the malevolent *A* destroys *B*'s life's work six months after *B*'s death, he does not *cause* something to happen to the living *B* six months earlier. The posthumous harm thesis, according to Pitcher, does not entail this misleading picture any more than a spatially distant harmful event (like the death of one's beloved son in an airplane crash in Australia, halfway around the world) entails the scientifically unacceptable thesis of instantaneous causation at a distance (as Pitcher puts it, "the plane crash sending out infinitely rapid waves of horror, as it were, diminishing [the father's] metaphysical condition").[20] At the moment his son was killed, the father's other-regarding interest in his son's well-being was totally and irrevocably defeated, and he was *ipso facto* in a harmed condition though he did not yet know it. But the accident did not reach out, as it were, and instantaneously smite the father in defiance of the known laws of physics. The reason why that unacceptable consequence does not follow is that the relation between the crash and the vicarious harm is not a relation of physical causation at all. Similarly, posthumous harms do not entail backward causation because they too do not entail physical causation at all.

Once we reject the model of physical causation, moreover, there is no reason to suppose that either vicarious or posthumous harms involve any notion of retroactivity that is offensive to common sense. The occurrence of the harmful posthumous event, in Pitcher's language, *makes it true* that the antemortem person is harmed, and that occurrence is in a sense *responsible* for the antemortem harm. But Pitcher quickly points out that the relevant senses of "make true" and "responsible" neither imply retroactivity nor are they in any way mysterious. The antemortem person was harmed in being the subject of interests that were going to be defeated whether he knew it or not. It does not become "retroactively true" that as the subject of doomed interests he is in a harmed state; rather it was true all along. Our *pity* for the harmed person, of course, can be unparadoxically retroactive. If we had known at the time before his death that the cause to which he had devoted his life was doomed all along, we would have been sorry for him then, as we feel sorry for him *now*, "in retrospect." But whatever causation *is* involved in the narrative is not retroactive. An event occurs after Smith's death that causes something to happen at that time. So far, so good; no paradox. Now, in virtue of the thing that was caused to happen at that time it is true that Smith was in a harmed condition before he died. It does not suddenly "become true" that the antemortem Smith was harmed. Rather it becomes apparent to us for the first time that it was true all along—that from the time Smith invested enough in his cause to make it one of his interests, he was playing a losing game. Pitcher provides his own example of the "unmysterious" character of the senses of "make true" and "responsible for" that are employed here: "If the world should be blasted to smithereens during the next presidency after Ronald Reagan's, this would make it true (be responsible for the fact) that even now, during Reagan's term, he is the penultimate president of the United States."[21] Similarly, the financial collapse of the life-insurance company through which I have protected my loved dependents, occurring, let us imagine, five minutes after my death, several years in the future, makes it true that my present interest in my children's security is harmed, and therefore, that *I* am harmed too, though I know it not. When that time comes, my friends might feel sorry not only for my children but for me too, though I am dead. If the present account is correct, there is no more paradox in this than in my feeling sorry for a living friend whose wife I know to be unfaithful and unloving though he has invested much of his own well-being in the marriage, or for another friend whose beloved daughter, unknown to him, must soon die of a rare disease.[22]

Doomed Interest and the Dating of Harm

How does the theory of posthumous harms lightly sketched above account for the harmfulness of death itself? The puzzles and doubts that remain, for the most part, have to do with the dating of harms, and we would be well advised not to seek more precision in answer to such questions than the subject matter permits. Consider first how we have already chosen to date "posthumous harms." Exactly when did the harmed state of the antemortem person, for which the posthumous event is "responsible," begin? I think the best answer is: "at the point, well before his death, when the person had invested so much in some postdated outcome that it became one of his interests." From that point on (we now know) he was playing a losing game, betting a substantial component of his own good on a doomed cause. Of course, the harm in question may not have been a *net harm*, since other equally important interests perhaps were flourishing, and many fulfillments were in store for him before death. But insofar as this one important interest was going to be defeated (that is, was actually doomed), he was in a harmed state.

Applying this model to the dating problems associated with the harm of death itself is a trickier matter. We should now say that it is the living person antemortem who is (usually) harmed directly by his own death. When then did his harmed condition begin? Presumably not at the moment of death itself, because that is when *he* ceased to be. Let us say then, still following the model of harmful posthumous events, that the harmed condition began at the moment he first acquired the interests that death defeats. Chief among these of course is the paramount welfare interest in remaining alive. But that interest is presupposed by most of his other interests, so he must have "acquired" it from the moment he acquired any others. It would follow that if it was going to happen that he would die at time t, he must have been in a harmed condition for almost all of his life before *t*—a conclusion that does not at first sight carry much conviction.

I think that the distinction between partial harm and net harm (or harm on balance) is the key to this and similar dating riddles. If John is going to be the victim of a fatal accident on his thirtieth birthday, then he is in at least a partially harmed condition from the time (many years earlier) when he acquires any interests at all. More specifically, he is in a partially harmed state from the time he acquires interests which themselves need more than thirty years to be fulfilled or satisfactorily advanced. But he has thirty years worth of other interests that will be advanced, promoted, and fulfilled, to his continual and repeated benefit. He is benefited in having the means to fulfill *them*, but harmed in lacking the means (as it turns out) of fulfilling those other interests that require more years of life. The degree of harmfulness of a person's premature death thus depends on *how* premature it is, given the interests that defined his own particular good. We now have at our disposal also an interpretation of the commonsense observation that "all life is tragic." Almost everyone will die with some interests that will be defeated by his death. And because of the inevitability of death, all of us are, while alive, in at least a partially harmed condition in that *those* interests are doomed, and thus generative of harm, from the time they are first acquired. But the person who will die at thirty is in a condition of greater harm on balance between ages of one and thirty than the person who will die at eighty is between the ages of one and eighty. That is because death defeats fewer interests, and especially fewer important interests, of the latter than of the former. Hence, we have an interpretation of still another commonsense maxim, that "Young deaths are more tragic than old ones." Other things being equal, a long life is more beneficial (less harmful) than a short one.

It is time now to summarize our conclusions in this and the previous sections about the harmfulness of death and certain posthumous events. Death can be a harm to the person who dies in virtue of the interests he had antemortem that are totally and irrevocably defeated by his death. The subject of the harm in death is the living person antemortem, whose interests are squelched. The fact of a person's death "makes it true" that his antemortem interests were going to be defeated and to that extent the antemortem person was harmed too, though his impending death was still unknown to him. Only the person who no longer has an interest in any goal that can be set back by his death is unharmed by death, and indeed such a person may even be the antemortem beneficiary on balance of his own death. The interests of a person that can be said to have "survived" his death are those ulterior interests that can still be thwarted or promoted by subsequent events. These include his publicly oriented and other-regarding interests, and also his "self-centered" interests in being thought of in certain ways by others. Posthumous harm occurs when one of the deceased's surviving interests is thwarted after his death. The subject of a surviving interest and of the harm or benefit that can accrue to it after a person's death is the living person antemortem whose interest it was. Events after death do not retroactively produce effects at an earlier time, but their occurrence can lead us to revise our estimates of an earlier person's well-being, and correct the record before closing the book on his life.

A Note on Posthumous Wrongs

Ernest Partridge denies not only that the dead can be harmed but also that they can be wronged, betrayed, or treated unfairly, on the grounds that they do not exist, and nonexistent beings are beyond all wronging. Nevertheless, he insists,[23] it is wrong to defame, cheat, or break promises to the dead; we may not simply do as we please with them. But the correct explanation of our duties toward persons now dead, he argues, does not imply that they have rights against us that we can violate. Rather there are general practices—making wills, insurance contracts, promises, truth-telling, among others—that most people, including *us now*, have an interest in preserving, and in the absence of rules imposing duties on us in respect to the dead, those useful practices would collapse, to our great collective loss. What would be the point of cherishing a person's memory, if he could be defamed with moral impunity by anyone? Those of us who care what memories of ourselves are left behind would feel insecure indeed while alive, if people generally did not accept the duty of truth-telling about the dead. There would be no point whatever in buying life insurance policies if the vendors could not be trusted to keep their promise made to the deceased when he was alive to pay his beneficiary at the appropriate time. Life insurance companies, in the absence of such trust, would be forced out of business, and all of us who *care* about our dependents would be left insecure and the dependents themselves highly vulnerable. If there were no acknowledged obligation to distribute a person's estate in accordance with the testimonial directions he left for us before his death, then there would be no point in making wills ourselves, and we would be deprived of something we value. We behave in certain appropriate ways toward the dead then because it is our duty to do so, and that duty is imposed by the rules that define certain practices that are highly useful to living people. The tendency of acts that are derelictions of these duties is to cause harm—not to people already dead (that, says Partridge, is impossible)—but rather to cause public harm, that is harm that consists in weakening the capacity of public practices to serve the interests of living people.

Rule-utilitarian arguments of this familiar kind[24] do indeed give the truth about our duties toward the dead, and nothing but the truth, but they do not give the whole truth. The very rules that impose duties on us as promisors, speakers, insurers, and testimonial instruction receivers confer, by the same token, *rights* on the living persons who are the corresponding promisees, parties talked about, insurance buyers, and testimonial instruction givers. These are the rights that can be violated after the right-holder's death by the wrongful behavior of those who violate their own duties. The duties in question are not without their corresponding claimants; a promise, for example, imposes a duty *to* the promisee, quite distinct from the more dilute and general duty toward all the rest of us who have an interest in protecting the general trust in promises. Its violation creates a quite distinct and powerful grievance in the right-holder (or his spokesman) that cannot wholly be derived from the more diffuse grievance the rest of us may have that "our practice" has been weakened or threatened. And indeed in some cases, where the violation is kept secret, there may be no such general consequences at all, yet the wrong to the party now deceased is clear and pointed. The practice may or may not be endangered; but only the right-holder has been betrayed.

It is absurd to think that once a promisee has died, the status of a broken promise made to him while he was still alive suddenly ceases to be that of a serious injustice to a victim, and becomes instead a mere diffuse public harm. Once we recall that the betrayed party is the person now dead as he was in his trusting state antemortem, all temptation to give this distorted account of the matter ceases. We no longer need embrace one absurdity to avoid an even greater one, namely that the wronged party is a corpse mouldering in the ground or a detached interest floating in the air.

CHAPTER ELEVEN

Eternal nothingness is O.K. if you're dressed for it.
    —Woody Allen, *Getting Even*

Reasons and Persons

Derek Parfit

Past or Future Suffering

The S-Theorist might claim that there is no need for argument. We cannot argue everything; some things have to be assumed. And he might say this about his present claim. He might say that, when we compare the questions "To whom does it happen?" and "When does it happen?," we see clearly that only the first question has rational significance. We see clearly that it is not irrational to care less about some pain if it will be felt by someone else, but that it *is* irrational to care less merely because of a difference in *when* some pain is felt by oneself.

Is this so? The bias towards the near is not our only bias with respect to time. We are also biased towards the future. Is this attitude irrational?

Consider *My Past or Future Operations:*

Case One. I am in some hospital, to have some kind of surgery. Since this is completely safe, and always successful, I have no fears about the effects. The surgery may be brief, or it may instead take a long time. Because I have to co-operate with the surgeon, I cannot have anaesthetics. I have had this surgery once before, and I can remember how painful it is. Under a new policy, because the operation is so painful, patients are now afterwards made to forget it. Some drug removes their memories of the last few hours.

I have just woken up. I cannot remember going to sleep. I ask my nurse if it has been decided when my operation is to be, and how long

Reprinted by permission from *Reasons and Persons* (Oxford: Clarendon Press, 1984): 165–85.

it must take. She says that she knows the facts about both me and another patient, but that she cannot remember which facts apply to whom. She can tell me only that the following is true. I may be the patient who had his operation yesterday. In that case, my operation was the longest ever performed, lasting ten hours. I may instead be the patient who is to have a short operation later today. It is either true that I did suffer for ten hours, or true that I shall suffer for one hour.

I ask the nurse to find out which is true. While she is away, it is clear to me which I prefer to be true. If I learn that the first is true, I shall be greatly relieved.

My bias towards the future makes me relieved here that my pain is in the past. My bias towards the near might, in the same way, make me relieved that some pain has been postponed. In either case, I might prefer some different timing for my ordeal even if, with the different timing, the ordeal would be much worse. Compared with an hour of pain later today, I might, like Proximus, prefer ten hours of pain next year. Or, as in this example, I might prefer ten hours of pain yesterday.

Is this second preference irrational? Ought I instead to hope that I am the second patient, whose pain is still to come? Before I discuss this question, I should explain one feature of the case: the induced amnesia.

Some writers claim that, if some part of my future will not be linked by memory to the rest of my life, I can rationally ignore what will happen to me during this period. For these writers, a double dose of amnesia is as good as an anaesthetic. If I shall have no memories while I am suffering, and I shall later have no memories of my suffering, I need not—they claim—be concerned about this future suffering. This is a controversial claim. But even if it is justified it does not apply to my example. This does not involve a *double* dose of amnesia. During my painful operation I shall have all my memories. It is true that I shall afterwards be made to forget the operation. But this does not remove my reason to be concerned about my future suffering. If we denied this, we would have to claim that someone should not be concerned when, already knowing that he is about to die, he learns the extra fact that he will die painfully. He will not later remember *these* pains.

If we imagine ourselves in the place of the patient who will suffer for an hour later today, most of us would be concerned. We would be concerned even though we know that we shall not later remember this hour of pain. And I can now explain why my case involves induced amnesia. This gives us the right comparison. If I have learnt that I am the second patient, I am in the following state of mind. I believe that I shall have an hour's pain later today, and I can imagine roughly how awful the pain is going to be. This is enough to make me concerned. If I have learnt instead that I am the first patient, I am in the strictly comparable state of mind. I believe that I did have ten hours' pain yesterday, and I can imagine roughly how awful the pain must have been. My state of mind differs only in the two respects that I am discussing. My belief has a different tense, being about the past rather than the future. And it is a belief about ten hours of pain rather than about a single hour. It would confuse the comparison if I did not just believe that I suffered yesterday, but could also remember the suffering. When I believe that I shall suffer later today, I have nothing comparable to memories of this future suffering. And memories of pain are quite various; some are in themselves painful, others are not. It therefore rids the example of an irrelevant and complicating feature if I would have about my past pain only what I would have about my future pain: a belief, with an ability to imagine the pain's awfulness.

The induced amnesia purifies the case. But it may still arouse suspicion. I therefore add:

Case Two. When I wake up, I do remember a long period of suffering yesterday. But I cannot remember how long the period was. I ask my nurse whether my operation is completed, or whether further surgery needs to be done. As before, she knows the facts about two patients, but she cannot remember which I am. If I am the first patient, I had five hours of pain yesterday, and my operation is over. If I am the second patient, I had two hours of pain yesterday, and I shall have another hour of pain later today.[1]

In Case Two there is no amnesia; but this makes no difference. Either I suffered for five hours and have no more pain to come, or I suffered for two hours and have another hour of pain to come. I would again prefer the first to be true. I would prefer my life to contain more hours of pain, if that means that none of this pain is still to come.

If we imagine ourselves in my place in these two cases, most of us would have my preference. If we did not know whether we have suffered for several hours, or shall later suffer for one hour, most of us would strongly prefer the first to be true. If we could make it true, we would undoubtedly do so. If we are religious we might pray that it be true. On some accounts, this is the one conceivable way of affecting the past. God may have made some past event happen only because, at the time, He had foreknowledge of our later backward-looking prayer, and He chose to grant this prayer. Even if we do not believe that we could in this way, through God's grace, cause our pain to be in the past, we would strongly prefer it to be in the past, even at the cost of its lasting ten times as long.

Is this preference irrational? Most of us would answer No. If he accepts this answer, the S-Theorist must abandon his claim that the question "When?" has no rational significance. He cannot claim that a mere difference in the timing of a pain, or in its relation to the present moment, "is not in itself a rational ground for having more or less regard for it."[2] Whether a pain is in the past or future is a mere difference in its relation to the present moment. And, if it is not irrational to care more about pains that are in the future, why is it irrational to care more about pains that are in the nearer future? If the S-Theorist admits as defensible one departure from temporal neutrality, how can he criticize the other?

The Direction of Causation

The S-Theorist might say: "Since we cannot affect the past, this is a good ground for being less concerned about it. There is no such justification of the bias towards the near."

This can be answered. We can first point out that we are still biased towards the future even when, like the past, it cannot be affected. Suppose that we are in prison, and will be tortured later today. In such cases, when we believe that our future suffering is inevitable, our attitude towards it does not fall into line with our attitude towards past suffering. We would not think, "Since the torture is inevitable, that is equivalent to its being already in the past." We are greatly relieved when such inevitable pains are in the past. In such cases the bias towards the future cannot be justified by an appeal to the direction of causation. Our ground for concern about such future pains is not that, unlike past pains, we can affect them. We know that we *cannot* affect them. We are concerned about these future pains simply because they are not yet in the past.

The S-Theorist might reply: "Such a justification need not hold in every case. When we are discussing a general attitude, we must be content with a general truth. Such attitudes cannot be 'fine-tuned.' Whether events are in the future in *most* cases corresponds to whether or not we can affect them. This is enough to justify the bias towards the future. If we lacked this bias, we would be as much concerned about past pains and pleasures, which we cannot affect. This would distract our attention from future pains and pleasures, which we can affect. Because we would be distracted in this way, we would be less successful in our attempts to get future pleasures and avoid future pains. This would be worse for us."

We could answer: "If this is true, there is another similar truth. If we were as much concerned about pains and pleasures in our *further* future, this would distract our attention from pains and pleasures in the nearer future. If we want to reduce our future suffering, we ought to pay more attention to possible pains in the nearer future, since we have less time in which to avoid or reduce these pains. A similar claim applies to future pleasures. Our need to affect the nearer future is more urgent. If your claim justifies the bias towards the future, this claim justifies the bias towards the near."

We could add: "We care more about the near future even in the special cases in which we cannot affect it. But these cases correspond to the special cases in which we cannot affect the future. Both these attitudes to time roughly correspond to these facts about causation. Your claims therefore cannot show that only one of these attitudes is defensible."

The S-Theorist might say: "You ignore one difference. We can act directly on the bias towards the near. If we are due to have one hour's pain later today, we may be able to postpone this pain, at the cost of making it worse. We may, like Proximus, exchange this pain for ten hours' pain next year. But we cannot exchange this pain for ten hours' pain yesterday. We cannot put future pains into the past, at the cost of making them worse. The important difference is this. Since we can affect both the near and the distant future, our bias towards the near often makes us act against our own interests. This bias is bad for us. In contrast, since we cannot affect the past, our bias towards the future never makes us act against our interests. This second bias is not bad for us. That is why only the second bias is defensible."

To this there are three replies: (1) This argument has a false premise. The fact that an attitude is bad for us does not show it to be irrational. It can at most show that we should try to change this attitude. If someone whom I love is killed, I should perhaps try, after a time, to reduce my grief. But this does not show that I have no reason to grieve. Grief is not irrational simply because it brings unhappiness. To the claim "Your sorrow is fruitless," Hume replied, "Very true, and for that very reason I am sorry."[3]

(2) Even if (1) is denied, this argument fails. It assumes that what matters is whether something is bad for us. This begs the question. The S-Theorist is condemning the bias towards the near. If we have this bias, we care more about our nearer future; and what will be, on the whole, worse for us may be better for us in the nearer future. If our bias is defensible, we can therefore deny the assumption that what matters is whether something will be bad for us. Since this assumption can be denied if our bias is defensible, it cannot help to show that our bias is *not* defensible.

(3) It has not been shown that the bias towards the near *is* bad for us. Because we have a more urgent need to affect the nearer future, the bias towards the near is in some ways good for us. But let us suppose that this bias is, on balance, bad for us. *So is the bias towards the future.* As I shall explain later, it would be better for us if we did not care more about the future. The argument above has another false premise. It is not true that the bias towards the future is not bad for us.

The S-Theorist must condemn the bias towards the near. If his criticism appeals to temporal neutrality, he must also criticize the bias towards the future. By appealing to facts about causation, the S-Theorist tried to avoid this conclusion. But this attempt has failed.

In condemning the bias towards the near, the S-Theorist might say: "Since our need to affect the near is more urgent, the bias towards the near is quite natural. It is not surprising that

Evolution gives this bias to all animals. But, since we are rational, we can rise above, and critically review, what we inherit from Evolution. We can see that this bias cannot be rational. That some pain is in the nearer future cannot be a *reason* to care about it more. A mere difference in timing cannot have rational significance."[4]

If the S-Theorist makes this claim, he must make a similar claim about the bias towards the future. He might say: "Since we cannot affect the past, it is natural to care about it less. But this bias cannot be rational. This is clearest when we cannot affect the future. That some inevitable pain is in the future, rather than the past, cannot be a *reason* to care about it more. It is irrational to be relieved when it is in the past."

In My Past or Future Operations, I would prefer it to be true that I did suffer for several hours yesterday rather than that I shall suffer for one hour later today. This is not a preference on which I could act. But this is irrelevant to the question of whether this preference is irrational. The S-Theorist cannot claim that it is *not* irrational *because* I cannot act upon it. He could say, "What an absurd preference! You should be grateful that you cannot act upon it." And this is what he *must* say, if he keeps his claim that our concern for ourselves should be temporally neutral. If he condemns the bias towards the near because it cannot have rational significance *when* some pain is felt, he must condemn the bias towards the future. He must claim that it is irrational to be relieved when some pain is in the past. Most of us would find this hard to believe. If the S-Theorist insists that we should be temporally neutral, most of us would disagree.

Temporal Neutrality

The S-Theorist might change his position. He might condemn the bias towards the near, not on the general ground that the question "When?" cannot have rational significance, but on a more particular ground.

He might switch to the other extreme, and claim that temporal neutrality is inconceivable. He might claim that it is inconceivable that we lack the bias toward the future. If this was true, he could again criticize only one of these two attitudes. It cannot be irrational to have some attitude if it is not conceivable that we lack this attitude. But, unlike the bias towards the future, the bias towards the near is clearly something that we could lack. We could be equally concerned about all the parts of our future. Some people are. The S-Theorist could claim that this is the only rational pattern of concern.

Is it conceivable that we might lack the bias towards the future? Our attitudes to the past could not be just like our attitudes to the future. Some emotions or reactions presuppose beliefs about causation. Since we cannot affect the past, these emotions and reactions could not be backward-looking. Thus we could not form an intention to have done something yesterday, or be firmly resolved to make the best of what lies behind us.

Are there mental states which are essentially forward-looking, in a way which cannot be explained by the direction of causation? This is a large question, to which I need not give a complete answer. It will be enough to consider the most important mental states that are involved in our bias towards the future.

One of these is desire. Some of our language suggests that desires are essentially forward-looking. Compare "I want to go to Venice next winter" with "I want to have gone to Venice last winter." The second claim is obscure.

Our language is here misleading. Consider *My Temporally Neutral Desire*:

I learn that an old friend is now dying in some distant country. We parted in anger, for which I now blame myself. After learning that my friend is dying, I have a strong desire to ask her to forgive me. Since she cannot be reached by telephone, the best that I can do is to send an express letter, asking to be forgiven, and saying goodbye. A week later, I do not know whether my friend is still alive, or has got my letter. My strongest desire is that she gets my letter before she dies.

If desires are essentially forward-looking, I must be held to be in two states of mind: a conditional desire, and a conditional hope. I must be said to want my friend, if she is alive, to get the letter before she dies, and to hope, if she is dead, that she got the letter before she died. But this description, even if linguistically required, is misleading. To distinguish here two states of mind, the desire and the hope, is to subdivide what is in its nature a single state. My "hope" is in its nature and its strength just like my "desire." What I want is that my friend's getting of this letter precedes her death. Provided that these events occur, in this order, I am indifferent whether they are in the past or the future.

Even if it changes the concept, it is therefore best to say that we can have desires about the past. And it is not clear that this is a change. For example, I may want it to be true that, in my drunkenness last night, I did not disgrace myself. And I may want this to be true for its own sake, not because of its possible effects on my future. Similarly, after reading the letters of Keats or van Gogh, I may want it to be true that they knew how great their achievements were.

In these examples I do not know what the truth is. Suppose that I do know that I disgraced myself last night. Can I want it to be true that I did not? It would be more natural to call this a *wish*. But this distinction also seems unimportant. When I learn that I disgraced myself, my desire that I did not becomes a wish. But the wish may be no weaker than the desire.

It may change the concept of desire if we claim that we can want something to be true that we know is false. We need not decide whether this change in our concept would be an improvement. I am discussing the different question of whether we can have desires about the past. I have claimed that we can, even though some of our language suggests that we cannot. We can express such desires with other parts of our language. We can say, as I have done, that we want it to be true that some event did or did not happen.

It may be objected that desires are essentially tied to possible acts. This is like the claim that "ought" implies "can." On this view, we cannot have desires on which it would be impossible to act. From this general claim we could deduce the special claim that we cannot have desires about the past, since we cannot affect the past.[5]

This general claim is false. There are, of course, close connections between desires and acts. If we strongly want something to be true, we shall try to find out whether we can make it true. And "the primitive sign of wanting is trying to get."[6] But the desire here comes first. We do not have to know whether we could make something true before we can want it to be true.

We can admit one way in which desires are tied to acts. If people could not act they could not have desires. We could not have the concept of desire unless we also had the concept of an act. But we can have a *particular* desire without being able to act upon it. We can want something to be true even when we know that neither we nor anyone else could possibly have made it true. The Pythagoreans wanted the square root of two to be a rational number. It is logically impossible that this desire be fulfilled. Since we can have desires that even an omnipotent God could not fulfill, particular desires are not tied to possible acts. This removes this ground for denying that we can have desires about the past.

We can next consider the mental states that are most important in this discussion: looking forward to some future event, and its negative counterpart, painful or distressing anticipation. These two mental states are essentially future-directed. But this may be another superficial truth. Could there be comparable states directed towards the past?

It may be thought that we actually have such backward-looking states. The bias towards the future does not apply to many kinds of event, such as those that give us pride or shame. But though the knowledge of a past achievement may give us pleasure, this is not analogous to looking forward. We are discussing our attitude, not to the *fact* that our lives contain certain kinds of event, but to our *experience* at other times of living through these events. For simplicity, I have been discussing attitudes to experiences that are merely in themselves pleasant or painful. Do we in fact look backward to past pleasures in the way that we look forward to future pleasures?

Once again, there is a complication raised by memories. These can be in themselves pleasant or painful. We may enjoy remembering pleasures, and dislike remembering pains. But neither of these is strictly analogous to the pains and pleasures of anticipation. We therefore need to consider our attitude to past pains and pleasures about which we know, but of which we do not have painful or pleasant memories.

Consider *My Past Ordeals*:

Case One. I am unusually forgetful. I am asked, "Can you remember what happened to you during May ten years ago?" I find that I can remember nothing about that month. I am then told that, at the start of that month, I was found to have some illness which required four weeks of immediate and very painful treatment. Since this treatment was wholly successful, I have no grounds for fear about the future. When I am reminded of this fact, it arouses a faint memory, which is not in itself painful.

I have been reminded, to my surprise, that ten years ago I had a month of agony. All that I have now is a faint memory of this fact, and an ability to imagine how bad my agony must have been. When I am reminded of this past ordeal, would I be upset? Would I have what corresponds to painful anticipation? I would not. I would react to this reminder with *complete indifference.*

If I learnt that, ten years from now, I shall have a month of agony, I would *not* be indifferent. I would be distressed. But I would be in no way distressed if I was reminded that, ten years ago, I had such a month.

Since we are biased towards the near, it may help to consider

Case Two. I wake up, on what I believe to be the 1st of May. It is in fact the 1st of June. I have just had a similar month of very painful but wholly successful treatment. So that I should not have painful memories, I was caused to forget this whole month.

I learn that I have just had a month of agony. Here too, I would not regard this as bad news. More exactly, I would regret the fact that a month of my life had to be wasted in this way. I might be somewhat anxious about the claimed success of this treatment. And I might have some fear that, if the induced amnesia does not last, I shall later have painful memories of this treatment. But I would not be at all distressed about the fact that, during this month, I was in agony. I would regard this recent agony with complete indifference. In contrast, if I learnt that I was about to have such an ordeal, I would be very distressed.

It may be an objection to Case Two that it involves induced amnesia. I therefore add

Case Three. In my actual life, I have often suffered severe pain. I can remember these pains, but these memories are not themselves painful. The worst suffering that I can remember lasted for three days in 1979.

When I remind myself of these three very painful days, I am not distressed at all. In the imaginary Cases One and Two, I believe that I would regard my past ordeals with indifference. In my actual life, I do in fact regard my past suffering with complete indifference.

I believe that, in this respect, most other people are like me. Unless their memories are painful, they regard their past suffering with indifference. I know a few people whose reaction is different. These people claim that, even if they have no painful memories, they find knowledge of their past pains mildly distressing. But I know of no one who has what fully corresponds to the pains of anticipation.

We do not in fact have this attitude to our past pains. And we do not look backward to pleasures in the way that we look forward to them. Could there be such mental states? Could "looking backward" to some past event be, except for its temporal direction, just like looking forward?

We might say: "We look forward to some future event when thinking about this event gives us pleasure. Thinking about a past event could give us similar pleasure. And to the pains of anticipation there could be corresponding pains of retrospection."

It may be objected: "You understate what is involved in looking forward. It is not merely true that the thought of future pleasures gives us pleasure. We *anticipate* these pleasures. Similarly, we anticipate pains. *Anticipation* cannot have a backward-looking counterpart."

We might answer: "We may be unable to imagine what it would be like to have this counterpart. But this does not show that it could not be had. Those who are congenitally blind cannot imagine what it is like to see."

This reply may not meet this objection. If this is so, our claims can be revised. Even if looking backward could not be *just like* looking forward, it could be equally cheering, or in the case of pains equally distressing. This would involve a change in our attitudes. But this change *is* conceivable. We can clearly describe someone who, in this respect, is unlike us. When such a person is reminded that he once had a month of agony, he is as much distressed as when he learns that he will later have such a month. He is similarly neutral with respect to enjoyable events. When he is told that he will later have some period of great enjoyment, he is pleased to learn this. He greatly looks forward to this period. When he is reminded that he once had just such a period, he is equally pleased. I shall call this imagined man *Timeless*.

This man is very different from us. But his description is coherent. We can therefore reject the suggestion made above. It is conceivable that we might lack the bias towards the future. Even if we could not be wholly temporally neutral, we could have been like Timeless.

Why We Should Not Be Biased Towards the Future

Our bias towards the future is bad for us. It would be better for us if we were like Timeless. We would lose in certain ways. Thus we should not be relieved when bad things were in the past. But we should also gain. We should not be sad when good things were in the past.

The gains would outweigh the losses. One reason would be this. When we look backward, we could afford to be selective. We ought to remember some of the bad events in our lives, when this would help us to avoid repetitions. But we could allow ourselves to forget most of the bad things that have happened, while preserving by rehearsing all of our memories of the good things. It would be bad for us if we were so selective when we are looking forward. Unless we think of all the bad things that are at all likely to happen, we lose our chance of preventing them. Since we ought not to be selective when looking forward, but could afford to be when looking backward, the latter would be, on the whole, more enjoyable.[7]

There would be other, greater gains. One would be in our attitude to aging and to death. Let us first consider the argument with which Epicurus claimed that our future non-existence cannot be something to regret. We do not regret our past non-existence. Since this is so, why should we regret our future non-existence? If we regard one with equanimity, should we not extend this attitude to the other?

Some claim that this argument fails because, while we might live longer, we could not have been born earlier. This is not a good objection. When they learnt that the square root of two was not a rational number, the Pythagoreans regretted this. We can regret truths even when it is logically impossible that these truths be false.

Epicurus's argument fails for a different reason: we are biased towards the future. Because we have this bias, the bare knowledge that we once suffered may not now disturb us. But our equanimity does not show that our past suffering was not bad. The same could be true of our past non-existence. Epicurus's argument therefore has force only for those people who both lack the bias towards the future, and do not regret their past non-existence. Since there are no such people, the argument has force for no one.

Though the argument fails, it may provide some consolation. If we are afraid of death, the argument shows that the object of our dread is not *our non-existence*. It is only our *future* non-existence. That we can think serenely of our past non-existence does not show that it is not something to regret. But since we do not in fact view with dread our past non-existence, we may be able to use this fact to reduce our dread, or depression, when we think about our inevitable deaths. If we often think about, and view serenely, the blackness behind us, some of this serenity may be transferred to our view of the blackness before us.

Let us now suppose that we lack the bias towards the future. We are like Timeless. We should then greatly gain in our attitude to aging and to death. As our life passes, we should have less and less to look forward to, but more and more to look backward to. This effect will be clearer if we imagine another difference. Suppose that our lives began, not with birth and childhood, but as Adam's did. Suppose that, though we are adults, and have adult knowledge and abilities, we have only just started to exist. We lack the bias towards the future. Should we be greatly troubled by the thought that yesterday we did not exist?

This depends on what is wrong with non-existence. Some think it in itself bad. But the more plausible view is that its only fault is what it causes us to lose. Suppose we take this view. We may then think it a ground for regret that our life is finite, bounded at both ends by non-existence. But, if we had just started to exist, we would not think that something bad was just behind us. Our ground for regret would merely be that we had missed much that would have been good. Suppose that I could now be much as I actually am, even though I had been born as one of the privileged few around 1700. I would then greatly regret that I was in fact born in 1942. I would far prefer to have lived through the previous two and a half centuries, having had among my friends Hume, Byron, Chekhov, Nietzsche, and Sidgwick.

In my imagined case, we are not biased towards the future, and we have just started to exist. Though we would regret the fact that we had not existed earlier, we would not be greatly troubled by the thought that only yesterday we did not exist. We would not regard this fact with the kind of dread or grief with which most actual people would regard the sudden prospect of death tomorrow. We would not have such dread or grief because, though we would have nothing good to look backward to, we would have our whole lives to look forward to.

Now suppose that our lives have nearly passed. We shall die tomorrow. If we were not biased towards the future, our reaction should mirror the one that I have just described. We should not be greatly troubled by the thought that we shall soon cease to exist, for though we now have nothing to look forward to, we have our whole lives to look backward to.

It may be objected: "You can look backward now. But once you are dead you won't be able to look backward. And you will be dead tomorrow. So you ought to be greatly troubled." We could answer: "Why? It is true that after we cease to exist we shall never be able to enjoy looking backward to our lives. We now have nothing at all to look forward to, not even the pleasures of looking backward. But it was equally true that, before we began to exist, we could not enjoy looking forward to our lives. Just after we began to exist, we had nothing at all to look backward to, not even the pleasures of looking forward. But that was then no reason to be greatly troubled, since we could then look forward to our whole lives. Since we can now look backward to our whole lives, why should the parallel fact—that we have nothing to look forward to—give us reason to be greatly troubled?"

This reasoning ignores those emotions which are essentially future-directed. It would not apply to those people for whom the joy in looking forward comes from making plans, or savouring alternatives. But the reasoning seems to be correct when applied to more passive types, those who take life's pleasures as they come. And, since this is partly true of us, this reasoning shows that we would be happier if we lacked the bias towards the future. We would be much less depressed by aging and the approach of death. If we were like Timeless, being at the end of our lives would be more like being at the beginning. At any point within our lives we could enjoy looking either backward or forward to our whole lives.

I have claimed that, if we lacked the bias towards the future, this would be better for us. This matches the plausible claim that it would be better for us if we lacked the bias towards the near. There is no ground here for criticizing only the latter bias. Both these attitudes to time are, on the whole, bad for us.

Since I believe that this attitude is bad for us, I believe that we ought not to be biased towards the future. This belief does not beg the question about the rationality of this bias. On any plausible moral view, it would be better if we were all happier. This is the sense in which, if we could, we ought not to be biased towards the future. In giving us this bias, Evolution denies us the best attitude to death.

Time's Passage

Return to my main question. Are these attitudes to time irrational? Most of us believe that the bias towards the future is not irrational. We are inclined to believe that it would be irrational to *lack* this bias. Thus we may be wholly unconvinced by the reasoning I gave in the case just imagined, where we are temporally neutral and shall die tomorrow. We can describe someone who does not much mind the prospect of death tomorrow, because he can now look backward to his whole life. But this attitude, though describable, may seem crazy, or to involve an absurd mistake.

It will help to take a simpler case, not involving non-existence and our attitudes to a whole life. This can be a variant of an earlier example, involving our imagined temporally neutral man. Consider *How Timeless Greets Good News*:

Case One. Timeless is in hospital for a painful operation that will be followed by induced amnesia. He wakes up, with no particular memories of the previous day. He asks his nurse when and for how long he will have to endure this painful operation. As before, the nurse knows the facts about two patients, but is unsure which he is. In either case, however, his operation needed to be unusually long, lasting a full ten hours. The nurse knows that one of the following is true. Either he did suffer yesterday for ten hours, or he will suffer later today for ten hours.

Timeless is plunged in gloom. He had hoped for a shorter operation.

When the nurse returns, she exclaims "Good News! You are the one who suffered yesterday."

Timeless is just as glum. "Why is that good news?" he asks. "My ordeal is just as painful, and just as long. And it is just as much a part of my life. Why should it make a difference to me now that my ordeal is in the past?"

The induced amnesia may be an objection to this case. I therefore add:

Case Two. Timeless has this operation, and has no amnesia. We visit him on the day before his ordeal, and on the day after. On the day after, Timeless is just as glum. "Why should I be relieved?" he asks. "Why is it better that my ordeal is in the past?"

Is Timeless making a mistake? Ought he to be relieved? Most of us would answer Yes. But it is hard to explain why, without begging the question. We might say, "If the ordeal was in his future, he would still have to undergo it. Since it is in his past, it is over and done with." This is not a further explanation of why Timeless is irrational. That he "still" has to undergo the pain merely repeats that it is in his future.

We might appeal here to what is called *time's passage*, or the *objectivity of temporal becoming*. We might say: "If his pain is in the future, it will get closer and closer until he is actually suffering the pain. But, if his pain is in the past, it will only get further and further away." Such remarks seem to express a deep truth. But this truth is curiously elusive. What is meant by the phrase "it will get closer and closer"? Does this not merely mean that, at future moments, the future pain will be closer to what will then be the present moment? But at past moments a past pain was closer to what was then the present moment. Where is the asymmetry?

It is natural, in reply, to use a certain metaphor: that of motion through time. We might say that we are moving through time into the future, or that future events are moving through time into the present, or that presentness, or the scope of "now," is moving into the future. "Now" moves down the sequence of historical events, "like a spot-light moving down a line of chorus-girls."

It may help to compare "now" with "here." For those who deny time's passage, or the objectivity of temporal becoming, "here" and "now" are strictly analogous. They are both relative to the thoughts, or utterances, of a particular thinker. "Here" refers to the place where this thinker is at some time, and "now" refers to the time at which some particular thought, one involving the concept "now," is thought. Both words could be replaced by "this," as in the announcer's jargon "at this place and time."[8]

Those who believe in time's passage would reject this analogy. They would admit that, in a Universe containing no thinkers, the concept "here" would lack application. But they claim that, even in such a Universe, it would still be true that certain things are happening *now*, and then be true that other things are happening *now*, and so on. Even in a lifeless Universe, the scope of "now" would still move through time from the past into the future.

The metaphor of motion through time may be indefensible. How fast do we move through time? We may not be satisfied with the only possible reply, "At a rate of one second per second." We may claim that, *if* either we or "now" can move through time, it must make sense for this motion to be faster or slower, but that this makes no sense.

The critics of the metaphor may be justified. But this may not show that there is no such thing as time's passage, or the objectivity of temporal becoming. Perhaps this is a categorical truth, at so deep a level that we should not expect that it could be explained, either by metaphors or in other terms.[9]

I shall not try to decide where, in this debate, the truth lies. I shall therefore consider both alternatives. Suppose first that, as some philosophers and physicists believe, time's passage is an illusion. If this is so, temporal neutrality cannot be irrational. In defending the Self-interest Theory, the S-Theorist must condemn the bias towards the near. If temporal neutrality cannot be irrational, the S-Theorist might return to his earlier view that such neutrality is rationally required. He must then claim that, just as it is irrational to be relieved when some unavoidable pain has been postponed, it is irrational to be relieved when it is in the past. We shall find this hard to believe.

Suppose, next, that we would be right to believe in time's passage, or the objectivity of temporal becoming. The S-Theorist might then retain his later view and appeal to time's passage. He must still condemn the bias towards the near. He might claim: "While you have excellent reasons to care less about the pains of others, you cannot rationally care less about pains of yours which lie further in the future. Mere distance from the present moment cannot have rational significance." The S-Theorist might now support this claim in a different way. He might abandon the appeal to temporal neutrality—the claim that mere timing cannot have rational significance. He might instead discriminate between different kinds of temporal relation.

We should remember here that most of us have a third attitude to time: the bias towards the present. If mere timing cannot have rational significance, it cannot be rational to care more about present pains. That I am *now* in agony cannot be a ground for being more concerned now about this agony. This may seem absurd. The requirement of temporal neutrality may seem least plausible when applied to the bias towards the present. How can it be irrational to mind my agony more while I am suffering the agony? Such a claim seems to undermine the whole structure of concern. Pain matters only because of what it feels like when we are *now* in pain. We care about future pains only because, in the future, they will be *present* pains. If future pains behaved like Alice's *Jam Tomorrow*, and remained perpetually future, they would not matter at all.[10]

The S-Theorist might now claim: "Of our three attitudes to time, one is irrational, but the other two are rationally required. We *must* care more about present pains, and we *cannot* rationally care about past pains, but we must *not* care less about pains that are in the further rather than the nearer future." This new view lacks the appeal of generality. There was an appealing simplicity in the claim that mere differences in timing—mere answers to the question "When?"—cannot have rational significance. But this new view, though less simple, may still be justified. The S-Theorist might claim that, on reflection, it is intuitively plausible. He might claim: "When we compare presentness, pastness, and distance in the future, it is clear that the first two are quite unlike the third. The first two have obvious rational significance, justifying a difference in our concern. But the third is obviously trivial."

These intuitions are not universal. Of those who are relieved when unavoidable bad events have been postponed, many do not believe that this relief is irrational. Or consider another effect of the bias towards the near: the mounting excitement that we feel as some good event approaches the present—as in the moment in the theater when the house-lights dim. This excitement would be claimed by many not to be irrational.

The S-Theorist might say: "Those who have these intuitions have not sufficiently considered the question. Those who *have* considered the question, such as philosophers, generally agree that it is irrational to care more about the nearer future."

As I have said, the agreement of philosophers may not justify their view. The Self-interest Theory has long been dominant. Since S has been taught for more than two millenia, we must expect to find some echo in our intuitions. S cannot be justified simply by an appeal to intuitions that its teaching may have produced.

If time's passage is not an illusion, the S-Theorist need not appeal only to our intuitions. He can claim that time's passage justifies the bias towards the future. If he is asked to explain why, he may find this difficult. There is, for instance, no suggestion that the past is unreal. It would be easy to see why, if the past was not real, past pains would not matter. It is not so obvious why, because time passes, past pains do not matter.

The S-Theorist might claim: "Suppose we allow the metaphor that the scope of 'now' moves into the future. This explains why, of the three attitudes to time, one is irrational, and the other two are rationally required. Pains matter only because of what they are like when they are in the present, or under the scope of 'now.' This is why we must care more about our pains when we are *now* in pain. 'Now' moves into the future. This is why past pains do not matter. Once pains are past, they will only move away from the scope of 'now.' Things are different with nearness in the future. Time's passage does not justify caring more about the near future since, however distant future pains are, they *will* come within the scope of 'now.'"

It is not clear that these are good arguments. The last, in particular, may beg the question. But the S-Theorist might instead claim that, in appealing to time's passage, we do not need arguments. He might claim that there is again no need for further explanation. It may be another fundamental truth that, since time passes, past suffering simply cannot matter—cannot be the object of rational concern. Timeless was not relieved to learn that his ordeal was in the past. This may not involve the kind of mistake that can be explained. The mistake may be so gross that it is beyond the reach of argument.

An Asymmetry

Perhaps, by abandoning the appeal to temporal neutrality, and instead appealing to time's passage, the Self-interest Theorist has strengthened his position. But we should consider one last kind of case. I call these the *Past or Future Suffering of Those We Love*:

Case One. I am an exile from some country, where I have left my widowed mother. Though I am deeply concerned about her, I very seldom get news. I have known for some time that she is fatally ill, and cannot live long. I am now told something new. My mother's illness has become very painful, in a way that drugs cannot relieve. For the next few months, before she dies, she faces a terrible ordeal. That she will soon die I already knew. But I am deeply distressed to learn of the suffering that she must endure.
A day later I am told that I had been partly misinformed. The facts were right, but not the timing. My mother did have many months of suffering, but she is now dead.

Ought I now to be greatly relieved? I had thought that my mother's ordeal was in the future. But it was in the past. According to the S-Theorist's new view, past pains simply do not matter. Learning about my mother's suffering gives me now *no* reason to be distressed. It is now as if she had died painlessly. If I am still distressed, I am like Timeless. I am making the mistake so gross that it is beyond the reach of argument.

This last example may shake the S-Theorist. He may find it hard to believe that my reaction is irrational. He might say: "How can it possibly matter to you whether your mother had those months of suffering? Even if she did, her suffering *is in the past*. This is not bad news at all." But, when applied to my concern for someone else, these remarks seem less convincing.

The S-Theorist might instead try to modify his view. He might say: "I should not have claimed that past pains simply do not matter. What is implied by time's passage is that they matter *less*." But this revision is indefensible. Once a pain is past, it is completely past. Being in the past is not a matter of degree. It is not plausible to claim that, since time passes, what is rational is to have *some* concern about past pain, but *less* than about future pain. And what should be claimed about My Past Ordeals? In these cases I regard my past suffering with complete indifference. Is this irrational? Ought I to be somewhat distressed, though less than I am about my future suffering? An appeal to time's passage cannot plausibly support this claim. And it is hard to believe that, in these cases, my indifference is irrational.

My examples reveal a surprising asymmetry in our concern about our own and other people's pasts. I would not be distressed at all if I was reminded that I myself once had to endure several months of suffering. But I would be greatly distressed if I learnt that, before she died, my mother had to endure such an ordeal.

This asymmetry is reduced in:

Case Two: Like Case One except that, though my mother suffered for several months, she is still alive, and is now in no pain.

I would be less distressed here to learn about my mother's past suffering. This difference can be explained. If my mother is like me, she now views with indifference her past ordeal. (We can suppose that her memories of this ordeal are not in themselves painful.) If there is an asymmetry in our concern about our own and other people's past suffering, it would not be surprising if this asymmetry was clearest in cases where the others were now dead. If my mother is still alive, my present attitude will naturally be affected by what I can assume to be her present attitude. Since I can assume that *she* now views with indifference her past suffering, this might reduce my concern about this suffering. But, if my mother is now dead, she does not now view with indifference her past suffering. Since my concern about her past suffering cannot be affected by her present attitude, this is when my concern shows itself in its purest form.

Does it make a difference whether her suffering lasted until her death? Consider:

Case Three. I learn that my mother suffered for several months, but that, before she died, she had a month free from pain. There was, within her life, a period in which her suffering was in the past, and thus no longer mattered to her.

If this is what I learn, would this make much difference to my concern? I believe that it would, at most, make a little difference. I would be deeply distressed to learn that my mother suffered for those months, even if I also knew that she had a month in which that suffering was in the past. What distresses me is not just to learn of my mother's *painful death*. If it was only this that distressed me, and I was not distressed to learn that she had to endure much suffering some months before she died, my reaction would be so special that it could perhaps be ignored. But my concern about the pasts of those whom I love, and who are now dead, is not merely a concern that they did not have painful deaths. I would be distressed to learn that, at any time within their lives, they had months of suffering of which I had not previously known. I believe that most people are, in this respect, like me.

Consider finally:

Case Four. The same as Case Three, except that I do not learn about my mother's suffering, since I knew about it at the time.

Even though I have always had this knowledge, I would continue to be saddened by the thought that, in my mother's life, there were several months of suffering. Once again, I believe that a similar claim applies to most other people. There is still a striking asymmetry with our attitude to our own past suffering, which most of us view with something close to indifference.

It may be objected: "If we draw distinctions, this asymmetry disappears. You ask whether, when it is in the past, suffering *matters*. This runs together different questions. It is one question whether you ought to *feel sympathy*, and another question whether you ought to *be concerned*. Whether suffering is in the past makes a difference, not to sympathy, but only to concern. We feel sympathy only for others. *This* is why you view your past suffering with indifference. You cannot sympathize with yourself. When you learn about your mother's past suffering, you do and ought to feel sympathy. But it would be irrational to be *concerned* about this past suffering, just as it would be irrational to be concerned about your own past suffering." [11]

These claims do not, I believe, remove the asymmetry. At the start of Case One, I am told that my mother will suffer for sev-

eral months before she dies. A day later this message is cor-
rected: she did suffer for several months before she died. On the
claims just stated, I should be greatly concerned on the earlier
day, when I believe that my mother's suffering will be in the
future. When I learn that it was in the past, I should cease to be
concerned, though I should still feel sympathy. When I cease to
have any concern, this should presumably greatly reduce my
distress, and also change its quality. But I am sure that, if this
imagined case occurred, my attitude would not be changed in
these two ways. I might be somewhat less distressed, but this
difference would not be great. Nor would my distress change its
quality.

Whether some event is in the past would and should affect
those of my emotions that are tied to possible acts. But, in these
cases, when I think that my mother's suffering is in the future,
there is nothing useful that I could do. I cannot even send her a
message. I cannot therefore have the kind of concern that is
active, searching for ways in which I can help the person for
whom I am concerned. In these cases, my concern can only be
passive. It can only be sadness and distress, with no impulse to
search for possible remedies. Because my distress would take
this form, its quality would not change when I learn that my
mother's suffering is in the past.

I admit that, when I learn this fact, I might be somewhat less
distressed. Just as my concern might be affected by my mother's
attitude, if she were alive, it might also be affected by my attitude to my own past suffering. This effect may partly remove
the asymmetry. In my concern about my own suffering, it makes
all the difference whether this suffering is in the future or the
past. It would not be surprising if this fact about my attitudes
affected my concern about the past suffering of those I love.
Since my concern about their past suffering cannot escape being
affected by my concern about my own past suffering, my concern about the sufferings of others can never take a wholly pure
or undistorted form. And, as I have claimed, when I learnt that
my mother's suffering was in the past, my concern would not be
much reduced.

On the objection given above, I have no concern about my
own past suffering because one cannot *sympathize* with oneself.
This claim does nothing to remove the asymmetry. It is merely a

redescription. It concedes that there *is* this difference between our attitudes to past suffering in our own lives and in the lives of those we loved.

This asymmetry makes it harder to defend the Self-interest Theory. An S-Theorist cannot plausibly claim that this asymmetry is rationally required. In particular, he cannot plausibly appeal here to time's passage. If time's passage justifies my complete indifference to my own past suffering, or even makes this indifference a rational requirement, the S-Theorist must claim the same about my concern for those I love. It is as much true, in the imagined case of my dead mother, that her suffering is in the past.

What should the S-Theorist claim about our attitudes to past suffering? He might claim: "There is not, here, one attitude that is uniquely rational. If you view your own past suffering with complete indifference, this is not irrational. But it would also not be irrational if knowledge of your own past suffering caused you great distress. Similarly, it would not be irrational if you were greatly distressed by the knowledge of your mother's past suffering. But it would also not be irrational if you viewed her suffering with complete indifference."

If the S-Theorist admits as not irrational this range of different attitudes towards the past, how can he defend his claim that, in our concern about the future, we ought to be temporally neutral? He must still make this claim. But if, in the case of past suffering, it would not be irrational either to care just as much, or to care less, or not to care at all, why in the case of future suffering is there only one attitude which is rational? Though there is no outright inconsistency, it is hard to believe a view which is so permissive in its claims about one range of attitudes to time, but so strict in its claim about another range.

CHAPTER TWELVE

BORIS: What is it like being dead?
VLADIMIR MAXIMOVICH: It's like—how can I
explain it? You know the boiled chicken at Tresky's
Restaurant?
BORIS: Yeah?
VLADIMIR MAXIMOVICH: It's worse.
—Woody Allen, *Love and Death*

Why Is Death Bad?

Anthony L. Brueckner and
John Martin Fischer

It seems that, whereas a person's death need not be a bad thing for him, it *can* be. In some circumstances, death is not a "bad thing" or an "evil" for a person. For instance, if a person has a terminal and very painful disease, he might rationally regard his own death as a good thing for him, or at least, he may regard it as something whose prospective occurrence should not be regretted. But the attitude of a "normal" and healthy human being—adult or child—toward the prospect of his death is different; it is *not* unreasonable in certain cases to regard one's own death as a bad thing for oneself.[1] If this is so, then the question arises as to *why* death is bad, in those cases in which it is bad.

If one believes in an afterlife, one could explain how death (conceived of roughly as the cessation of bodily functioning) can be bad insofar as it can involve eternal torment—an indefinitely long sequence of (highly) unpleasant experiences. Of course, on this sort of account, death *need not* be bad, even for a normal and healthy human being, since he may experience eternal bliss in the afterlife. If there is an afterlife, and for some it includes unpleasant experiences, then this would explain how death can be a bad thing, but it is controversial whether there is an afterlife. Since it is quite possible to deny the controversial assumption that there is an afterlife and yet regard death as a bad thing,

Reprinted by permission from *Philosophical Studies* 50 (1986): 213–23. We would like to thank Phillip Bricker for helping us to arrive at our explanation of why death is bad.

it would be desirable to produce an explanation of death's badness which does not presuppose that there are experiences after death. Many have thought that such an explanation can be given.

If death can be a bad thing for a person, though not in virtue of including unpleasant experiences of that person, then death is a bad thing for a person in a way that is different from the way in which, say, *pain* is a bad thing for a person. That is, some things which are bad (or evil) for a person (such as pain) are "experienced as bad by the person," whereas other things that are bad for a person (such as death) are not (ever) experienced as bad by the person.[2] Death, then, is assimilated to such bads as betrayal by a friend behind one's back, which, though never experienced as bad (one never finds out and suffers no bad consequences), are nevertheless bad for a person.[3]

Let us suppose that some things which are never experienced as bad by a person are nevertheless bad for the person. Death could then be an *experiential blank* and still be a bad thing for an individual. And one plausible explanation of why this is so is that death (though an experiential blank) is *deprivation* of the good things of life. That is, when life is, on balance, good, then death is bad insofar as it robs one of this good: if one had died later than one actually did, then one would have had more of the good things of life. This is the sort of explanation of death's badness that is adopted by Thomas Nagel.[4]

But a problem emerges. We intuitively think that it is appropriate to have *asymmetric* attitudes toward prenatal nonexistence and death. We think that it is reasonable to regard death as a bad thing in a way in which prenatal nonexistence is not. If death involves bad experiences in an afterlife, then this asymmetry could be explained. But we are assuming here that death's badness is *not* experienced as bad by the individual who dies. If this is so, how can we explain the intuitive asymmetry between prenatal and posthumous nonexistence? Both periods are, after all, experiential blanks. And it seems that prenatal nonexistence constitutes a deprivation in a sense analogous to that in which death is a deprivation: if a person had been born earlier than he actually was born, then he would have had more of the good things in life. (When it is supposed that one is born earlier here, we hold fixed the date of one's death. Similarly, when it is supposed above that one dies later, we hold fixed the date of one's birth.) Being born at the time at which one was born (rather than earlier) is a deprivation in the same sense as dying at the time when one dies (rather than later). Both Epicurus and Lucretius argued that our ordinary asymmetric attitudes are irrational, and since we do not regret prenatal nonexistence, we ought not regard death as a bad thing. If death is a bad insofar as it is a deprivation, the challenge posed by Epicurus and Lucretius is pressing: why should we treat prenatal and posthumous non-existence asymmetrically?

One way to respond to the challenge (and thus defend the Nagelian explanation of death's badness) is to say that, whereas one could (logically) have lived longer, it is logically impossible that one should have been born much earlier. Further, the claim is that it is irrational (or impossible) to regret that a proposition which is necessarily false is not true.[5] This response is un-satisfying. It is not clear that it is logically impossible that an individual should have been born substantially earlier than he actually was. It is not at all clear, for instance, that Socrates—the very same Socrates—could not (logically) have come into being ten years earlier than he in fact did. Why exactly should (roughly) the actual time of one's birth be an essential property of a person? Given that the essentiality of the actual time of birth is a *controversial* metaphysical claim, it is unsatisfying to use it as part of an explanation of the intuitive asymmetry.[6] The expla-nation will not be acceptable to anyone who denies the assump-tion.[7] If it is at least logically possible that one should have been born much earlier (and no reason has been offered to rule this out), then we still need to develop a response to the challenge raised by Epicurus and Lucretius (insofar as we cling to the ex-planation of death's badness in terms of deprivation).

Recently, Derek Parfit has suggested another response.[8] His position could be put as follows. We have a (not irrational) bias toward the future to the extent that there are cases where we are indifferent toward (or care substantially less about) our own past suffering but *not* indifferent toward our own future suffering. Since there are such cases, and the attitudes therein seem ra-tional, the general principle that it is always rational to have symmetric attitudes toward (comparable) past and future bads is false, and so it might be true that it is not irrational to have asymmetric attitudes toward our own past and future nonexistence (where such periods of nonexistence are taken to be *bads*). Thus, death could be considered a bad thing for us, and yet we need not assume symmetric attitudes toward death and prenatal nonexistence.

Consider Parfit's example:

I am in some hospital, to have some kind of surgery. Since this is completely safe, and always successful, I have no fears about the effects. The surgery may be brief, or it may instead take a long time. Because I have to co-operate with the surgeon, I cannot have anaesthetics. I have had this surgery once before, and I can remember how painful it is. Under a new policy, because the operation is so painful, patients are now afterwards made to forget it. Some drug removes their memories of the last few hours.

I have just woken up. I cannot remember going to sleep. I ask my nurse if it has been decided when my operation is to be, and how long it must take. She says that she knows the facts about both me and another patient, but that she cannot remember which facts apply to whom. She can tell me only that the following is true. I may be the patient who had his operation yesterday. In that case, my operation was the longest ever performed, lasting ten hours. I may instead be the patient who is to have a short operation later today. It is either true that I did suffer for ten hours, or true that I shall suffer for one hour.

I ask the nurse to find out which is true. While she is away, it is clear to me which I prefer to be true. If I learn that the first is true, I shall be greatly relieved.[9]

Parfit's claim is that it seems to be a deep-seated feature of us that we regard our own past and future sufferings asymmetrically. He does not explicitly defend the rationality of this sort of asymmetry, but he has pointed to a class of examples involving bads *other than death* in which it does not appear obviously unreasonable to hold asymmetric attitudes.[10]

Let us grant, for the sake of argument, that Parfit is correct about his example. The problem is that it cannot be extended to the case of death. The reason is that Parfit's case involves a bad for a person that is *experienced as bad by the person*. One's own pain is perhaps paradigmatic of such bads. But death is not a bad of this kind; indeed, the entire problem of justifying our intuitive asymmetric attitudes arises precisely because death is a bad for a person that is *not* experienced as bad by the person. Further, it seems that it is plausible to suppose that Parfit's conclusion will *only* apply to cases involving bads experienced as bad by the person. Cases that are structurally similar to Parfit's except involving bads *not* experienced as bad by the person yield *symmetric* attitudes.

Suppose, for instance, that you know that either some friends of yours have betrayed you behind your back nine times in the past or some friend will betray you behind your back once in the future. Here, it seems that you should prefer the one betrayal in the future (given that the betrayals are comparable, etc.). It also appears that, given a choice between being mocked once behind your back in the past and being similarly treated once in the future, you should be *indifferent*. (Of course, we assume here that you know that you can have no effect on the future events.)[11] These cases suggest that Parfit's point only applies to the class of bads experienced as bad by the person, and *not* to the class of bads (like death) that are *not* experienced as bad by the person.

Note that there are two different kinds of cases within the class of things that a particular person might reasonably regret (or wish would not happen or take to be bad), but that he himself does not experience as bad. One kind contains things that no person experiences as bad (such as death). Another kind contains things that are experienced as bad by *another* person (such as another's pain). If it is reasonable to take temporally symmetric attitudes toward regrettable things that we do not experience as bad and that *no one* experiences as bad, then it should not be surprising that we take temporally symmetric attitudes toward regrettable things that are experienced as bad *by others*. And Parfit has produced just such an example:

I am an exile from some country, where I have left my widowed mother. Though I am deeply concerned about her, I very seldom get news. I have known for some time that she is fatally ill, and cannot live long. I am now told something new. My mother's illness has become very painful, in a way that drugs cannot relieve. For the next few months, before she dies, she faces a terrible ordeal. That she will soon die I already knew. But I am deeply distressed to learn of the suffering that she must endure.

A day later I am told that I had been partly misinformed. The facts were right, but not the timing. My mother did have many months of suffering, but she is now dead.[12]

Parfit claims, about this example, that the new piece of information—that my mother's suffering is in the past—should *not* have a crucial impact on my attitude. Concerning the suffering of others it is rational to have temporally symmetric attitudes. This is precisely what one should expect in the light of the foregoing discussion of the appropriateness of temporally symmetric attitudes toward certain bads not experienced as bad by the person—those not experienced by *anyone*. The difference between our asymmetric attitudes toward another's past and future suffering and our asymmetric attitudes toward our own past and future suffering is a special case of the difference between our attitudes toward bads not experienced by us and bads experienced by us. If this is correct, it is appropriate to have temporally symmetric attitudes toward the class of regrettable things experienced by others, even if it is appropriate to have temporally asymmetric attitudes toward the class of regrettable things experienced by us.[13] Thus Parfit's own example highlights the inadequacy of the present response to the challenge posed by Epicurus and Lucretius, viz. the response suggested by Parfit's examples of temporally asymmetric attitudes toward experienced bads.

It might seem appealing to suggest that what makes death a bad thing for a person is that it is the deprivation of good things *already had* by the person. On this account, the asymmetry between our attitudes toward prenatal and posthumous nonexistence is due to the fact that the time before our birth cannot be conceived as a deprivation of good things we have *already had*, whereas the time after our death clearly can be so conceived. But why exactly should we care especially about the lack of good things we already have had, in comparison with the lack of good things we could have had, had we been born earlier?

The plausibility of the suggestion may come from a psychological truth which says that, in general, if a person has experienced a good thing and then been deprived of it, he tends to lament its absence (to "miss it") in a way in which a person who has never experienced the good *does not*. If a person has regularly drunk fine wines with dinner, he regrets the lack of a fine wine at tonight's dinner more than someone who has never had a fine wine with dinner.

But why would one regret the absence of something good to which one has grown accustomed? Presumably, because one tends to be *frustrated* by the lack of such goods—their absence causes *unpleasant experiences*. When a person accustomed to fine wines must do without, he is likely to have unpleasant experiences caused by the (partially involuntary) comparison of his present quite ordinary wine with his past delightful wines. In general, it *is* true that, when one is accustomed to a good thing, its absence causes unpleasant experiences and is therefore especially regrettable.

But clearly this principle is not applicable to death, since death deprives a person of goods *without* causing *any* experiences at all (according to our supposition). The psychological principle may apply to bads that are experienced as bad by a person (or that *cause* unpleasant experiences had by the person), but it does not apply to death, since it is *not* such a bad. So this explanation of our asymmetric attitudes suffers from the same problem as the above strategy. Suppose, on the other hand, that we do not appeal to the psychological principle and instead conceive of death as a bad that is *not* experienced. Then insofar as it is held that in regretting the prospect of death we regret the future deprivation of goods we have already had, it would be equally reasonable to regret the prenatal deprivation of such goods, goods that, we *now* know, could have graced our life had it begun earlier.

If death is taken to be a bad thing for a person, and it is appropriate to take symmetric attitudes toward past and future bads that are not experienced as bad by the person, then either we ought radically to revise our attitudes toward prenatal nonexistence, or we have not explained why death is a bad thing for a person. In *Annie Hall*, Woody Allen says, "We have two complaints about life. First, life is terrible. And second, life is too short." If life is terrible, it is—in the typical case—because of bad experiences. But if life is too short, why?

Imagine that you are in some hospital to test a drug. The drug induces intense pleasure for an hour followed by amnesia. You awaken and ask the nurse about your situation. She says that either you tried the drug yesterday (and had an hour of pleasure) or you will try the drug tomorrow (and will have an hour of pleasure). While she checks on your status, it is clear that you prefer to have the pleasure tomorrow. There is a temporal asymmetry in our attitudes to "experienced goods" that is parallel to the asymmetry in our attitudes to experienced bads: we are indifferent to past pleasures and look forward to future pleasures.

Perhaps it is this temporal asymmetry in our attitudes toward certain goods, and not the asymmetry in our attitudes toward bads, which explains our asymmetric attitudes toward prenatal and posthumous nonexistence. Death is a bad insofar as it is a deprivation of the good things in life (some of which, let us suppose, are "experienced as good" by the individual). If death occurs in the future, then it is a deprivation of something to which we look forward and about which we care—*future* experienced goods. But prenatal nonexistence is a deprivation of *past* experienced goods, goods to which we are indifferent. Death deprives us of something we care about, whereas prenatal nonexistence deprives us of something to which we are indifferent.

Thus we can defend Nagel's account of the badness of death by explaining the asymmetry in our attitudes toward prenatal and posthumous nonexistence. This explanation makes use of a principle clearly related to (but different from) Parfit's principle concerning the asymmetry in our attitudes toward past and future experienced bads. If we have asymmetric attitudes toward past and future experienced goods, then death is a bad thing in a way in which prenatal nonexistence is not.[14]

Let us end with a fanciful example that illustrates the present point. It is now 1985 and you will live eighty years in any case. Suppose you are given the following choice. Either you were born in 1915 and will die in 1995, or you were born in 1925 and will die in 2005. In each case, we will suppose, your life contains the same amount of pleasure and pain, distributed evenly through time. It is quite clear that you would prefer the second option—you want your good experiences in the future. Note that the periods before 1915 and after 2005 involve "experiential blanks" *in any case*. However, on the first option there is an "extra" blank between 1995 and 2005, and on the second option this extra blank is placed between 1915 and 1925. If one focuses simply on this experiential blank of ten years and asks whether it would be better to have the blank in the past or the future, it seems that one should not care. That is, as argued above, it is rational for a person to have temporally symmetric attitudes toward bads not experienced by him. Thus, our preference for the second option—living more in the future—cannot be explained directly by an alleged asymmetry in our attitudes toward experiential blanks. Rather, it is crucial that the placement of the "extra" experiential blank of ten years *determines* the temporal distribution of experienced goods, since we do have temporally asymmetric attitudes toward experienced goods.

Nagel is correct to assimilate death to a bad such as betrayal by a friend behind one's back—both bads do not involve unpleasant experiences. But the two sorts of bads are interestingly different. If death occurs later than it actually does, we will have a stream of good experiences in the future. The *alternative* to death is good experiences, whereas (in the typical case, at least) the alternative to a future betrayal behind one's back is *not* good experiences. Thus prenatal and posthumous nonexistence deprive us of things to which we have temporally asymmetric attitudes, whereas past and future betrayals do not. Death's badness is similar to the badness of betrayal behind one's back, but different in a way that explains why death is rationally regarded as worse than prenatal nonexistence.

CHAPTER THIRTEEN

Mr. Treadwell's sister died. Her first name was Gladys. The doctor said she died of lingering dread, a result of the four days and nights she and her brother had spent in the Mid-Village Mall, lost and confused.

A man in Glassboro died when the rear wheel of his car separated from the axle. An idiosyncrasy of that particular model.

The lieutenant governor of the state died of undisclosed natural causes, after a long illness. We all know what that means.

A Mechanicsville man died outside Tokyo during a siege of the airport by ten thousand helmeted students.

When I read obituaries I always note the age of the deceased. Automatically I relate this figure to my own age. Four years to go, I think. Nine more years. Two more years and I'm dead. The power of numbers is never more evident than when we use them to speculate on the time of our dying. Sometimes I bargain with myself. Would I be willing to accept sixty-five, Genghis Khan's age of dying? Suleiman the Magnificent made it to seventy-six. That sounds all right, especially the way I feel now, but how will it sound when I'm seventy-three?

It's hard to imagine these men feeling sad about death. Attila the Hun died young. He was still in his forties. Did he feel sorry for himself, succumb to self-pity and depression? He was the King of the Huns, the Invader of Europe, the Scourge of God. I want to believe he lay in his tent, wrapped in animal skins, as in some internationally financed movie epic, and said brave cruel things to his aides and retainers. No weakening of the spirit. No sense of the irony of human existence, that we are the highest form of life on earth and yet ineffably sad because we know what no other animal knows, that we must die. Attila did not look through the opening of his tent and gesture at some dog standing at the edge of the fire waiting to be thrown a scrap of meat. He did not say, "That pathetic flea-ridden beast is better off than the greatest ruler of men. It doesn't know what we know, it doesn't feel what we feel, it can't be sad as we are sad."

I want to believe he was not afraid. He accepted death as an experience that flows naturally from life, a wild ride through the forest, as would befit someone known as the Scourge of God. This is how it ended for him, with his attendants cutting off their hair and disfiguring their own faces in barbarian tribute, as the camera pulls back out of the tent and pans across the night sky of the fifth century A.D., clear and uncontaminated, bright-banded with shimmering worlds. —Don Delillo, *White Noise*

Death and the Value of Life

Jeff McMahan

Among the services that philosophers have traditionally attempted to provide is the manufacture of arguments intended to show that death is not or cannot be bad for those to whom it happens. In the first section of this paper I will contend that the most influential of these arguments fails to establish the conclusions which its defenders have sought from it. I will then devote the bulk of the paper to developing an account of why it is that death can be bad for those who die. Finally, I will sketch an apparent paradox which threatens this account and conclude by proposing a way of dissolving the paradox.

The Epicurean Argument

The Existence Requirement and the Wide and Narrow Experience Requirements

The argument I will consider derives from Epicurus.[1] Death, it is claimed, cannot be bad, or be a misfortune for the person

Reprinted by permission from *Ethics* 99, no. 1 (October 1988): 32–61. I have been helped in writing this paper by comments on earlier drafts by Matthew Buncombe, William R. Carter, Gerald Dworkin, Dorothy Grover, Thomas Hurka, Gregory Kavka, Brian Pike, Alan Mattlage, Robert McKim, Richard Mohr, and Jan Narveson. I am also greatly indebted to David Brink, Hugh Chandler, Timothy McCarthy, Derek Parfit, and Steven Wagner for exceptionally helpful comments and discussion. For discussion both of certain aspects of the problem of death that are not addressed in this paper and of certain objections that might be raised to the arguments developed here, see chap. 1 of my book, *The Ethics of Killing* (Oxford: Basil Blackwell, 1989).

who dies, for, when death occurs, there is no longer a subject to whom any misfortune can then be ascribed. This of course assumes, as I will assume throughout this paper, that death consists in the annihilation, or the ceasing to exist, of the person who dies.[2]

Call this the Epicurean argument. It presupposes the following principle:

The Existence Requirement. A person can be the subject of some misfortune only if he exists at the time the misfortune occurs.[3]

The Epicurean argument should be distinguished from a similar argument that is based on a principle that Epicurus seems also to have held—namely, the principle that an event can be bad for a person only if he experiences it as bad. Call this principle the *Narrow Experience Requirement.* It implies that, while the prospect of death can be bad for a person if the anticipation of it disturbs him, death itself cannot be bad for him since, when it occurs, he will not experience it and, *a fortiori,* will not experience it as bad.

The Narrow Experience Requirement should in turn be distinguished from the *Wide Experience Requirement,* which holds that an event can be bad for someone only if it in some way affects or makes a difference to his conscious experience. The difference between the two principles is that, while the Narrow Requirement implies that death cannot be bad for the person who dies, the Wide Requirement does not. For, although one does not experience death, it does affect one's experience—by limiting or ending it.

Obviously, then, to sustain the belief that death can be bad for the person who dies one needs to reject only the Narrow and not the Wide Experience Requirement. Yet the two are frequently conflated, so that it is often assumed that one must reject the Wide Requirement as well. This is a natural mistake, since the rejection of the Wide Requirement entails the rejection of the Narrow Requirement. Moreover, although the rejection of the Narrow Requirement does not entail the rejection of the Wide Requirement, the main objections to the Narrow Requirement also apply with equal force to the Wide Requirement. For example, the hypothetical cases in which people who long to be loved and admired and believe that they are, when in fact they are ridiculed and despised behind their backs, constitute counterexamples to both requirements.[4]

In my view these counterexamples provide sufficient grounds for rejecting the Narrow Requirement. But I will not press the objection here, since my target is instead the Epicurean argument. I mention the Narrow Requirement mainly to ensure that it is not confused with the Existence Requirement. To see how the two requirements diverge, consider the case of a person on holiday on a remote island. Back home, on Friday, his life's work collapses. But, because of the inaccessibility of the island, the bad news does not arrive until the following Monday. On the intervening Sunday, however, the man is killed by a shark; so he never learns that his life's work has come to nothing. While it is compatible with the Existence Requirement to suppose that he suffered a terrible misfortune when the collapse occurred, since he existed at the time, the Narrow Experience Requirement implies that this was not a misfortune for him since he was never aware of it. The Existence Requirement and the Narrow Experience Requirement are therefore quite different requirements, and the counterexamples that are often advanced against the latter leave the former, and therefore the Epicurean argument itself, entirely unscathed.

The Reconciliation Strategy

The obvious attraction of the Epicurean argument is that it is thought to have the welcome effect of undermining the idea that death is something to be feared. It is less often noticed, however, that, for the same reasons, the argument also threatens certain other commonsense beliefs that we are less eager to abandon—for example, that killing is wrong, that suicide can be rational or irrational, and so on. If we wish to salvage these latter beliefs, we must either reject the Epicurean argument or else show that the relevant beliefs are in fact compatible with the argument's conclusion. If we adopt the first option then obviously we will lose our ground for thinking that death should not be feared. I will argue that the most plausible way of pursuing the second option also has this consequence.

Though the two options are mutually exclusive, I will argue for them both. While I think the Epicurean argument should ultimately be rejected, the other option—which I will call the *reconciliation strategy*—is worth exploring as a fallback position in case the proposed reasons for rejecting the Epicurean argument prove unpersuasive.

Let us consider the reconciliation strategy first. It can be introduced by drawing on a comparison between death, or the ceasing to exist of a person, and the coming into existence of a person. It can be argued that, if a person's life would be worth living, then it would be good—not just impersonally, but good *for that person*—if he were to come into existence. The argument for this claim derives from the compelling commonsense view that it would be wrong, other things being equal, to bring a person into existence if his life could be expected to be utterly miserable. The most plausible explanation of why this would be wrong appeals to two claims: first, that to cause such a person to exist would be bad for that person, or would harm him; and second, that there is a general moral reason not to do what would be bad for people, or would harm them. But, if to be caused to exist with a miserable life can be bad for a person, then it should also be the case that to be caused to exist with a life that is worth living can be good for a person.

To deny this—to accept that to be caused to exist can be bad for a person but to deny that it can be good for a person—would, in the absence of some explanation, be unacceptably ad hoc. And it is difficult to imagine what sort of explanation could be given for the claim that there is an asymmetry of this sort. Moreover, the moral implications of supposing that there is such an asymmetry are likely to be quite implausible. For example, if it were possible to harm but not to benefit people by bringing them into existence, then any decision to have a child would carry a risk of harming the child but would not involve a possibility of benefiting him. Thus there would always be a moral presumption against having children. But it seems clear that there is no general presumption of this sort. So it seems safe to assume that, if causing a person to exist can be bad for that person, then it can also be good for him. It is, of course, possible to deny both these claims, but then one would need to find an alternative explanation of the fact that it would be wrong to cause a miserable person to exist.[5]

The point that emerges from this that is relevant to the reconciliation strategy is that, if we bring a person into existence with a life that is worth living, there is no problem in locating the beneficiary. He is here before us, enjoying the goods of life. There is thus no obvious incompatibility between the claim that it can be good for a person to come into existence and the Existence Requirement. There is, moreover, a relevant parallel here between starting to exist and continuing to exist. You might have died five years ago. But you did not; instead you continued to exist. If your life has been worth living, then it was good for you to have continued to exist. There is no problem in this case in locating the subject of this good fortune: you are the beneficiary of your continued existence, and you clearly exist during the time when this good fortune occurs. Hence it is not obviously incompatible with the Existence Requirement to claim that your continuing to exist is a good thing for you.

The claim of the reconciliation strategy is that continuing to live can be good for a person even if, as the Existence Requirement implies, death would not be bad for him. There is, however, a way in which the Epicurean might try to establish that the claim that continuing to live can be good is incompatible with the claim that death cannot be bad. This involves appealing to what has been called the *Comparative View*. The Comparative View is the view that any judgment about what is good or bad for a person must be implicitly comparative in the following way. The judgment that an act or event is *good* for someone implies that, if there is no relevant alternative that would be equally good or better, then the relevant alternative or alternatives to that act must be *worse* for that person. Similarly, the claim that an act or event is *bad* for someone implies that, unless there is some relevant alternative that would be as bad or worse, then any relevant alternative must be *better* for that person.[6]

The conclusion of the Epicurean argument—that death is not bad for those who die—together with the Comparative View, implies that the alternative to death—namely, continuing to live—cannot be good. This implication, if allowed to stand, will defeat the reconciliation strategy. Thus to defend the reconciliation strategy, we must reject the Comparative View.

One objection to the Comparative View is that it seems to lead to paradoxes.[7] Consider some person who continues to exist. The Existence Requirement itself (which for the moment we are treating as a fixed point in the argument) provides no ground for denying that continuing to exist is good for this person. And if continuing to exist is good for the person, then, given the Comparative View, it follows that ceasing to exist would have been worse for him. But suppose now that the actual outcome is that the person dies. According to the Existence Requirement, this is not bad for the person. Given the Comparative View, it then follows that it would not have been good, or better, for the person had he in fact continued to exist. A similar paradox arises when we consider the alternatives of coming into existence and not coming into existence.

The Comparative View thus has conflicting implications depending, it may seem, on which outcome we suppose to be the actual one. The Epicurean may reply, however, that the paradoxes derive, not from the Comparative View itself, but from our failure to evaluate the outcomes consistently. If (he might argue) we think that ceasing to exist cannot be bad, then we must accept that continuing to exist cannot be good, and we cannot change our minds about this when the actual outcome is continued existence rather than death. If we consistently hold that neither coming to exist nor not coming to exist is either good or bad, and that neither continuing to exist nor ceasing to exist is either good or bad, then the Comparative View will not lead to paradoxes.

The paradoxes to which I have called attention do not, therefore, immediately undermine the Comparative View. They do, however, help us to understand more clearly what is at issue here. The Epicurean starts with the Existence Requirement, infers that death cannot be bad for those who die, and then reasons via the Comparative View that continuing to exist cannot be good. The proponent of the reconciliation strategy starts with equal propriety with the claim that in most cases continuing to exist is good and then, seeing that an inconsistency arises when this claim is conjoined with both the Existence Requirement and the Comparative View, concludes that the Comparative View must be wrong. Thus to resolve this dispute, we must assess the relative plausibility of the Comparative Requirement and the claim that continuing to exist can be good.

As I suggested earlier, the claim that continuing to exist can be good is supported by the parallel between coming to exist and continuing to exist. I argued that it can be good for a person to come into existence and concluded that, if this is so, it can also be good for a person to continue in existence. This is, of course, a relatively weak case; no doubt more could be said. But for our purposes even a weak case will do. For there is no case for the Comparative View. The Comparative View takes a truth about standard cases of something being good or bad for a person and generalizes it, making it a necessary condition in all cases for something to be good or bad for a person. In standard cases, in which the person exists in both alternative outcomes, the Comparative View seems true as a matter of logic. But in the two nonstandard pairs of alternatives (coming to exist or not coming to exist and continuing to exist or ceasing to exist) in which the person exists in only one of the alternatives, there is no reason whatever to think that the Comparative View must be true. There is no reason to generalize from the standard to the nonstandard cases.

Since the Comparative View is without foundation in the two nonstandard cases, it should be rejected as a general necessary condition for something being good or bad for a person. The rejection of the view then allows us to reject the idea that never existing can be bad or worse for a person, while accepting that to come to exist can be good for a person. We can say that coming to exist can be good, even though it is not better than never existing—since the latter implies that never existing would be worse, which it would not be (at least if it were the actual outcome). This also allows us to concede the Epicurean claim that death is not bad for people, or worse for them than continuing to live, while at the same time accepting that continuing to live can be good for them. We can say that continuing to live can be a good thing for a person, though it is not better than dying. In short, we simply give up the comparative claims, while retaining the noncomparative ones. (If one insists on having a comparison, one could claim that, while never existing would not have been worse for me, it would not have been as good for me as existing has been, and similarly that, while dying would not be bad for me, it would not be as good for me as continuing to exist would be. These claims are true and unparadoxical, and therefore reinstate a comparative view of sorts, though not one which threatens the reconciliation strategy.)

Suppose we accept that continuing to live can be good for a

person even if death would not be bad for him. We could then claim that death would be bad—not bad for the person who dies, but bad in a quasi-impersonal way.[8] It would be bad because it would exclude what would be good for a person—namely, continuing to exist. Death would be bad in the same way that it is bad if a person whose life would have been worth living fails to come into existence. In both cases something which would be good for a person fails to occur, though in both cases the nonoccurrence of the good is not bad for the person who would have experienced it, since the nonoccurrence of the good involves—indeed perhaps consists in—the nonexistence of the person.

If death can be bad in this quasi-impersonal way, then this provides a sufficient basis for the important beliefs that seem to presuppose that death can be bad for the person who dies. If, for example, death can be bad because it excludes what would have been good for a person, then this will provide a foundation for the belief that killing is wrong, the belief that it is not irrational to fear death, the belief that suicide can be irrational, and so on.[9] In this way these important commonsense beliefs can be reconciled with the Epicurean claim that death cannot be bad for those who die.

The Existence Requirement

Despite the apparent success of the reconciliation strategy, it may seem that a more satisfactory way of preserving the relevant range of commonsense beliefs would be simply to reject the Epicurean argument. And this argument can be challenged directly. Consider again the case of the person whose life's work collapses while he is on holiday on a remote island. Suppose we agree that the fact that his life's work has come to nothing is a misfortune for him[10] On reflection, it seems hard to believe that it makes a difference to the misfortune he suffers whether the collapse of his life's work occurs shortly before he is killed or shortly afterward. Yet, according to the Existence Requirement, this difference in timing makes *all* the difference. If the collapse of his life's work occurs just before he dies, then, even though he never learns of it, he suffers a terrible misfortune. If, on the other hand, it occurs just after he dies, he suffers no misfortune at all. If we find this hard to believe then we may be forced to reject the Existence Requirement.

Most of us, however, will be disposed to do this anyway. The example is probably superfluous, since most of us find death itself a sufficient counterexample. Apart from suffering great pain, it is hard to think of a clearer example than death of something that most people believe to be in most cases bad for the person to whom it happens. The Epicurean simply denies what most of us believe. Death, he claims, cannot be bad for us because when it occurs we will not exist at all. But that is precisely what we object to: that we will not exist when we might otherwise be enjoying the benefits of life.

Death differs from never existing in one crucial respect. Never existing is not something that ever happens to actual people. *A fortiori*, there are no actual people for whom never existing can be bad. But death always happens to actual people. It can deprive actual people of what would otherwise be good for them. The Existence Requirement stands in the way of our being able to conclude from this that death can be bad for the actual people to whom it happens. But what authority does this principle have to overturn an evaluative inference so fundamental and compelling as this? The conflict here is analogous to a type of conflict that commonly arises in moral theory. For all of us there are certain convictions which constitute more or less fixed points in the system of our moral beliefs. When a conviction of this sort clashes with the dictates of some moral theory, the challenge from the theory must be more rationally compelling than the conviction itself if the conviction is to be justifiably dislodged. Theories seldom satisfy this demand. In the present case, the Existence Requirement also lacks the requisite rational force. Indeed, it seems, like the Comparative View, to be a simple misgeneralization from standard cases to an importantly different nonstandard case. In most instances it is a necessary truth that a person must exist to be the subject of some misfortune: I cannot, for example, suffer the pain of a toothache unless I exist. But death is obviously a special case. To insist that it cannot be an evil because it does not meet a condition that most if not all other evils satisfy is tantamount to ruling it out as an evil simply because it has special features.

It is important to notice, however, that if we reject the Existence Requirement, we may get the claim that death can be bad for those who die as part of a larger package that includes claims about posthumous benefits and posthumous harms. Death, when it is an evil, is a privative evil. In itself it has no positive or negative features, so when it is bad this must be because of what it deprives us of. But many people believe that people who have ceased to exist may also be subject to positive evils and misfortunes—as when a person's life's work is unjustly despised or neglected after her death—as well as positive benefits, as when an artist's works achieve the recognition they deserve which they never received during her lifetime. It seems that the only way we can reject both the Existence Requirement and the idea that we can be posthumously harmed and benefited is to accept some view, such as hedonism, which incorporates the Wide Experience Requirement. If we are hedonists we can believe that death is bad for the person who dies because it deprives him of valuable mental states, but we can reject the notion of posthumous harms and benefits on the ground that a dead person's mental status can no longer be affected. If, however, we do not accept the Wide Experience Requirement, then the rejection of the Existence Requirement would seem to commit us to the idea that numerous events that occur after our deaths can be either good or bad for us, or in or against our interests.

The Badness of Death

Given, then, that death can be bad, either for the victim or in quasi-impersonal terms, how are we to understand the loss or deprivation involved in death? The correct general answer to this question would seem to be that given by Nagel, which is that death, when it is bad, is bad because it deprives us of possible future goods.[11] The apparent simplicity of this answer, however, conceals a host of difficult problems. This section will be devoted to exposing the nature of these problems and proposing solutions to them.

One such problem is implicit in the following remarks of Nagel's: "Countless possibilities for [an individual's] continued existence are imaginable, and we can clearly conceive of what it would be for him to go on existing indefinitely. However inevitable it is that this will not come about, its possibility is still that of the continuation of a good for him, if life is the good we take it to be. . . . Death, no matter how inevitable, is an abrupt cancellation of indefinitely extensive possible goods. . . . If there is no limit to the amount of life that it would be good to have, then it may be that a bad end is in store for us all."[12]

If, however, the goods that would be possible for us were it not for death are conceived of as potentially unlimited, then it may seem that there is nothing to prevent the conclusion that our losses in death are infinite. But then, if the loss involved in death is infinite, and if the badness of death consists in what it deprives us of, how can we explain the common and compelling belief that it is in general worse to die earlier rather than later— for example, that it is worse, or more tragic, when someone dies at thirty than it is when someone dies at eighty?

What Death Deprives Us Of

What Nagel seems to be suggesting, in the passage quoted above, is that death is *always* bad for the person who dies relative to the possibilities for good that one could imagine his life containing had that life continued. What is unclear, however, is why one should think that a set of possibilities that are possible only in the sense of being imaginable constitutes a relevant alternative to death for purposes of comparison. Simply to point out that there is an imaginable possible future life that a person might have had if he had not died seems insufficient to show that he met with a bad end. For we can also imagine possible future lives that the person might have had which would not have been worth living, relative to which his death could be judged not to be bad, or even to be good. Since desirable future lives and undesirable future lives are all equally imaginable, there seems to be no more reason to judge the person's death to be bad than there is to judge it to be good. But unless there is some nonarbitrary way of selecting, from among the many imaginable lives the person might have had, the one which can be considered the relevant alternative to death for purposes of comparison, then Nagel's focus on what would have been imaginable in the absence of death provides no basis for the evaluation of an individual's death at all.

What is relevant in evaluating the badness of an individual's death is not what might have happened if he had not died, but what would in fact have happened. When we evaluate death relative to what would have happened in its absence, we find that it is clearly not the case that death is always infinitely bad because it deprives its victim of an "indefinitely extensive" set of possible goods. Rather, the possibilities for good of which a person is deprived by death are limited by the fact that, had he not died when and how he did, he would have been condemned by his biology and circumstances to die within a certain limited period of time thereafter. The relevant alternative to death for purposes of comparison is not continuing to live indefinitely, or forever, but living on for a limited period of time and then dying of some other cause. So, other things being equal, we measure the badness of death in terms of the quantity and quality of life that the victim would have enjoyed had he not died when and how he did. (I will later explain how other things might be relevantly unequal.)

This approach to determining the badness of death supports the common view that it is in general worse to die earlier rather than later.[13] As a rule, a person who dies at thirty would, had he not died, have enjoyed more goods before meeting with death from some other cause than a person who dies at eighty. This approach also supports the view that most of us take in cases in which it seems that death is not a bad thing for the person who dies, or is even a good thing. These are cases in which we feel that suicide would be rational, or euthanasia justified. The reason why death is not bad in these cases is that, if the person were not to die, the life that he would subsequently have would not be worth living. If, however, we assume with Nagel that death should be evaluated relative to the possibilities for good that would be imaginable in its absence, then it seems that we should regard death as an evil even in these cases. This makes it difficult to see how those who take Nagel's view can find cases in which suicide would be rational or in which euthanasia would even be conceptually possible.

Let us call the account of the badness of death that I have sketched the "revised possible goods account." In order to be able to explain our intuitive beliefs about the comparative badness of different possible deaths, this account requires further refinement. The necessary additions and qualifications will be developed in the following four subsections.

1. *Counterfactual Conditionals and the Problem of Specifying the Antecedent.* One problem that the possible goods account faces can best be introduced by means of an example. Consider the case of a thirty-year-old man who died today of cancer. Call him Mort. According to the possible goods account, our evaluation of Mort's death must be based on a counterfactual conditional claim to the effect that "such-and-such would have happened if. . . ." The natural candidate for the antecedent of the counterfactual is, of course, "if he had not died." But this is in fact hopelessly vague, for there are countless ways in which he might not have died. To imagine that his death did not occur we must imagine that its cause did not occur, or did not lead to its expected effect. Yet there are not only various ways of understanding what the cause of his death was, but there are also, for each way of conceiving of the cause of death, various ways in which it would have been possible for the cause not to have operated. Suppose, for example, that we say that the cancer was the cause of his death. Then to suppose that he might not have died is to suppose that he might have been cured of the cancer, or that he might never have been stricken with it in the first place, or that he might have lived on with it in a nonfatal form. In short, we must suppose that he might not have died from the cancer, but there are various ways in which this might happened.

Suppose, on the other hand, that we want to be more specific in identifying the cause of Mort's death. We might then say that the cause of his death was the immediate mechanism by which his death was brought about—a hemorrhage, for example. (This is what a pathologist who knew of Mort's condition would want to know if he were to ask what the cause of death was.) If this is how we conceive of the cause of death, then to hypothesize that he might not have died is to suppose that *this* cause of death might not have operated.

Which of these various ways of spelling out the antecedent ("if he had not died at *t*") is the one on which we should base our evaluation of Mort's death? Certainly our choice of interpretation will make a difference to what our evaluation will be. For our estimation of what would have happened to Mort had he not died will depend on how we understand the circumstances of his not dying. If not dying would have involved being cured of the cancer, then it may be true that had he not died, he would have lived a long and prosperous life. Relative to that understanding of the antecedent, then, Mort's death can be regarded as a terrible tragedy. But suppose that his not dying is understood in such a way that it would have involved only the absence of the immediate mechanism of death (the hemorrhage). In that case we may suppose that, had he not died when he did, he would have lived on for only a short period of time until his death would have been brought about by some alternative mechanism associated with the cancer. Relative to this understanding of the antecedent, Mort's death was not tragic, and it may even have been a good thing (if, e.g., the brief future he would otherwise have had would have been filled with suffering).

Mort's case is in a way paradoxical, for there is both a clear sense in which it is true that his death today was not tragic—indeed, was perhaps on balance a good thing—as well as a clear sense in which his death was tragic. We can see now that each of these claims is true relative to certain ways of specifying the antecedent and false relative to others. His death today was perhaps a good thing relative to living on for a few days in agony, but it was bad relative to continued life free from cancer.

It seems unsatisfactory, however, to be left with a multiplicity of different and superficially conflicting evaluations of his death. What we want is a single, general, context-independent evaluation that tells us whether, all things considered, his death was good or bad, period. Our problem, then, is to find a method for picking out the single most general, context-independent way of understanding the idea that he might not have died. Let us call this *the problem of specifying the antecedent*, since what we are trying to do, in effect, is to assign precise and determinate content to the phrase "if he had not died . . ." in such a way that the completed conditional, if true, will provide the most general and context-independent assessment of what Mort has been deprived of, or has been spared, by his death.

How might we discover a method of specifying the antecedent in this and all other cases in which we seek a single overall evaluation of a person's death? I see no alternative but to propose various methods and test them against our intuitions by exploring their implications for a range of cases. Before proposing what seems a promising candidate, I will introduce some further cases which will not only help to illuminate the structure of the problem but will also serve as useful tests for assessing the plausibility of proposed methods.

2. *The Problem of Causal Overdetermination*. There is a familiar problem in ethics, which is that it is often difficult to know how to evaluate an act that causes injury if, had the act not been done, some other cause would have operated around the same time to produce a relevantly similar injury to the same victim. Following Feinberg, I will way that these are cases in which injury to the victim is causally overdetermined.[14] A similar problem arises for the evaluation of death when death is causally overdetermined in this sense.

Consider the following case. Joe is twenty-nine and a half years old. Schmoe has just turned thirty. Both are run over by a bus as they step off the curb. Our initial reaction is to think of both deaths as terribly tragic, Joe's being perhaps slightly more tragic than Schmoe's because of his slightly younger age. But suppose that, while Schmoe was in robust good health, it is discovered during the autopsy that Joe had a silent, symptomless, but invariably fatal disease that would have killed him within two months had he not been mown down by the bus. Our response to the discovery of this fact is to revise our initial assessment of the badness of Joe's death. Joe's death now seems considerably less bad than it would have been had he not had the condition since, given the fact that he had the condition, all he lost in being hit by the bus was at most two months of further life. Our revised response is thus to think that Schmoe's death was the more tragic of the two, other things being equal, even though he was older than Joe.

The view that Joe lost only relatively little by dying in the accident is supported by the fact that it explains certain intuitions. Suppose that one knew about Joe's disease and that one was in a position to snatch either Joe or Schmoe, but not both, out of the path of the bus. It seems that it would be better to save Schmoe rather than Joe if other things, such as their importance to other people, were equal. The reason why it would be better to save Schmoe is simply that he would have more to lose by dying than Joe would.

This may seem straightforward. In fact it is not. When we learn the results of the autopsy, our inclination is to think that Joe's death was less bad than it initially seemed. But if we then report the results to Joe's grieving mother, it is very unlikely that she will find any grounds for consolation in the fact that he would soon have died anyway. She might reason as follows. Suppose that Joe had not been killed by the bus. Then he would have died sometime within the ensuing two months from the disease. What would we then have said of *that* death? If we were to ask what would have happened had he not then died from the disease, the answer could well be that he could have been expected to enjoy a long and fruitful life. In that case we would have said that his death from the disease was a terrible tragedy—a case of a young man cut down in his prime. But if death at so early an age from the disease would have been tragic, how can it be *less* bad when he is killed today by a bus at an even earlier age?

I will return to the question of Joe's misfortune below. I want now to introduce another case—the case of a young officer in the cavalry who was killed in the charge of the Light Brigade. This officer was among the leaders of the charge and was shot quite early by a soldier named Ivan. Suppose that, had he not been shot by Ivan, he would have been killed within a few seconds by a bullet fired by Boris, who also had him within his sights. Our natural response to this case is to say that the officer's death was a grave misfortune, depriving him of many years of life. Yet it would seem that this case is like that of Joe in being a case in which death within a relatively short span of time is causally overdetermined. Thus, if we accept that Joe lost at most two months in being hit by the bus, should we not also conclude that in this case all the officer lost in being shot by Ivan was a few seconds of life, so that his death was hardly a misfortune at all?

Obviously we cannot accept this. Yet in the case of Joe it is *not* implausible to regard his death in the accident as considerably less bad than it would have been had there been no other cause of death which would soon have killed him if the bus had not. Is there some difference between the cases which explains our differing reactions to them? I think that there is and that examining that difference will point us toward a plausible resolution of the problem of specifying the antecedent.

3. *A Proposal.* The solution I will offer to the problem of specifying the antecedent is based on a variant of the general analysis

of the truth-value of counterfactuals associated with the work of David Lewis and Robert Stalnaker.[15] What the variants of this form of analysis have in common is the view that a counterfactual conditional is true if and only if the consequent is true in the possible world (or in all of the possible worlds) in which the antecedent is realized that is (or are) closest to the actual world, where closeness is determined by the application of some similarity metric. I will simply assume that some theory of this sort is true and that the version that I appeal to is a reasonable candidate for the best version. I will not try to defend or even to make explicit all the details of this version.[16] Indeed, as will soon become apparent, the proposal I will advance raises far more problems of metaphysics than there is space to address here, so one should regard what follows as nothing more than a tentative sketch of a solution.

It is perhaps tempting to think that the solution to the problem of specifying the antecedent is given more or less directly by the Lewis-Stalnaker theory. One might think, for example, that we can identify the appropriate antecedent-world as the possible world in which the person does not die but which otherwise deviates minimally from the actual world (at least up to the time at which the person died in the actual world). This, however, would be a mistake. Return to the case of the cavalry officer. Suppose (what is not implausible) that the closest possible world in which the officer does not die from Ivan's bullet is one in which he is grazed by Ivan's bullet and then killed by Boris's bullet. In that case our answer to the question of what would have happened had the officer not died when and how he did will be that he would have lived for a few seconds, and then he would have been killed. This leads to the unacceptable conclusion that his actual death was hardly a misfortune at all.

In the case of the cavalry officer, as in the case of Mort, what we believe about what would have happened had he not died when and how he did depends on how we specify the cause of his death. If we single out the shot fired by Ivan as the cause and then ask what would have happened had the cause not operated (e.g., because Ivan's hand shook, or his gun jammed), we get the answer that the officer would soon have been killed by Boris. We might, however, identify the cause of the officer's death differently—for example, as his being shot in the charge.

If we ask what would have happened had he not been shot in the charge, the answer may well be that he would subsequently have led a long and happy life. Of course, as in the case of Mort, these two claims about what would have happened lead to radically divergent evaluations of the officer's death.

The problem of specifying the antecedent, then, is a problem about identifying and delimiting the cause of death. In asking what would have happened had a certain person not died, we are asking what would have been the case had the cause of his death not operated. The many different ways of specifying the antecedent thus correspond to different ways in which the chain of causation leading to the person's death might have gone off course or been disrupted—different ways, in short, in which various individually or jointly necessary conditions of the person's death might not have occurred. The problem of specifying the antecedent, therefore, is the problem of determining which elements from the totality of causally relevant factors in the etiology of death we should imagine not occurring when, in order to obtain a single overall evaluation of the death, we imagine what would have been the case had the victim not died.

Return now to the comparison between the case of the officer and the case of Joe. An important difference between the two cases would seem to be that, while the two potential causes of the officer's death (the threat from Ivan and the threat from Boris) both seem to be parts of the same causal sequence, the two potential causes of Joe's death (the bus accident and the fatal condition) are not. Hence in the possible world in which the entire causal sequence containing the immediate cause of the officer's death is absent, there are no other causes of death lurking in the foreseeable future. But if in Joe's case we subtract the causal sequence leading to his death in the bus accident, we do not thereby remove the other cause of death—namely, the fatal condition.

What this suggests is that we can secure the intuitively correct counterfactual claims in these cases if our formula for specifying the antecedent is to subtract the entire causal sequence of which the immediate cause of death is a part. Thus, if the entire causal sequence leading to the officer's being shot by Ivan had not occurred, then he would presumably have gone on to lead a long and prosperous life; whereas if the entire causal sequence leading to Joe's being hit by the bus had not occurred, he would still have died within two months of the condition. Because of this, we may regard Joe's death as less tragic than that of the officer.

This formula, while promising, requires considerable tightening up. One problem, for example, is to give sufficient content to the notion of a causal sequence to allow for the individuation of causal sequences in the way that the formula requires. Here is one suggestion for dealing with this problem. Let us define the *transitive cause* of an event E as follows. If C is the immediate or proximate cause of E, then the transitive cause of E is the set of all the events that form part of the chain of causes leading to C. This set is understood to be both complete and closed, in the sense that all and only the members of the set satisfy the following condition: if Ci is a member of the set and Cj is a cause of Ci, then Cj is a member of the set. Given the notion of transitive cause, we can now state more precisely what it means to imagine a possible world in which the entire causal sequence containing a certain death is absent. To imagine such a world is simply to imagine a world which is like the actual world except that the entire transitive cause of the death is absent, along with those events for whose occurrence some element or elements of the transitive cause were a necessary condition given the laws of causation that hold in the actual world. So, for example, if we imagine that the transitive cause of the officer's being shot by Ivan did not occur, we must presumably imagine that the Crimean War did not occur, in which case the threat from Boris would not have occurred either.

It is important to notice that the plausibility of this suggestion depends on our distinguishing between the cause of some event and the causally relevant conditions of that event. The transitive cause of E, as I understand it, consists of a chain of causes (namely, the cause of the cause of the cause . . . of E) and not the set of all the causally relevant conditions of E. For example, the transitive cause of the officer's death presumably includes the occurrence of the battle and thus the occurrence of the war, but not the event of Ivan's birth, or the presence of oxygen in the air for Ivan to breathe, or even the fact that the officer was not wounded and sent home just prior to the battle—though all of these are causally necessary conditions of the officer's actual death. If the transitive cause of the officer's death were to include these and all the other causally relevant conditions of his death, the proposal I am putting forward would obviously be hopelessly implausible.[17]

Having sketched certain theories, concepts, and distinctions on which my proposed solution to the problem of specifying the antecedent is based, I am now in a position to state the proposal in full. Let t be the time at which some person died. Our overall, objective evaluation of how bad or good his death was for him will be based on a counterfactual claim about what would have happened to him if he had not died at t. Let the antecedent of the relevant counterfactual be "if the entire transitive cause of his death had not occurred. . . ." To complete the counterfactual, we consult the possible world in which the antecedent is realized which is closest to the actual world up to t.[18] In assessing comparative similarity, we give nomological similarity lexical priority over factual similarity. That is, we hold the laws of causation constant across possible worlds.[19] Then we simply let the future unfold in this world in accordance with the laws of causation that hold in the actual world, and see how the person fares. If, for example, in the closest world in which the antecedent is realized the person goes on to live a long and happy life subsequent to t, then it is true that if he had not died he would have lived a long and happy life. His death was then bad in rough proportion to the amount of good that his life would have contained. (If the future is causally underdetermined by the present, then he may fare differently in different possible futures that are all compatible with running the closest antecedent-world forward in accordance with the laws of causation. In that case, the sum of the goods that would have been causally possible for the person will presumably exceed the amount of good that would have been contained in any single future life. Thus, in attempting to calculate the losses that the person suffers through death, we should presumably weight each good that would have been causally possible for him according to how probable its occurrence would have been had he lived. Again, however, there is no space to pursue this further complexity.)

This proposal provides what seem to be the intuitively correct answers in the cases we have considered so far. For example, it implies that the cavalry officer's death was tragic since, if the transitive cause of his death had never occurred, he would not have been threatened by either Ivan or Boris and so, we may assume, would have gone on to live a long and happy life. It also implies that Joe's death was significantly less bad than Schmoe's since, in the closest possible world in which the transitive cause of his death is absent, Joe would have lived on for at most two months; whereas, in Schmoe's case, removing the transitive cause of death would have left him with many years of life remaining. Finally, the proposal implies that Mort's death was a tragedy comparable to those suffered by the officer and by Schmoe, since the relevant counterfactual situation with which we compare his death is one in which he never contracts cancer in the first place.

It should be emphasized that these judgments represent only our most general, maximally context-independent evaluations of these deaths. As I noted earlier in introducing the problem of specifying the antecedent, there are many other possible evaluations of each of these deaths that are based on other imagined ways in which the causal chain leading to the death might have been interrupted so that the death would not have occurred. These alternative evaluations need not be mistaken. On the contrary, they can be quite important for certain purposes, such as guiding action at moments when, though it is not possible to prevent the entire transitive cause of some potential death, it nevertheless is possible to intervene in the causal chain in some other way. For example, the doctors may wish to know whether it would be in Mort's interests for them to avert the hemorrhage they predict will occur unless he is given a certain medication. Whether it would be in or against his interests depends at least in part on whether his death from the hemorrhage would be good or bad for him at that time (i.e., relative to what would be in store for him if, in his present condition, his death from the hemorrhage were to be prevented). In making this decision, the doctors should be guided by their assessment of what Mort's life would be like in the closest possible world in which the causal chain which will otherwise lead to his death is broken or diverted at the point at which it is possible for them to intervene.

So evaluations of this sort need not be wrong, and indeed are indispensable in a variety of decision-making contexts. But, unlike the evaluations that issue from the application of the procedure outlined above, they are essentially context dependent.

They can help to guide our action in relevant circumstances, but they do not tell us, for example, to what extent it is appropriate to feel pity for someone because he has died.

4. *Deprivation of Future Goods and the Global Evaluation of Lives.* I have claimed that the proposal sketched above gives the right answer in the case of Joe, but earlier I raised doubts about whether it is really our intuition that his death was less tragic than that of Schmoe. Even when we discover that Joe suffered from the fatal condition, we, along with his mother, retain our sense that he has suffered a terrible misfortune. And in fact we are right. Our mistake is to identify this misfortune with the event of his death. For it remains true that the event of his death was not itself a grave misfortune for him, since at most it deprived him of only two months of life. Rather, his misfortune consists in his having been deprived of a future in which there would be possibilities for good. It is because the absence of future possibilities for good (at least of an active or experiential kind) was in this case overdetermined, in that it was guaranteed by the disease quite independently of the bus accident, that the misfortune is not ascribable to his death alone. It is instead ascribable to the fact that he was killed by the bus *together with* the fact that if he had not been killed by the bus he would have died soon of the disease. It is this which is the proper object of his mother's great grief.

It may, however, be objected to this that the misfortune which I claim that Joe suffered is one that befalls us all, so that in the end we are all equally unfortunate, equally deprived. Consider, for example, the case of a person who dies from extreme old age, at the biological limits of human life. Call this person Gerry. It seems that Gerry's case is, according to my view, relevantly like Joe's. His death within a short span of time is overdetermined. Suppose that he died of a heart attack. Even if the transitive cause of the heart attack had not occurred, Gerry would nevertheless have died soon of some other cause associated with the fragility of old age.[20] For this reason most of us readily concede that his death was not a great misfortune for him; we acknowledge, in this case, that very few goods would have been causally possible for him had he not died. But, an objector might claim, the fact that he would have had little to look forward to had he not died is, according to my view, itself a great misfortune—precisely the same misfortune I have claimed that Joe suffered. But if Joe and Gerry both suffer this misfortune equally, and if neither one's death is particularly tragic, then it would seem that the problem raised in the passage from Nagel quoted above—namely, that we all suffer infinite losses—has reemerged in a slightly altered form. For it now seems that, on my view, we all *do* suffer infinite losses, though these losses are not attributable to death alone. But if this is right, how can we explain our feeling that Joe has suffered a greater misfortune than Gerry and is more deserving of our pity?

One reply to this challenge might appeal to the idea that the failure to realize some good is less bad the less causally possible it was to realize that good.[21] If that were true, then Joe would be the more unfortunate of the two because future goods were causally more possible for him than for Gerry, for whom the absence of future goods was multiply overdetermined by a variety of potential causes of death as well as by aging, disease, and so forth. But in fact this hardly seems to matter. Even if the absence of future possibilities for good were equally overdetermined in the two cases (e.g., if there were twenty Murder Inc. hit men independently trying to kill Joe when he was hit by the bus), we would still grieve more for him and think him more unfortunate than Gerry.

There is a better reply. This reply begins by embracing the allegedly absurd view that Gerry suffers a serious misfortune. Indeed, it is compatible with the view that ultimately we *all* suffer a great misfortune—even those of us who live the longest, richest lives. This is not the best of all possible worlds. We are all subject to aging beyond maturity, disease, injury, death, and so on. Were it not for these various evils, each of us would enjoy the prospect of an indefinitely extensive succession of possible goods. Perhaps it is this fact that Nagel has in mind in the quotation cited earlier. If so, his mistake is to think that the deprivation of future possibilities for good that we all suffer is attributable to death when it is in fact overdetermined by a package of evils of which death is only one.

The fact that we all suffer this deprivation equally does not, however, imply that we are all equally unfortunate. Consider again the comparison between Joe and Gerry. Even if their losses are ultimately the same, their gains from life have not been. The explanation of why there is less reason to grieve for Gerry is simply that he has had a fair share of life. Relative to reasonable expectations, he has had a rich and full life. Joe's life, by contrast, has fallen short of what he could reasonably have expected to gain from life.

Even though those who gain more from life than most of us *do* suffer a misfortune when they die or when their lives become such that death, in the circumstances, would be good for them, they are nevertheless seldom to be pitied. Feelings such as pity have to be adjusted to normal or reasonable expectations. Consider the case of someone who badly wants to travel to distant parts of the universe. It would be a mistake to suppose that he suffers no misfortune in being unable to do what he most wants to do (something which we would all agree to be well worth doing if it were possible—i.e., his desire, though idle, is not frivolous). But the fact that his desire is frustrated does not evoke pity. This is because pity is appropriate only in cases in which a person is unable to fulfill reasonable expectations given the circumstances of human life.[22]

If we assume that there is a limit to the amount of good that any life can contain, then it is natural to conclude that there is a correlation between what a person gains from life and what he loses when possibilities for good cease to be available to him. But, when we assess our lives relative to the possibility of a desirable immortality (which is what we do when we measure the misfortune inflicted on us jointly by aging, disease, physical vulnerability, death, etc.), it ceases to be true that, if other things (such as the quality of life) are equal, then the more a person gains from life, the fewer his losses will be when deprived of future possibilities for good. Since this correlation breaks down in this case, it is not unreasonable to measure the comparative misfortune that a person suffers in being deprived of future possibilities for good in terms of the extent to which the deprivation limits his gains from life rather than in terms of the extent to which it increases his losses.

There is, however, an objection to this claim. Consider the case of two elderly men, Faust and his friend Fred. Both have had lives of roughly equal length and quality. Faust is approached by Mephistopheles and given the elixir of youth—in this case with no penalty to be paid later on. The elixir gives

Faust the body of an eighteen-year-old. He then sets out joy-ously on a new life. But on the first day of the new life he and Fred are both run over by a bus. What should we say about this case? Both men suffer the misfortune of being deprived of future possibilities for good. Moreover, the limitation on their gains from life is the same in each case. Neither has gained more from life than the other. But surely Faust suffers a greater misfortune than Fred?

In fact Faust is no more unfortunate than Fred *in global terms*. It is true that Faust is killed just as he is about to embark on a second youth. What this means is that Faust's *death* is more tragic than Fred's. The event of his being hit by the bus is worse for Faust than being hit by the bus is for Fred. Thus if both Faust and Fred have been mortally injured by the bus and lie dying in their hospital beds, Faust will naturally feel greater bitterness about being hit by the bus than Fred will. It is often harder to bear the loss of some recently acquired good than it is never to acquire the good in the first place. But never to acquire some good is also a misfortune. So, just as Faust is unfortunate in having the benefits of the elixir snatched away from him, Fred is also unfortunate in never having been given the elixir.

I will now conclude this section by briefly considering one final problem case—a case which seems to pose a problem for any account of the badness of death. Suppose that there is a young woman who dies of a genetic condition that is both strongly incurable (in the sense that it is causally impossible to suppress its effects) and essential to her identity (in that any-one born without the condition would not have been *her*). Call this woman Genette. If we ask what would have happened if the transitive cause of her death had not occurred, the answer seems to be that she would never have existed. The possible world in which the transitive cause is absent is therefore not one in which she fares better than she does in the actual world. So it may seem that we are forced to conclude that she suffers no misfortune in dying of the condition, nor indeed in having the condition. Yet many of us share Nagel's intuition that death can be a misfortune even when it is strongly impossible that it should not occur.

I will not defend a particular solution to this problem, but will simply outline three possible responses, all of which have a certain plausibility. The first response is just to accept that Genette's death is not a misfortune on the ground that she has had the longest life that she could have. The second response concedes that there are no possible worlds in which she lives longer but rejects the inference that her death was not bad for her. This response appeals to counterpart theory. It holds that the truth-conditions for claims about what would have happened had she not had the condition are provided by closest possible worlds containing the closest counterpart to Genette in whom the genetic defect is absent. The fact that this counterpart would not, strictly speaking, be *Genette* would not necessarily undermine the relevance of events in these worlds to evaluative claims about Genette's life. According to some versions of counterpart theory, such as Lewis's, a counterpart in some possible world is never identical with the original object in the actual world.

The third response involves two deviations from the proposal advanced earlier. The first is that we should ask, not what would have happened if the transitive cause of Genette's death had not occurred, but instead what would have happened if the effects of her condition had been suppressed. The second is that we should allow that the closest possible world in which that antecedent is realized may contain some violation of the laws of causation that hold in the actual world. We may perhaps plead necessity in both cases. For example, the justification for the second deviation might be that, while we must preserve the laws of causation wherever possible, we are simply forced to admit closest possible worlds containing causal impossibilities when we consider antecedents which are themselves causally impossible. Consider for example, the claim that, if the law of universal gravitation were an inverse cube law rather than an inverse square law, objects would then attract one another less strongly at great distances and more strongly at short distances. This claim seems true, though the possible world which provides its truth-conditions is causally impossible. Notice, furthermore, that unless we make this concession we will be unable to sustain my earlier claim that we all suffer a misfortune in being physically vulnerable, susceptible to disease, and so on. If we accept that we are unfortunate in being vulnerable to injury, on the ground that if we were not, our lives would be both longer and happier, then we should be able to make the analogous claim in Genette's case that she is unfortunate in suffering certain effects of her condition, among which we include the fact that it leads to premature death.

Death and the Degree of Psychological Connectedness

Let us turn now to one final problem for the possible goods account. In general our belief is that death is worse the earlier it occurs. This seems to be implied by the possible goods account. For it would seem that, the earlier death occurs, the greater are the losses which the victim suffers and, correspondingly, the fewer are the gains which he derives from life. But many people feel that there are instances in which an earlier death is not worse for the victim, even if the whole of the life that is lost would have been well worth living. They believe that death at, say, one month after conception, or one month after birth, is not worse, or more tragic, than death at, say, twenty, or forty. Rather, death at twenty, or forty, is in fact *worse* than death before birth, or perhaps even in early infancy. How can this view be explained?

I think it is best explained by appealing to the theory which holds that the criterion of personal identity over time is psychological continuity.[23] According to this theory, continuing to exist as the same person over time essentially involves the holding of certain psychological relations—such as that between an experience and the memory of it, or that between an intention and the later act that carries it out. This presupposes that it is a necessary condition of being a person *at all* that an entity should have least some of the psychological states or characteristics that are the ingredients of these various relations. The theory is, moreover, reductionist. It holds that the existence of a person is ultimately reducible to the existence of a certain set of psychological events and the relations among them.

Since there is no mental life at all associated with a human fetus in the early stages of gestation, the fetus cannot be a person during this period. If, as I believe, personhood is an essential property, it follows that the fetus during this period cannot be the same individual as the person who would later exist if the fetus were to follow its natural path of development. Thus if a fetus dies early in its career, *it* suffers no loss at all. Since it has no mental life, its death cannot involve the loss of anything that

is of value to it at that time; and the loss of the future life that its
death involves is also no loss to it, since that life would not have
been *its* life but would instead have belonged to the person.[24]
Thus the reason why death at this early stage is not worse for
the victim than death at age twenty is that death at this stage is
not bad for the victim at all.

Later in the course of the development of a human fetus,
when the rudiments of a mental life begin to appear, a person
begins to develop. But the psychological attributes that are the
constituent elements of personhood do not appear all at once,
but instead appear gradually, so that the mental life that develops in association with the human organism becomes richer,
more sophisticated, and more unified as the organism matures
and develops. Since the existence of a person is nothing more
than the existence of certain psychological states and their inter-
relations, and since the appearance of the states and relations
that are constitutive of a person is a gradual process, the development or coming-into-existence of a person is also gradual.[25] It
seems to follow that the existence of a person can be a matter of
degree. During the period when the mental life associated with
the developing organism remains relatively primitive, the person does not yet fully exist. What exists is only a potential or
developing person—an entity in the process of becoming a person. Only when this sequence of mental activity reaches a
certain level of complexity and sophistication does the person
fully exist. There is, however, no determinate threshold of complexity and sophistication such that in passing the threshold the
person suddenly achieves full existence. Rather, there is a period during which, while what exists is clearly at least a potential
or developing person, it is indeterminate whether it has yet fully
become a person.[26]

Let us suppose that even one month after the birth of the
human organism the person is not yet fully realized. The one-
month-old infant is still only a potential, or developing, person.
If the infant dies, its losses will be less than those that a fully
developed person normally suffers through death. The future
life that is lost when the infant dies would have been the life of
a fully existing person, and hence it belonged only partially to
the infant itself. This helps to explain why death in early infancy
is not worse for the victim than, say, death at twenty. It is only

after a person becomes fully real that death is normally worse for him the earlier in his life it occurs.

A different though closely related way of supporting the same conclusion appeals to a reductionist view about what matters in personal survival. Most of those who accept the psychological continuity theory of personal identity believe that identity is not what matters in personal survival. What matters is not that there should later exist someone who is *me* but instead that there should later be someone with whom I am sufficiently closely psychologically connected. Psychological connectedness, in other words, provides the principal basis for egoistic concern about the future.[27] Psychological connectedness, however, is a matter of degree. This suggests that the weaker the psychological connections between a person now and the same person later, the weaker his grounds will be now for egoistic concern about his later life.

Even if we suppose—what seems doubtful—that a one-month-old human being can be regarded as a fully real person, there will be few, if any, direct psychological connections between the person at one month and the person later in life. Hence our grounds for concern about the infant's future life for *its* sake will be correspondingly weak. If the infant dies, there is a sense in which *its* losses are less than those that an adult human being normally suffers through death, since the future it loses would have been less closely connected to it in the ways that provide grounds for egoistic concern—or perhaps, in this case, grounds for concern for its sake. (Of course, the infant's death may mean the loss of a glorious future life. But the only loss that matters significantly where the infant—qua infant—is concerned is the loss of those parts of its future life with which it would have been psychologically connected.)

The Revised Possible Goods Account

What this appeal to the theory of personal identity suggests is that the possible goods account, to be plausible, cannot assess the losses involved in death by simply summing up the goods that life would likely have contained were it not for death. These goods must instead be weighted in such a way that the loss through death of some future good will count for more the closer the psychological connections would have been between the person as she was at the time of her death and as she would have been at the time at which she would have received or experienced the good.[28]

There are other ways in which the possible goods account can be revised or extended in order to be better harmonized with our common conception of the badness of death. It should, for example, make some provision for the importance of desire. While it seems implausible to suppose that one can fully account for the badness of death in terms of the fact that death frustrates so many of the victim's desires, it does seem to make a difference whether and to what extent the possible life which death prevents would have or might have contained experiences or activities that the victim actually cared about during his life.[29] So, for example, even if the possible life that is lost through death would have contained a rich variety of goods, and even if the victim would have cared about and valued these goods had he lived to experience them, his death may seem less tragic if these goods would have been ones that he cared little or nothing about while he was alive.

This might be partially explained in terms of the assumption that the change in values that would have been required for the person to come to appreciate the goods would have involved a weakening of psychological connectedness. But this is not a complete explanation. The desires and concerns a person has are important in assessing the badness of her death independently of the fact that desires and values are constituent elements in psychological connectedness. It is an important part of the explanation of the badness of death that death frustrates the victim's desires, retroactively condemns to futility her efforts to fulfill them, and generally renders many of her strivings vain and pointless.[30] In particular, death is worse to the extent that sacrifices have been made for the future, or to the extent that there has been an *investment* in the future.

Let me now review the results so far of our examination of the badness of death. Death is bad for a person (or developing person) at any point in his life, provided that the life that is thereby lost would on balance have been worth living. Other things being equal, the badness of death is proportional to the quality and quantity of the goods of which the victim is deprived. But, in assessing the goods of which the victim is deprived, we must weight them both according to the extent to which they were desired by the victim and according to how closely psychologically connected the person would have been at the time of acquiring them to himself at (and perhaps prior to) the time at which he in fact died. A short but perhaps helpful way of summarizing these results would be to say that death is worse the greater the potential unity and coherence of the life it disrupts.

It is perhaps worth emphasizing, in concluding this section, that, while the degree of unity and psychological connectedness in a life is relevant to assessing the value of the life or the extent to which the life is worth living, even a high degree of unity and connectedness is not a sufficient condition for a life's being well worth living. For not only can a life be highly unified and yet be of a very low quality, but it can also be highly unified around projects or aspirations that are trivial, absurd, contemptible, vile, or even evil. Thus the account I have sketched of the badness of death, and the implied account of the goodness of continued life, is merely formal. It is an account (and only a partial account at that) of the *structure* of the good life, and thus is compatible with different conceptions of the *content* of the good life. A more complete account would have to provide criteria for evaluating the meaningfulness of the different ways of living even highly unified lives.

A Paradox

As we have seen, the view I have developed implies that death at, say, thirty-five is normally worse than death at one month. This seems plausible, and coincides with our intuitions. For, when a person dies at thirty-five, the life she loses is normally one with which she would have been closely psychologically connected and in which she would have enjoyed many of the goods that she valued, desired, and strived for. But neither of these points is true in the case of the life that is lost when a person dies at one month. It therefore seems plausible to say that a thirty-five-year-old normally stands to gain more from continuing to live than a one-month-old does, and that a thirty-five-year-old loses more through death. And this provides good grounds for thinking that death is worse at age thirty-five than it is at one month.

Let us suppose, however, that there is a newborn baby with

a condition that, if untreated, will cause the baby to die at one month. The condition can be cured, but the treatment itself has the effect of making it inevitable that the person will die at the age of thirty-five. Should the baby's condition be treated? Most of us feel that, if the person's life could be expected to be worth living, then the baby ought to be treated. But this seems to indicate that we prefer for his sake that the person should die at thirty-five rather than at one month. But how can that be, given our earlier conclusion that death is worse at thirty-five than it is at one month?

We might say that to have more life that is worth living is always better than to have less, other things being equal. But that seems simply to restate the view that, if further life would be worth living, death is always worse the earlier it occurs. And that is what we have denied. We seem on the one hand to believe that death at thirty-five is worse, or more tragic, than death at one month. But now consideration of the case of the baby with the treatable condition leads us to believe that death is worse the earlier it occurs. We believe that it would be worse for this individual to die at one month than to die at thirty-five.

This paradox challenges the view about the badness of death that I have sketched because it seems to suggest that we feel compelled both to affirm and to deny the implications of that view. Is there a way in which the paradox might be dissolved? One suggestion might be that the paradox arises from our treating two different but superficially identical comparisons as if they were the same comparison. Consider, by way of analogy, the comparison between the following two choices. The first is a choice between death at a very early age—say at nine months after conception—and death at a much later age—say at thirty-five—for the *same person*. The second choice is between death at a very early age for one person and death at a much later age for *another* person. Both of these choices arise in a case in which a thirty-five-year-old woman who is nine months pregnant and will die unless a craniotomy is performed on the fetus. Suppose that, if the craniotomy is not performed, the baby will survive but, because of an inherited condition, will live to be only thirty-five. If we look just at the case of the fetus, we feel that it would clearly be worse for it to die now rather than at thirty-five. But if we compare the death of the mother now, at age thirty-five, with the death of the fetus now, most of us feel that the death of the mother would be the worse of the two.

While focusing on the case of the fetus alone might lead us to conclude that death at nine months after conception is worse than death at thirty-five, focusing on the comparison between the death of the fetus and the death of the mother tempts us to conclude that death at thirty-five is worse than death at nine months after conception. But, it might be argued, there is here only a surface paradox. For the terms of the two comparisons between death at nine months after conception and death at thirty-five are not the same. When we focus on the case of the fetus alone, we are comparing death at nine months with death at thirty-five rather than earlier, at nine months. In this case, therefore, choosing death at thirty-five would mean that the person would *gain* thirty-five years of life. But when we compare the death of the fetus with the death of the mother, we are comparing death at nine months rather than at thirty-five with death at thirty-five rather than much later, at the end of a full life. Death at thirty-five for the mother, unlike death at thirty-five for the person in the previous comparison, involves no gains. Hence it is not surprising that we get different answers in the two comparisons. Death at nine months *is* worse than death at thirty-five rather than at nine months; but is it *not* necessarily worse than death at thirty-five rather than at some much later time.

It may seem that the paradox as I stated it earlier trades on exactly the sort of confusion I have uncovered here. On the other hand, even here when we consider the case of the fetus alone we conclude that it would be worse for that individual to die at nine months after conception than to die at thirty-five, and this alone seems inconsistent with our earlier claim that pre-natal death is less bad for the victim than death at thirty-five. To dissolve the paradox completely it seems that we must recognize that the comparative badness of different possible deaths does not necessarily determine which death it would be worse to suffer. While it is usually worse for a person to suffer a worse death (e.g., to die at forty rather than at fifty), the case of the fetus suggests that it can sometimes be better to suffer a worse death. Similarly, it can also be worse to have a less bad death—for example, when death becomes less bad for a person because the life that he would otherwise have had has now become less good than it might have been. In the latter case, the fact that his death has become less bad may seem a double misfortune.

But how, it might be asked, could it be better to suffer a worse death if the badness of death is simply a function of the deprivation which the victim suffers? How, in other words, can it be better to be deprived of more? The proper response to these questions is, it seems, to note that there are two ways of assessing the deprivation involved in death. My claims above about the comparative badness of death in infancy and death in later life were relativized to persons-at-times. But the claims of this section, which seem to clash with those earlier claims, are of a different sort: they are claims about how death affects a life as a whole. The claim that death at thirty-five is worse than death in early infancy is a claim about the relative badness of death to persons at the time of death; while the claim that it is worse for a person to die in early infancy than at age thirty-five is a claim about the effect of death on the value of a person's life as a whole. Once we distinguish these two forms of evaluation, we can see that the two claims are in fact compatible and that there is no real paradox in the idea that it can be better for a person to suffer a worse death.

CHAPTER FOURTEEN

The thing to remember is that each time of life has its appropriate rewards, whereas when you're dead it's hard to find the light switch. The chief problem about death, incidentally, is the fear that there may be no afterlife—a depressing thought, particularly for those who have bothered to shave. Also, there is the fear that there is an afterlife but no one will know where it's being held. On the plus side, death is one of the few things that can be done as easily lying down.

—Woody Allen, *Without Feathers*

Annihilation

Steven Luper-Foy

I do not want to die—no; I neither want to die nor do I want to want to die; I want to live for ever and ever and ever.

—Miguel de Unamuno, *Tragic Sense of Life*

Like Unamuno, many people find it abhorrent to think that well within 90 years they are going to die and utterly cease to exist. Those who believe that they will *never* cease to exist (perhaps because they think of dying as a transition to an afterlife in which they will live forever) are usually happy about it, and would not willingly forgo the immortality they expect. People who look upon annihilation as a grim prospect certainly may be well aware that under certain circumstances it must be regarded as the lesser of the evils among which choice is limited.[1] They realize that it may be the only escape from a spate of creatively cruel torture, for example, and so a better option than suffering further pain. They may even be willing to say that if their lives were long enough and their possibilities exhausted, then insufferable boredom would set in.[2] And dying after a short life of (say) 100 years might be better than being forced to live on into

Reprinted by permission from *The Philosophical Quarterly* 37, no. 148 (July 1987): 233–52. Susann Luper-Foy, Curtis Brown, and the editors of *The Philosophical Quarterly* provided me with many important suggestions and criticisms; I want to thank them for their help.

a future that consists of an eternity of empty, indistinguishable days. But to acknowledge that there are worse fates than annihilation in the near future is not to deny that it is a terrible fate. Aside from a future filled with the agonies or boredom of the damned, a worse fate than no future at all is difficult to imagine. It *may* be that forever is longer than anyone would voluntarily live; but how many would refuse the chance to drink a potion that would allow them to live as long as they liked?

Even people who argue that dying is not a bad thing do not really seem to believe what they are saying.[3] More often than not, their anxiety to believe in the innocuousness of their demise prevents even brilliant thinkers from realizing that their arguments are inane. Epicurus's famous argument, for example, is about as absurd as any I have seen: "Death is nothing to us. It concerns neither the living nor the dead, since for the former it is not, and the latter are no more."[4] Make no mistake about it: when Epicurus speaks here of death, he means *annihilation*, and his claim is that annihilation is *nothing* to us. The self-deception of people like Epicurus is not conscious; we cannot relieve our anxiety by swallowing beliefs of whose inanity we are aware. But deception is nonetheless at work.

Let us assume with Epicurus that death means annihilation. Then can we truthfully say that death is *nothing* to us? I think not. Nor should we *want* to believe that the deaths we shall soon face are nothing to us, I shall argue. Once we see what we would have to be like in order to be truly as unconcerned about dying as Epicurus professed to be, we shall see that we are better off dreading our dying day. However, I shall suggest that there are steps we can take to ensure that if luck is on our side, dying will not be *as* bad a thing for us as it is capable of being. But few are so lucky.

The Misfortune of Dying

Why should anyone believe that dying (thought of as annihilation) is a misfortune? One suggestion begins with the observation that something is a misfortune for us if it thwarts our desires.[5] You would do me an evil if you stole my cherished pet, since thereby you prevent me from fulfilling my desire to live in peace with my pet. On the other hand, if all I wanted for my pet was that it lead a reasonably comfortable life, and it was not my wish that it be *me* who provided for its comfort, then you would do me no harm if you stole my pet so long as you saw to its well-being. In so doing you would not have thwarted my desires.

It seems reasonable to say, then, that whatever prevents me from getting what I want is a misfortune for me. But if something that thwarts my desires is an evil for me, then dying is an evil for me (though perhaps the lesser of all the evils that are inevitable in my circumstances), since it thwarts my desires. Of course, to say that dying thwarts my desires is to understand "thwarting my desires" liberally. An event can prevent me from fulfilling my desires not just by frustrating my attempts to fulfill them, but also by *removing* my desires. If an event pulls one of my desires out by the roots, it certainly does prevent me from fulfilling it. It is in this sense that dying thwarts my desires. It is a misfortune for me for the same reason that being forced to swallow a drug that washes away my desires (including my desire *not* to have swallowed the drug) is a misfortune for me.

We have said that dying is a bad thing for us since it frustrates our desires. However, a more accurate way to put matters is that dying is bad for us *if* it thwarts our desires. On the strength of the premise that what thwarts my desires is a misfortune for me, we cannot conclude that my dying is a bad thing for me unless I *have* desires that would be thwarted by my death. A death which comes when I have exhausted *all* of my ambitions will be a welcome release from a life destined to be one of excruciating emptiness.

An objection can even be made to the thesis that a death which frustrates its victim's desires is an evil. Suppose that at some point in our lives the only goals we *do* have left would fail to be rewarding or would even make us miserable if we were to achieve them. We would not judge something to be an evil for us if the only goals it frustrated or eradicated were ones which would prove to be unfulfilling or ones which would make us miserable if we were to accomplish them. So dying at a time that interrupts only our pursuit of such goals should not be regarded as a misfortune for us. But an important sort of death, it would seem, remains an evil, namely, one that prevents its victims from fulfilling *fulfilling* desires. Call such a death a *premature* one. Even prematurity as we have defined it is not an infallible sign of a regrettable end; however, it will serve us well enough.

Epicureans

The idea that a premature death is a misfortune for its victim seems rather obvious. I believe that it has been responsible for most of the anxiety which people (such as I) have felt about dying; it seems to them very likely that they are going to die prematurely even if they live to be 120 years old, which they will not. Their plans stretch far out into their futures, and they see no reason why a hundred years from now they would not plan ahead with equal fervor—if it were not for the realization that they cannot survive the inevitable physical breakdown of their bodies which is soon to take place.

Those of us who are uncomfortable or even bitter about dying are appalled by the cheerful indifference of people who are capable of agreeing with Epicurus's absurd claim that "death is nothing to us." What would people have to be *like* to really think that their deaths are nothing to them (assuming that their lack of concern is not simply due to their refusal to dwell upon "morbid" subjects)? The answer, as we shall see, is that to the extent that such people are understandable at all, they are rather coldhearted and passionless. Having said that, I nonetheless want to claim that they are worth careful study. By emulating a certain sort of "Epicurean," as I shall call an individual who is indifferent to dying, it may be possible for others to acquire a measure of equanimity in the face of death without adopting the less desirable characteristics of Epicureans. But before I describe the kind of Epicurean it would behoove us to become, I shall describe others whose ways we should shun.

Virtually the only thing worse than the prospect of spending eternity in unmitigated agony is the prospect of spending eternity in *even more intense* agony. It is obvious that dying would be better than either fate. But Epicureans could agree only if they were not completely indifferent to dying. To agree, they must be willing to admit that under some circumstances dying can be the best of all available alternatives because of the escape it provides. Yet this they cannot do. The fact that the Epicureans are *completely* indifferent to dying means that they never under any circumstances either want to die or want not to die, and that is possible only if under no circumstances do they prefer dying to anything nor anything to dying. This makes Epicureans considered as *completely* indifferent to dying extremely foreign; hence let us try to describe Epicureans whose indifference is somewhat limited. Our Epicureans are capable of thinking that dying is preferable to some alternatives, since it allows them to escape from an unbearable mode of life. But they remain incapable of thinking that there is an alternative than which dying is *worse*. For them, dying is no worse than (i.e., it is at least as good as) remaining alive no matter how utopian life might be. They believe that dying can be a good thing, but they cannot believe that it is ever a bad thing.

Because Epicureans prefer dying to various possibilities, they must be capable of having desires whose form can be expressed as follows:

I want the following to be the case: Were X not the case at given time *t*, then I would be dead at *t*.[6]

Call desires of this form *escape* desires. They set out conditions under which life is so bad that, according to the Epicureans, death is preferable. If Epicureans had no desires of this form, they would be incapable of ranking dying over living no matter what living entailed, even if living meant torture of the worst sort.

I think that we can make a further assumption about Epicureans, namely, even *they* must agree that a premature death, as we defined it, is a misfortune for its victim. It would be absurd for them to adopt an attitude of indifference when they face premature death, since that would entail being unconcerned about something that prevents them from fulfilling desires that they very much wish to fulfill.

Perhaps, however, it is hasty to think that the prospect of a premature death would dismay the otherwise unflappable Epicureans. Why couldn't they adopt the view that whatever causes us neither pain nor pleasure is a matter of indifference? This, in fact, was Epicurus's own hedonistic view:[7] something can be bad, he believed, only if it causes us pain; and something can be good only if it causes us pleasure. On the strength of the hedonistic criterion, Epicureans could claim that dying is nothing to us even if it does thwart our desires since it causes us neither pain nor pleasure. They would admit that the disease or aging process which causes us to die may be a bad thing; these causes of death may bring us experiences whose unpleasantness is formidable. But dying causes no sensations at all, they would point out. In fact, it brings about an end to all sensing. We lack even the opportunity to regret the fact that death has thwarted our desires; once we die, we experience neither pain, pleasure, nor regret for the simple reason that we experience nothing at all.

But isn't it a tragedy that death deprives us *even of the opportunity to experience, to delight, and to regret?*[8]

Consider the consequences of the hedonistic view. On this view, an event which *would* cause me great pain if I were to find out about it is a matter of indifference so long as I in fact never do. The fact that my spouse and children have fallen for the lies of my enemy and now hate me but are pretending not to is of no concern to me, according to hedonists, if my ignorance prevents that event from causing me any grief. Moreover, hedonists would cheerfully consent to being used in any way we like so long as we promise to precede their treatment with a drug that makes them *enjoy* what we do to them, or at least a drug that suppresses any unpleasant experiences that might otherwise result from the abuses we have planned for them. They could even be made to welcome our drugging away their free will so that they want to be our slaves.

At best, hedonistically inclined Epicureans could say that whatever *would* cause us neither pain nor pleasure if we *were* aware of it while not under the influence of powerful psychotropic drugs (or the like) is neither good nor bad. But this weakened sort of hedonism is not strong enough for their purposes. People who found out that their desires were going to be thwarted *would* be distressed by their discovery; they could not regard it as a matter of indifference. Nor could they be indifferent to that which thwarts their desires, and dying is one of the things that does.[9]

Epicureans never regard dying as a misfortune. But I have said that they would *have* to regard it as a misfortune if dying thwarted desires whose satisfaction would be fulfilling. Hence

Epicureans must not *have* any fulfilling desires that can be frustrated by death! Death for them can never be premature or else it *would* be a bad thing; therefore they must be so constituted that any time death comes it is mature. Assuming that Epicureans *have* goals, then either they are unfulfilling ones, or else they are ones that cannot be thwarted by death. If Epicureans had any other sort of goal, they could not be unconcerned about premature death.

But what would a desire that cannot be thwarted by death be *like*? One desire that obviously is impervious to death is the desire to *die*. Rather than being thwarted by my death, my goal to die is *achieved* through my death. Like the death wish, escape desires are also invulnerable to death. They are qualified desires for death: they say that if certain conditions are met, we wish to be dead. But they do not imply that there are any conditions under which we do *not* want to be dead. Hence death presents no obstacle to our satisfying them.

Nor does the list of relevant desires end there. Some of our aims are such that our chances of successfully accomplishing them are not really affected by what we do in the course of our lives or even by whether or not we *are* alive. Being alive does not help us achieve these ends; hence they cannot be thwarted by our deaths. Since the likelihood that such goals will be achieved does not depend on what we do with our lives, let us call these *independent* goals. Ones whose chances of being achieved do depend on our activities we can call *dependent* goals. My desire that the moon continue to orbit Earth, for example, is an independent goal; it cannot provide me any grounds for deploring death since the behavior of Earth and its satellite is unaffected by what I do in the course of my life.

Goals that have been dependent in the earlier part of my life can become independent as time passes. If at some point I fully accomplish my dependent goal of at least once visiting France, then thereafter it is independent. No matter what I do thereafter, I cannot make it more or less likely that at least once I set foot in France. Even my subsequent death would not reduce my chances of achieving that end. People whose dependent ends once made them vulnerable to premature death could therefore become less vulnerable by rendering those ends independent.

There is another, more interesting, type of desire that is invulnerable to our deaths. Suppose that we care about the situation at some future time, but only on the assumption that we shall be alive at that time; if we think that we shall be dead, we are indifferent about the situation. Suicidal depressants, for example, might take this view. They may strongly wish to be dead, and they may be totally indifferent to anything that may or may not happen once they *are* dead; yet they still may have the attitude that if they *are* to be alive, they should be well fed. They desire something—in this case being well fed—only on the assumption or condition that they will continue to be alive. It will be useful to characterize such conditional desires in a more formal way. My conditional desire concerning some situation X is one that takes the following form:

I want the following to be the case: Were I alive at *t*, X would be the case at *t*.[10]

Desires that are *not* in this way contingent on our being alive we can call *unconditional*.

Conditional desires are not independent desires. However, both dependent and independent goals are capable of being conditionalized, i.e., converted into conditional goals. Consider the dependent desire to be well fed, for example. As the case of the suicidal depressants mentioned a moment ago shows, it is entirely possible to possess a conditionalized desire to be well fed. My independent desire that the moon continue to orbit the sun can be conditionalized as well. I need only decide that what is important to me is the moon's orbit while I live.

The Epicurean Attitude Toward Life

As far as I can tell, the catalogue of desires that cannot be thwarted by death is limited to escape desires, independent desires, and conditional desires. Not one of the types of goals we have catalogued can be frustrated by death, and any other type of goal *would* be vulnerable to death. Epicureans must possess no fulfilling desires except the sort we have catalogued. This is the secret of their equanimity: since none of their fulfilling desires can be thwarted by death, Epicureans never regard death as a misfortune. Since limiting their desires to the catalogued sorts is the only way Epicureans could ensure that death is no evil for them, however, we shall want to consider what kind of person they have had to become as a result of that limitation. Only then can we decide whether it would be a good idea to follow their example.

Consider their motivation to take up the activities in which we normally engage. Since Epicureans never have any reason to avoid dying, it may appear that they have no reason to do *anything* (with the possible exception of committing suicide). But this is an important mistake. It is true that their independent desires cannot provide Epicureans grounds for any activities, since by definition these are desires about whose fulfillment Epicureans can do nothing of importance. However, conditional desires do provide strong reason for action. Such desires can enable Epicureans to take an interest in things for which life is a precondition. While indifferent to the prospect of dying in their sleep, Epicureans may take the attitude that if they *do* wake, their wakeful days should be spent in vigorous pursuit of an exciting career, in raising a family, etc. And for this to be possible, they will need to seek an education and work long hours in pursuit of a career.

But wouldn't they necessarily be indifferent to their health? No, since it would be eminently reasonable for them to want to spend their days—if days they will indeed spend—in the comparative comfort and convenience of health rather than the discomfort of disease. It is not necessary to want to *avoid* dying in order to want to do things that tend to make dying unlikely. The fact that our goals make our deaths unlikely can be an unintended side-effect. Even Epicureans who are no longer living out of inertia but who have developed a positive wish to die may be unable to commit suicide because of a strong aversion to pain.

Suppose that someone went around injecting Epicureans with painless but deadly poison. Wouldn't an Epicurean society have to be indifferent about that practice, since it would not interfere with any Epicurean's desires? No, precisely because it *would* interfere. It is true that an Epicurean cannot abhor these murders on the grounds that they are bad for their *victims*. But the murders could be abhorred (unless they involve the massacre of entire societies or the entire human race) because they deprive people of their loved ones. The murders are bad for the survivors, who wanted to share their lives (if lives they will lead) with the victims. Still Epicureans could condemn the murder of pariahs who play no positive role in society only on the grounds that if that sort of thing were permitted it might lead people to kill those who *do* have a role to play. Anyone who is inclined to condemn Epicureans on the grounds that they do not appreciate how bad murder is should, however, recall that the victims *themselves* are to their very cores genuinely indifferent to dying. How bad can it be to do something to someone who is incapable of anything except absolute indifference about what you plan to do? We non-Epicureans could object to the murdering of the pariahs on Utilitarian grounds (killing them eliminates future pleasure); just as we could object to the killing of infants and animals that *cannot assess* their fates; but since the pariahs *can*, and are indifferent about future pleasure, shouldn't their rational and informed assessments win out?

So far, adopting the Epicurean approach may not seem terribly unattractive. If something which is a bad thing for us, given our present desires, turns out to be inevitable, then why not alter our desires so that we no longer must regard the inevitable as an evil?[11] Dying is inevitable, so why not disarm it by limiting ourselves to the desires of Epicureans? Unfortunately, the indifference to dying that the Epicurean approach would secure us comes at a price most of us will not be willing to pay. The attraction of the Epicurean way of looking at things is that they do not care whether their lives are shorter than usual or longer than usual; death, whenever it comes, is nothing to them. However, Epicureans think that death is nothing to them only because they think that *life* is nothing to them. They are capable of their indifference to death only because they have pared down their concerns to the point that *life* is now a matter of indifference to them. For in avoiding all aspirations that can be thwarted by death, Epicureans have had to avoid all desires which are capable of giving Epicureans a reason for living. In order to maintain their unconcern about dying, they must avoid having any reason whatsoever for not dying. However, any reason for living is an excellent reason for not dying; so only if they avoid having any reason for living can they avoid having any reason for not dying.

The extent to which Epicureans have sabotaged their motivation for living can be brought out by examining the desires to which they are limited, desires that are invulnerable to death. Independent goals (unlike dependent ones) are incapable of giving us reason to remain alive and to avoid dying, since our lives and the things we do with our lives play no role toward the achievement of such goals. Conditional desires are similarly impotent; because they apply only on the assumption that we are alive, they cannot provide grounds for being alive. Like the other desires Epicureans possess, escape desires (as well as the death wish itself) are incapable of providing any reason to remain alive; on the contrary, escape desires provide reason to *die*. Beyond conditional, independent, and escape desires, the only other desires Epicureans can have are unfulfilling ones, and these are obviously as impotent as the others with respect to motivating Epicureans to live. Out of the desires possessed by Epicureans, then, a case for remaining alive cannot be built. Since they limit their desires to those listed above, and so consider dying at least as good as any other option, it is useful to characterize the Epicurean personality as *death-tolerant*.[12] By contrast, the personality of people who have unconditional desires that make living desirable can be called *life-affirming*.

Since Epicureans cannot allow themselves any motivation to live, they must ensure that they never think that it would be *good* to live. For to say that living is good certainly implies that it is preferable to dying, which is a view Epicureans must eschew. On their view, living no sort of life would be better than dying. A conception of a good or worthwhile life is a description of a life that would be good to live; such a conception Epicureans completely lack. (What they *can* have is a conception of a life such that it is a matter of indifference whether it is lived.) To make sure they do not develop one, moreover, they must be very selective in their activities. If an activity or set of activities promises to be so enjoyable that it threatens to make a life spent in pursuit of that activity *good*, then those who wish to retain a death-tolerant personality must abandon it in haste, or at least take steps which ensure that they do not enjoy what they do so much that they begin to show an interest in living. They must fill their lives with blander fare.

Nothing said here supports the claims, occasionally made, that life's being meaningful or worthwhile is due to the fact that we die,[13] or that life is *meaningless* because we die.[14] Both claims imply that it is due to death that life has the value it does, which is not true. A life can be made neither good nor bad by the fact that it will eventually end, any more than a car can be made good or bad by the fact that it will eventually be scrapped. A life has the value it does quite independently of the fact that it will end. In fact, *death* has the value it does due to the value of the life it ends. Speaking roughly, dying is a bad thing when living on would be good, and when living on would be bad, dying is good.

Because Epicureans are not interested in anything that could lead them to regard living as a good thing, they do not care about *anything* that they believe will happen after they die, ignoring what they care about through their independent desires, which (as we have seen) have no motivational power in the Epicureans' lives anyway. Those with a death-tolerant personality live out of inertia most of the time, acting only under the influence of their continual desires unless life becomes unpleasant enough to opt out of. But the interest they take in things through the agency of their conditional desires does not extend beyond what they believe to be the temporal boundaries of their lives. For given that their entire attitude about whether or not a given state of affairs X holds at some time *t* is conditional, then if they believed that they would be dead at *t*, then they would be indifferent about whether or not X would hold at *t*. This makes Epicureans peculiar people indeed. Out of her conditional desire for their well-being, an Epicurean mother may well be concerned about whether her children will survive an imminent catastrophe, but *only* if she assumes that she too will survive. Her conditional desires leave her completely indifferent to their welfare if she assumes that she will die. Nor does the peculiar pattern of her concern for her offspring end here. She may well place herself between a crazed beast and her children since she does not think that her life will be bearable to her if they die, and so is willing to risk her life in their defense. Her life means nothing to her in any case. But she is incapable of writing a will or taking out life insurance out of concern for her children's well-being after she dies, even if she knows that they will lead a horrible existence if she fails to act. Whether their lives go well or poorly after she dies is a matter of utter indifference to her.

Still less could Epicureans desire the welfare of future generations. Because their concern for others is conditional, Epicureans cannot believe that the welfare of future generations matters at all, though the welfare of their contemporaries may be important to them.

Nonetheless, it *is* conceivable that Epicureans have a conditional desire to spend their days working for the benefit of future generations. They could take the attitude that so long as they are to go on, they will work for the benefit of posterity. And an Epicurean mother could desire that, so long as she is alive tomorrow, she will spend it working to ensure that her children flourish after she dies. However, these attitudes are not to be mistaken for concern about what occurs after the Epicureans die. Epicureans just do not care what happens then. They are capable only of indifference about the well-being of posterity, and an Epicurean mother could not care less about the welfare of her children after she believes she will die. Therefore, even if Epicureans take an interest in *working for* the welfare of posterity, they remain indifferent to the welfare of posterity. It takes peculiar people to desire to spend time ensuring that some state of affairs holds in the future even though they are indifferent about whether that state of affairs comes to be. As a matter of psychological fact, it may be impossible. So since Epicureans must sustain their indifference about the future if they are to remain Epicureans, it may be impossible for them to want to spend time influencing the future.

It is worth noting that Epicureans will remain unconcerned about what occurs after their projected dying day if they adopt the hedonist claim that everything which does not actually cause them pain or pleasure is a matter of indifference. Hedonists of this sort are capable of caring about the welfare of their children, but only their welfare at times when the hedonist parents believe that they (the parents) will be alive. For they realize that dead parents can be caused neither pain nor pleasure by the fate of their children. Earlier I argued that hedonism is too implausible to sustain the judgment that premature death is no evil. Here we have a fresh reason to steer clear of hedonism: consistent hedonists exhibit a callousness which renders their view too unsavory to adopt.

There are still more reasons not to adopt a death-tolerant personality. Quite often, conditionalizing our desires would mutilate them so much that retaining the conditionalized versions of them is something we would not want to do or are psychologically unequipped to do. Consider, for example, the conditionalized form of our altruistic concern for the welfare of others. It is probably not really possible for us to care intensely about someone's welfare up to the point at which we believe that we shall die, yet be entirely indifferent to their welfare thereafter. Some of us could probably manage to be relatively unconcerned about anyone else's welfare at *any* time. Becoming utterly aloof in this way is probably the only way any of us could become death-tolerant, however, since none of us has the capacity to care intensely yet within sharply defined temporal boundaries.

Even the conditionalized form of a purely self-centered desire can be enormously peculiar. Our self-centered projects play an important role in our lives, and most of them can succeed only if we survive, either because we are an essential ingredient in them, as I am in my plan to become President of Money Bank, or my plan to lead a long life of adventure, or else because we play a key role in them. Hence we must conditionalize our concern for these projects if we are to emulate the Epicureans. But is a deep concern about such projects really consistent with the attitude that their failure is a matter of indifference so long as we do not live through their demise? How serious can I be about wanting to discover the cure for cancer if I am just as happy to fail so long as I do not live through my failure? The fact is that a conditionalized passion is not a passion, for we can conditionalize our passions in life only if we no longer take them seriously enough to want to live another day. Once conditionalized, they can no longer play any significant role in what might have been a worthwhile life.

Epicureanizing Our Desires

Dying is a constant threat to those of us who are unable or unwilling to abandon our concern for projects and lives whose welfare depends crucially on us, and so for us death is an evil. The strategy of the Epicureans, moreover, has proved to be unavailable to those of us who have a life-affirming personality, since they owe their indifference about longevity to their indifference to living. At best, life is a burden for those with a death-tolerant personality, something to be made as free of misery as possible; it is either a bore which they can take or leave, or a curse they would be better off without. Their view is not quite that *nothing* is anything to us, but it comes very close. Instead of succumbing to the despairing attitude that we have nothing to live for, we should be better off immersing ourselves in projects for which we *are* capable of living, and resign ourselves to the fact that we cannot persist in our endeavors for long.

Although we should not emulate the Epicureans we have described, it does seem to me that there *is* a type of Epicurean which we should strive to become. Unlike the ones we have discussed before, the Epicureans I have in mind are anxious to squeeze as much as possible out of life. But these neo-Epicureans (as I will call them) realize that one can squeeze out of a lifetime only as much as a lifetime can hold. If people's life expectancy can be increased, they are certainly in favor of doing so, since more can be squeezed into a longer life. The opportunity to live longer is a bad thing for *no* one. An abundance of life might make us less anxious to pack as much as possible into each moment of our lives, but what would be the harm of living at less frenzied a pace? And of course, if there are people who cannot find anything to do with their extended lives, suicide is always an option. But neo-Epicureans realize that they are forced to accept the life expectancy that is determined by the technology of their era in history. That technology, whether advanced or primitive, determines what for them is a normal lifetime.[15] Neo-Epicureans have impressed upon themselves the fact that unless further advances in life extension techniques can be expected, they cannot possibly expect much more than a normal lifetime, *and so they cannot allow their happiness to require more.* This they accomplish partly by making an effort to commit themselves only to projects that can come to fruition within the confines of a normally extended lifetime. They realize that it is reasonable to live one's life as if on the assumption that one will survive a normal lifetime, but not to plan life as if on the assumption that one will live beyond. Hence they try to make sure that their ambitions do not extend beyond a normal lifetime except in the form of *conditional* desires as well as escape desires.

But the neo-Epicureans could not limit their goals in this way without abandoning much of what makes life worthwhile. For example, they would have to forgo bringing children into the world—or at least avoid developing ties to any children they do produce—since their daughters and sons cannot be counted on to come to an end just as their Epicurean parents die. (Nor, presumably, would Epicurean parents want to ensure that their children would die on schedule if seeing to their demise *were* possible.) The only further alternative for Epicurean parents, caught in the predicament of being unable to reproduce for fear that they may become attached to their issue, is to conditionalize their concern for their children, to adopt the absurd attitude that a child's well-being is important while its parent is alive, but entirely a matter of indifference otherwise.

Rather than adopt one of these absurd approaches, the neo-Epicureans do allow themselves some ventures which will carry over beyond the reach of a normal lifetime. If they set out to raise children, they are prepared to care about the well-being of their families even when all of their children grow into adults. Yet as parents they realize that no matter what they (the parents) do in the course of a normal lifetime, their offspring could come to grief after the parents die. Neo-Epicureans, then, are not unconcerned about everything that happens after they die. But because they are not indifferent, they try to ensure that those of their concerns that their deaths might leave vulnerable are rendered invulnerable. For example, if they plan to have children, neo-Epicurean parents will see to it that the youngsters grow into relatively self-sufficient adults, or at least that the children's well-being does not depend on the survival of their parents beyond a normal lifetime, and so make sure that well before then they have fully equipped their children for life. Of course, neo-Epicureans also realize that they could die before they have equipped their children; but that does not stop from reproducing, so long as the odds are in favor of their surviving long enough. To help minimize the possible tragedy of leaving their children parentless, they will resort to devices such as insurance.

Neo-Epicureans have a similar approach to all of their other concerns which might be left vulnerable to what occurs after their deaths. They are not indifferent to these matters; instead, and because of their concern, they see to it that the goals they are concerned about are as invulnerable to their deaths as can be. All such goals neo-Epicureans convert to independent goals, so that the success of these projects is not made less likely by their deaths. In short, as their final years approach, neo-Epicureans make themselves completely dispensable to everything they care about. Not worried that the concerns of their lifetimes will come to a bad end with their deaths, they do not regret passing away. They have, we might say, *epicureanized* their desires. Death which comes before they have done what they have set out to do they hate with all their hearts, since it comes between them and what they consider dear. But death which comes after they have accomplished their goals or rendered their goals independent they do not grudge. It will catch the neo-Epicureans only with independent or conditional desires.

Being dispensable, however, is something that neo-Epicureans carefully postpone to the very end. Early on in life, they begin taking steps that will ensure that they will *be* dispensable, but—like a coffin—dispensability is something they want only when they die. For having our lives deeply intertwined with those of others is part of what makes life worthwhile. What neo-Epicureans want is not that their lives should have made no difference to anybody or anything. What they want is that their *deaths* should make no difference. To the extent that our being alive plays no important role in any of the matters we care about (and to the extent that we care about *nothing*), to that extent we have no reason to value our lives. It is the fact that we are indispensable to people and projects we care about that motivates us to live another day; we should undermine this motivation, therefore, only when we are prepared to die.

The neo-Epicurean approach to life is, I think, an attractive one. It allows those who can assume that their lifetimes will be normal to remain relatively calm about their future deaths without becoming aloof from life. But if I am not already a neo-Epicurean, should I become one? Or should I perhaps be content to admire them from afar? If I *already* take an interest in projects for the success of which I would have to live far beyond a normal lifetime, I can become a neo-Epicurean only if I give up or modify those undertakings. If I find myself engaged in the pursuit of such endeavors, *can* I do what it takes to become a neo-Epicurean even if I want to? Are our desires sufficiently within our control that we can give up certain ones of them if we wish, perhaps replacing them with more desirable ones?

Now of course we have some goals that we cannot modify, no matter how badly we might want to. To say that we should modify them is therefore absurd. (I am assuming that we are not willing to alter our desires using brainwashing or the like. More on that presently.) No one can give up the desire to avoid pure pain, for example, not even masochists. They seek the pleasure which accompanies an otherwise painful experience. Like the aversion to pain, a fondness for pleasures such as gastronomic and orgasmic ones is also something we all have by virtue of our very nature; we are *built* that way. Nor are all of our involuntary desires visceral. Some of them are manifestations in our conscious life of underlying needs. It is human nature, for example, to need the association of other people; that is why solitary confinement is such an effective punishment. Even if we never form the conscious desire for close ties with others—indeed, even if we think we prefer a life of complete solitude—we need them all the same; because of our human nature we would be miserable without them.

But not all desires are so deeply rooted as those that stem from underlying needs. And these shallower ambitions tend to be more malleable. My desire to acquire a cat, for example, is easily abandoned. To drop it, it may be sufficient for me to discover that I am violently allergic to fur. Whether I should change desires that are subject to voluntary manipulation is, therefore, an open question.

Even desires that are to some extent malleable cannot be changed under just any circumstances. Changing a desire is not like changing the position of our hands; we can move our hands at whim, but we cannot desire at whim. But usually we can make substantial changes in our desires when it is clear to us that it is rational for us to do so. The cat was out as soon as I saw that owning it meant suffering.

In speaking about modifications which we can or cannot make in our desires, I have been assuming that we do not resort to measures involving brainwashing or the chemical or surgical manipulation of our brains. However, I see no reason why in principle we should not make desirable changes in our scheme of desires using hypnosis, chemicals, or other sorts of artificial methods. In fact, such artificial methods are constantly invoked already. People who wish to give up smoking are well served by hypnotists who help them conquer their urge for cigarettes, for example. To countenance artificial methods is not to advocate *forced* manipulations of people's desires, of course, any more than to recommend hypnotism to a reluctant smoker is to kidnap and brainwash a smoker who is happy only with tobacco. The suggestion is just that *if* individuals decide that it really would be desirable to epicureanize their aspirations, they may as well use artificial means of doing so rather than limiting themselves to what they can achieve through sheer willpower.

In order for us to avoid forming a desire, or to abandon one we have already formed, it is often sufficient that we come to realize that we cannot possibly fulfill it. But not always. Moreover, the difficulty we have in abandoning desires we just cannot satisfy is sometimes overwhelming even when they are not involuntary. The desire for sight is not wired in, unlike the desire to avoid pain; those who are born blind and always convinced that the condition is irreversible may never develop any serious desire to see. To do so would cause them needless suffering and would be irrational. But I strongly doubt that blind people who have been able to see for most of their lives will ever cease to crave sight. They will always deeply resent their sightless condition. After all, so much of what they value depended on their being able to see, and only if they can completely overhaul their values can they become reconciled to their fate. Of course, the rational thing for them to do is to overhaul their desires, but it is nonetheless tragic that they should have to resort to modification, and the fact that modification is the rational course of action does not mean they can pursue it, or even that they will want to try.

People who are considering whether or not to become neo-Epicureans are in a position in many ways analogous to that of the newly blind. The main difference is that whereas the blind are missing out on something of which most normal human beings are capable, it has never been possible for any human being to live much more than a normal lifetime. The dying are going through something no one has ever been able to escape and which no one may ever be able to escape. In view of the inevitability of death, there can be no question that the rational course is to give up aspirations that we can accomplish only if we live more than a normal lifetime, but it is still tragic that we should have to let these hopes go, tragic that we should have to deal with the misfortune of death by abandoning things we care about. If we nonetheless manage to do so, or better yet, if we can manage to avoid ever forming aspirations that death is certain to defeat, then we shall be a good deal happier. And it is likely that the task of adjusting our desires will become considerably easier if we take seriously the fact that in wishing to do what cannot be accomplished within the confines of a maximally extended lifetime we are trying to attain the impossible. It is conceivable that research will yield life extension techniques; that would call for a readjustment of the plans we make for our lives. But to plan our lives on the assumption that such techniques will be forthcoming would only result in bitter disappointment.

Abandoning desires that cannot be satisfied within the span of a normal lifetime is something we can accomplish only to the extent that we have not already allowed what is dear to us to depend on the impossible being possible. If we have, we face the task of inventing for ourselves a new plan of life that can be realized within the more narrow confines of a normal lifetime, a task that may well prove to be too much for us. It will be those who have been reared with the promise of immortality always before them that will suffer most when they become convinced of their mortality. A good deal of anguish is in store for them unless they never really took that promise so seriously as to let anything dear to them depend on immortality.

Many will find the task of epicureanizing their desires difficult. But some parts of that task are easy to accomplish. Ensuring our own dispensability, for example, is a good deal easier than we perhaps would like to believe. It is rare indeed that people's lives are shattered irretrievably when their parents die, especially when their parents have lived a complete lifetime. It is even more rare that world affairs turn on whether or not particular individuals survive beyond a normal lifetime. For the most part, people are already dispensable; becoming so takes no effort at all. If we are indispensable, it is likely to be because we have developed strong ties to a small number of people in whose lives we play a very important role. It is likely to be because we are united with friends (including those we love) in mutually rewarding activities and our friends value the fact that it is *we* who are taking part in those activities with them.[16]

Even if we succeed in epicureanizing our desires and living long enough to see our projects through, we must still face the usual concomitants of dying: pain and physical breakdown. While it is not accurate to say that dying is a bad thing for us because of the pain and physical decline that lead up to it, this pain and decline certainly are bad things, and even those of us who manage to hold our withering bodies together long enough to achieve what passes as "old age" can rarely hope to avoid suffering terribly before we die.

Still, there is an obvious strategy for minimizing the agony that precedes dying. Supposing that we truly have accomplished our projects on schedule, then instead of waiting for nature to decide the course of events leading up to our death, we are better off taking our fates into our own hands. In many cases, painless suicide will be the best course. But planning for ourselves a painless suicide will require us to make the truly agonizing decision that our ventures are at an end and that further living would not be worthwhile. Making this decision could be the worst experience we shall ever undergo. But we may not be so lucky. What we should experience if we did not make it is likely to be worse.

Summary

We should not be indifferent about dying, any more that we should be indifferent about other misfortunes that will befall us. And a misfortune dying assuredly is for those of us whose endeavors make living a good thing. For dying prevents us from engaging further in those endeavors which we find so rewarding.

Nor should we *want* to be indifferent about dying, in view of what we would have to become in order to be indifferent to death whenever it may come. What we would have to do is to renounce the many ties, concerns and projects that make us life-affirmers. No longer could we pursue any fulfilling desire that would be thwarted if we were to die. But it is precisely *these* goals whose satisfaction makes life worth living. These are the ones that give us a reason to think that living is good. Any aspiration capable of motivating us to live is one we can achieve only if we are alive; inevitably, then, any such hope would be frustrated by our deaths. In the end, then, to become indifferent to death, to adopt a death-tolerant personality, requires that we give up all desires that give us reason to live. It requires that we become indifferent to life. But we are better off thinking that dying is bad than thinking that living cannot be good.

If we are doomed to undergo the misfortune of dying, we can at least make our destiny as tolerable as possible. We can allow ourselves to live life passionately, but according to a plan whereby everything we propose to do can be accomplished within the span of a normal lifetime. Concerns which transcend those limits we should occasionally allow ourselves as well, but only if we plan to render them invulnerable to our deaths. If we succeed in molding the scheme of our desires in this way, and if we die only after accomplishing what we have set out to do, then for us dying will not be such a bad thing. Whether we can say that it will not be a bad thing *at all* depends on what we think we could do with more time than is granted us.

CHAPTER FIFTEEN

BORIS: You get used to the taste of death.
ALEXI: What does it taste like?
BORIS: Like liver.

—Woody Allen, *Love and Death*

Epicurus and Annihilation

Stephen Rosenbaum

Steven Luper-Foy's recent article, "Annihilation,"[1] joins a stead-
ily growing body of writings attacking the Epicurean view of
death.[2] That view of death is the striking idea that "death is
nothing to us," in Epicurus's own insouciant words, that being
dead is not bad for us. Being deeply convinced that annihilation
is a terrible fate, Luper-Foy dismisses Epicurus's argument as
"inane" and "absurd."[3] However inane and absurd he may feel
Epicurus's reasoning was, he, like numerous others, takes the
argument seriously enough to devote considerable intellectual
effort to its defeat. He, like others, may believe that the view has
a vague plausibility. However, not only is the Epicurean idea
vaguely plausible but also it can be effectively defended.[4] Furthermore, it has far-reaching implications for many moral issues
concerning death and killing.[5] Defending the view is not simply
an engaging historical exercise, but an important philosophical
enterprise. In this essay, I wish to do two things: first, to sketch
the Epicurean view and the way in which one may support it;
second, to reveal the misconceptions that Luper-Foy has and to
use them as a basis on which to describe more fully the Epicurean view and what it entails.

The central principle in Epicurus's view about death is that
one's own death is not bad for one. However poorly he may
have expressed the idea, this reading is the only one that can
make any sense of his various urgings about death. The expres-

Reprinted by permission from *The Philosophical Quarterly* 39, no. 154 (January
1989): 81–90.

sion "one's own death" may, perhaps obviously, be taken in various ways. One should not understand Epicurus's view to be either of the following: (1) that the *process* of one's dying is not bad for one; or (2) that the *prospect* of one's dying or death is not bad for one. To take his view as the former would be an illegitimate way of making him appear foolish, since, so obviously, one's dying can be bad for one. Further, taking Lucretius as a useful source for interpretation,[6] there is good evidence that rather than dying, Epicurus meant "being dead." Lucretius clearly did not understand Epicurus to have argued that dying is not bad for one. Additionally, Epicurus's own painful dying[7] gave him opportunity to retract the view that one's dying is not bad for one, yet he did not retract, leading one to hypothesize that he did not take his argument to be about dying. Finally, if one took Epicurus to have argued against the badness of one's dying, one could never entertain the slightest hope of penetrating his somewhat cryptic comment that "Death, therefore, the most awful of evils, is nothing to us, seeing that, when we are, death is not come, and, when death is come, we are not."[8]

One should also not interpret him to have meant that the prospect of one's death is not bad for one, since he used death's not being bad for one to argue that the prospect of one's death should not disturb one, as follows:

Foolish, therefore, is the man who says that he fears death, not because it will pain when it comes, but because it pains in the prospect. Whatsoever causes no annoyance when it is present, causes only a groundless pain in the expectation.[9]

Also, to suppose that he might have been claiming that the prospect of death or dying is not bad for one or actually disturbs no one psychologically would be to attribute to him an insensitivity to psychological reality which he did not have. In fact, he argued precisely as he did in the endeavor to undermine what he knew to be actual human fears about death.

If Epicurus meant to argue neither that the process of one's dying is not bad for one nor that the anticipation of one's death is not bad for one, what did he mean? The only way to make sense of what he actually said and of what his disciples said is to understand him as having argued that one's *being dead* is not bad for one.[10] One can thus easily comprehend not only the plausibility of the apparent argument Epicurus gave for the view, but also the other comments he made. It is useful to recollect a major portion of the passage in which Epicurus discussed death:

Accustom thyself to believe that death is nothing to us, for good and evil imply sentience, and death is the privation of all sentience; . . . Death, therefore, the most awful of evils, is nothing to us seeing that, when we are, death is not come, and, when death is come, we are not.[11]

Far from being "absurd," this embodies an interesting argument, which bears reflection. The argument is roughly that since (a) something can be bad for a person only if the person can be affected by it; (b) a person cannot be affected by something after the person ceases to be; and (c) a person's being dead occurs after the person ceases to be; therefore, a person's being dead cannot be bad for the person.[12] Of course, one may well wonder just how psychologically effective this argument can be in assuaging the sentiments of those who are afraid of death. However, it is a philosophical view and worth consideration, even if it has only a limited, or no, psychological efficacy. The latter is a distinct issue.

The Epicurean view that one's death is not bad for one, that it is not an "evil," does not logically entail that one's death (being dead) lacks other features. For example, it does not entail that one's death cannot occur prematurely or that one does not prefer that one not be dead. Hence, one who accepts the Epicurean point about death can consistently prefer not to be dead, want not to be dead, or, more positively, prefer to continue living, for various important reasons. One could take various attitudes toward one's being dead while still believing that it is not bad for one. In fact, Epicurus himself, shortly following his notorious argument, remonstrated with those who might be tempted to minimize the desirableness of life, and made it clear that he had a positive attitude toward life. He said:

The wise man does not deprecate life nor does he fear the cessation of life. The thought of life is no offense to him, nor is the cessation of life regarded as an evil. And even as men choose of food not merely and simply the larger portion, but the more pleasant, so the wise seek to enjoy the time which is most pleasant and not merely that which is longest. And he who admonishes the young to live well and the old to make a good end speaks foolishly, not merely because of the desirableness of life, but because the same exercise at once teaches to live well and to die well. Much worse is he who says that it were good not to be born.[13]

Epicurus's view is that one's death is not bad for one and that thus one should not fear it, since fearing that which is not bad or evil for one is baseless. It is compatible with this to take the attitude that living well is desirable and to prefer to continue living to being dead. Epicurean hedonists would prefer living to not living on the ground that one can have pleasure, the highest good, both of the active and passive sort,[14] while one is alive, but that one is insentient and not able to experience any pleasures in death.

A consideration of the principal criticisms in Luper-Foy's paper will shed further light on the Epicurean view. (1) He takes the Epicurean expression that "death is nothing to us" to mean that the prospect of being dead is necessarily a matter of complete unconcern and total indifference to one who accepts the Epicurean view. (2) He argues that being dead ("annihilation") is, contrary to Epicurus's conclusion, sometimes a misfortune for the one who dies. (3) He argues that one who consistently adopts the Epicurean view of death could only have certain types of limited, unfulfilling desires, and correlatively, that the consistent Epicurean would have to live an undesirable and inhumane sort of life. I shall consider each of Luper-Foy's three main critical points in order.

Because of Epicurus's expression "death is nothing to us," Luper-Foy takes it that Epicureans must be unconcerned about and completely indifferent to their own prospective deaths, including the time at which they will die. That he so understands it is evident from several comments he makes, among which are these:

Those of us who are uncomfortable or even bitter about dying are appalled by the cheerful indifference of people who are capable of agreeing with Epicurus's absurd claim that "death is nothing to us."[15]

Also,

The fact that the Epicureans are *completely* indifferent to dying means that they never under any circumstances either want to die or want not to die.[16]

Taking the expression in this way is natural for one who takes it literally, and taking it literally is natural for one who does not try to place it in the context of a comprehensive understanding of Epicurean texts. However, understanding it correctly is to understand it as a rhetorically provocative and somewhat exaggerated way of expressing the basic idea about death. I have already explicated the Epicurean view about death and described it in a way that demonstrates the baselessness of Luper-Foy's supposition that Epicureans must be completely indifferent to their deaths, but it will be useful to comment explicitly on the expression "death is nothing to us."

This expression occurs at least four times in the *Letter to Menoeceus*[17] and at least once in the *Kuriai Doxai* (key doctrines) as well as once in the Vatican Sayings.[18] The use of this was important to Epicurus, and, so far as I can estimate, he used it to do several things. He used it (1) to express the idea that one's death (being dead) is not bad for one, the conclusion of the Epicurean argument, as I have interpreted it; (2) to express his own and others' acceptance of the view; (3) to express that he did not, nor did other Epicureans, regard the prospect of being dead as bad for them; and (4) to express the Epicurean lack of fear of death. Perhaps it was meant to do other things as well, but it clearly should not be taken to mean that Epicurus was completely indifferent to his death, especially in light of the remainder of the death passage in the *Letter to Menoeceus*, in which Epicurus expressed his positive view of the desirableness of life.[19] Therefore, Luper-Foy's interpretation of the phrase, "death is nothing to us," is too literal, and is not sufficiently sympathetic to the relevant texts.

Luper-Foy does not simply dismiss the core Epicurean idea that one's own death is not bad for one. He does argue directly against it by employing the principle that "whatever prevents me from getting what I want [whatever thwarts my desires] is a misfortune for me."[20] This principle seems reasonable to him, and he argues that

If something that thwarts my desires is an evil for me, then dying is an evil for me (though perhaps the lesser of all the evils that are inevitable in my circumstances), since it thwarts my desires,[21]

thus trying to prove the falsity of the Epicurean view. There are two difficulties with using this principle here. One is that its applicability to the Epicurean view is so questionable that additional argument is needed. The other is that it is plainly untrue.

The question of its applicability to death is one of which Luper-Foy is aware, and he does seem to pause over the question. The problem is that death's thwarting our desires is so un-like common thwartings of our desires that even if it were true (which, I shall argue, it is not) that what prevents desire fulfill-ment is bad for the person whose desires become unfulfillable, it is questionable whether preventing the fulfillment of desire by something which also removes the desire is bad for one. Death is like this. Not only does it prevent the fulfillment of the desire, but also it removes the desire, by removing the person. The per-son no longer exists to *have* the desire, fulfillable or not. The case of death is so very different from standard cases in which the thwarting of desire is bad for one that there should be some special argument that one's death is bad for one. Perhaps it can accurately be said that death thwarts desires we have at death. However, how can it be bad for us, since we then no longer exist to have those desires and to be frustrated in attempts to satisfy the desires? Luper-Foy does perhaps sense a problem here, and says:

An event can prevent me from fulfilling my desires not just by frustrat-ing my attempts to fulfill them, but also by *removing* my desires. . . . It is in this sense that dying thwarts my desires. It is a misfortune for me for the same reason that being forced to swallow a drug that washes away my desires (including my desire *not* to have swallowed the drug) is a misfortune for me.[22]

However, simply asserting that death is bad for me even though the desires it prevents me from fulfilling I no longer have (be-cause I no longer am) is no proper substitute for an argument that this is so. Nevertheless, some may take it that the example of being forced to swallow the drug could easily be turned into an effective argument, and Luper-Foy may have intended it as a sort of oblique argument. It is thus important to consider the case carefully. Is the case of being forced to swallow a drug that takes away one's desires, including the desire not to swallow the drug, really a case which shows that something is bad for us which thwarts our desires by removing them?

Suppose that the desire thwarted by taking the drug is the desire not ever to swallow any such drug or the desire to con-tinue having all of one's present desires up to the time at which they are fulfilled. One might say that my being forced to take the drug thwarts, i.e., prevents me from fulfilling, the desire to continue having all of my present desires up to the time at which they are fulfilled by the acquisition of their objects. It is not clear that this is bad for me or a misfortune for me at all. It is certainly not very much like creating obstacles to one's fulfilling one's desires, where one realizes that one cannot then fulfill the desires, but one continues to have them, and is thereby frustrated. Clearly, that sort of thing seems bad for one, since one winds up having unsatisfiable or unsatisfied desires. However, in the case of death thwarting one's desires, one winds up, so to speak, without having any desires. How then could death thwart my desires in a way that is bad for me? I do not see how it could, so I think that we need special arguments why death is bad for us, even if it may be thought to thwart our desires. The case of the swallowed drug does not seem to me to be such a special argument, for it is also not clearly a case in which thwarting one's desires is bad for one.

Perhaps some will think me insufficiently sensitive to the drug case. If this case seems to persuade some, I would suggest that its persuasiveness lies in the victim's *being forced* to swallow the drug. The expression "being forced" is highly tendentious, in that it seems obviously wrong to force someone to swallow a drug that would make such a significant alteration in the person. That it seems *wrong* is, I hypothesize, what makes it seem appropriate to characterize it as a misfortune or bad for the person to swallow the drug. To support this hypothesis, I offer a similar case in which a person voluntarily, but unwittingly, swallows a drug that has the effect of eradicating all the person's former desires, even the desire not to acquire any new desires until the old ones are satisfied. Suppose it also eradicates the person's memory of having had those old desires, so that the person will feel no frustration from the knowledge of having wanted to satisfy those old desires. As a result, the person comes to acquire new desires and new plans of action. It is not at all obvious that this act would be *bad for* the person, especially so, considering that the person might come to acquire desires which are, in an important sense, more appropriate, given the person's abilities and inclinations. We tend to think that persons to whom wrongs are done are thereby the subjects of misfortune, and this may be so. It is, however, a small but significant slip of logic to think that the act by which they are wronged is necessarily *bad* for them. It is quite possible to be wronged by a person committing an act which is good for one. The persuasiveness that Luper-Foy's case might have lies unsupported across this logical gap between wrong and bad.

Moreover, the principle on the basis of which he argues is itself mistaken. It is not correct to think that whatever thwarts one's desire is bad or evil for one. The very concept of something being bad for one is in need of some careful examination. However, it seems plain that it is not generally correct that what thwarts a person's desires is bad for the person. Suppose that a person for some reason desires to avoid being vaccinated against various diseases to which the person could succumb if not vaccinated—polio, smallpox, typhoid fever, or others. Thwarting this desire would be good for the person, for it would reduce the likelihood of suffering later. Some desires persons have would not be good to fulfill, and it would be good for those persons that those desires be thwarted (though this would not necessarily make it morally all right for someone to thwart those desires).

Luper-Foy is, however, aware of this objection, and dismisses it on the ground that the sort of death that would prevent the satisfaction of unfulfilling desires would not be an "important sort of death." His view is that

an important sort of death, it would seem, remains an evil, namely, one that prevents its victims from fulfilling *fulfilling* desires. Call such a death a *premature* one. Even prematurity as we have defined it is not an infallible sign of a regrettable end; however, it will serve us well enough.[23]

Apparently, to secure the applicability of the principle on the basis of which he argues, he is willing to restrict his claim about the badness of death to the deaths of those persons who die with unfulfilled desires, the fulfilling of which would be good for them. Then, of course, given the basis for the restriction, the principle would need to be qualified so that it would read: whatever prevents one from getting what one wants is bad for one, *provided that what one wants would fulfill one or be good for one.* But this too is incorrect, for suppose that someone prevents you from getting what you want but at the same time also succeeds in replacing your desires for that thing with a desire for something which would, in fact, be *more* fulfilling to you. (This happens, for example, when parents thwart a child's desire and also, by benevolent trickery, are able to replace the thwarted desire by another, "better" desire.) Then, I would judge, what has been done is not bad for you. The basic principle that Luper-Foy uses to argue against Epicureans is thus incorrect.

Having unsuccessfully tried to refute the Epicurean view, Luper-Foy goes on to describe the ways he thinks consistent Epicureans would have to think and to live, mistakenly thinking, as I have already pointed out, that Epicureans must be "completely indifferent" to their deaths. The greatest part of Luper-Foy's article is devoted to an extended renunciation of what he takes to be the consistently Epicurean way of life. He takes it that

> Epicureans . . . would *have* to regard it [dying] as a misfortune if dying thwarted desires whose satisfactions would be fulfilling. Hence Epicureans must not *have* any fulfilling desires that can be frustrated by death! Death for them can never be premature or else it *would* be a bad thing; therefore they must be so constituted that at any time death comes it is mature. Assuming that Epicureans *have* goals, then either they are unfulfilling ones, or else they are ones that cannot be thwarted by death.[24]

The sorts of goals or desires to which Luper-Foy thinks consistent Epicureans are limited are three: (1) "escape desires," to the effect that if living attains a certain degree of badness then death is preferable; (2) "independent desires," the satisfaction of which is independent of how and whether one continues to live; and (3) "conditional desires," that are somehow conditional on one's being alive.[25] The problem Luper-Foy sees with being restricted to desires of these types is that

> in avoiding all aspirations that can be thwarted by death, Epicureans have had to avoid all desires which are capable of giving Epicureans a reason for living. In order to maintain their unconcern about dying, they must avoid having any reason whatsoever for not dying. . . . [O]nly if they avoid having any reason for living can they avoid having any reason for not dying.[26]

Not only does he think that Epicureans can have no reason for living, but he also believes that they cannot consistently think their lives worthwhile or good.[27] This embodies a clever argument, and constitutes a very severe accusation which would indeed make the Epicurean view unattractive. Fortunately for the Epicureans, it rests on at least two incorrect premises. One I have already refuted. That is the principle that whatever prevents the satisfaction of fulfilling desires is bad for one.

There is, however, another mistaken assumption in this criticism, and it is important to expose it, for it bears on the conception of what gives one a (good) reason for living and of what makes one's life worthwhile. Luper-Foy believes that Epicureans have completely "sabotaged their motivation for living" by adopting the view that death is not bad for one.[28] It is worth considering this idea, because it is one many thoughtful persons are likely to have when confronting the Epicurean view. If one's death is really not bad for one, why not just kill oneself, and get it over with? Why go on living if one's death is not bad for one?

The second problem with this condemnation of the Epicurean way of life is Luper-Foy's supposition that one can have a reason for living a good and worthwhile life, only if one has desires of which death can prevent the satisfaction. That this supposition is incorrect or at least highly dubious may be shown by considering desires in a category that Luper-Foy finds immune to being thwarted by death. Conditional desires, desires to do certain things or desires that certain things be true on the condition that one continue to live would, it seems clear to me, provide a motivation for living, and could serve to make life as worthwhile as anything else.

"Conditional desires," Luper-Foy himself admits, "do provide strong reason for action." He goes on to say that

Such desires can enable Epicureans to take an interest in things for which life is a precondition. While indifferent to the prospect of dying in their sleep, Epicureans may take the attitude that if they *do* wake, their wakeful days should be spent in vigorous pursuit of an exciting career, in raising a family, etc. And for this to be possible, they will need to seek an education and work long hours in pursuit of a career.[29]

By admitting this, which seems to me correct in its description of the desires Epicureans can have, he undermines a crucial premise in his condemnation of the Epicurean life as worthless and mean. For if Epicureans have, on the basis of those conditional desires, motivation to act in various ways which give them pleasure and satisfaction, then they can have good and worthwhile lives. And life's being good and giving them pleasure constitutes an excellent reason for continuing to live, a reason not to die. Thus, Luper-Foy's view that consistent Epicureans are incapable of worthwhile lives is without adequate support.

It is interesting and important to note, too, that Luper-Foy is mistaken in other beliefs he has about what desires consistent Epicureans can and cannot have. He appears inconsistent in his discussion at several points. For example, he asserts that Epicureans cannot be at all concerned (unconditionally) about what happens in the future, as follows:

They [the Epicureans] are capable only of indifference about the well-being of posterity, and an Epicurean mother could not care less about the welfare of her children after she believes she will die.[30]

Apparently in haste to ridicule the Epicurean philosophy, he forgot that among the sorts of desires he rightly claimed Epicureans could consistently have were "independent desires," desires whose satisfactions "are not really affected by what we do in the course of our lives or even by whether or not we *are* alive."[31] The desires for the well-being of posterity and for the well-being of one's children, like so many (though, of course, not all) of the desires one has for the future, are like this, independent. Our desires that our children be well can be *fulfilled* after we die, although, of course, we cannot be *satisfied* by the fulfillment of those desires. Therefore, it is not true that consistent Epicureans cannot desire the welfare of their offspring or of future generations.[32]

Furthermore, if Luper-Foy had attended more closely to what Epicurus himself said about desires and the life of pleasure, he would have seen one clear reason why Epicureans might care about the future and have desires thwartable by death. This could have prompted a careful rethinking of his initial impressions about Epicureanism. In the *Letter to Menoeceus*, when Epicurus discussed pleasure at length, he remarked,

Since pleasure is our first and native good, for that reason we do not choose every pleasure whatsoever, but ofttimes pass over many pleasures when a greater annoyance ensues from them. And ofttimes, we consider pains superior to pleasures when submission to the pains for a long time brings us as a consequence a greater pleasure.[33]

Epicurus himself recommended courses of action, plans for life, which were future-regarding, involving goals that could easily be thwarted by death. One who prudently accepted a long sequence of pains for the sake of acquiring great pleasure in the future is essentially adopting a desire, a goal, and a plan that could be defeated by death. One might die, miss the future pleasure, and be stuck with having had only the long sequence of pains, thus being defeated in one's plans. This suggests that even though Epicurus regarded one's death as not bad for one, he felt he could consistently adopt a prudent plan of life, relying upon the expectation of a continued existence in the future. That he could consistently do this is due to the belief that one's death is not bad for one, even if it prevents one from achieving one's important, fulfilling goals and desires.

In John Stuart Mill's famous discussion of various misconceptions of Epicurean hedonism, Mill wrote that "such a theory of life excites in many minds . . . inveterate dislike." [34] Luper-Foy's article illustrates that the view still does excite "inveterate dislike." His expressed attitude is one of contempt and ridicule. However, it is not based on conclusions drawn through understanding and careful philosophical analysis of the view. A review of Mill's positive discussion of the Epicurean view would help to dispel many of the common misconceptions about hedonism generally, although Mill does not discuss the controversial idea about death. The Epicurean view of death may be distasteful to many, and hedonism may seem a shallow view. Both views may be incorrect, but Luper-Foy's arguments neither prove the falsity of the views nor present obstacles to their adoption.

CHAPTER SIXTEEN

DOCTOR: Why are you depressed, Alvy?

MOTHER: Tell Dr. Flicker. It's something he read.

DOCTOR: Something he read, huh?

ALVY: The universe is expanding.

DOCTOR: The universe is expanding?

ALVY: Well, the universe is everything, and if it's expanding, someday it will break apart and that would be the end of everything!

MOTHER: What is that your business? He stopped doing his homework.

ALVY: What's the point?

MOTHER: What has the universe got to do with it? You're here in Brooklyn! Brooklyn is not expanding!

DOCTOR: It won't be expanding for billions of years yet, Alvy. And we've gotta try to enjoy ourselves while we're here. Uh?

—Woody Allen, *Annie Hall*

Some Puzzles About the Evil of Death

Fred Feldman

The Puzzles

Death is nothing to Epicureans. They do not fear or hate death. They do not view death as a misfortune for the deceased. They think death is no worse for the deceased than is not yet being born for the as yet unborn. They say that ordinary people, who look forward to their deaths with dismay, are in this irrational. Why do they hold these odd views?

In his central argument for these conclusions, Epicurus says:

So death, the most terrifying of ills, is nothing to us, since so long as we exist, death is not with us; but when death comes, then we do not exist. It does not then concern either the living or the dead, since for the former it is not, and the latter are no more.[1]

The argument seems to turn on what has been called "The Existence Condition"—nothing bad can happen to a person at a time unless he exists at that time.[2] If we agree that the dead do not exist, we seem driven to the conclusion that nothing bad can

Reprinted by permission from *The Philosophical Review* 100, no. 2, (April 1991): 205–27. Many friends provided much-needed criticism and support, for which I am thankful. I am especially grateful to Gary Matthews for his encouragement on this and related projects. Earl Conee, John Fischer, Ed Gettier, Ned Markosian, Neil Schaefer, Harry Silverstein, and the editors of *The Philosophical Review* made helpful suggestions. Earlier versions were subjected to useful criticism at Montclair State College and Drew University.

happen to us once we are dead. It is just a small step then to the conclusion that death itself is not bad for those who die.

Although some may find reassurance in this ancient bit of reasoning, most of us cannot help but view it as sophistry. Except in cases in which continued life would be unbearable, death is taken to be a misfortune for the one who dies. We cry at funerals; we grieve for the deceased. Especially when a young person dies, we feel that she has suffered a great misfortune. And it apparently seems to most of us that our attitude is perfectly rational. So we have our first puzzle: how can being dead be a misfortune for a person, if she does not exist during the time when it takes place?

According to the most popular anti-Epicurean view, death is bad for a person primarily because it deprives him of certain goods—the goods he would have enjoyed if he had not died.[3] This so-called "Deprivation Approach" thus seems to require that we make a certain comparison—a comparison between (a) how well off a person would be if he were to go on living and (b) how well off he would be if he were to die. The claim is that when death is bad for a person, it is bad for him because he will be worse off dead than he would have been if he had lived. The second puzzle arises because it appears that any such comparison is incoherent. It seems to be, after all, a comparison between (a) the benefits and harms that would come to a person if he were to live, and (b) those that would come to him if he were to die. However, if he does not exist after his death, he cannot enjoy or suffer any benefits or harms after death. So there apparently is no second term for the comparison. Thus, the Deprivation Approach seems in a covert way to violate the Existence Condition, too.[4]

Suppose we find some coherent way to formulate the view that a person's death is a misfortune for him because it deprives him of goods. Then we face another Epicurean question: *when* is it a misfortune for him? It seems wrong to say that it is a misfortune for him while he is still alive—for at such times he is not yet dead and death has not yet deprived him of anything. It seems equally wrong to say that it is a misfortune for him after he is dead—for at such times he does not exist. How can he suffer misfortunes then?

Another problem confronts the anti-Epicurean. If we can find a coherent way to say that early death is bad for us because it deprives us of certain goods, then we probably will have found a coherent way to say that late birth also deprives us of certain goods—the goods we would have enjoyed if only we had been born earlier. Yet virtually nobody laments his late birth, or thinks it a misfortune that he was not born years or decades earlier. Lucretius presented a forceful statement of this puzzle. He said:

> Think too how the bygone antiquity of everlasting time before our birth was nothing to us. Nature therefore holds this up to us as a mirror of the time yet to come after our death. Is there aught in this that looks appalling, aught that wears an aspect of gloom? Is it not more untroubled than any sleep?[5]

So another puzzle that must be confronted is this: if early death is bad for us because it deprives us of the goods we would have enjoyed if we had died later, then why is not late birth just as bad for us? After all, it seems to deprive us of the goods we would have enjoyed if we had been born earlier.

There are other puzzles about the evil of death. Some of these will be addressed as we go along. But these are the main questions I mean to discuss here.

Metaphysical and Axiological Assumptions

Before I propose my answers to these questions, I should mention some of my metaphysical and axiological assumptions. First among these, perhaps, is the assumption that there are possible worlds. I am inclined to think that a possible world is a huge proposition fully describing some total way the world might have been, including all facts about the past, present, and future. Nothing I say here depends on this particular view about possible worlds. So long as it countenances an appropriate number of appropriately detailed possible worlds, any other coherent view will do as well.

I write as if a given individual may exist at several different possible worlds. This may seem controversial, but I think it is really not. Suppose Myron is an actual person. Suppose he actually smokes. I may ask you to consider some possible world in which Myron does not smoke. This may seem to commit me to the view that there are other worlds relevantly like our (concrete) world, and that in addition to being here in our (concrete) world, the actual concrete Myron (or perhaps a counterpart) is also located at these other places. That, it seems to me, would be strange.

In fact, however, I hold no such view. When I ask you to consider some world in which Myron does not smoke, I am just asking you to consider a huge proposition that fully describes some total way the world might have been, and which entails the proposition that Myron exists but does not smoke. Since it is more convenient to do so, I write in a "realistic" way about other possible worlds—as if they were giant, concrete planets far from Earth, but populated by many earthlings.

I assume that it makes sense to speak of the degree of similarity between possible worlds. Indeed, it seems to me that there are many similarity relations among possible worlds. Later I will have more to say about the details of the similarity relations that are most important for present purposes. However, if we have some particular similarity relation in mind, then it will make sense to speak of some world as being "most similar" in that way to a given world. Sometimes instead of speaking of similarity I speak of "nearness." It is just another way of expressing the same idea.[6]

Now let us briefly turn to axiology. Possible worlds can be evaluated in various ways. One sort of evaluation is "objective" and "non-relational." Suppose that the very simplest form of hedonism is true. According to this view, pleasure is intrinsically good and pain is intrinsically bad. Nothing else has any (basic) intrinsic value. Let us suppose that there is a way to measure the amount of pleasure contained in an episode of pleasure; let us suppose similarly that there is a way to measure the amount of pain contained in an episode of pain. Suppose further that the pleasure-measure and the pain-measure are commensurate, so that it makes sense to subtract amounts of pain from amounts of pleasure.[7] We can then say that the intrinsic value of a possible world is determined as follows: consider how much pleasure is experienced throughout the history of that world; consider how much pain is experienced throughout the history of that world; subtract the latter value from the former;

the result is the hedonic value of the world. The simplest form of hedonism says that the intrinsic value of a world is equal to the hedonic value of that world.[8]

Another way to evaluate worlds is equally "objective" but is "person-relative." That is, instead of asking how good a world is, we ask how good it is *for a certain person*. When I speak of how good a world is for a certain person, I mean to indicate the portion of that world's goods and evils that the individual in question enjoys and suffers at that world. Suppose again that the simplest form of hedonism is true. Then the value of a world, w, for a person, s, is determined in this way: consider how much pleasure s enjoys throughout his lifetime at w; consider how much pain s suffers throughout his lifetime at w; subtract the value of the latter from the value of the former. The result is the value of w for s, or $V(s,w)$.

I assume that these values can be expressed with numbers in such a way that higher numbers indicate greater value for the person; zero indicates neutrality for the person; negative numbers indicate badness for the person. Since $V(s,w)$ is a measure of how well s fares at w, I sometimes refer to this as s's "welfare level" at w.[9]

There is a question concerning a person's welfare level at worlds at which he does not exist. The proposed account leaves this value undetermined. Although it plays no role in my argument, I stipulate that if s fails to exist at w, then $V(s,w) = 0$. This thesis is suggested by the proposed account of relativized value, since if a certain person does not exist at a world then he enjoys no pleasure there and suffers no pain there.

In fact, I do not think that a person's real welfare level is determined in the simple-minded hedonistic way I have sketched. I am inclined to think that several other factors may contribute to determining how good a world is for a person. Among other things, I suspect that the amounts of knowledge and freedom that a person enjoys, as well as the extent to which he is forced to suffer injustice are also important. However, I prefer to proceed here on the pretense that hedonism is true. I have several reasons.

First and foremost, there is the historical reason. I am engaged in a debate with Epicurus about the evil of death. Epicurus was a hedonist. Some commentators have suggested that in order to answer Epicurus, we must reject his axiology—that his view about the evil of death is inextricably tied to his hedonism. I think this is a mistake. I want to show that, even if we accept the Epicurean axiology, we can still reject the Epicurean conclusion about the evil of death.

A second reason for assuming hedonism is strategic. The central intrinsic value-bearing properties associated with hedonism are ones that a person can have at a time only if he is alive and conscious then. I want to show how death can be an evil for the deceased even if this hedonistic axiology is assumed. Thus, I take myself to be trying to show that death may be an evil for a person even according to an axiology maximally hostile to this notion. If I succeed, it will be pretty easy to see how to extend the solution in the direction of more plausible axiologies.

It should be clear, then, that certain sorts of solution are ruled out by my axiological assumptions. I will not be able to say (as Thomas Nagel and others have suggested)[10] that death is bad in something like the way in which being the subject of nasty rumors is bad. Clearly enough, one can be the subject of nasty rumors even after one has died. If we think this is bad for a person, then we will want to say that one's welfare level at a world can be adversely affected by things that happen after one ceases to exist at that world. Another sort of example involves the failure of one's life projects. One's life projects may come unraveled after one has died. If we think this is bad for a person, then we can cite another way in which one's welfare level at a world may be reduced by things that occur after one's death.

These claims about welfare levels are controversial, and strike me as being implausible. I would rather stick to a much more hard-nosed axiology—an axiology according to which one's welfare level at a world is determined entirely by things that happen during one's life there. Thus (for purposes of illustration) I have adopted a form of simple hedonism. According to this view, if a person never learns of nasty rumors, and never suffers from them, then they do not affect his welfare level. If a person never learns that his life project has come to naught, and never suffers from this frustration, then it does not affect his welfare level. Only pains and pleasures can affect a person's welfare level at a world—and these he must experience during his life.

A final advantage of the hedonistic axiology is its simplicity.

If we assume that the fundamental bearers of intrinsic value are experiences of pleasure and experiences of pain, and we assume that these are in principle subject to unproblematic quantification, then the determination of a person's welfare level at a possible world becomes quite straightforwardly a matter of simple arithmetic. To find s's welfare level at w, just subtract the amount of pain s suffers at w from the amount of pleasure s enjoys at w. Although the axiology is admittedly quite crude, its simplicity makes it especially useful for illustrative purposes.

I assume that any statement to the effect that something is good (or bad) for a person can be paraphrased by a statement to the effect that some *state of affairs* is good (or bad) for the person. Furthermore, I assume here that a state of affairs (such as the state of affairs of *Myron smoking*) is just a proposition (in this case, the proposition *that Myron smokes*). Thus, for present purposes, it makes no difference whether we say that a certain state of affairs obtains, or whether we say that a certain proposition is true.

In any case, instead of saying that smoking (apparently an activity) would be bad for Myron, we can say instead that *that Myron smokes* (a state of affairs) is bad for Myron. Instead of saying that a bowl of hot soup (apparently a physical object) would be good for me, we can say that what would be good for me is *that I have a bowl of hot soup*, and thus again represent the thing that is good for me as a state of affairs. I prefer to write in this way, since it induces a sort of conceptual tidiness and uniformity.

I am also going to assume that when a person dies, he goes out of existence. In fact, I think this assumption is extremely implausible. No one would dream of saying that when a tree dies, it goes out of existence. Why should we treat people otherwise? My own view is that a person is just a living human body. In typical cases, when the body dies, it continues to exist as a corpse. So the thing that formerly was a person still exists, although it is no longer alive (and perhaps no longer a person). Of course, I recognize that some people go out of existence at the moment of death—for example, those located at Ground Zero at the moment of a nuclear blast. For present purposes, I will assume that everyone does. Once again, I do this in part for historical reasons—Epicurus seems to have accepted this view about death and nonexistence—and in part for strategic reasons. I want to show how death can be bad for the deceased even on the assumptions (a) that things that directly affect a person's welfare level can happen to that person only at times when he exists, and (b) that death marks the end of existence for the deceased.[11]

Things That Are Bad for People

The central question here is how a person's death can be bad for him. The claim that someone's death is bad for him is an instance of a more general sort of claim—the claim that some state of affairs is bad for some person. It would be surprising if it were to turn out that we need two independent accounts of what's meant by statements to the effect that something is bad for someone: one account of the meaning of such a statement when the relevant object is the person's death, and another account of the meaning of such a statement when the relevant object is something other than the person's death. Surely the statement about death ought to be nothing more than an interesting instance of the general sort of statement. So let us consider the more general question first, and then focus more narrowly on the specific case concerning death. What do we mean when we say that something would be bad for someone?

It seems to me that when we say that something would be bad for someone, we might mean either of two main things. One possibility is that we mean that the thing would be *intrinsically* bad for the person. So if someone says that a state of affairs, p, is intrinsically bad for a person, s, he presumably means that p is intrinsically bad, and s is the subject or "recipient" of p. Given our assumed hedonistic axiology, the only things that could be intrinsically bad for someone would be his own pains. Thus, *Dolores suffering pain of intensity 10 from t_1 to t_3* would be intrinsically bad for Dolores.

On the other hand, when we say that something would be bad for someone, we might mean that it would be "all things considered bad" for him. At least in some instances, this seems to mean that he would be all things considered worse off if it were to occur than he would be if it were not to occur. In this case, the thing itself might be intrinsically neutral. The relevant consideration would be the extent to which it would lead to or prevent or otherwise be connected with things that are intrinsically bad for the person. Consider an example. Suppose we are interested in the question whether moving to Bolivia would be bad for Dolores. Intuitively, this question seems to be equivalent to the question whether Dolores would be worse off if she were to move to Bolivia than she would be if she were to refrain from moving to Bolivia. Letting "*b*" indicate the state of affairs *Dolores moves to Bolivia*, we can say this: *b* would be all things considered bad for Dolores if and only if she would be worse off if *b* obtained than she would be if *b* did not obtain. Now, if we employ the standard account of the meaning of subjunctive conditionals, together with the assumptions about values of worlds for individuals, we can rewrite this as follows: *b* would be all things considered bad for Dolores if and only if the value for Dolores of the nearest possible *b*-world is less than the value for her of the nearest possible ~*b*-world.[12]

Correspondingly, to say that a state of affairs would be all things considered good for a person is to say that she would be better off if it were to obtain than she would be if it were to fail to obtain. More exactly, it is to say that her welfare level at the nearest possible world where it obtains is higher than her welfare level at the nearest possible world where it does not obtain.

If we make use of the abbreviations introduced above, we can restate these claims as follows:

D1: *p* would be good for *s* if and only if ($\exists w$) ($\exists w'$) (*w* is the nearest *p*-world & *w'* is the nearest ~*p*-world & $V(s,w) > V(s,w')$)

D2: *p* would be bad for *s* if and only if ($\exists w$) ($\exists w'$) (*w* is the nearest *p*-world & *w'* is the nearest ~*p*-world & $V(s,w) < V(s,w')$)

If we make use of our assumption that worlds have numerical values for individuals, then we can say precisely *how bad* or *how good* something would be for someone. Suppose that if Dolores were to move to Bolivia the rest of her life would be a nightmare. Considering all the pleasures and pains she would ever experience (including the ones she has already experienced), her life would be worth +100 points. Thus, the value for Dolores of the nearest world in which she moves to Bolivia is +100. Suppose on the other hand that the value for her of the nearest world in which she does not move to Bolivia is +1,000. Then she would be 900 units worse off if she were to move to Bolivia. That tells us precisely how bad it would be for her to move to Bolivia. The value for her of moving to Bolivia is -900. So the general principle says that to find the value for a person of a state of affairs, subtract the value for him of the nearest world where it does not obtain from the value for him of the nearest world where it does obtain.

Precisely the same thing happens in the case of a state of affairs that would be good for a person. Suppose it would be good for Dolores to move to Boston. To find out how good it would be for her, consider the value for her of the nearest world in which she does move to Boston. Suppose it is $+1,100$. Consider the value for her of the nearest world in which she does not move to Boston. Suppose it is $+1,000$. Subtract the value for her of the latter from the value for her of the former. The result ($+100$) is the value for Dolores of moving to Boston.

In its most general form, then, the principle may be formulated as a principle about the overall value (good, bad, or neutral) of states of affairs for persons. The overall value of a state of affairs for a person is the result of subtracting the value for him of the nearest world where it does not occur from the value for him of the nearest world where it does occur. In other words:

D3: The value for s of $p = n$ if and only if $(\exists w)\,(\exists w')$ (w is the nearest p-world & w' is the nearest $\sim p$-world & $V(s,w)$ minus $V(s,w') = n$).

The Evil of Death

The application of these ideas to the case of one's own death is straightforward. Suppose we are wondering whether it would be bad for a certain person, s, to die at a certain time, t. Then we must ask about the value for s of the possible world that would exist if s were to die at t; and we must compare that value to the value for s of the possible world that would exist if s were not to die at t. If the death-world is worse for s than the non-death-world, then s's death at t would be bad for s; otherwise, not.

Let us consider a typical example to see how this works. Suppose I am thinking of taking an airplane trip to Europe. Suppose I am worried about accidents, hijackings, sabotage, etc. I think I might die en route. I think this would be bad for me. D3 directs us to consider the nearest possible world in which I do die en route to Europe on this trip, and to consider my welfare level at that world. I see no reason to suppose that interesting parts of my past are any different at that world from what they are at the actual world. So I assume that all my past pleasures and pains would be unaffected. The main difference (from my perspective) is that in that world I suffer some terminal pain and then a premature death, and never live to enjoy my retirement. Let us suppose that that world is worth + 500 to me— + 500 is the result of subtracting the pain I there suffer from the pleasure I there enjoy. Next D3 directs us to consider the nearest world in which I do not die en route to Europe on this trip. The relevant feature of this world is that I do not die a painful and premature death in an airplane accident. Suppose I there do live to enjoy many happy years of retirement. Let us suppose my welfare level at that world is + 1,100. D3 implies that my death on this trip would have a value of − 600 for me. It would be a terrible misfortune.

Two points deserve mention here. One is the fact that D3 is a proposal concerning how *good* or *bad* a state of affairs is for a person, and not a proposal concerning the extent to which a state of affairs *benefits* or *harms* a person. I am inclined to suspect that the concepts of benefit and harm are in certain important ways different from the concepts of being good for and being bad for a person. One such respect might be this: it might be that it is impossible for a person to be harmed or benefited by things that happen at times when he no longer exists. It is nevertheless still possible that something bad or something good for a person might occur at a time when the person no longer exists. D3 is not intended to have any direct implications concerning harm and benefit. It is intended to be restricted to the concepts of being good for a person and being bad for a person.

The second point is that nothing I have said here implies that death is always bad for the one who dies. Suppose a person is suffering from a painful terminal disease. Suppose he is considering suicide, and is inclined to think that death might be a blessing. He might be right. If his welfare level at the nearest world where he thus commits suicide is higher than his welfare level at the nearest world where he does not commit suicide, then committing suicide would be good for this person.[13] My point in formulating D3 is simply to show how it is possible for a person's death to be bad for him, not that everyone's death must be so.

Perhaps we can now see where Epicurus went wrong in his argument for the conclusion that one's death cannot be bad for him. Perhaps Epicurus was thinking that the only states of affairs that are bad for a person are the ones that are *intrinsically* bad for him. Since (given our axiological assumptions, which are intended to be relevantly like his) death is not intrinsically bad for anyone, it would follow that death is never bad for the one who dies. But even the most fervent hedonist should acknowledge a distinction between things that are intrinsically bad for a person (which he will take to be pains) and things that are bad for the person in other ways. D3 is designed to calculate an important sort of *non-intrinsic* value. It tells us the degree of *overall* badness for a person of a state of affairs. Even though my death on my imagined European trip would not be intrinsically bad for me, D3 tells us that it would be overall bad for me.

Another possibility is that Epicurus was thinking that if a state of affairs would be bad for a person, then it must at least *cause* something intrinsically bad for him. Since (given our axiological and metaphysical assumptions) nothing intrinsically bad can happen to me after my death, my death cannot cause anything intrinsically bad for me. Thus, Epicurus might have concluded that my death cannot even be extrinsically bad for me. However, D3 does not calculate extrinsic value by focusing exclusively on intrinsic goods and evils that would befall the person *as a result* of the state of affairs. Rather, it calculates the value of a state of affairs for a person by considering what would happen (whether as consequence or not) if the state of affairs were to occur, as compared to what would happen (whether as consequence or not) if it were to fail to occur. Thus, according to D3, my death would be bad for me not because it would cause me to suffer pain, and not because it would itself be intrinsically bad for me. Rather, it would be bad for me because it would deprive me of 600 units of pleasure that I would have had if it had not happened when it did. More precisely, it would be bad for me because my welfare level at the nearest world where it occurs is 600 points lower than my welfare level at the nearest world where it does not occur.

Some Proposed Answers

At the outset, I mentioned some questions about the evil of death. These were prompted by the Epicurean challenge. I will now attempt to answer those questions.

The first question was the question how, given that he does not exist after he dies, being dead can be a misfortune for a person. The simple answer is this: a state of affairs can be bad for a person whether it occurs before he exists, while he exists, or after he exists. The only requirement is that his welfare level at the nearest world where it occurs is lower than his welfare level at the nearest world where it does not occur. It may be interesting to consider an example in which something bad for a person occurs *before* the person exists. Suppose my father lost his job shortly before I was conceived. Suppose that as a result of the loss of his job, my parents had to move to another town, and that I was therefore raised in a bad neighborhood and had to attend worse schools. I would have been happier if he had not lost his job when he did. In this case, the fact that my father lost his job was bad for me—even though I did not exist when it occurred. It was bad for me because the value for me of the nearest world where he did not lose his job is greater than the value for me of the actual world (which, on the assumption, is the nearest world where he did lose his job). The same may be true of cases involving things that will happen after I cease to exist (although, of course, such cases will illustrate *deprivation* of happiness, rather than *causation* of unhappiness).

It should be clear, then, that the plausibility of the Existence Condition derives from a confusion. Given our hedonistic axiology, it would be correct to say that nothing *intrinsically* bad can happen to a person at a time unless he exists at that time. You cannot suffer pains at a time unless you then exist. However, even on the same axiology, the *overall* value version of the thesis is not true. That is, it would not be correct to say that nothing *overall* bad for a person can happen at a time unless he exists at that time. Perhaps some Epicureans have been induced to accept the Existence Condition because they fail to notice this distinction.[14]

The second puzzle concerns an allegedly illegitimate comparison. It may seem that I am maintaining that when a person's death is bad for him, it is bad for him because he is worse off being dead than he would have been if he had stayed alive. Yet this suggests that there is some degree of "bad-offness" that he endures while dead. However, since he does not exist while he is dead, he can have no degrees of "bad-offness" then. The question, then, is this: doesn't my answer presuppose an illegitimate comparison?

My answer presupposes no such comparison. I am not proposing that we compare a person's welfare level during life to his welfare level during death. I have assumed that one's welfare level at a world is determined entirely by pleasures and pains that one experiences during one's life at that world. Thus, the comparison is a comparison between one's welfare level (calculated by appeal to what happens to one during his life) at one possible world with his welfare level (also calculated by appeal to what happens to him during his life) at another possible world. I have provisionally agreed that nothing intrinsically good or bad can happen to a person at times when he does not exist.

In effect, then, my proposal presupposes what Silverstein calls a "life-life comparison." [15] To see how this works, consider again the example concerning my imagined death en route to Europe. My proposal requires us to compare the values for me of two lives—the life I would lead if I were to die on the plane trip and the life I would lead if I were not to die on the plane trip. Since (according to our assumptions) the shorter life is less good for me, my death on that trip would be correspondingly bad for me.

The third puzzle was a puzzle about dates. I have claimed that a person's death may be bad for her because it deprives her of the pleasures she would have enjoyed if she had lived. One may be puzzled about just *when* this misfortune occurs. The problem is that we may not want to say that her death is bad for her during her life, for she is not yet dead. Equally, we may not want to say that it is bad for her after her death, for she does not exist then.

In order to understand my answer to this question, we must look more closely into the question. Suppose a certain girl died in her youth. We are not concerned here about any puzzle about the date of her death. We may suppose we know that. Thus, in one sense, we know precisely when the misfortune occurred.

Nor are we concerned about the dates of any pains she suffered as a result of that death. We assume that there are none. The present question is, rather, a question about when her death is a misfortune for her. If Lindsay is the girl, and d is the state of affairs of *Lindsay dying on December 7, 1987*, then the question is this: "Precisely when is d bad for Lindsay?" I have proposed an account of the evil of death. According to that account, when we say that d is bad for Lindsay, we mean that the value for her of the nearest world where d occurs is lower than the value for her of the nearest in which d does not occur. So our question comes to this: "Precisely *when* is it the case that the value for Lindsay of the nearest world in which d occurs is lower than the value for her of the nearest world in which d does not occur?"

It seems clear to me that the answer to this question must be "eternally." For when we say that her death is bad for her, we are really expressing a complex fact about the relative values of two possible worlds. If these worlds stand in a certain value relation, then (given that they stand in this relation at any time) they stand in that relation not only when Lindsay exists, but at times when she does not. If there were a God, and it had been thinking about which world to create, it would have seen prior to creation that d would be bad for Lindsay. In other words, it would have seen that the value for Lindsay of the relevant d-world is significantly lower than the value for Lindsay of the relevant $\sim d$-world. And it would have seen this even though Lindsay did not yet exist at that pre-creation moment.

A final puzzle concerns the fact that we feel that early death is a greater misfortune for the prematurely deceased than is "late birth" for the late born, even though each may deprive us of as much happiness as the other.

Suppose Claudette was born in 1950 and will die somewhat prematurely in 2000 as a result of an accident. We may want to say that her premature death will be a misfortune for her. Consider the nearest possible world (call it "w3") in which she does not die prematurely. Suppose that at w3 she lives happily until 2035. Since she has 35 extra years of happiness in w3, her welfare level there is higher than her welfare level in the actual world. D3 yields the result that her premature death is bad for her. But now consider the claim that Claudette suffered an equal misfortune in not having been born in 1915. This fact seems to deprive her of 35 happy years too—the years from 1915 to 1950 when she was in fact born. Yet we feel uncomfortable with the idea that her late birth is as great a misfortune for Claudette as her premature death. Why is this?

Consider the state of affairs of *Claudette being born in 1915*. Call it "*b*." In the actual world *b* is false. Consider the nearest world where *b* is true.[16] (In other words, consider what would have happened if Claudette had been born 35 years earlier.) Call this world "w4." I see no reason to suppose that Claudette lives any longer in w4 than she does here in the actual world. Any such change in lifespan strikes me as being superfluous. I am inclined to suppose that Claudette's welfare level in w4 is slightly lower than her welfare level in the actual world—after all, in w4 she probably endures hard times during the Great Depression, and maybe even catches measles, whooping cough and other diseases that were rampant in those days. If she has just 50 years to live, she is better off living them in the second half of the twentieth century, rather than 35 years earlier. Thus, given my intuitive sense of how to calculate what would have happened if Claudette had been born earlier, it follows that early death is worse for Claudette than late birth. Her late birth deprived her of very little value; her early death would deprive her of a lot.

The proposed reply to Lucretius's challenge is thus based on an asymmetry between past and future. When I am asked to consider what would happen if Claudette were to die later, I hold her birthdate constant. It has already occurred, and I tend to think that unnecessary differences in past history are big differences between worlds. Thus, it is more natural for me to suppose that if she were to die later, it would be because she lives longer. On the other hand, when I am asked to consider what would have happened if she had been born earlier, I do not hold her deathdate constant. Instead, I hold her lifespan constant, and adjust the deathdate so as to accommodate itself to the earlier birthdate.

Someone might claim that I have made an unfair comparison. They might want to insist on holding lifespans constant. They might say that Claudette would be better off living longer if the extra time were tacked on to the end of her life. They might say that Claudette would not be any better off if the extra time were tacked on to the beginning of her life. (That is, if she were born in 1915 instead of 1950 but lived until 2000 anyway.) The question is vexing, since it is hard to discern Claudette's welfare levels in the appropriate worlds. My own inclination is to say that if she lives 85 happy years in each world, then her welfare level at the one is equal to her welfare level at the other. In this case, I cannot see why anyone would think it would be better for her to have the 35 years tacked on at the end of her life rather than at the beginning. When the comparison is fair, D3 generates what seem to me to be the correct results. And the results are that the deprivation of 35 happy years of life is a bad thing, whether these years would have occurred before the date at which Claudette was in fact born, or after the date on which she in fact died.

There are, after all, two ways in which we can rectify the apparently irrational emotional asymmetry. On the one hand, we can follow Lucretius and cease viewing early death as a bad thing for Claudette. On the other hand, we can at least try to start viewing late birth as a bad thing. My suggestion is that in the present case, the latter course would be preferable.

I think it must be granted that our emotional reactions toward pleasures lost by early death are quite different from our emotional reactions toward similar pleasures lost by late birth. If my proposal is right, this emotional asymmetry is irrational. To see this, consider a variant of the case involving Claudette. Suppose (to make the case very "clean") that Claudette never experienced any pleasures or pains, but that if she had died later, she would have enjoyed one especially great pleasure ("the Late Pleasure") in her old age. Suppose similarly that if she had been born earlier, she would instead have enjoyed an equally great pleasure ("the Early Pleasure"). In either case, her life would have contained exactly one pleasure.

Given natural assumptions, my proposal yields the result that Claudette's late birth was just as bad for her as was her early death. Yet I suppose that at times near the end of her life, Claudette and her friends would have been more upset about her impending early death than they would have been about her late birth. Perhaps this emotional asymmetry is to be explained by the fact that we tend to think that the past is fixed, whereas the future is still open. Thus, we may feel that there is no point in lamenting the fact that Claudette missed the Early Pleasure. On the other hand, we may feel that there was a "real chance" that she might have enjoyed the Late Pleasure. Her loss of that seems a greater misfortune.

Another possibility is that we have what Derek Parfit has called "a bias toward the future." Once they are past, we become indifferent toward our pleasures and pains; while they are still in the future, we care deeply about them.[17] If hedonism is true, this sort of asymmetry is wholly irrational. Nevertheless, it might be a deep-seated feature of human psychology.

I want to emphasize the fact that my central proposal here concerns a value-theoretic question, not a question in psychology. I mean to be discussing the question about the relative evil of early death and late birth. I have not attempted to answer the psychological question about the differences in the ways in which we react to early death and late birth. If my proposal is right, then (to a large extent) our emotional reactions may be irrational.

An Objection and a Reply

In "Death and the Value of Life," Jeff McMahan considers and rejects an account of the evil of death very much like the one I mean to defend.[18] He cites a number of difficulties for any such view. One concerns a young cavalry officer who is shot and killed in the charge of the Light Brigade. According to the story, the officer was shot by someone named "Ivan." McMahan stipulates that if the officer had not been killed by Ivan's bullet, he would have died just a few seconds later by a bullet fired by Boris. McMahan says that "our answer to the question of what would have happened had the officer not died when and how he did will be that he would have lived for a few seconds, and then he would have been killed. This leads to the unacceptable conclusion that his actual death was hardly a misfortune at all."[19]

McMahan goes on to offer various revisions of the original proposal, but these seem to me to be changes for the worse (and I explain why below). It seems to me that D3 generates appropriate results.

It is important to distinguish several different things that happen in this example. Let us call the gallant officer "Herbert," and let us suppose the time of his death was 3:30 p.m., October 25,

1854—or "*t.*" Here are some states of affairs that we should distinguish:

P1: Herbert dies at exactly *t*.

P2: Herbert dies near Balaclava.

P3: Herbert dies in the charge of the Light Brigade.

P4: Herbert dies as a result of being shot by Ivan.

P5: Herbert dies in his youth.

It should be clear that we have five different states of affairs here. In fact, each is logically independent of each of the others. Furthermore, it should come as no surprise if some of these are worse for Herbert than others. Given the details of the story, it turns out that P1 and P4 are not very bad for Herbert. Neither of these deprived Herbert of much happiness, since if he had not been killed at *t* by Ivan, he would have been killed seconds later by Boris. It is hard to see why this calls for any alteration of D3. These states of affairs seem to me not to be very bad for Herbert. The real tragedy here is not that he died exactly at *t*, or that he died as a result of being shot by Ivan; the real tragedy is that he died so young. Thus, P5 should be the focus of our attention.

We must consider the nearest possible world in which P5 does not occur. Let us call it "w5." What sort of life does Herbert live there? Perhaps in w5 Herbert is one of the few survivors of the charge; perhaps he is wounded, but recovers and goes on to live a long and happy life. Of course, I do not know precisely what happens to Herbert in w5—but it is reasonable to suppose that in w5 Herbert's welfare level is significantly higher than it is here in the actual world. After all, in w5 Herbert does not die in his youth, but is otherwise as much as possible like he is here in the actual world. In any case, according to D3, the badness of P5 for Herbert is equal to the difference in value for Herbert between w5 and the actual world. This might be a significant difference. He might have led a long and happy life if he had not died in his youth.

I mentioned earlier that I think that McMahan's view is less plausible than D3. On McMahan's proposal, we are asked to consider what happens in a world far more distant than w5. McMahan asks us to consider the nearest world *in which the whole causal sequence leading up to Herbert's death* fails to occur. As McMahan remarks, in the example cited, this may mean considering a world in which the Crimean War does not occur.[20] This strikes me as being implausible. To see how it could go wrong, suppose that Herbert loved excitement. If there had been no Crimean War, he would have sought excitement elsewhere. He would have taken up mountain climbing, and would have been killed in 1853. Given these assumptions, McMahan's proposal yields the surprising result that being killed in the Crimean War was *good* for Herbert. It seems to me to make much more sense to consider a nearer world—a world in which the Crimean War occurs, Herbert participates, but does not die a premature death. w5 is supposed to be such a world, and Herbert is better off in w5 than he is in the real world.

Conclusion

I have attempted to formulate a coherent answer to the ancient challenge set by Epicurus. I have claimed that there is nothing paradoxical about the idea that death may be bad for the one who dies. My answer is a version of the traditional view that death is bad (when it is bad) primarily because it deprives the deceased of goods—the goods he would have enjoyed if he had lived. I have attempted to provide my answer within a predominantly Epicurean framework. I have assumed that hedonism is true, and I have assumed that when a person dies, he goes out of existence. I have attempted to show that even if we grant these assumptions, we can still maintain that death can be evil for the deceased. I have furthermore attempted to show that if we formulate our account properly, we can provide satisfactory answers to some puzzling questions: "How can death be bad for the deceased if he does not exist when it occurs?" "When is death bad for the deceased?" "Is there an illegitimate comparison between the welfare of the nonexistent and the welfare of the existent?" "Why is death worse than prenatal nonexistence?" Along the way, I have also discussed the merits of some other proposed solutions to the puzzles.

CHAPTER SEVENTEEN

MICKEY: Do you realize what a thread we're all hanging by?

GAIL: Mickey, you're off the hook. You should be celebrating.

MICKEY: Can you understand how meaningless everything is? Everything! I'm talking about . . . our lives, the show . . . the whole world, it's meaningless.

GAIL: Yeah . . . but you're not dying!

MICKEY: No, I'm not dying now, but, but you know, when I ran out of the hospital, I, I was so thrilled because they told me I was going to be all right. And I'm running down the street, and suddenly I stop, 'cause it hit me, all right, so you know, I'm not going to go today. I'm okay. I'm not going to go tomorrow. But eventually, I'm going to be in that position.

GAIL: You're realizing this now?

MICKEY: Well, I don't realize it now, I know it all the time, but, but I managed to stick it in the back of my mind . . . because it-it's a very horrible thing to . . . think about!

GAIL: Yeah. What?

MICKEY: Can I tell you something? Can I tell you a secret?

GAIL: Yes, please.

MICKEY: A week ago, I bought a rifle.

GAIL: No.

MICKEY: I went into a store, I bought a rifle. I was gonna . . . You know, if they told me that I had a tumor, I was going to kill myself. The only thing that mighta stopped me, *might've*, is my parents would be devastated. I would, I woulda had to shoot them, also, first. And then, I have an aunt and uncle, I would have . . . You know, it would have been a bloodbath.

GAIL: Tch, well, you know, eventually it, it is going to happen to all of us.

MICKEY: Yes, but doesn't that ruin everything for you? That makes everything . . . you know it, it just takes the pleasure out of everything. I mean, you're gonna die, I'm gonna die, the audience is gonna die, the network's gonna—The sponsor. Everything!

GAIL: I know, I know, and your hamster.

MICKEY: Yes!

GAIL: Listen kid, I think you snapped your cap. Maybe you need a few weeks in Bermuda, or something. Or go to a whorehouse! No?

—Woody Allen, *Hannah and Her Sisters*

Well-Being and Time

J. David Velleman

A person can fare well either over an extended period or at a
particular moment. We evaluate how well a person fares over an
extended period when we speak of him as having a good day, a
good year, or a good life, or when we speak of such a period as
going well for him. We evaluate how a person fares at a particular moment when we say that he is doing well just then. We
favor different idioms in these two kinds of evaluation: we are
more inclined to speak of a person as having a good life than as
having a good moment; and, conversely, we are more inclined
to use the terms "welfare" or "well-being" to express how well
things are going for him at a particular moment than to evaluate
how well his life goes as a whole. Nevertheless, evaluations of
both kinds are judgments of relational value—of what is good
for the person or good in relation to his interests—and so they
are both judgments of the person's welfare.[1]

What is the relation between the welfare value[2] of a temporal
period in someone's life and his welfare at individual moments
during that period? And what is the relation between the value
of a period and that of the shorter periods it comprises? Is a
good day just a day during which one is frequently well off?[3] Is
a good week just a week in which the good days outweigh the
bad? Is a good life just a string of good years?

Reprinted by permission from *Pacific Philosophical Quarterly* 72, no. 1 (March
1991): 48–77. For comments on earlier drafts of this paper, I am indebted to
Elizabeth Anderson, Fred Feldman, Jonathan Lear, Brian Leiter, Peter Railton,
Connie Rosati, Michael Slote, and Nicholas White.

The answer to these questions would be yes if well-being were additive. If the welfare value of a time-period in one's life were equivalent to the sum of momentary well-being that one enjoyed during that period, then a good period would indeed be a period during which one was, on balance, well off, and a good life would be a life composed, on balance, of good periods. But I doubt whether well-being is additive in this way.

Of course, I do not mean to rule out the possibility that the amount of momentary welfare accruing to someone during his life and the welfare value of that life might turn out to be the same. I am simply saying that their being the same would ordinarily be an accident, because the welfare value of a life is not in general determined by, and cannot be inferred from, the amount of momentary well-being that the life contains.[4]

Here I am not merely denying that the value of a life can be computed by the addition of values antecedently assigned to its constituent moments. Computing the value of the whole in this manner, by composition, might be impossible only because the values of the parts had to be computed, inversely, by decomposition. If the only way to assess someone's well-being at a particular moment was to compute the fraction of his life's value that was being realized at the time, then the value of the whole would have to be computed first, and couldn't be derived from the values of the parts.[5] In that case, however, well-being might still be additive in the sense that interests me, since the values of the parts and the value of the whole might still be such that the latter had to equal the sum of the former. What I wish to deny is that well-being is additive in even this sense.

My claim thus militates equally against evaluating a whole life by composition and evaluating its parts by decomposition. In my view, just as assigning values to someone's moments of existence and adding them will not necessarily yield the value of his life; so assigning a value to his life and dividing it among his moments of existence will not necessarily yield their values, either.

My strategy will be to criticize these alternative computations in turn. First I shall presuppose a rough understanding of momentary well-being, and I shall argue, on rather intuitive grounds, that the value of a life need not be the sum of the momentary well-being enjoyed within it. Then I shall argue, on more theoretical grounds, against regarding a person's well-being at a particular moment as a currently realized fraction of his life's value. In neither phase of the argument will I presuppose any particular theory of individual well-being; rather, I will apply what I take to be commonsense notions of faring well, either over one's entire life or within the confines of a particular moment.

Intuitively speaking, the reason why well-being is not additive is that how a person is faring at a particular moment is a temporally local matter, whereas the welfare value of a period in his life depends on the global features of that period. More specifically, the value of an extended period depends on the overall order or structure of events—on what might be called their narrative or dramatic relations.[6]

Consider two different lives that you might live. One life begins in the depths but takes an upward trend: a childhood of deprivation, a troubled youth, struggles and setbacks in early adulthood, followed finally by success and satisfaction in middle age and a peaceful retirement. Another life begins at the heights but slides downhill: a blissful childhood and youth, precocious triumphs and rewards in early adulthood, followed by a midlife strewn with disasters that lead to misery in old age. Surely, we can imagine two such lives as containing equal sums of momentary well-being. Your retirement is as blessed in one life as your childhood is in the other; your nonage is as blighted in one life as your dotage is in the other.

Yet even if we were to map each moment in one life onto a moment of equal well-being in the other, we would not have shown these lives to be equally good. For after the tally of good times and bad times had been rung up, the fact would remain that one life gets progressively better while the other gets progressively worse; one is a story of improvement while the other is a story of deterioration. To most people, I think, the former story would seem like a better life-story—not, of course, in the sense that it makes for a better story in the telling or the hearing, but rather in the sense that it is the story of a better life.[7]

Note that I am not committed to the truth of this value judgment, in particular. I offer it merely as an intuitively plausible illustration of the possibility that periods containing equal sums of momentary welfare can have different overall welfare values. (The same goes for most of the value judgments offered below.) Even those who do not agree with the present value judgment, or can imagine disagreeing with it, will at least acknowledge that it is a reasonable judgment to entertain; whereas it would be ruled out *a priori* if well-being were additive.

One who thinks that a life's value is the sum of the momentary well-being enjoyed therein may seek to explain the outcome of this thought experiment as due to subconscious assumptions that violate the experiment's terms. That is, one may claim that a preference between lives stipulated to contain equal amounts of momentary well-being must arise from a silent refusal to grant the stipulation. Those who prefer the uphill climb to the downhill slide, one may say, are simply assuming that the highs and lows encountered in maturity are more extreme than those encountered in childhood, and that the intensifying effects of age, or mitigating effects of youth, make the goods of one life better and the evils of the other life worse.

But I doubt whether our preference between these lives can be traced to a denial of their supposed symmetry. We do not necessarily assume that the best retirement is better than the best childhood, or that the miseries of age are worse, at their worst, than the miseries of youth. If asked why we prefer the life of improvement, we would be unlikely to express such views; we would be more likely to say, "A life that gets better is, other things being equal, better than a life that gets worse."[8] We would then be expressing a preference between trends, as opposed to sums, of momentary well-being, a preference that is entirely natural and yet at odds with the view that a life's value is the sum of the values of its constituent moments.

This preference can be further sustained by reflection on the counterintuitive consequences of the opposing view.[9] If the value of a life were additive, then a life could be forever spoiled or saved by its initial segment. Every year of well-being would raise the minimum value to which one's life could possibly fall; every year of suffering would lower the maximum value to which one's life could possible rise. An unfortunate childhood would therefore make for a bad start in life, not only by leaving one emotionally or physically ill-equipped for future challenges, but also by permanently lowering the level of lifetime well-being to which one could reasonably aspire. Conversely, a fortunate childhood would provide not only the personal resources with which to succeed in the future but also so much lifetime well-being in the bank, so to speak, ensuring the value of one's life against subsequent reverses. But surely, we do not think, after reading the first few chapters of a biography, that they have placed limits on how well or how badly the subject's life might possibly turn out. We do not think, "He's already fifteen years to the good," or ". . . fifteen years in the hole," as if registering credits or debits that will necessarily be reflected in the subject's final accounts. Yet we do think that we know how well the person fared during the first fifteen years of his life.

My remarks thus far may differ only slightly from, and add only slightly to, what Michael Slote has said in his essay, "Goods and Lives."[10] There Slote offers an example closely resembling the cases I have discussed:

A given man may achieve political power and, once in power, do things of great value, after having been in the political wilderness throughout his earlier career. He may later die while still "in harness" and fully possessed of his powers, at a decent old age. By contrast, another man may have a meteoric success in youth, attaining the same office as the first man and also achieving much good; but then lose power, while still young, never to regain it. Without hearing anything more, I think our natural, immediate reaction to these examples would be that the first man was the more fortunate.[11]

Slote goes on to say that our natural reaction to such a case "seems to suggest a time preference for goods that come late in life."

Whether Slote is describing the phenomenon that I have in mind depends on how this last remark is to be interpreted. On the one hand, a preference for goods that come late in life may reflect the view that one and the same commodity, as measured in purely descriptive terms, often adds more to one's well-being if it is received later. In that case, however, the preference in question is perfectly compatible with the view that a life's value is the sum of the momentary well-being enjoyed therein. For even if a particular quantity of pleasure or money or fame gives a greater boost to one's momentary welfare if it is received later in life, what the commodity adds to one's total momentary welfare, whenever it is received, may still exhaust its contribution to the value of one's life overall. On the other hand, the goods among which Slote's temporal preference discriminates might be equilibrated as goods rather than as commodities—that is, in terms of their impact on one's welfare at the time of their receipt. In that case, the preference reflects the view I am defending, that one and the same increment in one's momentary well-being may have greater or lesser effect on the value of one's life, depending on when and how it occurs. Although Slote sometimes appears to favor the former view,[12] only the latter would place him in disagreement with Henry Sidgwick's principle that "a smaller present good is not to be preferred to a greater future good"[13]—a principle with which Slote claims to disagree. I shall therefore interpret Slote's "pure time preference" as implying that a life's value is not equivalent to a sum of momentary well-being.

I hope to build on Slote's observations in two ways. First, I would like to suggest a deeper explanation than Slote's for the preferences cited in his article. While I agree with Slote that two benefits of equal momentary value may contribute differently to the welfare value of one's life, I doubt whether they can do so merely because of their timing. They can do so, I think, because they can belong to different life stories, which coincidentally place them at different times.

Second, I hope to draw out the consequences of this phenomenon for various issues in moral psychology and moral philosophy. Among the issues I shall discuss are the evil of death, the nature of prudence, and the value of desire-satisfaction.

Consider the theoretical conclusion that Slote hopes to illustrate with the case cited above:

When a personal benefit or good occurs, [it] may make a difference to how fortunate someone is (has been), quite independently of the effects of such timing in producing other good things and of the greater importance we attach to the distinctive goals and interests of certain life periods. And I believe, in particular, that what happens late in life is naturally and automatically invested with greater significance and weight in determining the goodness of lives.[14]

While I agree with Slote's evaluative intuitions about the case, I do not agree with this explanation of them. The reason why later benefits are thought to have a greater impact on the value of one's life is not that greater weight is attached to what comes later. Rather, it is that later events are thought to alter the meaning of earlier events, thereby altering their contribution to the value of one's life.

Suppose that we drew one of Slote's politicians behind a veil of ignorance about his life and put to him the following proposition. He is to have ten years of political success, but he can choose whether his fortunate decade is to occur in his fifties or his thirties. How strong a preference would he have between the alternatives thus described? I suspect that he would be indifferent.[15] If he had any preference at all, it would be neither as strong nor as stable as the preference he would have if we described the alternative careers more fully, as they are described in Slote's example. Merely postponing a fixed amount of well-being until later in life would not strike him as an obvious means of making it more valuable; indeed, he might reasonably regard well-being as more valuable if enjoyed in youth. Surely, then, the preference elicited by Slote's example must depend on something other than the effects of mere timing.[16]

In order to reproduce the preference elicited by Slote's example, we would have to tell the aspiring politician that the later successes being offered to him would be the culmination of a slow ascent, whereas the earlier successes would be the prelude to a sudden decline. That is, we would have to tell him, not only about the timing of the rewards in question, but also about their place in a larger trend. He would not care whether a particular bundle of goods was to be encountered early or late in the game; what he would care about is whether they were to be encountered at the top of a chute or the top of a ladder.

Why would a person care about the placement of momentary goods on the curve that maps his changing welfare? The answer, I believe, is that an event's place in the story of one's life lends it a meaning that is not entirely determined by its impact on one's well-being at the time. A particular electoral victory, providing a particular boost to one's current welfare, can mean either that one's early frustrations were finally over or that one's subsequent failures were not yet foreshadowed, that one enjoyed either fleeting good luck or lasting success—all depending on its placement in the trend of one's well-being. And the event's meaning is what determines its contribution to the value of one's life.[17]

The meaning attached to a quantity of momentary well-being is determined only in part by its place in the overall trend.[18] The meaning of a benefit depends not only on whether it follows or precedes hardships but also on the specific narrative relation between the goods and evils involved. Slote's politician would have experienced an improvement in his well-being whether his years of toil were capped by electoral victory or merely cut short by his winning the lottery and retiring young. But the contribution of these alternative benefits to the overall value of his life would not be determined entirely by how well-off each would make him from one moment to the next. Their contribution to his life's value would also be determined by the fact that the former would be a well-earned reward, and would prove his struggles to have been a good investment, whereas the latter would be a windfall in relation to which his struggles were superfluous. Thus benefits that would effect equal improvements in his momentary well-being might contribute differently to the value of his life, by virtue of lending and borrowing different meanings in exchange with preceding events.

The most familiar illustration of this principle is the commonly held belief in the importance of drawing lessons from one's misfortunes. If a life's value were a sum of momentary well-being, learning from a misfortune would be no more important than learning from other sources, since every lesson learned would add so much value and no more to the sum of one's well-being. On being invited to learn from a personal tragedy, one would therefore be entitled to reply, "No, I think I'll read a book instead." Edification would offset the losses incurred in the tragedy, but its having been derived from the tragedy would not render edification more valuable, either intrinsicially or extrinsically. Any lesson of equal value would offset one's losses equally.[19]

The point of learning from a misfortune, surely, is to prevent the misfortune from being a total loss. Learning from the misfortune confers some value on it, by making it the means to one's edification. But how could this be the point? The instrumental value of a means is not to be counted as additional to the intrinsic value of the end. (Otherwise, we would be obliged to pursue our ends as circuitously as possible, so as to accumulate the most instrumental value along the way.) Since the value of a means is not additional to that of the end, turning a misfortune into a means of learning a lesson does not produce any more value than that inherent in the lesson itself, a value not necessarily greater than that of any alternative lesson one might have learned. So how can the point of learning from a misfortune, in particular, be to confer instrumental value on it?

The answer, I believe, is that conferring instrumental value on a misfortune alters its meaning, its significance in the story of one's life. The misfortune still detracted from one's well-being at the time, but it no longer mars one's life story as it formerly did. A life in which one suffers a misfortune and then learns from it may find one equally well-off, at each moment, as a life in which one suffers a misfortune and then reads the encyclopedia. But the costs of the misfortune are merely offset when the value of the latter life is computed; whereas they are somehow canceled entirely from the accounts of the former. Or rather, neither misfortune affects the value of one's life just by adding costs and benefits to a cumulative account. The effect of either misfortune on one's life is proportionate, not to its impact on one's continuing welfare, but to its import for the story. An edifying misfortune is not just offset but redeemed by being given a meaningful place in one's progress through life.[20]

The same point can be illustrated with other examples. In one life your first ten years of marriage are troubled and end in divorce, but you immediately remarry happily; in another life the troubled years of your first marriage lead to eventual happiness as the relationship matures. Both lives contain ten years of marital strife followed by contentment; but let us suppose that in the former, you regard your first ten years of marriage as a dead loss, whereas in the latter you regard them as the foundation of your happiness.[21] The bad times are just as bad in both lives, but in one they are cast off and in the other they are redeemed. Surely, these two decades can affect the value of your life differently, even if you are equally well off at each moment of their duration. From the perspective of your second marriage, you may reasonably think that your life would have gone better if you could have made your first marriage work out; and you may reasonably think so without thinking that the first marriage, if successful, would have been better from day to day than the second. You can simply think that a dead-end relationship blots the story of one's life in a way that marital problems do not if they lead to eventual happiness.

Of course, your desire for a successful first marriage is fulfilled in the latter life, whereas in the former it is given up and replaced by the desire for a successful second marriage. In a sense, then, the former life differs from the latter by virtue of containing more unfulfilled desires. Doesn't this difference in desire fulfillment explain the difference in perceived value between these lives?

I doubt whether a difference in desire fulfillment can do this explanatory job. Suppose, for example, that in both versions of the story your early desire to achieve happiness with your first mate was accompanied by an equally strong, competing desire to start afresh with someone else. The only difference between these desires, let us say, was that during your ten years of trying to fulfill the former, the latter remained an idle yearning on which you never acted. Now the two endings of your story no longer differ in respect to the fulfillment of your youthful desires: each ending fulfills one and frustrates one of the desires that you harbored throughout your first marriage. Do they consequently result in equally valuable lives? I am inclined to say not. For I am still inclined to prefer the ending in which your initial efforts are redeemed over the ending in which they are abandoned. Fulfilling a desire on behalf of which you have struggled may be more important than fulfilling a desire in which you have made no investment. Hence desire fulfillment per se is not what is valuable; what is valuable is living out a story of efforts rewarded rather than efforts wasted.[22]

Insofar as the fulfillment of one's past desires is valuable, I am inclined to say, its value depends on that of life stories in which desires are eventually fulfilled. For I cannot see how a difference in the fulfillment of past desires can yield any difference in momentary well-being. Let us cancel the assumption that you always wanted to change mates, and return to the assumption that the beginning of your story, in either version, includes only a desire to make a go of your first marriage—a desire that is fulfilled in one version but abandoned in the other. The question remains when you are rendered worse off, in the version that involves a second marriage, by the abandonment of your hopes for the first. Once you abandon those hopes, you acquire new ones—for success in the second marriage—and these are richly fulfilled. You are therefore just as well off in your second marriage, from day to day, as you would have been in your first, had it flourished. To be sure, you are no longer achieving what your former self wanted you to achieve—namely, success in the first marriage—but this failure can hardly make your former self worse off retroactively. The daily well-being of your former self is a feature of the past, beyond alteration. Failure to fulfill your previous desires thus impinges on your interests without affecting your welfare at any particular moment.

Oddly enough, several philosophers have affirmed the possibility of retroactive effects on well-being—often in order to explain when a person suffers the evil of death.[23] According to these philosophers, a person's death can make him worse off during the immediately preceding portion of his life, by preventing the fulfillment of the desires he has during that period.

These philosophers argue that our resistance to the idea of being currently harmed by future events is based on the false assumption that one cannot be harmed by things that do not affect one's conscious experiences. But acknowledging the possibility of unexperienced harms should not necessarily lead us to acknowledge the possibility of present harms due to future events. For even if a person's current welfare is not determined entirely by facts within his experience, it may still be determined entirely by facts within the present.

This restriction on the determinants of momentary well-being cannot be inferred directly from the impossibility of backward causation. Future events could affect one's present well-being if present well-being were a relation between one's present desires and the states of affairs that fulfilled or failed to fulfill them. In that case, retroactively harming someone would no more require retrograde causation than retroactively "making a liar" of him. But momentary well-being is ordinarily conceived as a temporally local matter, determined by a person's current circumstances, whether experienced or unexperienced. We think of a person's current well-being as a fact intrinsic to the present, not as a relation that he currently bears to his future. We do not say, of a person who dies in harness, that he fared progressively worse toward the end, simply because he was acquiring more and more ambitions that would go unfulfilled. Nor do we say, of a person raised in adversity, that his youth was not so bad, after all, simply because his youthful hopes were eventually fulfilled later in life.[24] We might say that such a person's adulthood compensated for an unfortunate youth, but we would not say that it made his youth any better. Because the belief in retroactive welfare effects would entail such judgments, it strikes me as highly counterintuitive.

Thus, the reason why it is generally in your interests to promote the fulfillment of your current desires for the future cannot be that their future fulfillment will make you better off now. Nor can it be that their future fulfillment will make you better off then—that is, better off than you would be if you replaced them with different desires that got fulfilled.[25] The reason why it is in your interests to promote the fulfillment of your current desires for the future is rather that a life story of ambitions conceived, pursued, and fulfilled may be a better life story than one of ambitions conceived, discarded, and replaced. And the one life is better than the other even though they may include equal amounts of momentary well-being.[26]

My view of lifetime well-being provides a different explanation from Slote's for the discrepancy in our attitudes toward early and late stages in life. My explanation begins with the observation that events in a person's life can borrow significance from both preceding and succeeding events. A particular success can be either a windfall or a well-earned reward, depending on the amount of effort that preceded it; the expenditure of a particular effort can be either a good investment or a waste, depending on the degree of success that ensues. Retrospective significance—that which is gained from subsequent events—is often responsible for the discrepancy between total momentary well-being and lifetime value. For when subsequent developments alter the meaning of an event they can alter its contribution to the value of one's life, but they cannot retroactively change the impact that it had on one's well-being at the time.

From the perspective of practical reasoning, in which the past is fixed but the future remains open, earlier events seem more susceptible to retroactive changes of significance. Even after the events of one's youth have occurred, their import for one's life story remains undetermined, since the events from which they will gain significance or to which they will lend significance lie primarily in the future. By contrast, the events of one's old age occur in the determinate context of one's past, with which they exchange fixed implications that are unlikely to be significantly modified in what remains of one's life. Thus, one looks forward to a lifetime in which to redeem one's youth, but confronts events of middle age as having a single, determinate significance once and for all.

The result is, not that later events are more important, but that one sees less latitude for arranging them within the requirements of a good life. By middle age, one finds oneself composing the climax to a particular story—a story that is now determinate enough to be spoiled. Virtually any beginning might have been the beginning of a good life; but given one's actual beginnings, there may now be only a few good ways of going on.[27]

Because one will confront one's prime with relatively narrow criteria of success, one is required to devote more care to planning it and to ensuring that it turns out as planned. The extraordinary attention paid to this stage in life may be misinterpreted as indicating that it is more important—that the events of middle age contribute more to a life's value than events at other stages. The reason for paying more attention to one's prime, however, is not that the possibilities at middle age are worth more than at other stages but rather that in relation to a fixed youth, fewer of the possibilities will result in a life that's any good at all.

My account of the value judgments canvassed above amounts to the claim that the value of one's life is what might be called a strongly irreducible second-order good.[28] A second-order good is a valuable state of affairs consisting in some fact about other goods. Of course, corresponding to every good that someone might attain is the potential fact of his having thereby attained something good; and his having attained something good would undeniably be a good state of affairs consisting in a fact about other goods. There is therefore a second-order good corresponding to every attainable good of the first order. But such a second-order good is reducible to the first-order good implicated in it, in the sense that it has no value over and above that of the implicated first-order good. That is, when someone attains a good, he is not enriched by its value plus some additional value attaching to the fact of his having thereby attained something good. (If he were, then he would be infinitely enriched, since the second-order good would generate a good of the third order, and so on *ad infinitum*.)

In order for a second-order good to be irreducible, it must at least possess value over and above that of its component first-order goods. A possible example of such a good in the realm of social value is that of a just distribution of benefits. Some people think that there can be value in redistributing benefits among the members of a society even if the redistribution does not increase the total amount of good accruing to individuals. This thought implies that the resulting distribution has a value over and above that of the goods being distributed, and hence that the new distribution is an irreducible second-order good.

There is yet a stronger form of irreducibility that may or may not attach to a second-order good whose value is additional to that of its components. Consider two possible views about the second-order value of a just distribution. On the one hand, we might judge that a distribution of individual benefits has a second-order value that depends entirely on the proportions among the shares of benefits distributed; on the other hand, we might judge that the justice of a distribution, and hence its value, depends on whether individuals deserve their shares by dint of their actions or characters. The first view implies that the value of a just distribution, though additional to that of the benefits distributed, can still be computed from the amounts in which those benefits are distributed. The view thus implies that facts about second-order value are still, in a sense, reducible to facts about mere quantities of first-order goods. By contrast, the second view implies that no facts about quantities of first-order goods can fully determine the facts about second-order value, since the latter also depend on facts about the conduct and characters of individuals. The second view thus implies that the second-order value of a just distribution is irreducible in a stronger sense.

The existence of second-order goods that are irreducible in either sense entails the existence of more than one dimension of value. If social justice is an irreducible second-order good, for example, then there must be a dimension of value other than total individual welfare—a dimension of social value, as it might be called—along which value can be produced even while total individual welfare remains constant.

In the case of distributing benefits among the periods in someone's life, however, the corresponding implication may initially seem odd. If we regard a particular temporal distribution of well-being as having irreducible second-order value for a person, we would seem committed to claiming that its value lies along a dimension distinct from that of total individual well-being, since we shall have said that value can be produced by a redistribution that leaves total well-being constant. Yet the distribution in question is supposed to be good specifically for the person, and so its value would seem to lie along the dimension of individual well-being rather than along any alternative dimension. We are therefore confronted with a puzzle. If a temporal redistribution of benefits produces no additional benefits for the person, how can it be beneficial to him? How can a person be better off under an arrangement that affords him no additional benefits?

The answer to this question is that the value of a temporal distribution of benefits need not lie along a dimension of value distinct from that of individual well-being; its dimension of value must be distinct only from that of *momentary* individual well-being, since momentary benefits are the benefits whose total remains constant under the envisioned redistribution. Thus, regarding a temporal distribution of benefits as an irreducible second-order good requires the assumption that a person's well-being has both a synchronic and a diachronic dimension. The value of someone's life lies along the dimension of diachronic welfare, which is distinct from, and irreducible to, how well off he is at each moment therein.

Here we find, in a new guise, the value judgment with which I began—namely, that two lives containing equal sums of momentary well-being need not be equally good lives if their momentary benefits stand in different temporal or, more generally, different narrative relations. We can now see what this intuitive judgment implies: it implies that self-interest is not a unitary dimension of value. Rather, a person has two distinct sets of interests, lying along two distinct dimensions—his synchronic interests, in being well off at particular moments, and his diachronic interests, in having good periods of time and, in particular, a good life.

Although Slote regards a life's value as weakly irreducible, he does not regard it as irreducible in the stronger sense.[29] Slote analyzes the values of lives in terms of weights assigned to momentary goods in accordance with the time of their occurrence. He says that some periods of life are more important than others, and hence that the goods and evils occurring in those periods are accorded greater weight when the value of a life is computed. His view therefore amounts to the claim that facts about the value of a life can be reduced to facts about the amounts and temporal order of the momentary benefits enjoyed therein—in short, to facts about temporal patterns of momentary benefits.

In my view, however, the facts about a life's value are not even reducible to this extent. Some of the value judgments considered above are incompatible with any reduction of diachronic well-being to synchronic well-being, no matter how sophisticated an algorithm of discounting and weighting is applied. Because an event's contribution to the value of one's life depends on its narrative relation to other events, a life's value can never be computed by an algorithm applied to bare amounts of momentary well-being, or even to ordered sequences of such amounts, in abstraction from the narrative significance of the events with which they are associated. How the value of one's life is affected by a period of failure combined with a period of success, for example, cannot be computed merely from the timing of these periods and the amounts of well-being they contain. Their impact on the value of one's life depends as well on the narrative relations among the successes and failures involved. Were one's travails in the political wilderness ended by ascent to high office? or were they ended by a lucky ticket in the lottery and a round-the-world cruise? Was one's perseverance through rocky times vindicated or discredited by the particular way in which one eventually attained domestic happiness? Our evaluative intuitions about the importance of learning from misfortunes, or of salvaging one's projects, thus imply that the value of a life is more strongly irreducible than Slote suggests.

The degree of irreducibility between second- and first-order goods determines the degree of independence between the corresponding dimensions of value. If we analyze the second-order value attaching to different patterns of benefits in terms of weights attached to those benefits, we shall continue to regard diachronic well-being as reducible to synchronic well-being, albeit by means of a time-weighted algorithm. The implication will therefore remain that the greater weight attached to some goods and evils, because of their occurring at important times, can be offset by a greater amount of goods and evils occurring at times of less importance. The second-order value of a benefit's timing will thus be conceived as exchangeable for a greater amount of that or any other first-order benefit.

Thus, if the problem with a downward trend in well-being were that more importance attached to what happens in one's prime, then there would have to be some amount of childhood happiness that was sufficient to compensate for midlife misfortunes even after the appropriate weights had been applied. Childhood well-being would still amount to so much credit earned toward a good life, even if that credit was computed at a discounted rate. Hence a life that took a slide would still be a good one if it started from a sufficient height.

If we suppose, however, that the second-order value of a life is simply not computable from the amounts and temporal order of the momentary benefits that it contains, then we must conclude that some second-order goods may not be exchangeable for goods of the first order (and vice versa). That is, there may be some undesirable turns of plot whose disvalue simply cannot be offset by greater amounts of momentary well-being in the associated prelude or denouement. I find this implication more consonant with our evaluative intuitions than the implications of Slote's view. It explains why we think that the value of someone's life remains almost entirely undetermined even after he has passed an especially happy or unhappy childhood; and why we are inclined to perceive some wisdom in Solon's refusal to declare Croesus happy without knowing how his life would ultimately turn out.[30]

I therefore favor the principle that a person's self-interest is radically divided, in the sense that he has an interest in features of his life that are not at all reducible to, and hence cannot be exchanged with, patterns of momentary well-being. Let me briefly suggest two possible applications for this principle.

First, I think that this principle, if correct, justifies a revision in the philosophical conception of prudence and imprudence.[31] Imprudence has traditionally been conceived as an irrational preference for momentary goods that are closer in time, and prudence as a rational indifference toward the timing of such goods. Prudence and imprudence have thus been conceived as dispositions to value momentary goods differently. In my view, however, we should consider the hypothesis that imprudence is rather an undue concern for momentary goods altogether; and prudence, a rational appreciation for the second-order value of a good life—a disposition that cannot be constituted out of any appreciation for patterns of momentary goods. According to this hypothesis, a person can be imprudent no matter how carefully he balances momentary goods of the present against those of the future, if he does so without regard to the value of the resulting life, a value not reducible to temporal distributions of momentary goods; and a person can be prudent even if he pursues present benefits at the expense of future benefits, so long as the value of his life is thereby enhanced. Preferring the lesser but nearer good to that which is greater but more remote may sometimes be the prudent thing to do, if done in the service of one's irreducible second-order interest in a good life.

A second application for the principle of divided self-interest has to do with the evil of death. A prevalent view about death is that it is bad for a person if, but only if, his continued survival would add to his accumulation of momentary well-being. The choice between heroic medical treatment and passive euthanasia is therefore frequently said to require so-called quality-of-life considerations. Whether days should be added to or subtracted from a patient's life is to be judged, according to the prevalent view, by whether the days in question would be spent in a state of well-being or hardship.[32]

In my view, however, deciding when to die is not (despite the familiar saying) like deciding when to cash in one's chips—not, that is, a decision to be based on the incremental gains and losses that one stands to accumulate by staying in the game. It is rather like deciding when and how to end a story, a decision that cannot be dictated by considerations of momentary well-being. Hence a person may rationally be willing to die even though he can look forward to a few more good weeks or months;[33] and a person may rationally be unwilling to die even though he can look forward only to continued adversity. The rationality of the patient's attitude depends on whether an earlier or later death would make a better ending to his life story.

Thus far I have presupposed a prior understanding of what it is to be well off at a particular moment, and I have argued that the value of a person's life is not reducible to his momentary well-being, so understood. The reader might be moved to object, however, that I am not entitled to my initial presupposition. One might think that the only legitimate conception of a person's well-being is that of his life's value; and that any conception of his well-being at a particular moment must therefore be illegitimate insofar as it fails to capture the portion of his life's value being realized at that moment.

I shall argue against this suggestion on grounds more theoretical than those of my previous arguments. First I shall offer a more theoretical explanation of why a person's momentary well-being might fail to be additive. The reason, I shall claim, is that a person's well-being at each moment is defined from the perspective of that moment, and values defined from different perspectives cannot necessarily be added together. This explanation will prompt the suggestion that the successive perspectives defining momentary well-being simply distort the true values of things, which are properly defined from the comprehensive perspective of an entire life. I shall then argue against this suggestion, by defending the independent validity of momentary perspectives. Finally, I shall explore some further implications of these theoretical results.

That momentary well-being might not add up should come as no surprise: values are rarely additive. Notoriously, the value of two things together need not be the sum of their individual values.[34] The value of having two egg rolls on one's plate is less than the sum of the values of having one or the other of them; and the value of having one egg roll and a dollop of plum sauce is more than the sum of the values of having either an egg roll or plum sauce alone. To be sure, the value of having two egg rolls is indeed the sum of their marginal values: marginal values are additive. But marginal values are additive only because they are defined by decomposition of total value, to begin with. That is, the marginal value of one's second egg roll is defined as the amount by which its acquistion increases one's total well-being; and this definition guarantees that the acquisition of a second egg roll increases one's well-being by the addition of its marginal value. The point previously made by saying that the values of egg rolls are not additive can then be made by saying that the marginal values of two successive egg rolls are not the same.

Of course, what is currently at issue is not additivity in the value of some commodity such as food but additivity in well-being itself. The question is not whether two egg rolls are twice as good as one but whether being well off at two different times is twice as good as being well off at one time. And we might have thought that although successive helpings of food can vary in their impact on one's well-being, and hence in their marginal value, successive helpings of well-being cannot.

This thought might have been correct if the helpings in question were defined in relation to the same context of evaluation. But since helpings of momentary well-being are defined in relation to different contexts, they are not additive at all. Let me explain.

The reason why the marginal value of successive egg rolls varies is that the value of acquiring an egg roll depends on the context in which the acquistion occurs. One's second egg roll is worth less than the first because it is acquired in the context of one's already having the first. Of course, once the second egg roll is assigned a marginal value, that value need not be further adjusted because of its being acquired in the context of the well-being that is already, so to speak, on one's plate; the egg roll's marginal value already reflects the only adjustment necessitated by the context.

Nevertheless, we often restrict the context in which judgments of value are made. For example, we make distinct assessments of how well off someone is in different respects—assessments of his financial well-being, say, or his emotional well-being, and so on. And such evaluations are made within restricted contexts. An assessment of someone's financial well-being may take account of the diminishing marginal value of dollars:³⁵ his second million need not be thought to make him twice as well off, financially speaking, as the first. But our assessment of someone's financial well-being does not take account of interactions between his finances and other goods. The impact of a million dollars on someone's overall well-being may depend not only on how much wealth he already has but also on his emotional state or his health. But the potential interactions between wealth and these other goods are screened off from assessments of specifically financial well-being. Two people with equal assets and liabilities (and, perhaps, similar attitudes towards money) are judged to be equally well off, financially speaking, even if those assets and liabilities affect their overall welfare differently, by virtue of their differing emotional or physical circumstances.³⁶

Consequently, we cannot compute a person's overall well-being at a particular moment by adding up his concurrent financial well-being, emotional well-being, physical well-being, and so on. The problem is not simply that we do not know how to commensurate among wealth, health, and sanity—that is, how to bring these commodities under a common unit of value for the purposes of addition and subtraction. The problem is that such restricted assessments of well-being are made in isolation from potential interactions among the goods involved. Our assessment of the person's financial well-being does not reflect how his emotional and physical circumstances affect the marginal value of his wealth; our assessment of his emotional well-being does not reflect how his physical and financial circumstances affect the marginal value of his sanity; and so forth. Thus, even if we could establish an equivalence of value between a helping of financial well-being and a helping of physical well-being, we would not have established that the combination of the two was worth twice as much as either one alone, since our measures of financial and physical well-being would not reflect potential interactions between the values of the underlying commodities.

We can easily forget this limitation on evaluative calculations if we imagine value itself to be a commodity. If we picture financial well-being as an elixir distilled from piles of money, we shall think of it as having an independent existence; and we shall then be inclined to think that when financial well-being is added to the values distilled from physical health or emotional stability, the resulting brew must simply be the sum of its ingredients. But an amount of financial well-being is not a quantity of stuff; it is rather a property of one's financial state. Indeed, it is a property that one's financial state possesses only in relation to other possible financial states, just as one's overall well-being at a particular moment is a relation of one's overall state to the other states that one might be in. And there is no reason to assume that the relation of one's overall state to its possible alternatives can be computed from the relations of its parts or aspects to theirs.

The problem of compounding values is analogous, in many respects, to problems in the compounding of chances. Notoriously, the probability of a person's having the trait *p or q* is not necessarily equal to the probability of having *p* plus that of having *q*, since the latter probabilities may not be independent; and for the same reason, the probability of having the trait *p and q* is not necessarily equal to the product of the probabilities of having the component traits. Consequently, we cannot estimate how unusual a person is by compounding the degrees to which he is physically unusual, psychologically unusual, socially unusual, and so on. The product of these probabilities may not reflect the extent to which the person possesses physical and psychological traits that are individually rare but often combined, or vice versa. This computation would therefore count someone with red hair and a hot temper as doubly unusual,[37] even if these two unusual traits tend to go hand in hand; and it would correspondingly underestimate the rarity of someone who is both beautiful and modest. In estimating how physically unusual a person is, we do take account of interactions among the probabilities of physical traits (red hair and freckles); in estimating how psychologically unusual he is, we take account of interactions among the probabilities of psychological traits (hot temper and romantic passion); but in neither case do we consider interactions between physical and psychological probabilities. Because these estimates of probability are thus confined to different contexts, they cannot be added or multiplied together.

In short, calculating someone's overall well-being by adding up his physical and emotional welfare is no more appropriate than calculating how unusual he is by compounding his physical and emotional quirkiness. My view is that momentary well-being lacks additivity for the same reasons. Estimates of momentary well-being are made within a restricted context—namely, the context of the events and circumstances of the moment. How well off someone is judged to be at one moment does not reflect potential interactions between the value of what obtains and happens then and the value of earlier or later events. Hence evaluations made in the context of one moment cannot be added to evaluations made in the context of another. Being well off on two occasions does not necessarily make a person doubly well off, any more than being both physically and psychologically unusual makes him doubly unusual.[38]

Again, we shall tend to forget this limitation on evaluative calculations if we imagine an amount of momentary well-being as a quantity of stuff, derived from the facts of the moment but then having an independent existence of its own. In reality, one's well-being at each moment is a relation between the facts of the moment and alternative possibilities; and there is no reason to assume that the relations of successive facts to their alternatives determine the relation of the entire succession to its alternatives.

My claim that momentary well-being is assessed from a restricted perspective might seem to undermine my earlier claim that a person's self-interest is divided. Doesn't my latest argument show that a person's synchronic interests are divided from his diachronic interests only in the sense that his financial interests, say, are divided from his interests as a whole? Either division, one might think, is merely an artifact of the restrictions placed on the context in which synchronic or financial interests are assessed: a person's interests, comprehensively considered, are still unified.

Although I agree that the division between synchronic and diachronic interests results from the difference between the perspectives from which they are assessed, I hesitate to assume that the more comprehensive of these perspectives has exclusive authority. In the case of a person's financial interests, of course, I am inclined to say that insofar as they diverge from his interests overall, they should be regarded as a figment of a restricted perspective and should be ignored. Although a person can limit his attention and concern to financial matters from time to time, the resulting value judgments, even if correct, have no independent authority on which to stand in competition with more comprehensive judgments of his interests.

A person's synchronic interests, however, strike me as having an independent claim that is not necessarily overridden by that of his diachronic interests. The reason, I think, is that a person himself has both a synchronic and a diachronic identity. The perspectives from which synchronic interests are assessed, unlike the financial perspective, are not optional points of view that a person may or may not adopt from time to time. They are perspectives that a person necessarily inhabits as he proceeds through life, perspectives that are partly definitive of who he is. An essential and significant feature of persons is that they are creatures who naturally live their lives from the successive viewpoints of individual moments, as well as from a comprehensive, diachronic point of view.

To think that the more comprehensive of these perspectives must have greater authority is, I believe, to mistake how perspectives bear on questions of relational value. When we choose between competing theories about one and the same phenomenon, the more comprehensive theory may be preferable, other things being equal. But the different perspectives currently in play are not competing theories about the same phenomenon; they are partly constitutive of different phenomena—that is, different modes of relational value. Because well-being is a relational value, it is constituted, in part, by a point-of-view—namely, the point of view inhabited by the creature whose well-being is in question. What is good for that creature, in particular, depends on what point of view it inhabits by virtue of being the particular creature it is.

Thus, although the perspective of a particular creature is less comprehensive than that of the entire universe, evaluations relative to the creature's perspective are not any less authoritative than those relative to the universe's point of view. Evaluations relative to a particular creature's perspective are authoritative about what is good for that creature; and what is good for a particular creature is really and truly good for that creature, even if it is not good for the universe. These two perspectives are not two competing theories about one and the same mode of value; they are constitutive of two different modes of value.

Similarly, evaluations from the perspective of a single moment in someone's life need not be less authoritative than those that are relative to the perspective of his life as a whole. Both are judgments of relational value, which is constituted in either case by a particular point of view; and evaluations relative to either point of view are authoritative about what is good from that point of view.

The question, then, is not whether what is good from the perspective of a moment in someone's life is really good, since it really *is* good from that perspective. The question is rather whether the perspective in question has a subject—whether there really is a creature whose perspective it is and who therefore is the subject of the values it constitutes. To this latter question, I think, the answer is yes. By virtue of being who you are, you unavoidably occupy successive momentary viewpoints as well as a diachronic one; and just as what is good from the latter viewpoint is good for you as protagonist of an ongoing life, so what is good from the former viewpoints is good for you as subject of successive moments within that life.[39]

Note that in arguing for the validity of synchronic perspectives, I am not defending or attacking any thesis about time preferences.[40] I am not trying to show that one is entitled to take a greater interest in the present moment than in other moments in one's life. In my view, no one momentary perspective takes precedence over any other. My brief is on behalf of all momentary perspectives equally, against the assumption that their deliverances are to be overridden by those of the diachronic perspective that subsumes them. I am trying to show that the value something has for someone in the restricted context of a single moment in his life is a value that genuinely accrues to him as the subject of that moment, even if interactions with events at other times result in its delivering a different value to him in his capacity as the protagonist of an entire life. The good that something does you now is not just the phantom of a restricted method of accounting; it is an autonomous mode of value.

If I am right about the autonomy of synchronic interests, then a person's well-being at a particular moment cannot be computed from the fraction of his life's value being realized at the time, any more than the value of the whole can be computed from the values of its parts. To assess the benefits that someone is currently receiving in terms of their share in the value of his life would be to evaluate everything in the more comprehensive context. Such a method of evaluation might be appropriate for Tralfamadorians, who do not live one moment at a time,[41] but it is not appropriate for human beings. Just as evaluating a life by adding up the values of its component moments entails neglecting the perspective that encompasses the unity of those moments, so evaluating moments in a life by dividing up the value of the whole entails neglecting the perspectives that preserve their individuality. Each moment in a life is, momentarily, the present. And for a human being, the present is not just an excerpt from a continuing story, any more than the story is just a concatenation of moments.[42]

What if a creature cannot adopt a perspective that encompasses a particular combination of goods? How then do we assess what value the combination has for him or how the values of its components interact?

Consider a nonhuman animal, such as a cow or a pig. I assume that a cow cannot conceive of itself as a persisting individual and consequently cannot conceive of itself as enjoying different benefits at different moments during its life. What the cow cannot conceive, it cannot care about; and so a cow cannot care about which sequences of momentary goods it enjoys. The cow cannot care twice as much about faring well at two distinct times than it cares about faring well right now—not because it can care only less than twice as much, but rather because it cannot care at all, being unable to conceive of itself as persisting through a sequence of benefits.

The upshot is that any judgment we make about the value that a particular sequence of benefits has for a cow will bear no relation to how the cow would or should or even could feel about that sequence of benefits. And this result seems incompatible with even a weak form of internalism about value, which would at least rule out the possibility that something can be intrinsically good for a subject if he is constitutionally incapable of caring about it. I am not sympathetic to stronger versions of internalism, which make a thing's intrinsic value for someone contingent on his being disposed to care about it under specified or specifiable conditions; but I am inclined to think that unless a subject has the bare capacity, the equipment, to care about something under some conditions or other, it cannot be intrinsically good for him.[43]

Of course, we can adopt yet a weaker form of internalism, which allows for intrinsic goods that the subject cannot care about, so long as they are compounded out of goods that he can. But this version of internalism will be unstable, for two reasons.

One reason is that this version will commit us to constrain some of our judgments about intrinsic relational value within the bounds of internalism and yet to make other, similar judgments that exceed the same bounds. If we assume that what cannot be of concern to a creature can nevertheless have intrinsic value for that creature, provided that it is divisible into components that can be of concern, then we shall need to adopt some method for combining the values of the components. In order to add up the momentary goods enjoyed by a cow, for example, we shall have to make some assumption about how the values of those goods interact, so that we can compute their combined value. And this assumption will constitute another judgment of intrinsic relational value. To suppose that a cow's momentary well-being consists in this or that feature of its current circumstances is one value judgment; but to suppose that the values of the cow's good moments can be combined in this or that way is a further value judgment, a judgment to the effect that two moments containing the relevant feature are this much or that much better for the cow than one.

Whether we say that one moment of such-and-such a kind is good for a cow, or that two such moments are thus-and-so much better for the cow, we are making a judgment of intrinsic relational value. Yet the proposed version of internalism will say that the validity of the former judgment depends on the cow's ability to care about the object of evaluation, whereas the validity of the latter does not. On what grounds can this distinction be drawn? Surely, whatever intuitive reasons we have for applying the internalist constraint to the first value judgment are likely to be reasons for applying it to the second.

Another, related instability in the resulting view is that it is at odds with a fundamental intuition about relational value— namely, that the value something has for a particular creature is somehow grounded in or determined by that creature's point of view.[44] Insofar as we commit ourselves to combining the values accruing to a subject from goods whose combinations exceed his comprehension, we shall find ourselves making relational value judgments that are not appropriately related to the subject's perspective. There is nothing about the perspective of a cow that supports one assumption rather than another about how the value of two momentary benefits stands to the value of either benefit alone, given that sequences of such benefits are beyond the cow's ken and thus, as it were, nothing to the cow. The combined value would therefore have no claim to represent what is good for the cow, or what is good from the cow's perspective.[45]

Note that this problem is equally acute for all possible assumptions about how the cow's momentary benefits should be combined. Even the assumption that two equally good moments in the cow's life are twice as valuable as one presupposes a flat curve of marginal value;[46] and this presupposition has no basis in the cow's point of view. Such a straight-forward method of adding benefits may have the advantages of simplicity and salience in comparison with other methods, but these advantages should not be mistaken for truth. In respect to truth, any method of combining the values of a cow's good and bad moments will be purely arbitrary and consequently defective, insofar as it fails to represent what values things have specifically for the cow rather than from some other perspective.

I therefore think that we should refuse to combine the momentary benefits and harms accruing to a cow; we should conclude, instead, that a cow can fare well or ill only at particular moments. Good and bad things can befall a cow, but they are good or bad for it only at particular times and thus bear only a time-indexed sort of value. There is no timeless dimension of value along which the cow progresses by undergoing successive benefits and harms. Hence the various benefits accruing to a cow at different moments must not add up to anything at all, not even to zero: they must simply be unavailable for addition.

As before, if we imagine the cow's momentary well-being as a commodity, then we shall be puzzled by the claim that amounts of this commodity cannot be added together. But once we realize that the cow's momentary well-being is a relation that the cow's current state bears to other possible states, the air of mystery is dispelled. For there is nothing odd about the suggestion that a relation obtaining between momentary states of a cow cannot obtain between sequences of those states. One moment can be better or worse for a cow than another moment, but one sequence of moments cannot be better for a cow than another sequence, because a cow cannot care about extended periods in its life. This conclusion seems mysterious only if we imagine one moment as better for the cow than another by virtue of containing more of a special stuff that cannot help but accumulate.

For a lower animal, then, momentary well-being fails not only of additivity but of cumulability by any algorithm at all. Consequently, the totality of this subject's life simply has no value for him, because he cannot care about it as such, and because its constituent moments, which he can care about, have values that do not accumulate.

This conception of a lower animal's interests is supported, I think, by its fruitfulness in accounting for our intuitions about the moral difference between killing animals and killing people. For in relation to an animal's interests, as I have now described them, the traditional Epicurean arguments about death are correct. That is, there is no moment at which a cow can be badly off because of death, since (as Lucretius would put it) where death is, the cow is not;[47] and if there is no moment at which a cow is harmed by death, then it cannot be harmed by death at all. A premature death does not rob the cow of the chance to accumulate more momentary well-being, since momentary well-being is not cumulable for a cow; nor can a premature death detract from the value of the cow's life as a whole, since a cow has no interest in its life as a whole, being unable to care about what sort of life it lives.

Of course, a person can care about what his life story is like, and a premature death can spoil the story of his life. Hence death can harm a person but it cannot harm a cow.[48]

Generous tears filled Gabriel's eyes. He had never felt like that himself towards any woman but he knew that such a feeling must be love. The tears gathered more thickly in his eyes and in the partial darkness he imagined he saw the form of a young man standing under a dripping tree. Other forms were near. His soul had approached that region where dwell the vast hosts of the dead. He was conscious of, but could not apprehend, their wayward and flickering existence. His own identity was fading out into a grey impalpable world: the solid world itself which these dead had one time reared and lived in was dissolving and dwindling.

A few light taps upon the pane made him turn to the window. It had begun to snow again. He watched sleepily the flakes, silver and dark, falling obliquely against the lamplight. The time had come for him to set out on his journey westward. Yes, the newspapers were right: snow was general all over Ireland. It was falling on every part of the dark central plain, on the treeless hills, falling softly upon the Bog of Allen and, farther westward, softly falling into the dark mutinous Shannon waves. It was falling, too, upon every part of the lonely churchyard on the hill where Michael Furey lay buried. It lay thickly drifted on the crooked crosses and headstones, on the spears of the little gate, on the barren thorns. His soul swooned slowly as he heard the snow falling faintly through the universe and faintly falling, like the descent of their last end, upon all the living and the dead.   —James Joyce, *Dubliners*: "The Dead"

Reference Matter

Notes

Fischer: Introduction

1. For some interesting philosophical discussions of the possibility of an afterlife, see C. J. Ducasse, *A Critical Examination of the Belief in Life After Death* (Springfield, Ill., 1961); Antony Flew, *Body, Mind, and Death* (New York, 1964); Terence Penelhum, *Survival and Disembodied Existence* (London, 1970); and John Hick, *Death and Eternal Life* (New York, 1977).

2. For a thorough and enlightening discussion of various criteria and concepts of death on which I have relied considerably, see Karen Grandstrand Gervais, *Redefining Death* (New Haven, 1986). See also Douglas Walton, *On Defining Death* (Montreal, 1979); and Fred Feldman, *Confrontations with the Reaper* (New York, 1991).

3. For discussions of the brain-death criterion, see especially Ad Hoc Committee of the Harvard Medical School to Examine the Definition of Brain Death, "A Definition of Irreversible Coma," *Journal of the American Medical Association* 205 (Aug. 1968): 337–40; Robert M. Veatch, "Brain Death: Welcome Definition or Dangerous Judgment?" *The Hastings Center Report* 2 (Nov. 1972): 10–13; "The Whole-Brain-Oriented Concept of Death: An Outmoded Philosophical Foundation," *Journal of Thanatology* 3 (1975): 13–30, and *Death, Dying, and the Biological Revolution* (New Haven, Conn., 1976); and Gervais, *Redefining Death*.

4. For a discussion of this sort of account of the underlying concept of death, see Feldman, *Confrontations with the Reaper*.

5. For the biological approach, see, e.g., Lawrence C. Becker, "Human Being: The Boundaries of the Concept," *Philosophy and Public Affairs* 4 (Summer 1975): 335–59, and David Lamb, "Diagnosing Death," *Philosophy and Public Affairs* 7 (Winter 1978): 144–53.

6. Some who believe that moral considerations are relevant to generating an account of death are Hans Jonas, *Philosophical Essays: From Ancient Creed to Technological Man* (Englewood Cliffs, N.J., 1974); Howard Brody, *Ethical Decisions in Medicine*, 2d ed. (Boston, 1981), and "Brain

Death and Personal Existence: A Reply to Green and Wikler," *Journal of Medicine and Philosophy* 8 (1983): 187–96; and Veatch, *Death, Dying, and the Biological Revolution.*

7. For such an approach, see Michael Green and Daniel Wikler, "Brain Death and Personal Identity," *Philosophy and Public Affairs* 9 (Winter 1980): 105–33. For discussions, see Brody, "Brain Death and Personal Existence"; George J. Agich and Royce P. Jones, "Personal Identity and Brain Death: A Critical Response," *Philosophy and Public Affairs* 15 (Summer 1986): 267–74; and Gervais, *Redefining Death.*

8. For an extensive discussion of the President's Commission's report, see Gervais, *Redefining Death.*

9. For an interesting discussion of such worries, see Thomas Nagel, "The Absurd," in *Mortal Questions* (New York, 1979).

10. Similarly, in John Boorman's film *Zardoz*, bored immortals who live in a bell-like glass structure (after a nuclear holocaust) eventually choose to leave the structure, and they die in ecstasy.

11. Immortality is one of the most salient themes in science fiction. (For a list of some of the classic treatments of this subject, see Part Two of the Bibliography.) There is a tremendous diversity in the depictions of immortality in science fiction. One major dichotomy is between individualistic and non-individualistic models of immortality. In a non-individualistic model, persons somehow "fuse" into quasi-organisms that persist indefinitely; see, e.g., Arthur C. Clarke, *Childhood's End* (New York, 1976) and *The City and the Stars* (New York, 1977), and Greg Bear, *Blood Music* (New York, 1986). This sort of non-individualistic model may well run afoul of Williams's criteria for the desirability of immortality.

12. Undeniably, there are radically different attitudes to immortality. In the film *The New Leaf*, Walter Matthau asks (about the sort of immortality gained by fame after one's death), "If you can't be immortal, why live at all?" But Woody Allen asks, in *Getting Even*, "If man were immortal, do you realize what his meat bills would be?"

13. Williams says: "EM, of course, is in a world of people who do not share her condition, and that determines certain features of the life she has to lead, as that any personal relationship requires peculiar kinds of concealment. That, at least, is a form of isolation which would disappear if her condition were generalized. But to suppose more generally that boredom and inner death would be eliminated if everyone were similarly becalmed, is an empty hope: it would be a world of Bourbons, learning nothing and forgetting nothing, and it is unclear how much could even happen" (p. 82). Yes, if a "becalmed" and detached condition is generalized, this does not improve matters for anyone. But if others who are vital and open to life are allowed to be immortal along with the individual in question, then his prospects are considerably improved.

14. For a thorough discussion of such matters, see Derek Parfit, *Reasons and Persons* (Oxford, 1984).

15. In Robert Heinlein's novel *Time Enough for Love* (New York, 1974), the protagonist, Lazarus Long, faces precisely the same sort of

decision as confronted by EM (in the Capek play). And he makes precisely the opposite decision, opting for a kind of immortality.

16. Two useful collections about this topic are John Lachs and Charles E. Scott, eds., *The Human Search* (New York, 1981), and Oswald Hanfling, ed., *Life and Meaning: A Reader* (Oxford, 1987). See also Nagel, *Mortal Questions* and *The View from Nowhere* (Oxford, 1986), and Robert Nozick, *Philosophical Explanations* (Cambridge, Mass., 1981).

17. For very interesting discussions of why death is a tragedy for persons (as opposed to non-persons) and alternative explanations of this putative truth, see Ruth Cigman, "Death, Misfortune, and Species Inequality," *Philosophy and Public Affairs* 10 (Winter 1981): 47–64, and David Velleman, "Well-Being and Time" (Chapter 17 in this volume). For some discussions of the distinctive features of personhood, especially insofar as persons are taken to be *free* and morally responsible agents, see Harry Frankfurt, "Freedom of the Will and the Concept of a Person," *Journal of Philosophy* 68 (1971): 5–20; Gary Watson, "Free Agency," *Journal of Philosophy* 72 (1975): 205–20; Charles Taylor, "Responsibility for Self," in Amelie Rorty, ed., *The Identities of Persons* (Berkeley, Calif., 1976); and Susan Wolf, "Sanity and the Metaphysics of Responsibility," in F. Schoeman, ed., *Responsibility, Character, and the Emotions* (Cambridge, Engl., 1987). In addition to Schoeman's, other recent collections pertaining to the free-will aspect of personhood are Gary Watson, ed., *Free Will* (Oxford, 1982), and John Martin Fischer, ed., *Moral Responsibility* (Ithaca, N.Y., 1986). It might be fruitful to explore the relationship between the properties associated with the free-will/moral responsibility feature of personhood and the properties associated with the right-to-life/tragedy-to-die feature of personhood. Why is it plausible to suppose—if it is indeed plausible to suppose this—that the two sets of properties and their associated features are really aspects of one kind of thing?

18. For discussions of such desires, which allegedly are associated with "agent-relative" reasons for action, see Parfit, *Reasons and Persons*, and Nagel, *The View from Nowhere*.

19. See John Perry, "The Importance of Being Identical," in A. Rorty, ed., *The Identities of Persons*.

20. For this sort of argument, and an alternative picture of death's badness, see Cigman, "Death, Misfortune, and Species Inequality."

21. There is an argument that distributive justice is an essentially historical (as opposed to current-time-slice) notion in Robert Nozick, *Anarchy, State, and Utopia* (New York, 1971). For an argument that ascriptions of moral responsibility depend essentially on historical considerations and not just on current-time-slice features of an agent (e.g., purely structural features of an agent's motivational system), see John Martin Fischer, "Responsiveness and Moral Responsibility," in Schoeman, ed., *Responsibility, Character, and the Emotions*. For an interesting argument that certain normative features do not supervene on current-time-slice properties, see Velleman, "Well-Being and Time" (Chapter 17). If our lives get their meaning from their narrative structure, later events can affect the meaning of earlier events, and thus the normative

properties of temporal slices need not depend solely on their temporally nonrelational features.

22. Even Nagel is not entirely confident in this position; see p. 370 n. 3. (Nagel here describes an interesting objection to the position developed by Robert Nozick.)

23. There is an interesting response in Ishtiyaque Haji, "Pre-Vital and Post-Vital Times," *Pacific Philosophical Quarterly* 72 (Sept. 1991): 171–80.

24. One might distinguish a more subjective "desire-frustration" theory from a more objective "interest-thwarting" theory. For the first, see Pitcher, "The Misfortunes of the Dead" (Chapter 9). For the second, see Feinberg, "Harm to Others" (Chapter 10). On both of these approaches it might be possible to say that the harm of death takes place when the desire or interest is formed (and thus while the "ante-mortem" person still exists). But the claim that the harm takes place while the ante-mortem person still exists is less plausible on the deprivation theory.

25. For useful and illuminating discussions of these connections, see Philip E. Devine, *The Ethics of Homicide* (Ithaca, 1978); Jeff McMahan, *The Ethics of Killing* (Oxford, 1989); and Feldman, *Confrontations with the Reaper*.

26. For classic philosophical discussions of this topic, see Philippa Foot, "Euthanasia," *Philosophy and Public Affairs* 6 (Winter 1978): 85–112; and Joel Feinberg, "Voluntary Euthanasia and the Inalienable Right to Life," *Philosophy and Public Affairs* 7 (Winter 1978): 93–123.

27. For an enlightening discussion, see Warren Quinn, "Abortion: Identity and Loss," *Philosophy and Public Affairs* 13 (Winter 1984): 24–54.

28. For a development of this sort of argument, see Don Marquis, "Why Abortion Is Immoral," *Journal of Philosophy* 86 (Apr. 1989): 183–202. For critical discussions, see Ann E. Cudd, "Sensationalized Philosophy: A Reply to Marquis's 'Why Abortion Is Immoral,'" *Journal of Philosophy* 87 (May 1990): 262–64; Peter K. McInerney, "Does a Fetus Already Have a Future-Like-Ours?" ibid., 264–68; and Alastair Norcross, "Killing, Abortion, and Contraception: A Reply to Marquis," ibid., 268–77.

29. Ann Cudd takes this tack in "Sensationalized Philosophy: A Reply to Marquis's 'Why Abortion Is Immoral.'"

Murphy: Rationality and the Fear of Death

1. *Montaigne's Essays*, trans. Donald Frame (Stanford, Calif., 1958), p. 56. Montaigne is here paraphrasing a remark made by Cicero. The thought, of course, goes back much further—at least to Socrates.

2. There is also an element of superstitious fatalism in this remark that I shall not pursue.

3. Spinoza agrees with the Stoics and Epicureans that the fear of death is irrational. He disagrees with them, however, on the question of how the fear is to be extinguished. The Stoics and Epicureans coun-

sel that we should desensitize ourselves to death by thinking of it constantly (a thought shared by Montaigne). Spinoza, on the other hand, suggests that we should try to avoid thinking of death entirely, to forget about death in the pursuit of the values of life. As Woody Allen has remarked, "It is impossible to experience one's own death objectively and still carry a tune" (*Getting Even* [New York, 1972], p. 31).

4. Jung, "The Soul and Death," in Herman Feifel, ed., *The Meaning of Death* (New York, 1959), pp. 3–15.

5. Psychiatrist Elisabeth Kübler-Ross raises this question in her book *On Death and Dying* (New York, 1969).

6. I am grateful to Barbara Levenbook for forcing me to see the importance of drawing a distinction between two senses in which a fearing may be irrational.

7. This concept of profit, of course, is not to be understood in any monetary sense, or even necessarily in terms of any external accomplishments. It is meant to include such things as personal satisfaction and feelings of self-worth, self-respect, and integrity.

8. Foot, "Morality as a System of Hypothetical Imperatives," *Philosophical Review* 81, no. 3 (July 1972): 310.

9. A few comments about this analysis, not worth making in the text, are perhaps worth making in a note:

i. The phrase "state of affairs" is here meant to include both things and events. Normally persons fear future events, bad happenings to them, but it is possible to fear things (e.g. nonpoisonous spiders now in the room) quite independently of any belief that these things will *do* anything at all. (It could plausibly be argued that all fears of the latter sort are intrinsically irrational.)

ii. The concept of "reasonable belief" is introduced into the first two conditions for the following reason: It is obvious that a fear of S can be rational even if it is false that S obtains or is harmful so long as P believes that S obtains or is harmful and provided that this belief is reasonable. If a neighbor, for a joke, comes to my door disguised as a bandit and pretends he is going to shoot me, my fear is rational if I have no grounds for believing that it is my neighbor or that I am being fooled.

iii. By "reasonable belief" I simply mean a belief for which one has good grounds of evidence.

iv. The second condition stipulates P must believe that S is not easily avoided and is *very* undesirable, etc. This is because it would be absurd for P to claim that he feared S and then admit that he believed that S was nothing but a very minor inconvenience or that he could avoid S with no trouble at all.

v. Finally, it should be noted that, though P must himself hold the beliefs included in the first two conditions, P does not have to hold a belief in conditions (3) or (4). Typically, a person who is really afraid would not be in a position to entertain complex propositions of this nature. It is enough that (3) and (4) be true or at least reasonable for someone (e.g. the person evaluating the fears of P) to believe them.

10. Freud, "Thoughts on War and Death," *Collected Papers*, vol. 4, trans. Joan Riviere (New York, 1959), p. 306 [emphasis added].

11. It is possible that Socrates may not have literally accepted such beliefs but was rather simply using certain traditional and metaphorical language as his way of evincing courage.

12. Lucretius, following Epicurus, writes as follows: "It does not concern you dead or alive: alive, because you are; dead, because you are no more. . . . Where death is, I am not." In addition to making the point that death is not necessarily painful, he also seems to be raising the conceptual puzzle noted by Wittgenstein: "Death is not an event in life" (*Tractatus*, 6.4311). The difficulty here is the following: If death is a misfortune, how is it to be assigned to a *subject* at all? When a person is alive, he has not died; when he has died, he no longer exists as a subject to which any attributes (including misfortunes) can be assigned. Lucretius also raises a temporal puzzle about the fear of death—namely, we regard as bad a future in which we will not exist, but none of us lament the fact that there was a time before our birth when we did not exist. These puzzles are interestingly discussed in an exchange between Thomas Nagel and Mary Mothersill, and I do not want to go over this ground again here. See Nagel, "Death" (Chapter 4 in this volume).

13. "Are there great variations in the awareness or fear of death from person to person, from epoch to epoch, from culture to culture? If so, how are these variations to be explained? Surprisingly, very little attention has been given to these questions. The most interesting and almost the only hypothesis on this topic is that of Huizinga and Paul-Louis Landsberg. According to these authors, the consciousness of death has been most acute in periods of social disorganization, when individual choice tends to replace automatic conformity to social values; they point especially to classical society after the disintegration of the city-states; to the early Renaissance, after the breakdown of feudalism; and to the twentieth century. This hypothesis has yet to be confirmed or disconfirmed by careful historical and anthropological study. However, it is true that late antiquity, the early Renaissance, and the twentieth century have made unusually great contributions to the literature on death" (Robert G. Olson, "Death," in Paul Edwards, ed., *Encyclopedia of Philosophy*, 2: 307–9 [New York, 1967]). Freud, in *Collected Papers*, thought that major wars were the primary historical stimulus to reflection on death, and the breakdown of traditional religion and its comforts is also probably a factor.

14. James Rachels, ed., *Moral Problems* (New York, 1975), pp. 381–82. I suspect that Mothersill is correct when she says that this way of thinking captures only *one sort* of fear of death. Many writers have traced at least part of the fear to the supposed impossibility of imagining one's own death and the resulting fear of "the void" or "nothingness." I do not feel competent to discuss this possible aspect of the fear of death and simply refer the reader to the following: Paul Edwards, "My Death," in Edwards, ed., *Encyclopedia of Philosophy*, 5: 416–19, and

James van Evra, "On Death as a Limit," *Analysis* 31 (April 1971): 170–76.

Although I cannot pursue the point at any length here, I believe that the account I am offering of the death of a person and the fear of such death (i.e., the fear of death as the fear that self-defining projects will be aborted) provides a partial explanation for the analogy that seems to obtain between death and sex—e.g. the common and rather convincing literary and poetic characterization of sexuality (particularly orgasm) in metaphors of death and dying. (Thomas Mann's *Death in Venice* is just one of many obvious examples that could be given.) Sexual orgasm involves a total immersion in the present and a corresponding loss of that future-orientation required for self-defining projects. There are, of course, obvious differences: "loss of self" in sexual orgasm is temporary and is typically surrounded by intense sensual pleasure—both features, alas, missing in death. In spite of this, however, the analogy is provocative. The analogy of sex with death may explain why the prospect of intense sexual intimacy contains (at least for some persons) an element of fear. Also, the analogy may help to explain why death is not just fearful but is (again, at least for some persons) seductive. For surely it must sometimes appear attractive and tempting to be freed from all those elaborate projects that define us, freed from all the responsibilities they impose, and freed from the enormous effort involved in carrying them through—attracted and tempted, in other words, by that "letting go" so seductively characterized by Emily Dickinson ("After Great Pain a Formal Feeling Comes").

15. "Paradoxically but understandably," writes psychiatrist Theodore Lidz, "it is those who have never been able to live, either because others have restricted them or because of their own neurotic limitations, who may fear death the most" (*The Person* [New York, 1968], p. 502).

16. On this analysis, Caesar's attitude (as portrayed by Shakespeare) might not be so purely "philosophical" after all. It could be argued that Caesar (because of his "tragic flaw" of pride) *recklessly* risked his life (i.e., stepped into danger that was both physically and morally avoidable) and thus revealed himself as more imprudent than courageous. His attitude of *che sarà, sarà* was perhaps inappropriate to the actual circumstances in which he expressed it. This, at any rate, is one possible interpretation, and I mention it here to point out that a complete analysis of the rationality of fearing death would have to consider the following question: For the fear of death to be rational or prudent, do the as-yet-unfulfilled projects themselves have to be rational—i.e., is *any* projection of oneself into the future (however irrational) enough to make rational or prudent the fear of death aborting it? Suppose one of my uncompleted projects is to play a full-length golf course with a score of less than seventy-five. In addition to the high probability that I could never do this, the project might seem irrational for another reason— namely, the triviality of such an achievement. One could also regard as trivial Caesar's desire to play to the hilt the role of fearless general and

head of state. One wants to be as tolerant as possible, of course, with respect to differences in human desires and projects, but there are perhaps limiting cases. I am grateful to Anthony D. Woozley for pointing out this complexity to me.

17. There is a sense in which the person who (a) sees that his fears are irrational, (b) lacks the capacity to overcome them on his own, but (c) has the capacity to seek out therapeutic help may legitimately be blamed if he does not seek out such help and praised if he does. Successful psychotherapy is often a long and painful process, requiring a kind of close self-examination that most people would prefer to avoid. Seeking it out when needed can thus be a moral achievement for which moral praise is merited. It could, of course, be suggested that the fear of death is far too common, too "normal," to be characterized as neurotic; contrary to what Caesar says, the fear does not seem "strange" at all. There are two responses that can be made to this suggestion. First, though a certain fear of death is indeed common (not to mention prudentially desirable), the extreme and self-damaging forms of this fear (the only forms properly called neurotic) are not. Second, extreme and self-damaging attitudes are properly called neurotic no matter how common or "normal" they are. For example, it is not implausible to suggest that most living Americans experience deep neurotic conflicts with respect to their sexual behavior.

18. *Montaigne's Essays*, pp. 53, 60–64.

19. Lael Tucker Wertenbaker, *Death of a Man* (New York, 1950), p. 10. Quoted in R. F. Holland, "Suicide," in Rachels, *Moral Problems*, p. 358. For a more philosophically grandiose elaboration of a similar view, see sec. 36, "Morality for Physicians," of Friedrich Nietzsche's *Twilight of the Idols*.

20. It is frequently suggested that some people are too weak to face death honestly and it is better that these people derive some support and happiness from comforting illusions. This is perhaps true. But those who make this suggestion should do so with a certain sense of regret; for the suggestion, even if benevolently motivated, involves a patronizing and degrading response to those people for whose benefit it is made. Would anyone want this said of *himself*?

Nagel: Death

1. It is sometimes suggested that what we really mind is the process of *dying*. But I should not really object to dying if it were not followed by death.

2. It is certainly not true in general of the things that can be said of him. For example, Abraham Lincoln was taller than Louis XIV. But when?

3. I confess to being troubled by the above argument, on the grounds that it is too sophisticated to explain the simple difference between our attitudes to prenatal and posthumous nonexistence. For this reason I suspect that something essential is omitted from the account of the badness of death by an analysis that treats it as a deprivation of

possibilities. My suspicion is supported by the following suggestion of Robert Nozick. We could imagine discovering that people developed from individual spores that had existed indefinitely far in advance of their birth. In this fantasy, birth never occurs naturally more than a hundred years before the permanent end of the spore's existence. But then we discover a way to trigger the premature hatching of these spores, and people are born who have thousands of years of active life before them. Given such a situation, it would be possible to imagine *oneself* having come into existence thousands of years previously. If we put aside the question whether this would really be the same person, even given the identity of the spore, then the consequence appears to be that a person's birth at a given time *could* deprive him of many earlier years of possible life. Now while it would be cause for regret that one had been deprived of all those possible years of life by being born too late, the feeling would differ from that which many people have about death. I conclude that something about the future *prospect* of permanent nothingness is not captured by the analysis in terms of denied possibilities. If so, then Lucretius's argument still awaits an answer. I suspect that it requires a general treatment of the difference between past and future in our attitudes toward our own lives. Our attitudes toward past and future pain are very different, for example. Derek Parfit's writings on this topic have revealed its difficulty to me.

Williams: The Makropulos Case

1. At the University of California, Berkeley, under a benefaction in the names of Agnes and Constantine Foerster.

2. Lucretius, *De Rerum Natura III*, 870f., 898f.

3. Ibid., 1091.

4. Ibid., 830.

5. Obviously the principle is not exceptionless. For one thing, one can want to be dead: the content of that desire may be obscure, but whatever it is, a man presumably cannot be *prevented* from getting it by dying. More generally, the principle does not apply to what I elsewhere call *non-I desire*: for an account of these exceptions, see "Egoism and Altruism" in my *Problems of the Self* (Cambridge, Engl., 1973), pp. 260ff. They do not affect the present discussion, which is within the limits of egoistic rationality.

6. Sophocles, *Oedipus at Colonus*, 1224f.

7. Nagel, "Death" (Chapter 4 in this volume).

8. However, my argument does not in any sense imply Utilitarianism; for some further considerations on this, see the final paragraphs of this chapter.

9. Aristotle, *Ethica Nicomachea*, 1096^{b} 4.

10. This is one possible conclusion from the dilemma discussed in "The Self and the Future" in my *Problems of the Self*, pp. 46–63. For the point, mentioned below, of the independence of physical pain from psychological change, see p. 54.

11. For a detailed discussion of closely related questions, though in a different framework, see Derek Parfit, "Personal Identity," *Philosophical Review* 80 (Jan. 1971): 3–27.

12. Stuart Hampshire, "Spinoza and the Idea of Freedom," in Hampshire, *Freedom of Mind* (Oxford, 1972), pp. 183ff.; the two quotations are from pp. 206–7.

13. Hampshire, "Disposition and Memory," in *Freedom of Mind*, pp. 160ff.; see esp. pp. 176–77.

14. Unamuno, *Del sentimiento trágico de la vida*, trans. J. E. Crawford Flitch (London, 1921). Page references are to the Fontana Library edition, 1962.

15. An affirmation that takes on a special dignity retrospectively in the light of his own death shortly after his courageous speech against Millan Astray and the obscene slogan "!Viva la Muerte!" See Hugh Thomas, *The Spanish Civil War* (Harmondsworth, 1961), pp. 442–44.

Silverstein: The Evil of Death

1. Feinberg, "Harm and Self-Interest," in P. M. S. Hacker and J. Raz, eds., *Law, Morality and Society: Essays in Honour of H. L. A. Hart* (Oxford, 1977), p. 300.

2. There are in fact grounds for questioning whether Epicurus *consistently* adheres even to the Epicurean view itself. For example, insofar as Epicurean morality holds that death is *neutral* or *indifferent* for the person who dies (i.e., that death is on the midpoint of the evaluative continuum between good and evil), it presupposes that the claim "death is an evil for the person who dies" is false rather than incoherent. For to say that this claim is incoherent, on the ground that the alleged evil lacks a subject, is to imply that death cannot coherently be assigned *any* value for the person who dies, including indifference (see pp. 104–5). Perhaps the most reasonable thing to say here is that our distinction between falsity and incoherence is simply alien to Epicurus's philosophical milieu.

3. Versions of the standard argument are given in L. S. Sumner, "A Matter of Life and Death," *Noûs* 10 (May 1976): 157–60; Bernard Williams, "The Makropulos Case: Reflections on the Tedium of Immortality" (Chapter 5 in this volume); and Thomas Nagel, "Death" (Chapter 4 in this volume). (Parenthetical page references to these authors will be to these articles.) Nagel's central argument, however, goes significantly beyond the standard argument and will be considered in the next section. Instructive portions of Williams's argument are discussed further below.

4. Sumner, though conceding that death is a "peculiar sort" of loss, nonetheless contends that "the only condition essential to any loss is that *there should have been a subject who suffered it*" (p. 160)—i.e., a subject who exists up to the point of loss. Sumner gives no argument for this view and, unless he is thinking merely of the idiomatic—and irrelevant—sense where "to lose one's life" is just a substitute for "to cease to exist," it seems plainly false. There is no literal loss of *x* unless there

is some being who has lost x, i.e., unless the loser exists after the point of loss; there is no "subject" who "suffers" a loss if there is no loss so long as there is a subject. But even if Sumner could adequately defend—or justifiably stipulate—a literal sense of "loss" according to which his claim were true, that would not, of course, be sufficient to defend the standard argument; he would also have to show, against the Epicurean view, that this "peculiar sort" of loss, like ordinary sorts of loss, can intelligibly be regarded as an evil for the loser.

5. It might be argued that "a longer life is better than a shorter" is not deemed incoherent by the Epicurean view because it is life-life comparative and, hence, that the Epicurean view does not conflict *substantively* with common sense, but merely implies that S_1 should be reworded along the lines of "the (short) duration of A's life is an evil for A." But while A lives, his life is temporally open-ended and thus has no (completed) duration; and when his life has a duration, a duration that could then be evaluated, A no longer exists. Hence, the argument underlying the Epicurean view applies with equal force to either formulation. Moreover, as I shall argue at the conclusion of this chapter, the evaluation not only of the duration of life but of duration in general is intelligible in the first place only if one adopts a conceptual framework that is sufficient in any case to undermine the Epicurean view.

6. Moreover, the conflation discussed above can occur in discussions of desire as easily as in discussions of value, as another section of Williams's argument illustrates: "If I [prudentially] desire something, then, other things being equal, I prefer a state of affairs in which I get it from one in which I do not get it, and . . . plan for a future in which I get it rather than not. But one future, for sure, in which I would not get it would be one in which I was dead. . . . [F]rom the perspective of the wanting agent it is rational to aim for states of affairs in which his want is satisfied, and hence to regard death as something to be avoided; that is, to regard it as an evil" (pp. 76–77). The conflation here occurs in Williams's use of the claim that "If I [prudentially] desire something, then . . . I prefer a state of affairs in which I get it from one in which I do not get it." This claim is noncontroversial—and non-question-begging—only if "state of affairs . . . in which I do not get it" is interpreted as "state of affairs . . . in which I (exist but) lack it," i.e., only if the claim is interpreted, in effect, as life-life comparative ("If I desire something, then, other things being equal, I prefer a life that contains it to a life that lacks it"). But, on this interpretation, the claim is entirely compatible with the Epicurean view. The claim conflicts with this view only if it is interpreted as life-death comparative, i.e., only if "state of affairs . . . in which I do not get it" means, or includes, "state of affairs . . . in which I do not exist." But on this interpretation the claim is, in the present context, both controversial and question-begging. Thus, the argument is persuasive only if one conflates these two interpretations.

7. Cf., e.g., Philip E. Devine, *The Ethics of Homicide* (Ithaca, 1978), p. 20.

8. The morality of killing is another area where the Epicurean view has implications that are seriously disturbing; its acceptance would wreak havoc, in my opinion, with our considered judgments on this issue. I lack the space to discuss this problem here, but the reader is invited to consider whether he can construct a plausible theory that both (a) does not rely, even indirectly (via, e.g., the notion of a "right to life"), on the idea that death is an evil for the person who dies; and yet (b) yields tolerable results concerning the killing of persons without yielding unacceptable results on other matters. (Utilitarianism is the obvious first suggestion. But though it satisfies [a]—it either uses a "recipientless" concept of value or focuses on the value of one's death for "Society"—it does not begin, despite the contortions of some of its followers, to satisfy [b].)

9. Although this is the weakest formulation consistent with the Epicurean view, it also appears to be the strongest to retain plausibility. For it seems clear, on the one hand, that at least "extrinsic" values may entirely antedate their recipients—e.g., if A is born blind as a result of a drug his mother took the day before he was conceived, there is no difficulty in saying that her consumption of the drug was an evil for A. On the other hand, we cannot deny that a value may *partially* postdate its recipient—e.g., World War II was clearly an evil for those who suffered and then died in its early stages.

10. See, e.g., John Woods, "Can Death Be Understood?" in J. King-Farlow and W. R. Shea, eds., *Values and the Quality of Life* (New York, 1976), pp. 157–76.

11. The fact that this weaker version is more plausible is shown not merely by cases of the sort Nagel considers, cases where A lacks the appropriate feeling because he is ignorant of x, but also, and more simply, by cases where A is perfectly aware of x but lacks the appropriate feeling for other reasons. For example, if A does not suffer from the unfair loss of his job because his religious sect has taught him to be concerned only with "spiritual" matters, of if A gets no joy from being awarded the Nobel Prize in physics, an award he has sought all his life, because of misfortunes in his personal life, it nonetheless seems patently intelligible to regard these things as an evil for A and a good for A, respectively.

12. Certain philosophers would claim that neither posthumous nor spatially distant events can be the objects of feeling or experience and, hence, that A-relative value can reside only in A's "immediate sensations." But we need not debate this sort of phenomenalism here; if we can show that S_1 has the same kind and degree of intelligibility as corresponding claims concerning events spatially distant from A, then we shall have satisfactorily resolved the Epicurean dilemma, for we shall have resolved the problems *peculiar* to the Epicurean view.

13. As Epicurus himself puts it: "That which is not distressing when it is present is painful in vain when it is anticipated" (quoted in Fred D. Miller, Jr., "Epicurus on the Art of Dying," *Southern Journal of Philosophy* 14 [Summer 1976]: 170).

14. Quine, "Physical Objects," typescript (read, among other places, at the Western Washington University Philosophy Colloquium, March 1978), pp. 7–9.

15. A typical instance of this sort of objection, applied to posthumous events, is the following:

A posthumous event itself, as distinct from one's thought about it, can never be an object of joy, suffering, etc. For it is always possible, at least in principle, that one's beliefs, hopes, etc., about the event—beliefs that mediate between it and one's joy, suffering, etc.—will turn out to be false, i.e., that the anticipated posthumous event will never take place. But since one's joy, suffering, etc. will be the same whether these beliefs are true or not, it cannot be the posthumous event itself, even where it actually occurs, which is the object of joy, suffering, etc.

And exactly the same objection can, of course, be applied to spatially distant events. For example, one would suffer from a false report of a spatially separated friend's death in exactly the same way that one would suffer from a true one; hence, by the same argument, one's friend's death cannot itself be the object of one's suffering, even where it actually occurs. Insofar, then, as we can justifiably reject such arguments when they are applied to spatial distance, we can justifiably reject them when they are applied to temporal distance.

16. Whereas my definition of "atemporal predicate" restricts the applicability of the phrase "atemporal value" to causes where the relevant predicate *must* be construed atemporally, one might, of course, adopt an alternative definition according to which "atemporal value" could be applied to any case where the relevant predicate *can* be construed atemporally. But since any predicate *can* be so construed, this would trivialize the notion of "atemporal value"; we would not have to regard all values as atemporal and could not distinguish, as Nagel presumably wishes to do, between atemporal and temporal values.

Rosenbaum: *How to Be Dead and Not Care*

1. Thomas Nagel, "Death" (Chapter 4 in this volume).

2. Since completing this paper, I have learned of a recent paper that undertakes a defense of Epicurus. O. H. Green, "Fear of Death," *Philosophy and Phenomenological Research* 43 (Sept. 1982): 99–105.

3. Diogenes Laertius, *Lives of Eminent Philosophers*, vol. 2 (Cambridge, Mass., 1925), p. 651 (Bk. X, 124–25).

4. Ibid.

5. In fact, there is reason to expect him not to have carefully distinguished these. He wrote more for popular accessibility than for careful philosophical discussion.

6. Lucretius, *De Rerum Natura* (Cambridge, Mass., 1975), p. 254 (Bk. III, 861–68). There are many comments that prove this, but see "Scire licet nobis nil esse in morte timendum," at line 866. This use of the phrase "in morte" is not eccentric, for its literary use antedates

Lucretius by some 150–200 years. It occurs, for example, in the Plautus play *Captivi*, at line 741: "post mortem in morte nihil est quod metuam mali."

7. Hereafter, I shall use "death" to mean being dead, unless the context makes it clear that it is used otherwise.

8. But one might wish to review J. M. Hinton's work, *Experiences* (Oxford, 1973), pt. I, where there is a useful discussion of the various senses in which the term is used.

9. Diogenes Laertius, *Lives*, p. 611 (Bk. X, 82).

10. Mary Mothersill, "Death," in J. Rachels, ed., *Moral Problems* (New York, 1971), p. 378.

11. Harry Silverstein, "The Evil of Death" (Chapter 6 in this volume, p. 95).

12. Nagel, "Death," p. 65.

13. The same point is made by Silverstein, "The Evil of Death"; see, e.g., p. 120.

14. Nagel, "Death," p. 64.

15. L. S. Sumner, "A Matter of Life and Death," *Noûs* 10 (May 1976): 160.

16. Lucretius, *De Rerum Natura*, pp. 253, 265 (Bk. III, 830–42, 972–77).

17. Nagel, "Death," p. 67.

18. Ibid.

19. Silverstein, "The Evil of Death," p. 110.

20. Ibid.

21. Ibid.

22. Ibid., p. 111.

23. Lucretius, *De Rerum Natura*, p. 257 (Bk. III, 870–86).

Yourgrau: The Dead

1. In Nagel, *Mortal Questions* (New York, 1979).

2. W. V. Quine, "Quantifiers and Propositional Attitudes," in *The Ways of Paradox* (Cambridge, Mass., 1979).

3. In conversation with the author.

4. Ibid.

5. It was of course Bertrand Russell who announced, in "On Denoting," that his Theory of Descriptions enabled one to paraphrase away all apparent reference to the nonexistent. But his claim that descriptive phrases never refer, but at best "denote," does not survive scrutiny. (See my "Russell and Kaplan on Denoting," *Philosophy and Phenomenological Research* 46, no. 2 [Dec. 1985.]) Moreover, it is surely too much to expect one's ontology to flow from one's semantics; the question of *what is* is not settled by the truth about "the." (Russell did have internal objections to the theory of nonexistents. But on these matters see below.)

6. Nagel, "Death" (Chapter 4 in this volume).

7. Ibid., p. 67.

8. Silverstein, "The Evil of Death" (Chapter 6 in this volume).

9. Arthur Prior had no use for this conception of the past as a mere place where the dead enjoy full ontological privileges. See his "The Notion of the Present," in J. T. Fraser et al., eds., *The Study of Time* (New York, 1972). Prior extended his displeasure to Special Relativity, if it is taken to imply this repugnant doctrine.

10. Lewis, *Counterfactuals* (Cambridge, Mass., 1973).

11. Yourgrau, "On Time and Actuality: The Dilemma of Privileged Position," *British Journal for the Philosophy of Science* 37 (Dec. 1986): 405–17.

12. Ĉapek, "The Inclusion of Temporal Becoming in the Physical World," in Ĉapek, ed., *The Concepts of Space and Time* (Boston, 1976); Sklar, "Time, Reality, and Relativity," in R. Healey, ed., *Reduction, Time and Reality* (New York, 1981); Popper, *The Open Universe* (Totowa, N.J., 1982). Ĉapek seems to accept Special Relativity but questions the excessive Eleaticism of the standard interpretations. Sklar discerns, at the heart of Special Relativity itself, a verificationist slide on which there seems no natural stopping place, short of a kind of "point-solipsism."

13. Parsons, *Nonexistent Objects* (New Haven, Conn., 1980). I have noted among some philosophers the feeling that the theory of nonexistents, even if logically impeccable, is not to be taken seriously from a philosophical point of view—that it is, as it were, a mere metaphysical daydream. This attitude compares with that of sober theorizers in the past toward the relation of the new non-Euclidean geometries to an account of physical reality. But, just as Einstein's physics has shown that these new geometries are more than mathematical toys, we will come to see, I believe, that the theory of nonexistents is a tool for serious metaphysics and not a mere plaything for bored logicians.

14. Wittgenstein, *Tractatus Logico-Philosophicus*, trans. D. F. Pears and B. F. McGuiness (London, 1974), 6.4311.

15. C. Parsons, "Objects and Logic," esp. sec. 6.

16. Ibid., p. 506.

17. For a discussion of the role of "grasping" Platonic senses in Frege's philosophy, see my "Frege, Perry, and Demonstratives," *Canadian Journal of Philosophy* 12, no. 4 (1982): 725–52, as well as "The Path Back to Frege," *Proceedings of the Aristotelian Society* (ns) 87 (1986–87): 169–210.

18. Donnellan, "Speaking of Nothing," *Philosophical Review* 82 (Jan. 1974): 3–32; Kripke, "Naming and Necessity," in D. Davidson and G. Harman, eds., *Semantics of Natural Language* (Boston, 1972), republished as *Naming and Necessity* (Cambridge, Mass., 1980); page references will be to the 1972 edition.

19. S. Kripke, "Semantical Considerations on Modal Logic," *Acta Philosophica Fennica* 16 (1963): 83–94.

20. Ishiguro, "Possibility," *Proceedings of the Aristotelian Society* (suppl.) 54 (1980): 73–87.

21. Ibid., pp. 79, 85.
22. Kant, *Critique of Pure Reason*, A599 B627.
23. Ishiguro, "Possibility," p. 86.
24. Bealer, "Review of Parsons' *Nonexistent Objects*," *Journal of Symbolic Logic* 59 (June 1984): 652–55.
25. For some sensible advice about not letting our formalism set artificial limits to our ontological horizons, see Paul Benacerraf, "Skolem and the Skeptic," *Proceedings of the Aristotelian Society* (suppl.) (1985): 85–116.
26. Gödel, "What Is Cantor's Continuum Problem?" in P. Benacerraf and H. Putnam, eds., *Philosophy of Mathematics*, 2nd ed. (New York, 1983), pp. 483–84.
27. For discussion of such five-dimensional "modal-Minkowski" space-time diagrams, see my "On Time and Actuality."
28. Kripke, "Is There a Problem About Substitutional Quantification?" in G. Evans and J. McDowell, eds., *Truth and Meaning* (New York, 1977), p. 412.
29. Rosen, *The Limits of Analysis* (New Haven, Conn., 1980), p. 84.
30. McTaggart, "The Unreality of Time," *Mind* 17 (1908): 457–84.
31. Jeffrey, "Coming True," in C. Diamond and J. Teichman, eds., *Intention and Intentionality* (Ithaca, 1979).
32. Thomason, "Indeterminist Time and Truth-Value Gaps," *Theoria* 36, no. 3 (1970): 264–81. See also my "On the Logic of Indeterminist Time," *Journal of Philosophy* 82, no. 10 (1985): 548–59.
33. David Kaplan, "Demonstratives: An Essay on the Semantics, Logic, Metaphysics, and Epistemology of Demonstratives and Other Indexicals," in J. Almog, J. Perry, and H. K. Wettstein, eds., *Themes from Kaplan* (New York, 1989): 481–563; John Perry, "Frege on Demonstratives," *Philosophical Review* 86, no. 4 (Oct. 1977): 474–97. For a collection of essays on demonstratives that speaks to a number of issues in this paper, see my edited volume *Demonstratives* (Oxford, 1990).
34. See Note 17 above.
35. Mellor, *Real Time* (New York, 1981); he wields Perry's semantics for "now" as a club to beat down the A-series.
36. See Note 33 above.
37. Kripke, "Naming and Necessity," p. 293.
38. For Putnam's version of Kantian (transcendental) idealism, see his *Reason, Truth and History* (New York, 1981). See also his "Reference and Truth," in *Realism and Reason* (New York, 1983), where he coins the phrase "existentially given" (p. 73), a marvelous neo-Kantianism in which ontology and epistemology are rolled into one.
39. I discuss this issue at length in *The Disappearance of Time: Kurt Gödel and the Idealistic Tradition in Philosophy* (New York, 1991).

Pitcher: The Misfortunes of the Dead

1. Aristotle, *Nicomachean Ethics*, bk. I, chap. xi. The translation is by J. A. K. Thomson.

2. Nagel, "Death" (Chapter 4 in this volume, p. 64). Joel Feinberg mentions a similar case in "Harm and Self-interest," in P. Hacker and J. Raz, eds., *Law, Morality and Society: Essays in Honour of H. L. A. Hart* (Oxford, 1977).

Feinberg: Harm to Others

1. A possible model for understanding this indeterminacy is that proposed in another context by W. D. Falk in "Morality, Self, and Others," in J. Feinberg, ed., *Reason and Responsibility*, 5th ed. (Belmont, Calif., 1981). Speaking of the concept of the distinctively moral and the controversy over whether it applies to wholly self-regarding conduct, Falk notes that there is a tendency in ordinary thought to say the one thing and a conflicting tendency to say the other: "This disagreement exhibits a kind of shuttle-service between rival considerations known as the dialectic of a problem. It may be that this shuttle service is maintained by a cleft in the very concept of morality. This concept may have grown from conflicting or only partially overlapping observations, not fully reconciled in ordinary thinking" (p. 52).

2. See Barbara Levenbook, "Harming Someone After His Death," *Ethics* 94 (1984): 407–19.

3. See Ernest Partridge, "Posthumous Interests and Posthumous Respect," *Ethics* 91 (June 1981): 243–64, for a forceful use of this technique in a thorough rebuttal of my earlier arguments for the harmfulness of death. See also Mary Mothersill's relentless criticisms of Thomas Nagel in her article "Death" in J. Rachels, ed., *Moral Problems* (New York, 1971).

4. See Epicurus, *Letter to Menoeceus*, in C. Bailey, ed., *Epicurus: The Extant Remains* (Oxford, 1926). For ingenious attempts to resolve the epicurean paradox, see Thomas Nagel, "Death," and Harry D. Silverstein, "The Evil of Death" (Chapters 4 and 6, respectively, in this volume). Nagel's views especially have influenced my own.

5. Levenbook, "Harming Someone After His Death," is very convincing on this point.

6. See my "Harm and Self-Interest," in P. M. S. Hacker and J. Raz, eds., *Law, Morality and Society* (Oxford, 1977), p. 308.

7. Partridge, "Posthumous Interests and Posthumous Respect," p. 246.

8. Ibid., p. 260.

9. W. D. Ross, *Foundations of Ethics* (Oxford, 1939), p. 300.

10. This judgment is probably too confident if understood to extend to cases where what is wanted is expected to cause actual *disappointment*. Derek Parfit has reminded me of the distinction between cases where fulfillment *cannot possibly* produce satisfaction because the person will never be in a position to know that his want has been fulfilled, and cases where fulfillment can produce satisfaction but in fact will not. In the former case, all would agree that the important thing is that what we want to happen will happen (our desire will be fulfilled). But in the

latter case, if people know or confidently expect that fulfillment will not only "not cause joy" but will actually produce disappointment, it is not so clear, as Parfit points out, that the important thing is "to get what one wants." There is some question, however, whether the existence of the want could even survive such conditions.

11. The most vivid example I know in literature of "positively harmful" death is that foreseen by Pip at the hands of the villainous Orlick in Charles Dicken's *Great Expectations*, chap. 52 (Penguin edition, p. 436). Orlick is about to murder Pip and dispose of his body in a kiln in a remote marsh. "I'll put your body in the kiln," he says. "I won't have a rag of you, I won't have a bone of you, left on earth. . . . Let people suppose what they may of you, they shall never know nothing." Pip's reaction is revealing: "My mind, with inconceivable rapidity, followed out all the consequences of such a death. Estella's father would believe I had deserted him, would be taken, would die accusing me; even Herbert would doubt me, when he compared the letter I had left for him, with the fact that I had called at Miss Haversham's gate for only a moment; Joe and Biddy would never know how sorry I had been that night; none would ever know how I had suffered, how true I had meant to be, what an agony I had passed through. The death close before me was terrible, but far more terrible than death was the dread of being misremembered after death. And so quick were my thoughts, that I saw myself despised by unborn generations—Estella's children and their children—while the wretch's [Orlick's] words were yet on his lips."

12. C. D. Broad, "Egoism as a Theory of Human Motives," in *Ethics and the History of Philosophy* (London, 1952), p. 220.

13. Ibid., p. 221.

14. Aristotle, *Nicomachean Ethics*, trans. J. A. K. Thomson (Baltimore, 1953), 1.10.

15. Ibid., first paragraph. Aristotle's primary concern in this chapter, however, was not to show that a person's interests can be affected after his death, but rather that well-being, whether before or after death, cannot be utterly destroyed by the caprice of events, but at worst, only somewhat tarnished. The point about interests surviving death he simply assumed as beyond need of argument.

16. George Pitcher, "The Misfortunes of the Dead" (Chapter 9 in this volume).

17. Ibid., p. 161.

18. Ibid., p. 162.

19. Ibid., p. 168.

20. Ibid., p. 165.

21. Ibid., p. 168.

22. In this last example, Pitcher would say that the loving father is already harmed by the impending death, quite apart from whether he knows the facts yet or not. See his own example of Bishop Berkeley's son.

23. The remainder of this paragraph summarizes the argument suggested by Partridge, "Posthumous Interests and Posthumous Respect," pp. 254–61.

24. See my article "The Forms and Limits of Utilitarianism," *Philosophical Review* 76 (July 1967): 368–81. I call arguments like the one sketched above "Actual-Rule Utilitarian," as opposed both to "Ideal-Rule Utilitarian" arguments and to "Generalization" arguments.

Parfit: Reasons and Persons

1. This version of the case was suggested to me by G. Harman.

2. Rawls, *A Theory of Justice* (Cambridge, Mass., 1971), p. 293.

3. Hume, "The Sceptic," in *Essays* (Oxford, 1963), p. 177.

4. I repeat some remarks of R. Nozick's.

5. A subtler version of this objection is advanced in Edidin, "Temporal Neutrality and Past Pains," *Southern Journal of Philosophy* 20 (Winter 1982): 423–31. I do not fully answer Edidin's objection.

6. Anscombe, *Intention* (Ithaca, 1957), p. 68.

7. I believe that these gains would themselves outweigh the losses described by the S-Theorist at the start of "The Direction of Causation" section above.

8. These remarks are over-simplified. Even if we deny time's passage, we can admit that "now" can be applied to descriptions of a lifeless Universe. Event X is "now" relative to Event Y if they both occur at the same time.

9. Cf. Pears, "Time, Truth, and Inference," in A. Flew, ed., *Essays in Conceptual Analysis* (London, 1966), p. 249: "And, because time is a category, and figures unobtrusively in all our experience, it is possible to define the past and the future in many different ways and yet none of these definitions is very convincing. For the sentences which give the logical relations of temporal words exhibit a curious feature. They are . . . as it were, weak tautologies. And they are weak tautologies not only because we are so accustomed to using temporal words correctly that we need no strong reminders, but also because their structure is peculiar. For most tautologies are constructed like columns, by placing terms squarely on top of one another like marble drums. But the tautologies which give the logic of temporal words put their terms together like the stones of a vault. No single conjunction of terms is indispensable or could stand alone. But together they form the vaulted ceiling on which the fresco of knowledge is painted."

10. These remarks are too crude. Even if, in the present, some experience is either neutral, or even unpleasant, it can be remembered with great joy. Proust, in *The Sweet Cheat Gone* (trans. C. K. Scott-Monerief [London, 1949]), p. 97, writes: "At a much later date, when I went over gradually, in a reversed order, the times through which I had passed before I was so much in love with Albertine, when my scarred heart could detach itself without suffering from Albertine dead, then I

was able to recall at length without suffering that day on which Albertine had gone shopping with Francoise instead of remaining at the Trocadero; I recalled it with pleasure, as belonging to a moral season which I had not known until then; I recalled it at length exactly, without adding to it now any suffering, rather, on the contrary, as we recall certain days in summer which we found too hot while they lasted, and from which only after they have passed do we extract their unalloyed standard of fine gold and imperishable azure." Or, on p. 107: "An impression of love is out of proportion to the other impressions of life, but it is not when it is lost in their midst that we can take account of it. It is not from its foot, in the tumult of the street and amid the thronging houses, it is when we are far away, that from the slope of a neighboring hill, at a distance from which the whole town has disappeared, or appears only as a confused mass upon the ground, we can, in the calm detachment of solitude and dust, appreciate, unique, persistent and pure, the height of a cathedral." It would be possible to live a life of great backward- and forward-looking happiness even if one never, in the present, found any pleasure in any of one's experiences.

11. This objection was suggested to me by J. Broome, R. Swinburne, and J. Thomson.

Brueckner and Fischer: Why Is Death Bad?

1. This does not imply that it is rational to *preoccupy* oneself with one's own death or to focus one's attention upon it constantly.

2. Something is "experienced as bad by a person" roughly speaking insofar as that thing causes unpleasant experiential episodes in the person (and perhaps the person believes that the thing is causing such experiences).

3. Thomas Nagel discusses such bads in "Death" (Chapter 4 in this volume). Also, Robert Nozick discusses similar examples in "On the Randian Argument," in J. Paul, ed., *Reading Nozick* (Totowa, N.J., 1981), pp. 218–22.

4. Nagel, "Death."

5. Ibid., pp. 67–68.

6. Even if one—controversially—held that generation from such and such gametes is an essential property of an individual, this would not commit one to the further essentialist claim in the text.

7. Nagel himself is unsatisfied with this response (see p. 370, n. 3). He points out that "It is too sophisticated to explain the simple difference between our attitudes toward prenatal and posthumous nonexistence." To explain his doubts, he presents an example (attributed to Robert Nozick) in which it is granted that it *is* logically possible that an individual be born years before he is actually born (by prematurely "hatching" the spore from which one develops), and yet it seems that even here the intuitive asymmetry is justified. Thus, the logical impossibility of being born earlier cannot *explain* the asymmetry in our attitudes.

8. Derek Parfit, "Reasons and Persons" (Chapter 11 in this volume).
9. Ibid., pp. 193–94.
10. Nagel seems to have been aware of some version of Parfit's claim. Given his worries about the view that it is logically impossible that one should have been born much earlier than one actually was, Nagel admits that "Lucretius's argument still awaits an answer." He continues: "I suspect that it requires a general treatment of the difference between past and future in our attitudes toward our own lives. Our attitudes toward past and future pain are very different, for example. Derek Parfit's writings on this topic have revealed its difficulty to me" ("Death," p. 370, n. 3).
11. So a *symmetric* attitude towards past and future betrayals involves *preference* for one betrayal over several comparable ones regardless of when they occur and *indifference* between two comparable betrayals regardless of when they occur.
12. Parfit, "Reasons and Persons," p. 213.
13. Parfit says: "My examples reveal a surprising asymmetry in our concern about our own and other people's pasts. I would not be distressed at all if I was reminded that I myself once had to endure several months of suffering. But I would be greatly distressed if I learnt that, before she died, my mother had to endure such an ordeal" (ibid., p. 214). This asymmetry is not the same as the asymmetry between my attitudes toward my own past and my own future, yet the two asymmetries are connected as follows. The first asymmetry consists in my indifference to my own past suffering paired with my concern for another's past suffering. Given my concern for my own future suffering, it follows that I have asymmetric attitudes toward my own past suffering and my own future suffering. Given my concern for another's future suffering, it follows that I have symmetric attitudes toward another's past suffering and another's future suffering. Thus the contrast between temporally asymmetric attitudes regarding my own suffering and temporally symmetric attitudes regarding another's suffering stems from the "surprising" asymmetry Parfit notes above. But the contrast in question, which arises from the "surprising" asymmetry, is precisely what one should expect given the discussion in the text: the contrast matches up with the contrast between bads that one experiences and bads that one does not.
14. Although Parfit focuses on examples involving temporally asymmetric attitudes toward pain, he speaks of our "bias toward the future" with respect to experienced goods such as pleasure as well. So he would endorse the principle about temporally asymmetric attitudes toward experienced goods, which grounds the foregoing explanation of the asymmetry in our attitudes toward prenatal and posthumous nonexistence. Although this explanation is consistent with Parfit's remarks in the passages surrounding his discussion of Epicurus on death, that discussion itself does not indicate that he had the explanation in mind: "Epicurus's argument fails for a different reason: we are biased towards

the future. Because we have this bias, the bare knowledge that we once suffered may not now disturb us. But our equanimity does not show that our past suffering was not bad. The same could be true of our past non-existence. Epicurus's argument therefore has force only for those people who both lack the bias towards the future, and do not regret their past non-existence. Since there are no such people, the argument has force for no one" ("Reasons and Persons," pp. 205—6). In any case, it is crucial to see that only the principle about temporally asymmetric attitudes toward experienced *goods* such as pleasure will afford an explanation of why death is bad. The principle about experienced *bads* that is suggested by Parfit's examples, it has been argued, will not generate such an explanation.

McMahan: Death and the Value of Life

1. Epicurus, "Letter to Menoeceus," 124b–127a, in Russel M. Geer, ed., *Epicurus: Letters, Principal Doctrines, and Vatican Sayings* (Indianapolis, 1964).

2. Strictly speaking, death is a biological phenomenon—something that happens to living organisms. Since I believe that persons are not identical with their organisms, I believe that persons can cease to exist in other ways than through death (e.g., a person will cease to exist if he loses consciousness irreversibly, and there are cases in which this is compatible with his organism's continuing to exist and even continuing to live); and, though this never in fact happens, it is in principle possible for persons to survive the deaths of their organisms. As things are, death is a sufficient condition of the ceasing to exist of a person, but not a necessary condition. In this chapter my concern is with the ceasing to exist of persons. But for convenience I will treat the death of a person as if it were equivalent to the ceasing to exist of a person.

3. The Existence Requirement does not, of course, require that the person exist when the cause of the misfortune occurs.

4. See, e.g., Thomas Nagel, "Death" (Chapter 4 in this volume; p. 64), and James Rachels, *The End of Life: Euthanasia and Morality* (Oxford, 1986), pp. 46–48. An equally damaging objection to both Experience Requirements is that they have trouble accounting for the fact that experiential states such as happiness and unhappiness can be rational or irrational, appropriate or inappropriate. See Jeff McMahan, *The Ethics of Killing* (Oxford, 1989), chap. 1.

5. One alternative possible explanation appeals to the idea that it is wrong, other things being equal, to do what makes the outcome worse in impersonal terms by increasing the net amount of whatever it is that we regard as bad—suffering, for instance. Thus we might object to causing a miserable person to exist on the ground that this produces an uncompensated increase in the amount of suffering in the world. If we appeal to this alternative explanation, then we will be able to develop a way of reconciling the conclusion of the Epicurean argument with the various commonsense beliefs which it threatens that is analogous to the

way developed in the text. The difference is that, according to the alternative account, death will be impersonally bad rather than what I call quasi-impersonally bad (see n. 8 below).

6. The Comparative View is both christened and advocated by Jan Narveson in "Future People and Us," in R. Sikora and B. Barry, eds., *Obligations to Future Generations* (Philadelphia, 1978), p. 48.

7. Here I draw on the argument of my "Problems of Population Theory," *Ethics* 92 (Oct. 1981): 104–5.

8. I call the badness of death as it is here understood "quasi-impersonal" to distinguish it both from the badness of events that are bad because of their effects on people and from the badness of events that are bad in a fully impersonal way—that is, bad for reasons that are independent of considerations of effects on particular people.

9. One could appeal to a parallel reconciliation strategy to show that suicide can also be rational: e.g., in cases in which death would be quasi-impersonally good, excluding what would be bad for a person.

10. The Epicurean, it seems, can reject this claim only by appealing to the Narrow Experience Requirement. He cannot appeal to the Wide Requirement, since this is incompatible with the Existence Requirement.

11. Nagel, "Death," pp. 62–64. If, as I suggested above, there can be posthumous benefits, then death does not deprive us of all possibilities for good. It deprives us only of possibilities for goods of an active or experiential kind. This and other related points are made by Frances Myrna Kamm in her *Morality, Mortality* (Oxford, forthcoming), in a chapter entitled "Death and Later Goods."

12. Nagel, "Death," pp. 68 and 69.

13. As his text makes clear, Nagel himself believes that it is normally worse to die earlier rather than later. It is not clear, however, how he thinks this can be rendered consistent with his belief that even those who die of extreme old age thereby suffer a loss of indefinite possibilities for good. Below I will suggest a way of reconciling his various intuitions.

14. Joel Feinberg, "Wrongful Life and the Counterfactual Element in Harming," *Social Philosophy and Policy* 4 (Autumn 1986): 145–78. Normally the phrase "causal overdetermination" is reserved for cases in which two or more individually sufficient causes operate simultaneously to bring about some event.

15. See Robert C. Stalnaker, "A Theory of Conditionals," *American Philosophical Quarterly*, monograph no. 2 (1968), and David Lewis, *Counterfactuals* (Cambridge, Mass., 1973).

16. I suspect, though I cannot prove this, that my proposal could be reformulated without significant loss in terms of other variants of the general theory of counterfactuals.

17. I have no analysis of the distinction between cause and causal condition to offer, nor any view about whether the distinction marks a real difference or is simply context-dependent. I here rely on our intuitive sense of what counts as a cause and what counts as a causal condition.

18. Lewis contends that there may be more than one closest possible world in which the antecedent is realized. I must ignore this complication here.

19. Unless, perhaps, we are forced to consider causally impossible worlds by the fact that the antecedent itself is causally impossible. (More on this later.) In insisting that we alter matters of fact before we alter the causal structure of the actual world, I am assuming a version of the similarity theory that many writers, including Lewis, would reject. For arguments in favor of banning miracles in closest antecedent-worlds, see Jonathan Bennett, "Counterfactuals and Temporal Direction," *Philosophical Review* 93 (Jan. 1984): 57–91, esp. sec. 7.

20. I assume that we may rule out counterfactual claims based on antecedent-worlds in which the aging process is arrested or reversed on the ground that any such world would be insufficiently similar to the actual world in terms of any plausible similarity metric to provide truth-conditions for a counterfactual.

21. Compare Nagel, "Death," p. 68, where he appears to suggest that whether (and perhaps to what extent) the failure to realize some future good counts as a misfortune depends on how possible the relevant good is.

22. Our evaluation of a person's global good or ill fortune should thus be relativized to our perception of the norm for a certain sort of human life. This should not be confused with the common but nevertheless unacceptable idea that we should evaluate a person's death relative to the possibility of his living out a lifespan that is normal for persons in his society. Among the various objections to the latter idea is the fact that it seems to entail that death cannot be bad for those who have already lived longer than the normal lifespan.

23. This theory is most persuasively developed in Derek Parfit's *Reasons and Persons* (Oxford, 1984), pt. 3. For the purposes of this paper I will assume that this theory is true. It is not, however, strictly necessary for my argument that we should accept this theory. Although the claims that are essential to my argument—e.g., that it can be rational for a person to discount for diminished psychological connectedness—are probably best supported by this theory, they are in principle compatible with certain other theories. Hence one is not necessarily committed by the acceptance of my argument to any particular theory of personal identity.

24. It might be objected that, since my present physical organism is certainly the same organism as the fetus with which it is physically continuous, the claim that *I* am not identical with that fetus implies that I am not my physical organism. I accept this objection. Since to live, it would seem that I cannot be identical with my organism. This, however, may be compatible with the claim that there is a further sense in which I am my organism. To borrow an old analogy, the sense in which I am my organism is the same sense in which a statue is the clay of which it is made. Just as the statue is constituted by the clay without being identical with it, so I consist of or am constituted by my organism

without being identical with it. (These issues are ably discussed by W. R. Carter in "Do Zygotes Become People?" *Mind* 91 [Jan. 1982]: 77–95, and in "Once and Future People," *American Philosophical Quarterly* 17 [Jan. 1980]: 61–66, and by Warren Quinn in "Abortion: Identity and Loss," *Philosophy and Public Affairs* 13 [Winter 1984]: 24–54, though both of these writers defend a different position from that advocated here. I discuss the issue of the relation between persons and their organisms, as well as the other issues raised in this section, in considerable detail in *The Ethics of Killing*, chap. 2.)

25. For a cogent defense of the view that persons, even if they are substances, come into existence gradually, see Quinn, "Abortion," pp. 33–40.

26. Compare Parfit, *Reasons and Persons*, sec. 79.

27. Ibid., chap. 12, esp. secs. 89 and 90. Although psychological connectedness is what matters most, a simple argument suggests that psychological continuity also matters. Suppose that I am now psychologically connected with myself at t_1 but not with myself at t_2. Suppose that, because of the lack of any connections, I do not now have any direct concern about what happens to me at t_2. I nevertheless realize that at t_1, I will care about what happens to me at t_2, since at t_1 I will be connected to myself at t_2. Thus, since I now care about my interests at t_1, I now have an indirect reason for caring what happens to me at t_2, since what happens to me at t_2 will matter to me at t_1.

28. It might be argued that these implications of the theory of personal identity themselves imply that personal growth, evolution, and improvement are, in prospect at least, undesirable because they would involve a weakening of psychological connectedness and hence reduce the value to oneself now of goods that one might acquire or experience in the future. Two points may be made in reply. First, personal growth and improvement need not involve any weakening of psychological connectedness, since changes in one's character can occur in fulfillment of one's earlier desires and intentions. In these cases the relevant changes actually constitute psychological connections that bind the later person more closely to his earlier self. Thus a life in which there is substantial change and diversity will, if the diverse elements are connected by threads of desire and intention, be unified in a deeper and richer way than a life in which one's character remains static. Second, even in cases in which personal improvement simply *happens* to a person, and so may involve some weakening of psychological connectedness, it may still be desirable, all things considered. For the weakening of connectedness may be outweighed by the greater importance of, e.g., an enhancement of virtue or rationality.

29. On the claim that the badness of death can be explained solely in terms of the frustration of desire, see McMahan, *The Ethics of Killing*, chap. 1, and the references to other works, such as Bernard Williams, cited there.

30. This point has been well expressed by Michael Lockwood, who writes, "Set against an ideal of human life as a meaningful whole, we

can see that premature death can, as it were, make nonsense of much of what has gone before. Earlier actions, preparations, planning, whose entire purpose and rationale lay in their being directed towards some future goal, become, in the face of an untimely death, retrospectively pointless—bridges, so to speak, that terminate in mid-air, roads that lead nowhere" ("Singer on Killing and the Preference for Life," *Inquiry* 22 [Summer 1979]: 167). This point, and the point about desire, reinforce the explanation developed above of the view that death very early in life is not worse than death later in life.

Luper-Foy: Annihilation

1. Unamuno is the only person I know of who would insist that there is *nothing* worse than dying: "And I must confess, painful though the confession be, that in the days of the simple faith of my childhood, descriptions of the tortures of hell, however terrible, never made me tremble, for I always felt that nothingness was much more terrifying. . . . It is better to live in pain than to cease to be in peace" (*Tragic Sense of Life* [New York, 1954], pp. 43–44). I find his adamancy refreshing.

2. Bernard Williams presses this point in "The Makropulos Case" (Chapter 5 in this volume).

3. Montaigne gathers a marvelous collection of inanities in "That to Philosophize Is to Learn to Die," *The Complete Works of Montaigne*, trans. D. Frame (Stanford, 1943), pp. 56–68.

4. Epicurus, *Letter to Menoeceus*.

5. This suggestion is due to Thomas Nagel, "Death" (Chapter 4 in this volume).

6. Or, alternatively,

If I (now) believed that X were not the case at a given time *t*, then I would (now) want to be dead at *t*.

These two possible formulations of escape desires differ in that the first (given in the body of the paper) characterizes escape desires in terms of the form of their *contents*, whereas the second (given above) characterizes them in terms of the conditions under which we shall *have* them. Both, however, rely on subjunctive conditionals.

7. According to Epicurus, "All good and evil consists in sensation, but death is deprivation of sensation. . . . For we recognize pleasure as the first good innate in us, and from pleasure we begin every act of choice and avoidance, and to pleasure we return again, using the feeling as the standard by which we judge every good" (*Letter to Menoeceus*).

8. Galileo Galilei is reported by Unamuno (in *The Tragic Sense of Life*) to have remarked that "Some perhaps will say that the bitterest pain is the loss of life, but I say there are others more bitter; for whosoever is deprived of life is deprived at the same time of the power to lament, not only this, but any other loss whatsoever." No doubt it is confused to support the claim that things exist that are worse than death by ad-

ducing a consequence of death, but at least Galileo recognized that loss
of the ability to lament would be lamentable.

9. Below I point out that even hedonism cannot help avoid a very
unappealing callousness. I might note that there is another reason, often attributed to Epicurus, for denying that dying can be a bad thing
for us. The objection is that "having died" can never correctly be *attributed* to anyone, since before people die, "having died" is not true of
them, and after they die they have ceased to exist, so that nothing remains for "having died" to be a property of. Hence "having died" does
not refer to a property anyone can have, and so it cannot be a misfortune for us to have that property. (Arguably, this is what Wittgenstein
had in mind when he remarked in *Tractatus*, 6.4311, that "death is not
an event in life.") But this is a mere sophism. Just as I can have properties by virtue of what goes on outside my *spatial* boundaries (for example, being attacked by a cat), so I can have properties by virtue of
what is going on outside my temporal boundaries. Thus it is partly due
to events that occurred before I came into existence that "having been
conceived" and "born after Aristotle" are both true of me. And it is
partly due to events that will take place after I die that "will have his
will read" and "will die" are true of me. Death is not an event in life,
but it *is* the event by which a life ends.

10. Alternatively,

If I (now) believed that I would be alive at *t*, then I should (now) want
X to be the case at *t*.

Notice that the contents of conditional desires are the contrapositions
of escape desires. Contrapositions of subjunctive conditionals are not
equivalent to each other, however. For an explanation, see David Lewis,
Counterfactuals (Cambridge, Mass., 1973), p. 35. The notion of a conditional desire is essentially Williams's; see his "The Makropulos Case."

11. This view has been advocated in one form or another by a great
number of people for a good while. It is the third "Noble Truth" of
Gautama Siddhartha (563–483 B.C.) and is echoed in the following melancholy advice by the tenth-century Buddhist Iama Milarepa: "All
worldly pursuits have but the one unavoidable and inevitable end,
which is sorrow: acquisitions end in dispersion; buildings, in destruction; meetings, in separation; births, in death. Knowing this, one
should from the very first renounce acquisition and heaping-up, and
building and meeting. . . . Life is short, and the time of death is uncertain" (from W. Evans-Wentz, *Tibet's Great Yogi: Malarepa* [New York,
1969]). The Roman Stoic Epictetus (ca. A.D. 50–130), who lived about
three centuries after Epicurus, also suggests that we alter our desires
so that we need not regard the inevitable as a bad thing: "Ask not that
events should happen as you will, but let your will be that events
should happen as they do, and you shall have peace. If . . . you try to
avoid only what is unnatural in the region within your control, you will
escape from all that you avoid; but if you try to avoid disease or death
or poverty you will be miserable (from *The Manual of Epictetus*, in

W. Oates, ed., *The Stoic and Epicurean Philosophers* [New York, 1940], pp. 468–84).

12. Indeed, we might just as well call the Epicurean personality death-*wishing* in view of the facts that conditional desires are much like escape desires and the latter are qualified death wishes. What is plausible about Freud's theory is captured by the view that many people are quite death-tolerant.

13. Williams says this rather casually in "The Makropulos Case."

14. In *My Confessions*, trans. Leo Weiner (London, 1905), Tolstoy seems to suggest that life would be meaningless if we died: "But the answer in this sphere of knowledge to my question what the meaning of my life was, was always: 'You are what you call your life; you are a temporal, accidental conglomeration of particles. The inter-relation, the change of these particles, produces in you that which you call life. This congeries will last for some time; then the interaction of these particles will cease, and that which you call life and all your questions will come to an end.' With such an answer it appears that the answer is not a reply to the question. I want to know the meaning of my life, but the fact that it is a particle of the infinite not only gives it no meaning, but even destroys every possible meaning."

15. For a description of the (primitive) status of research into life extension, see R. Parker and H. Gerjouy, "Life-span Extension: The State of the Art," in R. Veatch, ed., *Life Span* (San Francisco, 1979), pp. 1–27.

16. For an elaboration of the notion of friendship, see my paper, "Competing for the Good Life," *American Philosophical Quarterly* 23 (1986): 167–77.

Rosenbaum: Epicurus and Annihilation

1. Luper-Foy, "Annihilation" (Chapter 14 in this volume).

2. Thomas Nagel, "Death" (Chapter 4 in this volume); Mary Mothersill, "Death," in J. Rachels, ed., *Moral Problems* (New York, 1971); Bernard Williams, "The Makropulos Case: Reflections on the Tedium of Immortality" (Chapter 5 in this volume); Harry Silverstein, "The Evil of Death" (Chapter 6 in this volume); George Pitcher, "The Misfortunes of the Dead" (Chapter 9 in this volume); Anthony L. Brueckner and John Martin Fischer, "Why Is Death Bad?" (Chapter 12 in this volume); and Palle Yourgrau, "The Dead" (Chapter 8 in this volume).

3. Luper-Foy, "Annihilation," p. 272. Such an approach is not unheard of among contemporary commentators on Epicurus's view. Richard Rorty describes the Epicurean view as a "vacuity" in "The Contingency of Selfhood," *London Review of Books* 8 (May 1986): 11. Mary Mothersill dismisses the Epicurean view as one that "will hardly bear looking into, but may have been intended as little more than an eristic flourish" ("Death," p. 378). Philosophers have not explored Epicurus's view very deeply, and it is fair to note that Luper-Foy's reaction is not unusual in this respect.

4. O. H. Green, "Fear of Death," *Philosophy and Phenomenological Research* 43 (Sept. 1982): 99–105. See also Stephen E. Rosenbaum, "How to Be Dead and Not Care: A Defense of Epicurus" (Chapter 7 in this volume).

5. Stephen E. Rosenbaum, "The Harm of Killing: An Epicurean Perspective," in R. Baird et al., *Contemporary Essays on Greek Ideas: The Kilgore Festschrift* (Waco, Tex., 1987).

6. See Rosenbaum, "How to Be Dead and Not Care."

7. Diogenes Laertius, "Epicurus," *Lives of Eminent Philosophers*, vol. 2 (Cambridge, 1975), p. 549. Hereafter cited in the usual way: D.L., X, 22 (but followed by a parenthetical page reference for this volume).

8. D.L., X, 126 (p. 651).

9. Ibid.

10. For a fuller development of this point, see Rosenbaum, "How to Be Dead and Not Care."

11. D.L., X, 126 (p. 651).

12. For a defense of this argument, see Rosenbaum, "How to Be Dead and Not Care."

13. D.L., X, 126 (pp. 651–53).

14. D.L., X, 136 (p. 661).

15. Luper-Foy, "Annihilation," p. 272.

16. Ibid.

17. D.L., X, 124–25 (p. 651).

18. D.L., X, 139 (p. 665).

19. D.L., X, 126 (p. 651).

20. Luper-Foy, "Annihilation," p. 271.

21. Ibid.   22. Ibid.

23. Ibid.   24. Ibid., pp. 274–75.

25. Ibid., pp. 273–76.   26. Ibid., p. 278.

27. Ibid., p. 279.   28. Ibid.

29. Ibid., p. 277.   30. Ibid., p. 281.

31. Ibid., p. 275.

32. Epicurus's will shows that he was concerned with the welfare of future generations (D.L., X, 16–22 [pp. 545–49]). Diogenes Laertius reports, also, in his description of the Epicurean *sophos*, that the wise man "will have regard to . . . the future" (D.L., X, 120 [p. 645]).

33. D.L., X, 129 (p. 655).

34. John Stuart Mill, *Utilitarianism* (Indianapolis, 1957), p. 11.

Feldman: Some Puzzles About the Evil of Death

1. Epicurus, *Letter to Menoeceus*, trans. C. Bailey, in *The Stoic and Epicurean Philosophers*, edited and with an introduction by Whitney J. Oates (New York, 1940), pp. 30–31. Lucretius presents essentially the same argument. See *On the Nature of Things*, trans. H. A. J. Munro, and Oates, ed., *The Stoic and Epicurean Philosophers*, p. 131.

2. Jeff McMahan, "Death and the Value of Life" (Chapter 13 in this volume), p. 234. He calls it "The Existence Requirement."

3. I am by no means the first to defend this sort of answer. Similar views are defended (or at least discussed with some enthusiasm) by a number of philosophers. See, for example, McMahan, "Death and the Value of Life"; Thomas Nagel, "Death" (Chapter 4 in this volume); Roy Perrett, *Death and Immortality* (Dordrecht, 1987); L. S. Sumner, "A Matter of Life and Death," *Noûs* 10 (May 1976): 145–71; Douglas Walton, *On Defining Death* (Montreal, 1979); and Bernard Williams, "The Makropulos Case: Reflections on the Tedium of Immortality" (Chapter 5 in this volume).

4. For a vigorous defense of the claim that the standard view involves an illegitimate comparison, see Harry Silverstein, "The Evil of Death" (Chapter 6 in this volume).

5. Lucretius, *On the Nature of Things*, p. 134.

6. The *locus classicus* of many of these ideas is David Lewis, *Counterfactuals* (Cambridge, Mass., 1973).

7. I attempted to present a clear formulation of this view about axiology in *Doing the Best We Can: An Essay in Informal Deontic Logic* (Dordrecht, 1986). See especially sec. 2.2.

8. I doubt that many moral philosophers would endorse anything like this simplest form of hedonism. Indeed, I would not endorse it either. My point here is primarily to indicate something about the structure of an axiological view—it should yield an ordering of worlds in terms of value. In an attempt to make this conception most obvious, I have assumed that there is a value function taking us from worlds to numbers. This structural approach is consistent with a wide variety of substantive axiological theories.

9. It should be obvious that in interesting cases, no one could possibly calculate the value of a world for a person. On the other hand, we could have reason to believe that worlds of a certain specified sort would be uniformly *worse* for someone than worlds of some other specified sort.

10. Nagel discusses this idea in his now-classic paper, "Death." A similar approach to the evil of death is suggested by George Pitcher in "The Misfortunes of the Dead" (Chapter 9 in this volume).

11. Some commentators suppose that we stop existing when we die but we do not stop "being." They also suppose that appealing to the existence/being distinction helps solve the problem about the evil of death. For an example of this approach, see Palle Yourgrau's "The Dead" (Chapter 8 in this volume). In this paper I have made no such distinction.

12. I am suppressing consideration of certain complexities. One that should be addressed concerns cases in which there is no unique nearest world in which a certain state of affairs occurs—several worlds are tied for this distinction. What shall we say then?

Suppose that at the real world Dolores does not move to Bolivia. Then the real world is the nearest world in which she does not move to Bolivia. Suppose that among worlds in which she does move to Bolivia, there are two that are equally near and most near the real world. Then

I want to say this: if each of these worlds is worse for Dolores than the real world, then moving to Bolivia would be bad for her; if each is better for her than the real world, then moving to Bolivia would be good for her; if one is better and the other is worse, then it is not the case that moving to Bolivia would be good for her, and it is not the case that moving to Bolivia would be bad for her; moving to Bolivia might be good for her and might be bad for her.

If all the nearest *b*-worlds have the same value for Dolores, then we can use this value when we compute the value of *b* for Dolores. On the other hand, if the nearest *b*-worlds differ in value for Dolores, then the computations become more problematic. One possibility would be to make use of the average value for Dolores of these nearest *b*-worlds. Another possibility would be to say that the value of *b* for her might be the result of subtracting the value for Dolores of the real world from the value for her of one of them, and it might be the result of subtracting the value for her of the real world from the value for her of another. In such a case, we would have to say that there is no number, *n*, such that the value of *b* for Dolores equals *n*.

In what follows, I shall write as if there is always a unique nearest world. My main points are not affected by this simplifying assumption.

13. I think these remarks provide the basis for a reply to one sort of argument concerning the alleged irrationality of suicide. Some have said that suicide is always irrational since it is impossible to calculate the value of death for the deceased. See, for example, John Donnelly's "Suicide and Rationality," in Donnelly, ed., *Language, Metaphysics, and Death* (New York, 1978), and Philip Devine's *The Ethics of Homicide* (Ithaca, 1978), esp. p. 25. If what I have said here is right, the calculations are in principle possible, and some suicides are perfectly rational.

14. In "How to Be Dead and Not Care: A Defense of Epicurus" (Chapter 7 in this volume), Stephen Rosenbaum proposes an interpretation of the Epicurean argument. He suggests that one crucial premise is "A state of affairs is bad for a person *P* only if *P* can experience it at some time" (p. 121). I would say that the premise is ambiguous. If taken to mean that a state of affairs is *intrinsically* bad for a person only if he can experience it, then (assuming hedonism or any other "experience-based" axiology) the premise may be true—but it is not relevant to the claim that death is bad for the one who dies, since it is most reasonable to take this as the claim that death is *extrinsically* bad for the one who dies. If the claim is understood in this more plausible way as the claim that a state of affairs can be *extrinsically* bad for a person only if he can experience it, then, as I have attempted to show, the premise is false.

15. Silverstein, "The Evil of Death," p. 99.

16. In "Death" (p. 68), Thomas Nagel claims that late birth does not deprive anyone of anything, since no one could have been born much earlier than she was in fact born. This provides the basis for a quick answer to Lucretius. Derek Parfit makes a similar claim in *Reasons and Persons* (Oxford, 1984), p. 351. The argument might be based on the essentiality of origins. However, with the development of techniques

for the cryopreservation of sperm and eggs, the view seems false. Even if we grant the controversial claim that each person has her origins essentially, we have to acknowledge that once the relevant sperm and egg have been frozen, it is in principle possible for her to be conceived at any time in the next thousand of years or so. I grant, of course, that the issue of the essentiality of origins deserves independent discussion. I simply assume that it makes sense to speak of what would have happened if Claudette had been born earlier. This makes it possible to look more deeply into the puzzle suggested by Lucretius.

17. Parfit, *Reasons and Persons* (see also Chapter 11 in this volume). An interesting proposal based on some Parfittian ideas can be found in "Why Is Death Bad?" by Anthony Brueckner and John Martin Fischer (Chapter 12 in this volume).

18. McMahan discusses what he calls "the revised possible goods account." This is relevantly like my proposal. He claims that it runs into the "problem of specifying the antecedent" (p. 245).

19. Ibid., p. 249.

20. "If we imagine that the transitive cause of the officer's being shot by Ivan did not occur, we must presumably imagine that the Crimean War did not occur, in which case the threat from Boris would not have occurred either" (ibid., p. 251).

Velleman: Well-Being and Time

1. In this paper I assume that a person's welfare is defined by his interests, or what is good for him. According to some theories of the good, however, a person can have interests that do not bear on his well-being, since his interests are not all self-regarding, and his well-being depends only on the fulfillment of self-regarding interests. These theories imply that what has value for a person and what improves that person's welfare are not necessarily coextensive. In my view, proponents of such theories should recognize two distinct ways of measuring the relational value attaching to a person's life: first, the extent to which the life fulfills the person's interests, broadly construed; and second, the extent to which the life fulfills the person's self-interest, or welfare interests. Although I ignore this distinction, I believe that it could be introduced into my arguments with only a loss of simplicity. (Thanks to Peter Railton for bringing this point to my attention.)

2. Henceforth I shall frequently drop the modifier and speak simply about the value of someone's life. In all cases, however, I shall be referring to the welfare value of the life—that is, how well it goes for the person living it—rather than to its being morally praiseworthy, aesthetically pleasing, or endowed with significance. (See also notes 7 and 17 below.) I shall also refer to the welfare value of someone's life as his "lifetime well-being."

3. Amartya Sen interprets the phrase "being well off" as referring to something other than well-being. "The former," he says, "is really a concept of opulence" ("Well-Being and Freedom," the second lecture in "Well-Being, Agency and Freedom: The Dewey Lectures 1984," *Jour-*

nal of Philosophy 82 [1985]: 195ff.). Without necessarily rejecting Sen's intuitions about the meanings of these terms in ordinary parlance, I shall stipulate, for the purposes of the present paper, that "being well off" refers to the state of having well-being.

4. This statement requires one minor qualification. I can imagine a kind of life whose welfare value would be determined by the amount of momentary welfare accruing to its subject. This would be a life with virtually no narrative structure at all—say, the life of someone who is maintained, from birth to death, in a state of semiconsciousness and inactivity. That this particular life would be only as good as the sum of its good and bad moments is perfectly compatible with my claim that a life's value is not *in general* a function of momentary well-being.

5. I believe that James Griffin denies additivity in this sense. He initially says, "We can never reach final assessment of ways of life by totting up lots of small, short-term utilities. . . . It has to take a global form: this way of living, all in all, is better than that" (*Well-Being: Its Meaning, Measurement and Moral Importance* [Oxford, 1986], pp. 34–35). But Griffin then goes on to say that the values of a life's components should be assessed in terms of the components' contributions to the value of the whole, in such a way that "aggregation" is preserved (see esp. p. 36). Thus, Griffin's objection to the "totting-up model," as he calls it, is an objection to computing values by composition rather than decomposition. (See also pp. 88, 104–5, 144–46.)

6. The notion that the value of a life depends on its narrative structure appears in many works, including Alasdair MacIntyre's *After Virtue* (Notre Dame, Ind., 1984), chap. 15, and Charles Taylor's *Sources of the Self: The Making of the Modern Identity* (Cambridge, Mass., 1989), pp. 47ff.

7. Michael Slote has pointed out to me that my view is at risk of being confused with a view sometimes attributed to Nietzsche, to the effect that literary or aesthetic considerations determine the value of a life. (See Alexander Nehamas, *Nietzsche: Life as Literature* [Cambridge, Mass., 1985].) I am grateful to Brian Leiter for guidance on this subject.

8. Our preferences among trends in well-being are not confined to that for improvement over deterioration. I think that one may have reason to prefer variety and intensity to consistency and moderation—that is, a life of great joys and sorrows to one of uninterrupted contentment—even if the sum of momentary well-being were the same in both lives; or there may be reasons supporting the opposite preference. (Amartya Sen favors equality of well-being among the different moments in one's life. See "Utilitarianism and Welfarism," *Journal of Philosophy* 76 [1970]: 407f.). As I have said, my argument does not depend on showing one such preference to be more rational than another. I am arguing against a view that would deny the possibility of reasons supporting either preference, given the equal amounts of momentary well-being accumulated in the two lives.

9. The point made in this paragraph is borrowed from Connie Rosati, who makes it in a somewhat different context. See her "Mortality, Agency, and Regret" (forthcoming). Rosati has pointed out to me that

people sometimes regret having started too late on a particular career or relationship, as if the value of their lives has been permanently reduced by this delay in their success or happiness. But I am not committed to denying that there can ever be a bad start that permanently depresses the value of one's life. I am committed only to denying that early misfortunes necessarily depress the value of one's life, as they necessarily would if well-being were additive. What's more, I suspect that the view of well-being as additive cannot properly account for the cases that Rosati has in mind. What these people regret is not the level of well-being that they enjoyed in youth but rather their delay in embarking on a particular project that (as they now realize) will provide an important theme or plot for their life's story. Hence their regrets can be understood only as an attitude toward the narrative structure of their lives.

10. Slote, *Goods and Virtues* (Oxford, 1983), originally published in *Pacific Philosophical Quarterly* 63 (1982): 311–26. Recently the additivity of well-being has also been challenged by John Bigelow, John Campbell, and Robert Pargetter in "Death and Well-Being," *Pacific Philosophical Quarterly* 71 (1990): 119. Nick White has pointed out to me that an early argument against the additivity of well-being appears in C. I. Lewis's *An Analysis of Knowledge and Valuation* (La Salle, Ill., 1946), chap. 16. In reading Lewis, I have difficulty separating (1) the claim that the juxtaposition of events in a life affects the value of the whole; (2) the claim that it affects the intrinsic character of the events themselves, which are colored by the recollection and anticipation of other events; and (3) the claim that the value of a life depends on its character as a diachronic *experience* that is not reducible to a succession of momentary experiences. My defense of (1) does not depend on claims like (2) or (3). My argument can thus be viewed as a generalization of Lewis's, in which I abstract from Lewis's experiential conception of value.

11. Slote, *Goods and Virtues*, pp. 23–24.

12. E.g., when saying that "a good may itself be greater for coming late rather than early in life" (ibid., p. 25).

13. Sidgwick, *The Methods of Ethics* (Indianapolis, 1981), p. 381.

14. Slote, *Goods and Virtues*, p. 23.

15. Here I am assuming that the veil of ignorance deprives the subject of information about his current age. For if he knew that he was currently in his forties, then he may have a preference arising out of what Derek Parfit calls the bias toward the future in "Reasons and Persons" (Chapter 11 in this volume). Note, then, that the time preferences considered by Slote are different in structure from those considered by Parfit. Parfit is concerned with a preference between past and future, wheres Slote is concerned with a preference between early and late. As the subject's temporal relation to an event changes, the former preference yields a different attitude toward the event, but the latter does not.

Connie Rosati has suggested to me that a person might prefer earlier success because it would be a sign of genius. But this suggestion strikes me as only proving my point. The person so described would not prefer earlier success merely by virtue of its timing; he would prefer it only because he values the meaning of some story that its early occurrence would subserve.

16. Bigelow, Campbell, and Pargetter also express doubts about Slote's treatment of this case. See "Death and Well-Being," pp. 122–23.

17. To say that the meaning of an event determines its contribution to the value of one's life is not to equate a valuable life with a meaningful one. To be sure, meaningfulness is a valuable characteristic in a life, and it, too, is probably a function of the life's narrative structure. But we can conceive of meaningful lives that are not particularly good ones for the people who live them; and we may be able to conceive of good lives that are not particularly meaningful. What's more, the meaning, or narrative role, that determines an event's contribution to a life's value, in my view, must not be confused with the event's meaningfulness, in the evaluative sense. To say that a particular increment in momentary well-being adds more to the value of a particular life if it has the meaning of a well-earned reward than that of a windfall is not to say that rewards are necessarily more meaningful events; it is simply to say that their contribution to the life's value depends on their being rewards.

18. Here I disagree with Bigelow, Campbell, and Pargetter, who believe that the value of someone's life, though not reducible to the sum of the momentary well-being enjoyed throughout that life, nevertheless supervenes on the pattern of the person's momentary well-being through time. (See "Death and Well-Being," pp. 127–28, 136–37.) Indeed, these authors believe that momentary well-being just *is* that property—whatever it may be—whose profile through time determines the value of a person's life (p. 128). My reasons for rejecting this view are expounded in greater detail below.

19. In some cases, of course, what we hope to learn from a misfortune is how to avoid repeating some mistake that occasioned it. But why do we think it more important to learn how to avoid repeating a past mistake than to learn a different lesson, about how to avoid committing a novel mistake? The reason is not that we regard the consequences of a repeated mistake as necessarily worse than those of a mistake committed for the first time. We might prefer committing a novel mistake to repeating a past mistake even if their consequences would be equally bad. Surely, the reason is that we regard the story of committing the same mistake repeatedly as worse than that of committing different mistakes—a value judgment that depends on more than the momentary costs of the mistakes themselves.

One might think that our interest in learning from misfortunes, and the mistakes that occasion them, is based on the assumption that the mistakes a person has already committed are the ones that he is most likely to commit in future, and hence that lessons learned from them are the ones that are most likely to be useful. I disagree. We value learning from mistakes even if we know that the opportunity to repeat them will never arise. And we value learning from misfortunes, such as grave illnesses or freak accidents, that are not in any way attributable to mistakes.

Finally, one might think that learning from a misfortune is valuable only because it is a means to a more pleasant consciousness of the misfortune—a means of "coming to terms" or "making peace" with it. But why not simply forget about the misfortune entirely, or turn one's thoughts to something else? If making peace with a misfortune were valuable only as a means to pleasurable consciousness, then any alternative pleasure would serve just as well. Making peace with a misfortune is valuable not just because it entails acquiring so much peace of mind but because it entails acquiring peace of mind in a way that draws a fitting conclusion to one's past. (All of the objections considered in this note were suggested to me by Connie Rosati.)

20. Charles Taylor remarks on our concern for whether the past "is just 'temps perdu' in the double sense intended in the title of Proust's celebrated work, that is, time which is both wasted and irretrievably lost, beyond recall, in which we pass as if we had never been" (*Sources of the Self*, p. 43). Taylor goes on to say that our desire to prevent the present from becoming lost in this sense is a desire for "the future to 'redeem' the past, to make it part of a life story which has sense or purpose." Taylor continues: "A famous, perhaps for us moderns a paradigm, example of what this can mean is recounted by Proust in his *A la recherche du temps perdu*. In the scene in the Guermantes's library, the narrator recovers the full meaning of his past and thus restores the time which was 'lost' in the two senses I mentioned above. The formerly irretrievable past is recovered in its unity with the life yet to live, and all the 'wasted' time now has a meaning, as the time of preparation for the work of the writer who will give shape to this unity" (pp. 50–51).

21. Of course, we can also imagine a life in which an unsuccessful first marriage teaches you lessons instrumental to the success of your second. But in that case, I would claim, your life would be better than it would have been if the first marriage had been a dead loss.

22. Peter Railton has pointed out to me that I seem to be appealing to a desire that was omitted from my calculation of desire-fulfillment—namely, your desire for a life in which your efforts are rewarded. But I do not think that your desire for a life in which your efforts are rewarded is contingent on the assumption of your having that desire in the life under consideration.

23. These philosophers include Joel Feinberg ("Harm to Others," Chapter 10 in this volume) and Bigelow, Campbell, and Pargetter ("Death and Well-Being," pp. 134–35, 138). Note that in rejecting the notion of retroactive effects on a person's momentary well-being, I do not necessarily reject the notion that the value of a person's life can be influenced by events after his death. The reason is that I regard the value of a person's life as a feature of his life story, and a person's life story may not end at his death.

24. Indeed, I do not see how Feinberg or Bigelow et al. can say that such a person's life gets better at all if, in adulthood, he desires that his youth had gone differently.

25. Many philosophers have noted the absence of any rational requirement to satisfy desires that one had in the past (Derek Parfit, *Reasons and Persons* [Oxford, 1984], Chap. 8; Richard Brandt, "Two Concepts of Utility," in H. B. Miller and W. H. Williams, eds., *The Limits of Utilitarianism* [Minneapolis, 1982], p. 180). To my knowledge, these philosophers do not raise the further question of why one has any present reason to promote the fulfillment of one's desires for the future, given that one may have no reason to promote their fulfillment at the time. See also Amartya Sen, "Plural Utility," *Proceedings of the Aristotelian Society* 81 (1981): 202–4.

26. C. I. Lewis offers many suggestive remarks to the effect that striving and achieving have value only as related to each other in a diachronic whole (*Analysis of Knowledge and Valuation*, pp. 498ff.). As I have noted, however, Lewis's remarks often rely on the notion that the *experiences* of striving and achieving suffuse one another or add up to an irreducible diachronic experience.

27. Subsequently, such constraints may relax to some extent, since the events of one's retirement may be less intimately related to the other events in one's life than those occurring at the culmination of one's active career. A life story that has only one fitting climax may have more than one fitting denouement.

28. As Michael Stocker points out, the value of a life is what Moore would have called an "organic whole" (*Plural and Conflicting Values* [Oxford, 1990], pp. 300–302, 323).

29. The same goes for Bigelow, Campbell, and Pargetter, who argue that the value of someone's life supervenes on the pattern of his momentary well-being through time. They say, "Surely if two people have had the same temporal well-being at all times of their lifespans of equal length, they are to be seen to have had equal global well-being" ("Death and Well-Being," p. 137). I say, Surely not. For if one person's later good fortune redeemed his earlier sufferings and the other's did not, the value of their lives might well differ.

30. Herodotus, I. 30–33. This story is cited by Aristotle (*Nicomachean Ethics* I.x.1–2), whose final definition of happiness (at I.x.15) also betrays an inclination to agree with Solon to some extent.

31. Some philosophers seem to regard "prudence" as synonymous with "self-interested rationality" or "practical wisdom." In this paragraph I am discussing prudence in a narrower sense, in which it denotes a specific aspect of practical wisdom—namely, a rational attitude toward the future.

32. For a clear presentation of this view, see Fred Feldman, "Some Puzzles About the Evil of Death" (Chapter 16 in this volume). Feldman's own view on the matter may not correspond to the view that he presents in this paper, since the paper adopts a simplistically additive hedonism merely for the sake of arguing with Epicureans. What Feldman does believe is that the evil of a particular death must be computed as the difference between the value of the actual life in which it occurs and that of the same life in the nearest possible world in which the death does not occur. I do not in general accept this method of com-

puting the value of events in someone's life, since I believe that events have a momentary value that is distinct from their contribution to the value of the subject's life as a whole. Since death has no momentary disvalue, however, my view about it coincides with Feldman's. I discuss this subject further below.

33. Griffin expresses doubts about this view in note 33, p. 355, of *Well-Being*.

34. See Griffin, *Well-Being*, pp. 36, 144–46.

35. In speaking of financial well-being, of course, I am assuming that wealth has intrinsic value for a person. Nothing in my argument depends on this assumption. Emotional, social, or physical well-being can be substituted in my arguments, *mutatis mutandis*, for financial well-being.

36. Assessments of emotional, physical, and professional well-being thus involve what Sen would call "informational constraints"—that is, constraints on which sorts of information are relevant. In Sen's terms, the reason why people with equivalent financial holdings have the same level of financial well-being is that they belong to the same "iso-information set" as defined by the applicable informational constraint. See "Moral Information," the first lecture in "Well-Being, Agency and Freedom," pp. 169–84.

37. For ease of expression, I have chosen to compare probabilities on a logarithmic scale. That is, I call p doubly unlikely in relation to q if the probability of p is equal to the probability of q squared.

38. See the preceding note.

39. This argument is in the same spirit as the following remarks of Thomas Nagel's: "Human beings are subject to . . . motivational claims of very different kinds. This is because they are complex creatures who can view the world from many perspectives . . . and each perspective presents a different set of claims. Conflict can exist within one of these sets, and it may be hard to resolve. But when conflict occurs between them, the problem is still more difficult . . . [Such conflicts] cannot, in my view, be resolved by subsuming either of the points of view under the other, or both under a third. Nor can we simply abandon any of them. There is no reason why we should. The capacity to view the world simultaneously from [different points of view] is one of the marks of humanity" ("The Fragmentation of Value," in *Mortal Questions* [New York, 1979], p. 134). (Here I have made strategic deletions from Nagel's remarks in a way that may exaggerate their similarity to my view.)

40. I am therefore making a somewhat different point from one made by Bernard Williams. When Williams says, "The correct perspective on one's life is *from now*," he is criticizing the principle that one should "distribute consideration equally over [one's] whole life" ("Persons, Character and Morality," in A. Rorty, ed., *The Identities of Persons* [Berkeley, Calif., 1976], pp. 209, 206).

41. Kurt Vonnegut, *Slaughterhouse Five* (New York, 1969), p. 23: "The Tralfamadorians can look at all the different moments just the way we look at a stretch of the Rocky Mountains. . . . They can see how

permanent all the moments are, and they can look at any moment that interests them. It is just an illusion we have here on Earth that one moment follows another one."

42. C. I. Lewis also defends the autonomy of momentary value (*Analysis of Knowledge and Valuation,* pp. 503ff.). Again, Lewis's argument is based on an experiential conception of value.

43. I defend this view in "An Essay on Internalism" (manuscript). Note that internalism applies only to matters of intrinsic value. Obviously, something that's beyond a person's powers of comprehension can still be good for him extrinsically, since it can be conducive to things that are good for him intrinsically.

44. Of course, the intuition expressed here may not be independent of that expressed in internalism. Indeed, there are some interpretations of internalism according to which the two intuitions are one and the same. I separate them here because I regard internalism as resting on a rather different intuition. See my "Essay on Internalism."

45. This point follows most clearly from desire-based conceptions of well-being, which will define how valuable different sequences of harms and benefits are for a cow in terms of how much the cow wants those sequences, or would want them under some ideal conditions. Since a cow cannot care about sequences of harms and benefits, and would not be able to care about them except under conditions that transformed it into something other than a cow, these definitions imply that temporal sequences cannot be assigned a value specifically for a cow.

Although my point thus follows from desire-based conceptions of relational value, it does not presuppose that relational value is desire-based. Judgments of relational value must somehow be relativized to the subject's perspective—if not by being made to depend on the subject's actual or counterfactual desires, then by some other means. And any strategy for relativizing evaluations of temporal sequences to the perspective of a cow will run into the same obstacle—namely, that the perspective of a cow does not encompass temporal sequences at all.

One might think that Peter Railton's version of the desire-based conception would have the resources to circumvent this problem, since it would define what is good for the cow in terms of what an idealized cow would want its actual self to desire ("Moral Realism," *Philosophical Review* 95 (1986): 163). The idealized cow, one might think, could acquire the ability to conceive of, and form preferences among, temporal sequences of harms and benefits while still doing so on behalf of its cognitively limited and hence fully bovine self. This suggestion strikes me as out of keeping with Railton's theory, for various reasons, of which one will suffice for now. The cognitively enhanced cow, once fully informed, would realize that its actual self was unable to want temporal sequences of harms and benefits, and would therefore not bother wanting its actual self to have any such desires.

46. See Griffin, *Well-Being,* p. 145: "Even when one does tot up, say, many small-scale pleasures to get an overall aggregate value, the value of the life containing these many local pleasures is fixed in comparison

with competing forms of life, and so the finally effective magnitudes are fixed by global desires." My point is that a cow is incapable of having the requisite global desires.

47. *De Rerum Natura*, III, 870f., 898f., cited by Bernard Williams in "The Makropulos Case: Reflections on the Tedium of Immortality" (Chapter 5 in this volume), p. 75.

48. Here I am not saying that a premature death is bad for a person because he wants or would want his life to be longer. Rather, I am saying that because a person *can* want his life to be longer, the judgment that a premature death is bad for him satisfies the requirements of internalism. To cite a person's actual or potential desires as evidence that a value judgment is compatible with internalism is one thing; to cite those desires as the value judgment's truth-makers is quite another.

These brief remarks on the evil of death were inspired by Thomas Nagel's essay "Death" (Chapter 4 in this volume). Nagel points out that the Epicurean argument assumes that if death harms its victim, it must harm him at a particular time. Nagel argues that this assumption is false. (So does Fred Feldman, in "Some Puzzles About the Evil of Death.") My claim is that although the assumption is indeed false in application to persons (which is the application that Nagel has in mind), it is true in application to lower animals.

Bibliography

PART ONE

The following works include most of those cited in the preceding chapters as well as a selection of books and articles with particular relevance to the issues raised in this volume.

Ad Hoc Committee of the Harvard Medical School to Examine the Definition of Brain Death. "A Definition of Irreversible Coma." *Journal of the American Medical Association* 205 (August 1968): 337–40.

Agich, George J. "The Concepts of Death and Embodiment." *Ethics in Science and Medicine* 3 (1976): 95–105.

Agich, George J., and Royce P. Jones. "Personal Identity and Brain Death: A Critical Response." *Philosophy and Public Affairs* 15 (Summer 1986): 267–74.

Allen, Woody. *Getting Even*. New York, 1966.

———. *Without Feathers*. New York, 1972.

Almog, Joseph, John Perry, and Howard Wettstein, eds. *Themes from Kaplan*. Oxford, 1989.

Anderson, Ray S. *Theology, Death and Dying*. New York, 1986.

Annas, George J. "Defining Death: There Ought to Be a Law." *The Hastings Center Report* 13 (February 1983): 20–21.

Annas, Julia. "Epicurus on Pleasure and Happiness." *Philosophical Topics* 15 (1987): 5–21.

Ariès, Philippe. *Western Attitudes Toward Death*. Trans. Patricia M. Ranum. Baltimore, 1974.

Baird, Robert M., et al. *Contemporary Essays on Greek Ideas: The Kilgore Festschrift*. Waco, Tex., 1987.

Barrett, William. *Irrational Man: A Study in Existential Philosophy*. Garden City, N.J., 1958.

Barry, Brian. *Political Argument*. New York, 1965.

Bataille, George. *Death and Sensuality*. New York, 1962.

———. *Le Mort*. Paris, 1967.

———. *La pratique de joie devant la mort*. Paris, 1967.

———. *Visions of Excess*. Minneapolis, 1985.

Bealer, George. "Review of Parsons' *Nonexistent Objects*." *Journal of Symbolic Logic* 59 (June 1984): 652–55.

Becker, Ernest. *The Denial of Death*. New York, 1973.

Becker, Lawrence C. "Human Being: The Boundaries of the Concept." *Philosophy and Public Affairs* 4 (Summer 1975): 335–59.

Benn, Stanley. "Freedom and Persuasion." *Australasian Journal of Philosophy* 45 (December 1967): 259–75.

Bennett, Jonathan. "Counterfactuals and Temporal Direction." *Philosophical Review* 93 (January 1984): 57–91.

Bernat, James L., Charles M. Culver, and Bernard Gert. "Defining Death in Theory and Practice." *The Hastings Center Report* 12 (February 1982): 5–9.

Bigelow, J., J. Campbell, and R. Pargetter. "Death and Well-Being." *Pacific Philosophical Quarterly* 71 (June 1990): 119–40.

Blanchot, Maurice. *L'Amite*. Paris, 1971.

———. *Foucault/Blanchot*. New York, 1987.

Brandt, Richard. "Two Concepts of Utility." In Miller and Williams, eds., *The Limits of Utilitarianism*.

Broad, C. D. *Ethics and the History of Philosophy*. London, 1952.

Brody, Howard. "Brain Death and Personal Existence: A Reply to Green and Wikler." *Journal of Medicine and Philosophy* 8 (1983): 187–96.

———. *Ethical Decisions in Medicine*. 2d ed. Boston, 1981.

Bultmann, Rudolf. *Life and Death*. Trans. P. H. Ballard, D. Turner, and L. A. Garrard. London, 1965.

Camus, Albert. *The Myth of Sisyphus and Other Essays*. Trans. Justin O'Brien. New York, 1955.

———. *Resistance, Rebellion, and Death*. Trans. Justin O'Brien. New York, 1960.

Canadian Government. "Criteria for the Determination of Death." Ottawa, 1981.

Čapek, Milic, ed. *The Concepts of Space and Time*. Boston, 1976.

Capron, Alexander M., and Joanne Lynn. "Defining Death: Which Way?" *The Hastings Center Report* 12 (April 1982): 43–44.

Carter, W. R. "Do Zygotes Become People?" *Mind* 91 (January 1982): 77–95.

———. "Once and Future Persons." *American Philosophical Quarterly* 17 (January 1980): 61–66.

Cartwright, Ann, et al. *Life Before Death*. Boston, 1973.

Castañeda, Hector-Neri. "Conventional Aspects of Human Action, Its Time, and Its Place." *Dialogue* 19 (September 1980): 436–60.

Choron, Jacques. *Death and Western Thought*. New York, 1963.

———. *Modern Man and Mortality*. New York, 1963.

Cigman, Ruth. "Death, Misfortune, and Species Inequality." *Philosophy and Public Affairs* 10 (Winter 1981): 47–64.

Cooper, John. "Friendship and the Good in Aristotle." *Philosophical Review* 86 (July 1977): 290–315.

Cudd, Ann E. "Sensationalized Philosophy: A Reply to Marquis's 'Why Abortion Is Immoral.'" *Journal of Philosophy* 87 (May 1990): 262–64.
Delillo, Don. *White Noise*. New York, 1986.
Demske, James M. *Being, Man and Death: A Key to Heidegger*. Lexington, Mass., 1970.
Devine, Philip E. *The Ethics of Homicide*. Ithaca, 1978.
Diamond, Cora, and Jenny Teichman, eds. *Intention and Intentionality*. Ithaca, 1979.
Donnellan, Keith. "Speaking of Nothing." *Philosophical Review* 82 (January 1974): 3–32.
Donnelly, John, ed. *Language, Metaphysics, and Death*. New York, 1978.
Ducasse, C. J. *A Critical Examination of the Belief in Life After Death*. Springfield, Ill., 1961.
Eddin, Aron. "Temporal Neutrality and Past Pains." *Southern Journal of Philosophy* 20 (Winter 1982): 423–31.
Edwards, Paul. *Death and Existentialism*. New York, 1977.
——. "Existentialism and Death: A Survey of Some Confusions and Absurdities." In Morgenbesser, Suppes, and White, eds., *Philosophy, Science, and Method*.
——. "Heidegger and Death as 'Possibility.'" *Mind* 84 (1975): 548–66.
——. "Heidegger and Death: A Deflationary Critique." *The Monist* 59 (April 1976): 161–86.
——. "My Death." In Paul Edwards, ed., *Encyclopedia of Philosophy*, vol. 5, pp. 416–19. New York, 1967.
Eliade, Mircea. *The Myth of Eternal Return*. Trans. Willard R. Trask. New York, 1954.
Enright, D. J., ed. *The Oxford Book of Death*. Oxford, 1987.
Falk, W. D. "Morality, Self, and Others." In Feinberg, ed., *Reason and Responsibility*.
Feifel, Herman, ed. *The Meaning of Death*. New York, 1959.
Feinberg, Joel. "The Forms and Limits of Utilitarianism." *Philosophical Review* 76 (July 1967): 368–81.
——. "Harm and Self-Interest." In Hacker and Raz, eds., *Law, Morality and Society*.
——. *Harm to Others*. Oxford, 1984.
——. "Voluntary Euthanasia and the Inalienable Right to Life." *Philosophy and Public Affairs* 7 (Winter 1978): 93–123.
——. "Wrongful Life and the Counterfactual Element in Harming." *Social Philosophy and Policy* 4 (Autumn 1986): 145–78.
——, ed. *Reason and Responsibility*. 5th ed. Belmont, Calif., 1981.
Feldman, Fred. *Confrontations with the Reaper*. New York, 1991.
——. *Doing the Best We Can: An Essay in Informal Deontic Logic*. Dordrecht, 1986.
——. "On Dying as a Process." *Philosophy and Phenomenological Research* 1 (December 1989): 375–90.
——. "F. M. Kamm and the Mirror of Time." *Pacific Philosophical Quarterly* 71 (March 1990): 23–27.
Ferrater Mora, José. *Being and Death*. Berkeley, 1965.
Flew, Antony. *Body, Mind, and Death*. New York, 1964.

406   Bibliography

———. "Can a Man Witness His Own Funeral?" *Hilbert Journal* 54 (1956): 242–50.

Flew, Antony, and A. MacIntyre. *New Essays in Philosophical Theology.* New York, 1964.

Foot, Philippa. "Euthanasia." *Philosophy and Public Affairs* 6 (Winter 1978): 85–112.

Fraser, J. T., et al., eds. *The Study of Time.* New York, 1972.

Freud, Sigmund. "Thoughts on War and Death." *Collected Papers*, vol. 4. Trans. Joan Riviere. New York, 1959.

Fulton, Robert, ed. *Death and Identity.* New York, 1965.

Furley, David. "Nothing to Us?" In Schofield and Striker, eds., *The Norms of Nature.*

Geer, Russel M., ed. *Epicurus: Letters, Principal Doctrines, and Vatican Sayings.* Indianapolis, 1964.

Gervais, Karen Grandstrand. *Redefining Death.* New Haven, 1986.

Glover, Jonathan. *Causing Death and Saving Lives.* Middlesex, Engl., 1977.

Gosling, J. C. B., and C. C. W. Taylor. *The Greeks on Pleasure.* Oxford, 1984.

Green, Michael, and Daniel Wikler. "Brain Death and Personal Identity." *Philosophy and Public Affairs* 9 (Winter 1980): 105–33.

Green, O. H. "Fear of Death." *Philosophy and Phenomenological Research* 43 (September 1982): 99–105.

Griffin, James. *Well-Being: Its Meaning, Measurement and Moral Importance.* Oxford, 1986.

Grover, Dorothy. "Death and Life." *Canadian Journal of Philosophy* 17 (December 1987): 711–32.

———. "Posthumous Harm." *Philosophical Quarterly* 39 (July 1989): 334–53.

Hacker, P. M. S., and J. Raz, eds. *Law, Morality and Society: Essays in Honour of H. L. A. Hart.* Oxford, 1977.

Haji, Ishtiyaque. "Pre-Vital and Post-Vital Times." *Pacific Philosophical Quarterly* 72 (September 1991): 171–80.

Halley, M. Martin, and William F. Harvey. "Medical and Legal Definitions of Death." *Journal of the American Medical Association* 204 (March 1968): 423–25.

Hampshire, Stuart. *Freedom of Mind.* Oxford, 1972.

Healy, Richard, ed. *Reduction, Time and Reality.* New York, 1981.

Heidegger, Martin. *Being and Time.* Trans. John Macquarrie and Edward Robinson. New York, 1962.

Hick, John. *Death and Eternal Life.* New York, 1977.

High, Dallas M. "Death: Its Conceptual Elusiveness." *Soundings* 55 (1972): 438–58.

Hinton, J. M. *Experiences.* Oxford, 1973.

Hoffman, Piotr. *Doubt, Time, Violence.* Chicago, 1986.

———. *The Human Self and the Life and Death Struggle.* Gainesville, Fla., 1983.

Hornsby, Jennifer. *Actions.* London, 1980.

Hunsinger, George. *Kierkegaard, Heidegger, and the Concept of Death.* Stanford, Calif., 1969.

Institute of Society, Ethics and the Life Sciences—Task Force on Death and Dying. "Refinements in Criteria for the Determination of Death." *Journal of the American Medical Association* 221 (1972): 48–53.

Ishiguro, Hidé. "Possibility." *Proceedings of the Aristotelian Society* (supplementary) 54 (1980): 73–87.

James, William. *The Varieties of Religious Experience.* New York, 1902.

Jaspers, Karl. *Philosophie.* Berlin, 1932.

———. *Way to Wisdom.* Trans. Ralph Manheim. New Haven, Conn., 1951.

Jeffrey, Richard. "Coming True." In Diamond and Teichman, eds., *Intention and Intentionality.*

Jonas, Hans. *Philosophical Essays: From Ancient Creed to Technological Man.* Englewood Cliffs, N.J., 1974.

Jung, Carl. *Memories, Dreams, Reflections.* New York, 1961.

———. "The Soul and Death." In Feifel, ed., *The Meaning of Death.*

Kamm, Frances Myrna. *Morality, Mortality.* Oxford, forthcoming.

———. "Why Is Death Bad and Worse Than Pre-natal Non-existence?" *Pacific Philosophical Quarterly* 69 (June 1988): 161–64.

Kaplan, David. "Demonstratives." In Almog, Perry, and Wettstein, eds., *Themes from Kaplan.*

Kaufmann, Walter, ed. *Existentialism from Dostoevsky to Sartre.* New York, 1956.

King-Farlow, J., and W. R. Shea, eds. *Values and the Quality of Life.* New York, 1976.

Kleinig, John. "Crime and the Concept of Harm." *American Philosophical Quarterly* 15 (January 1978): 27–36.

Kluge, Eike-Henner W. *The Practice of Death.* New Haven, Conn., 1975.

Koestenbaum, Peter. *The Vitality of Death: Essays in Existential Psychology and Philosophy.* Westport, Conn., 1971.

Korein, Julius, ed. *Brain Death: Interrelated Medical and Social Issues.* New York, 1978.

Kübler-Ross, Elisabeth. *Death: The Final Stage of Growth.* New York, 1986.

———. *On Death and Dying.* New York, 1969.

Ladd, John, ed. *Ethical Issues Relating to Life and Death.* New York, 1979.

Lamb, David. *Death, Brain Death and Ethics.* Albany, N.Y., 1985.

———. "Diagnosing Death." *Philosophy and Public Affairs* 7 (Winter 1978): 144–53.

———. "Reply to Professor Wikler.' *Journal of Medical Ethics* 2 (1984): 102.

Le Sidaner, Jean-Marie, ed. *La Mort.* Paris, 1978.

Levenbook, Barbara. "Harming Someone After His Death." *Ethics* 94 (April 1984): 407–19.

Lewis, C. I. *An Analysis of Knowledge and Valuation.* LaSalle, Ill., 1946.

Lewis, David. *Counterfactuals.* Cambridge, Mass., 1973.

Lewis, Hywel D. *The Self and Immortality.* London, 1973.

Lidz, Theodore. *The Person.* New York, 1968.

Lockwood, Michael. "Singer on Killing and the Preference for Life." *Inquiry* 22 (Summer 1979): 157–70.

Long, A. A. *Hellenistic Philosophy*. 2d ed. Berkeley, 1986.

MacIntyre, Alasdair. *After Virtue*. Notre Dame, Ind., 1984.

Marcel, Gabriel. *Présence et immortalité*. Paris, 1959.

Marquis, Don. "Why Abortion is Immoral." *Journal of Philosophy* 86 (April 1989): 183–202.

Matthews, Gareth. "*De Anima* B2-4 and the Meaning of *Life*." In Nussbaum and Rorty, ed., *Essays on Aristotle's "De Anima."*

McInerney, Peter K. "Does a Fetus Already Have a Future-Like-Ours?" *Journal of Philosophy* 87 (May 1990): 264–68.

McMahan, Jeff. *The Ethics of Killing*. Oxford, 1989.

———. "Problems of Population Theory." *Ethics* 92 (October 1981): 96–127.

Mellor, D. H. *Real Time*. New York, 1981.

Merlan, Philip. *Studies in Epicurus and Aristotle*. Wiesbaden, 1960.

Miller, Fred D., Jr. "Epicurus on the Art of Dying." *Southern Journal of Philosophy* 14 (Summer 1976): 169–77.

Miller, H. B., and W. H. Williams, eds. *The Limits of Utilitarianism*. Minneapolis, 1982.

Mitsis, Phillip. *Epicurus' Ethical Theory*. Ithaca, N.Y., 1988.

———. "Epicurus on Death and the Duration of Life." *Proceedings of the Boston Area Colloquium on Ancient Philosophy* 4 (1988): 295–314.

Momeyer, Richard M. *Confronting Death*. Bloomington, Ind., 1988.

Morgenbesser, S., P. Suppes, and M. White, eds. *Philosophy, Science, and Method*. New York, 1969.

Mothersill, Mary. "Death." In Rachels, ed., *Moral Problems*.

Nagel, Thomas. *Mortal Questions*. New York, 1979.

———. *The View from Nowhere*. Oxford, 1986.

Narveson, Jan. "Future People and Us." In Sikora and Barry, eds., *Obligations to Future Generations*.

Nehemas, Alexander. *Nietzsche: Life as Literature*. Cambridge, Mass., 1985.

New Jersey Supreme Court. "Opinion on the Matter of Karen Quinlan." 70 N.J. 10, 335A 2d, 647. 1976.

Norcross, Alastair. "Killing, Abortion, and Contraception: A Reply to Marquis." *Journal of Philosophy* 87 (May 1990): 268–77.

Nozick, Robert. *Anarchy, State, and Utopia*. New York, 1971.

———. "On the Randian Argument." In Paul, ed., *Reading Nozick*.

———. *Philosophical Explanations*. Cambridge, Mass., 1981.

Nussbaum, M., and A. Rorty. *Essays on Aristotle's "De Anima."* Oxford, forthcoming.

Nussbaum, Martha C. "Mortal Immortals: Lucretius on Death and the Voice of Nature." *Philosophy and Phenomenological Research* 50 (December 1989): 303–51.

Oates, Stephen B. *Let the Trumpet Sound: The Life of Martin Luther King, Jr.* New York, 1982.

Olson, Robert G. "Death." In Paul Edwards, ed., *Encyclopedia of Philosophy*, vol. 2, pp. 307–9. New York, 1967.

Parfit, Derek. "Personal Identity." *Philosophical Review* 80 (January 1971): 3–27.

———. *Reasons and Persons.* Oxford, 1984.

Parsons, Charles. "Objects and Logic." *The Monist* 65 (October 1982): 491–516.

Parsons, Terence. *Nonexistent Objects.* New Haven, Conn., 1980.

Partridge, Ernest. "Posthumous Interests and Posthumous Respect." *Ethics* 91 (January 1981): 243–64.

Paul, Jeffery, ed. *Reading Nozick.* Totowa, N.J., 1981.

Pears, D. F. "Time, Truth, and Inference." In Flew, ed., *Essays in Conceptual Analysis.*

Penelhum, Terence. *Survival and Disembodied Existence.* London, 1970.

Perrett, Roy W. *Death and Immortality.* Dordrecht, 1987.

Popper, Karl. *The Open Universe.* Totowa, N.J., 1982.

President's Commission for the Study of Ethical Problems in Medicine and Biomedical and Behavioral Research. *Defining Death: Medical, Legal and Ethical Issues in the Determination of Death.* Washington, D.C., 1981.

Prior, Arthur. "The Notion of the Present." In Fraser et al., eds., *The Study of Time.*

Puccetti, Roland. "The Conquest of Death." *The Monist* 59 (April 1976): 249–63.

Quinn, Warren. "Abortion: Identity and Loss." *Philosophy and Public Affairs* 13 (Winter 1984): 24–54.

Rachels, James. *The End of Life: Euthanasia and Morality.* Oxford, 1986.

———, ed. *Moral Problems: A Collection of Philosophical Essays.* New York, 1971. 2d ed., 1975.

Rilke, Rainer Maria. *The Book of Hours.* Trans. A. L. Peck. London, 1961.

Rist, J. M. *Epicurus: An Introduction.* Cambridge, Engl., 1972.

———. "Pleasure: 360–300 B.C." *Phoenix* 28 (Summer 1974): 167–79.

Rorty, Amelie O. "Fearing Death." *Philosophy* 58 (April 1983): 175–88.

———, ed. *The Identities of Persons.* Berkeley, Calif., 1976.

Rorty, Richard. *Contingency, Irony, and Solidarity.* New York, 1989.

———. "The Contingency of Selfhood." *London Review of Books* 8 (May 1986): 11.

Rosenbaum, Stephen E. "Epicurus on Pleasure and the Complete Life." *The Monist* 73 (January 1990): 21–41.

———. "The Harm of Killing: An Epicurean Perspective." In Baird et al., *Contemporary Essays on Greek Ideas.*

———. "The Symmetry Argument: Lucretius Against the Fear of Death." *Philosophy and Phenomenological Research* 50 (December 1989): 353–73.

Rosenberg, Jay. *Thinking Clearly About Death.* Englewood Cliffs, N.J., 1983.

Ross, W. D. *Foundations of Ethics.* Oxford, 1939.

Ryle, Gilbert. *The Concept of the Mind.* New York, 1949.

Sartre, Jean-Paul. *Being and Nothingness.* Trans. Hazel E. Barnes. New York, 1956.

———. *La Nausée.* Paris, 1938.

Schleifer, Ronald. *Rhetoric and Death: The Language of Modernism and Postmodern Discourse Theory.* Chicago, 1990.

Schofield, M., and G. Striker, eds. *The Norms of Nature.* Cambridge, Engl., 1986.

Schrodinger, Edwin. *What Is Life? & Mind and Matter.* New York, 1967.

Sen, Amartya. "Plural Utility." *Proceedings of the Aristotelian Society* 81 (1981): 193–215.

———. "Utilitarianism and Welfarism." *Journal of Philosophy* 76 (September 1970): 463–89.

Shibles, Warren. *Death: An Interdisciplinary Analysis.* Whitewater, Wis., 1974.

Sidgwick, Henry. *The Methods of Ethics.* Indianapolis, 1981.

Sikora, Richard and Brian Barry, eds. *Obligations to Future Generations.* Philadelphia, 1978.

Sklar, Lawrence. "Time, Reality, and Relativity." In Healy, ed., *Reduction, Time, and Reality.*

Slote, Michael A. "Existentialism and the Fear of Dying." *American Philosophical Quarterly* 12 (January 1975): 17–28.

———. *Goods and Virtues.* Oxford, 1983.

Smart, Ninian. "Philosophical Concepts of Death." In Toynbee et al., *Man's Concern with Death.*

Sorabji, Richard. *Time, Creation, and the Continuum.* Ithaca, N.Y., 1983.

Stocker, Michael. *Plural and Conflicting Values.* Oxford, 1990.

Stoppard, Tom. *Rosenkrantz and Guildenstern Are Dead.* (New York, 1967).

Striker, Gisela. "Commentary on Mitsis." *Proceedings of the Boston Area Colloquium on Ancient Philosophy* 4 (1988): 323–28.

Sumner, L. S. "A Matter of Life and Death." *Noûs* 10 (May 1976): 145–71.

Taylor, Charles. *Sources of the Self: The Making of the Modern Identity.* Cambridge, Mass., 1989.

Tillich, Paul. *The Courage to Be.* New Haven, Conn., 1952.

Toynbee, Arnold, et al. *Man's Concern with Death.* London, 1968.

Unamuno y Jugo, Miguel de. *Del sentimiento trágico de la vida.* Trans. J. E. Crawford Flitch. London, 1921.

Van Evra, James. "On Death as a Limit." *Analysis* 31 (April 1971): 170–76.

Veatch, Robert M. "Brain Death: Welcome Definition or Dangerous Judgment?" *The Hastings Center Report* 2 (November 1972): 10–13.

———. "Death." *Theoretical Medicine* 5 (1984): 197–207.

———. *Death, Dying, and the Biological Revolution.* New Haven, Conn., 1976.

———. "The Definition of Death: Ethical, Philosophical, and Policy Confusion." Paper delivered at the Illinois Wesleyan University Symposium on Brain Death, 1976.

———. "Maternal Brain Death: An Ethicist's Thoughts." *Journal of the American Medical Association* 248 (September 1982): 1102–3.

———. "The Whole-Brain-Oriented Concept of Death: An Outmoded Philosophical Foundation." *Journal of Thanatology* 3 (1975): 13–30.

Walton, Douglas N. *Brain Death: Ethical Considerations*. West Lafayette, Ind., 1980.
————. *On Defining Death*. Montreal, 1979.
Wikler, Daniel. "Correspondence: Brain Death." *Journal of Medical Ethics* 10 (1984): 101–2.
Wild, Douglas. *The Challenge of Existentialism*. Bloomington, Ind., 1955.
Williams, Bernard. *Problems of the Self*. Cambridge, Engl., 1973.
Wollheim, Richard. *The Thread of Life*. Cambridge, Mass., 1984.
Woods, John. "Can Death Be Understood?" In King-Farlow and Shea, ed., *Values and the Quality of Life*.
Wyschogrod, Edith, ed. *The Phenomenon of Death*. New York, 1973.
Yourgrau, Palle. *The Disappearance of Time: Kurt Gödel and the Idealistic Tradition in Philosophy*. New York, 1991.
————. "On Time and Actuality: The Dilemma of Privileged Position." *British Journal for the Philosophy of Science* 37 (December 1986): 405–17.

PART TWO

The following is a highly selective list of science fiction that treats topics relevant to immortality. In preparing this list, I am indebted to Professor George Slusser, Department of Comparative Literature and director of the Eaton Program for Science Fiction and Fantasy Studies, University of California, Riverside. All of the material cited below is available in the Eaton Collection of Science Fiction and Fantasy Literature, Rivera Library, University of California, Riverside. Note that the novels are listed by reference to available editions, not necessarily to initial publication.

Aldiss, Brian. *Greybeard*. New York, 1965.
Anderson, Poul. *Tau Zero*. New York, 1970.
Asimov, Isaac. *The End of Eternity*. Garden City, N.J., 1955.
————. *Foundation and Earth*. New York, 1986.
Barjavel, Rene. *The Immortals*. New York, 1975.
Bear, Greg. *Blood Music*. New York, 1986.
Benford, Gregory. *Against Infinity*. New York, 1984.
————. *Great Sky River*. New York, 1988.
————. *Tides of Light*. New York, 1989.
Binder, Eando. *Anton York, Immortal*. New York, 1965.
Blish, James. "At Death's End." *Astounding Science Fiction* (May 1954): 6–63.
————. *Cities in Flight*. New York, 1982.
Campbell, John W., and Don A. Stuart. "Twilight." *Astounding Science Fiction* (November 1934): 44–58.
Clarke, Arthur C. *Childhood's End*. New York, 1976.
————. *The City and the Stars*. New York, 1977.
Curval, Philippe. *Cette chere humanite* [Brave Old World]. Paris, 1976.
Dick, Philip K. *Ubik*. London, 1969.
Farmer, Philip Jose. *The Fabulous Riverboat*. New York, 1971.

——. *Gods of the Riverworld.* New York, 1985.
——. *To Your Scattered Bodies Go.* New York, 1971.
Gallun, Raymond Z. *The Eden Cycle.* New York, 1974.
——. *People Minus X.* New York, 1957.
Gibson, William. *Count Zero.* New York, 1987.
——. *Neuromancer.* New York, 1984.
Gunn, James. *The Immortals.* New York, 1979.
Haldeman, Joe. *Buying Time.* New York, 1987.
Hawthorne, Nathaniel. "Dr. Heidegger's Experiment." *Twice-Told Tales.* Boston, 1837.
Herbert, Frank. *The Eyes of Heisenberg.* New York, 1966.
——. *The Heaven Makers.* New York, 1970.
——. *The Lazarus Effect.* New York, 1983.
Heinlein, Robert A. "All You Zombies." *Magazine of Fantasy and Science Fiction* (March 1959): 5–15.
——. *I Will Fear No Evil.* New York, 1970.
——. *Methusaleh's Children.* New York, 1958.
——. *Time Enough for Love.* New York, 1974.
Jeury, Michel. *Le Temps uncertain* [Chronolysis]. Paris, 1973.
Keller, David. "Life Everlasting [Part 1]." *Amazing Stories* (July 1934): 9–34.
——. "Life Everlasting [Part 2]." *Amazing Stories* (August 1934): 10–41.
Knight, Damon. "Dio." *Infinity Science Fiction* (September 1957).
——. "Stranger Station." *Magazine of Fantasy and Science Fiction* (December 1956): 3–24.
——. "World Without Children." *Galaxy Science Fiction* (December 1951): 4–70.
Lafferty, R. A. "Nine Hundred Grandmothers." In *Nine Hundred Grandmothers.* New York, 1982.
Manning, Laurence. *The Man Who Awoke.* New York, 1933.
Moskowitz, Sam, ed. *Masterpieces of Science Fiction.* Cleveland, Ohio, 1967.
Niven, Larry. *Ringworld.* New York, 1970.
——. *The Ringworld Engineers.* New York, 1980.
Pohl, Frederick. *Drunkard's Walk.* New York, 1960.
——. *Gateway.* New York, 1977.
——. *Heechee Rendezvous.* New York, 1984.
Russell, Eric Frank. *Sentinels from Space.* New York, 1953.
Schmitz, James H. *The Demon Breed.* New York, 1968.
——. *The Tale of 2 Clocks.* New York, 1968.
——. *The Universe Against Her.* New York, 1964.
Shaw, Bob. *One Million Tomorrows.* New York, 1970.
Sheckley, Robert. *Immortality, Inc.* New York, 1978.
Shelley, Mary. "The Mortal Immortal." In Moskowitz, ed., *Masterpieces of Science Fiction.*
Silverberg, Robert. *The Book of Skulls.* New York, 1972.
——. "Born with the Dead." *Magazine of Fantasy and Science Fiction* (April 1974): 4–66.
——. *To Live Again.* New York, 1978.

Simak, Clifford. *Way Station*. New York, 1973.
———. *Why Call Them Back from Heaven?* New York, 1980.
Smith, Cordwainer. *Norstrilla*. New York, 1975.
Smith, E. E. "Doc." *Children of the Lens*. Reading, Pa., 1954.
———. *First Lensman*. Reading, Pa., 1950.
———. *Galactic Patrol*. Reading, Pa. 1950.
———. *Gray Lensman*. Reading, Pa. 1951.
Smith, George O. *Highways in Hiding*. New York, 1956.
Spinrad, Norman. *Bug Jack Barron*. New York, 1969.
Stapledon, Olaf. *Last and First Men, and Star Maker*. New York, 1968.
Steiner, Kurt. *Le disque raye*. Paris, 1970.
Sterling, Bruce. *Schismatrix*. New York, 1985.
Tucker, Wilson. *The Time Masters*. New York, 1953.
Van Vogt, A. E. *The Players of Null-A*. New York, 1966.
———. *The Weapon Makers*. New York, 1952.
———. *The World of Null-A*. New York, 1945.
Weinbaum, Stanley. *The Black Flame*. New York, 1948.
Wilhelm, Kate. *The Nevermore Affair*. New York, 1966.
Zelazny, Robert. *Isle of the Dead*. New York, 1969.
———. *Nine Princes in Amber*. New York, 1986.
———. *This Immortal*. New York, 1980.

Index

In this index and "f" after a number indicates a separate reference on the next page, and an "ff" indicates separate references on the next two pages. A continuous discussion over two or more pages is indicated by a span of page numbers, e.g., "57–59." *Passim* is used for a cluster of references in close but not consecutive sequence.

Library of Congress Cataloging-in-Publication Data

The Metaphysics of death / edited, with an introduction, by John
Martin Fischer.
    p.   cm.—(Stanford series in philosophy)
Includes bibliographical references and index.
ISBN 0-8047-2046-0 (cl.)   ISBN 0-8047-2104-1 (pbk.)
    1. Death.   I. Fischer, John Martin, 1952–.   II. Series.
BD444.M429   1993
128'.5—dc20
92-36933   CIP